HOW THE FEW BECAME
THE PROUD

TITLES IN THE SERIES

The Other Space Race: Eisenhower and the Quest for Aerospace Security

An Untaken Road: Strategy, Technology, and the Mobile Intercontinental Ballistic Missile

Strategy: Context and Adaptation from Archidamus to Airpower

Cassandra in Oz: Counterinsurgency and Future War

Cyberspace in Peace and War

Limiting Risk in America's Wars: Airpower, Asymmetrics, and a New Strategic Paradigm

Always at War: Organizational Culture in Strategic Air Command, 1946–62

Transforming War

PAUL J. SPRINGER, EDITOR

To ensure success, the conduct of war requires rapid and effective adaptation to changing circumstances. While every conflict involves a degree of flexibility and innovation, there are certain changes that have occurred throughout history that stand out because they fundamentally altered the conduct of warfare. The most prominent of these changes have been labeled "Revolutions in Military Affairs" (RMAs). These so-called revolutions include technological innovations as well as entirely new approaches to strategy. Revolutionary ideas in military theory, doctrine, and operations have also permanently changed the methods, means, and objectives of warfare.

This series examines fundamental transformations that have occurred in warfare. It places particular emphasis upon RMAs to examine how the development of a new idea or device can alter not only the conduct of wars but their effect upon participants, supporters, and uninvolved parties. The unifying concept of the series is not geographical or temporal; rather, it is the notion of change in conflict and its subsequent impact. This has allowed the incorporation of a wide variety of scholars, approaches, disciplines, and conclusions to be brought under the umbrella of the series. The works include biographies, examinations of transformative events, and analyses of key technological innovations that provide a greater understanding of how and why modern conflict is carried out, and how it may change the battlefields of the future.

HOW THE FEW BECAME

CRAFTING THE MARINE CORPS MYSTIQUE, 1874–1918

THE PROUD

HEATHER VENABLE

NAVAL INSTITUTE PRESS

ANNAPOLIS, MARYLAND

NAVAL INSTITUTE PRESS
291 Wood Road
Annapolis, MD 21402

Library of Congress Cataloging-in-Publication Data

Names: Venable, Heather P., author.
Title: How the few became the proud : crafting the Marine Corps mystique,
    1874–1918 / Heather P. Venable.
Description: Annapolis, MD : Naval Institute Press, [2019] | Series.
    Transforming war | Includes bibliographical references and index.
Identifiers: LCCN 2019018011 (print) | LCCN 2019020165 (ebook) | ISBN
    9781682474822 (ePDF) | ISBN 9781682474822 (ePub) | ISBN 9781682474686
    (hardcover : alk. paper)
Subjects: LCSH: United States. Marine Corps—History. | Marines—United
    States—History. | United States. Marine Corps—Organization.
Classification: LCC VE23 (ebook) | LCC VE23 .V46 2019 (print) | DDC
    359.9/6097309034—dc23
LC record available at https://lccn.loc.gov/2019018011

♾ Print editions meet the requirements of ANSI/NISO z39.48-1992 (Permanence
of Paper).
Printed in the United States of America.

27 26 25 24 23 22 21 20 19   9 8 7 6 5 4 3 2 1
First printing

Interior design and composition: Alcorn Publication Design

Contents

List of Illustrations viii

Preface ix

Introduction 1

PART I. CRAFTING THE CORPS' IDENTITY

1. Inspiration and Articulation: Othering the Navy 19
2. Internalization: Image and Identity in Imperial Wars, 1898–1905 53
3. Refinement and Elaboration: The Navy's Impact on the Corps' Early Publicity Efforts 80
4. Intensification and Dissemination: The Recruiting Publicity Bureau's Influence on the Corps' Image and Identity 102

PART II. DEPLOYING THE CORPS' IDENTITY

5. Differentiation: How the Marine Corps Engendered Landing Parties, 1908–1918 119
6. Democratization: From Boot Straps to Shoulder Straps, 1914–1918 136
7. Hypermasculinization: Every Male a Rifleman, Every Female a Clerk 174

Epilogue 196

Notes 201

Bibliography 293

Index 323

Illustrations

"Who Am I?" 7

Uncle Sam 16

"Prize Money! Prize Money!" 31

"Wanted for the United States Marine Corps!" 32

"The Signaling at Cuzco Well" 57

"Recruiting Marines" 85

"What's a Good Title for This?" 105

"Soldiers of the Sea" 132

"Pull together men—the Navy needs us" 133

"Democracy's Vanguard" 134

"Preparing for the Tour" 143

Advertisement 144

"Story of the Shoulder Strap" 150

Farewell Dinner 157

"Man Wanted—To Fit This Hat" 159

"If You Want to Fight! Join the Marines" 178

"Gee!! I wish I were a man . . ." 180

Cover, September 1918 188

"Hurdling the Hatches" 190

Cover, November 1918 192

Preface

As it happened only once, I still remember the night in elementary school when my father returned home late at night by himself. I heard his laughter resound throughout our home as he described to my mother the initial scenes of *Full Metal Jacket*, which depict a recruit's initial training during boot camp. The scenes some might watch in shock or disgust resonated with my father and his fellow Marines in the audience, reminding them of what they proudly endured to become members of a self-proclaimed elite institution.[1]

My father often joked that he decided to enlist in the Marine Corps to avoid being drafted into the Army, which wasn't tough enough for him. Most Marines assume that their historical predecessors had similar attitudes, that this kind of rhetoric has always characterized Marines. Early on in my research into the nineteenth-century Marine Corps, however, I realized this was not the case. For more than half of its existence, the Marines largely self-identified as soldiers. Neither the Marines nor the public at large considered service in the Corps something distinct from service in the other branches of the military.

This work explores developments pertaining to the Marine Corps' identity and image, and focuses primarily on the late nineteenth and early twentieth centuries. Although these developments largely coalesced within a decade of the Spanish-American War, Marines certainly refined and expanded on them in subsequent decades. The end result is that love for the Corps came to rest at the center of many Marines' identities as a kind of deep emotional attachment that seems virtually antithetical to popular understandings of the relationships individuals historically have had with military institutions. Similarly, the Corps' publicity efforts became preoccupied with fostering the country's affection for the Corps.

This work owes much to those who have provided guidance and wisdom over the years. From my days at the University of Hawai'i,

I am particularly grateful to Margot Henriksen. At Duke University, Alex Roland, Richard Kohn, Laura Edwards, Jocelyn Olcott, and Susan Thorne challenged and improved my writing and ideas. At Air Command and Staff College, John Terino's enthusiasm and inspiring leadership have done much to help me through the final stages of this project while providing a wonderful environment in the Department of Airpower. Jordan Hayworth and Jared Donnelly read drafts and provided significant insights, along with Sebastian Lukasik and Paul Springer, who greatly motivated me to keep moving forward. Donny Seablom always supported me when I needed to vent or laugh. Ryan Wadle loyally and efficiently read draft after draft, and his ideas about the Navy during this time period have greatly improved this work. I am also grateful to financial support from the Marine Corps Heritage Foundation as well as Air Command and Staff College. All errors herein are my own. Finally, this work would not exist without my parents, Temple and Cecilia Pace, who have so selflessly supported me, along with the other Marines and future Marines in my family, especially Kyle, Braylen, and Kieran.

HOW THE FEW BECAME
THE PROUD

Introduction

In 1918, after visiting hospitals in France filled with wounded Marines, one sergeant proclaimed, "It means something these days to be a Marine."[1] Impressed by the bravery and pride of the men he encountered, the sergeant implied that the public finally recognized and appreciated the Marine Corps. He also suggested that the horrific combat losses his fellow Marines had endured had not dimmed their identification with the Marine Corps or their belief in the cause for which they were fighting, describing a recently wounded Marine who waved to him with the stump of his arm, eager to demonstrate his pride in his great sacrifice.[2]

To the anonymous sergeant, the Marine epitomized a fighter, eager to charge into battle with his bayonet against treacherous Germans armed with machine guns. His Marines had "set a pace for the American Army that the National Army will have difficulty to excel." It was not enough for the Marines to do their part in defeating the Germans—they also must outdo the Army in the process. The sergeant also believed in the "value of traditions." Indeed, it was the sense of wanting to belong, to "be considered a thorough Marine," that he believed had driven those wounded Marines to the "pinnacle of achievement, from which [the Corps] might never be ousted."[3] Responsible for touring the field hospitals to ensure that wounded Marines received their pay, this sergeant surveyed the human costs of war and found much to celebrate.

This sergeant's views also accorded with the institution's leadership and the Recruiting Publicity Bureau's rhetoric. The Corps included the letters in congressional testimony showing the lengths to which the institution had gone to pay wounded Marines. The letters subsequently received some elaboration before being published the following year in a collection entitled *"Dear Folks at Home": The Glorious Story of the United States Marines in France as Told by Their Letters from the*

Battlefield (1919), which epitomized the increasingly triumphant and assumedly intense identification of Marines with their institution.[4]

But it had not always meant something to be a Marine, or at least anything positive. In 1875, for example, Marine officer Henry Clay Cochrane bemoaned in the popular *Army and Navy Journal* that Marines were neither "respected nor respectable." A headline in the *Saint Louis Post-Dispatch* printed more scathing headlines, including "A Corps of Frauds" and "A Branch of Service in which There Is Nothing but Rottenness." A Kentucky paper similarly characterized the Corps as "very useless and corrupt."[5]

For good reason, then, after the Civil War, Marine officers worried about their institution's survival or its potential merger with the Army. In response, Marines took steps to reform the Corps' image, particularly when Capt. Richard Collum created a written historical record that stressed his institution's antiquity and extensive contributions to the nation. In effect, they began to make it mean something to be a Marine.

Some historians have viewed the Corps' earliest histories as short-term responses undeserving of detailed analysis.[6] On the contrary, these histories epitomize the individual efforts of many Marines to craft and refine an image for the Corps for external consumption while strengthening the institution's internal identity. These dual processes helped to shape the Corps' institutional culture, which is defined here as the "pattern of shared basic assumptions learned by a group as it solved its problems of external adaptation and internal integration, which has worked well enough to be considered valid and, therefore, to be taught to new members as the correct way to perceive, think, and feel in relation to these problems."[7] This definition highlights the external and internal focus of the Corps' efforts as it sought to ensure its existence and the way the Corps began to consciously institutionalize these ideas.

The Marines' approach contrasted greatly with their counterparts in the Navy and Army, who drew on history in their efforts to professionalize while Marines reactively looked to the past in seeking to resolve their ongoing existential crisis. As renowned scholar of organizational culture Edgar Schein has argued, institutions must envision a "shared concept of its ultimate survival problem, from which usually is derived their most basic sense of core mission, primary task, or 'reason to be.'"[8] The Corps had two primary missions from its establishment: keep order at sea and participate in combat, either as sharpshooters or as participants in landing parties. These two missions provided the Corps with a tenuous claim because the requirement to police naval vessels in particular originated from the aping of British customs, which many U.S. naval officers found objectionable. The presence of Marines, they believed, inhibited the development of a truly American Navy.

By privileging seemingly pragmatic aspects of military institutions like mission and technology, historians largely have ignored naval officers' efforts to fashion an identity for the Navy that did not include the Marines. As Carl Builder has shown, culture permeates matters such as strategy and planning that one often assumes are driven by purely rational thinking.[9] Marine and naval officers at times shared the same vision of eliteness, which led to competing institutional cultures.

The tension between the institutions intensified during periods of technological change, but it owed just as much to the need to fashion a distinctively American Navy as it did to "practical" justifications. The Navy might not need the Marine Corps to do its job, but its relationship with the Corps—even from a position of superior power—critically influenced its own cultural development. With its existence challenged continually by some in the Navy as well as elsewhere, the Corps struggled to establish a strong culture, particularly because it did not have the institutional infrastructure to agree on deeply embedded assumptions about why it existed in the first place.

The extent to which the relationship between the Corps and the Navy sparked identity formation ebbed and flowed. Between the end of Reconstruction and the onset of the Spanish-American War, issues of identity increasingly shaped the relationship between the Navy and the Corps. In part, this increase can be explained by the rise of navalism, or the commitment to building a first-rate Navy for imperial purposes. This trend resonated powerfully with naval officers, who then similarly sought to improve their branch's image. The United States built an imperial navy, Mark Shulman argues, not because it saw any strategic necessity but because it wanted an imperial navy.[10]

A first-class Navy needed first-rate sailors. Naval officers arrived at this realization a decade or so after a handful of Marine officers concluded that, in an era when the Marine Corps was anything but elite, an elite image could resolve the Corps' continuing existential crises. Indeed, an improved reputation was the only solution, as no mission could provide the Corps with the stability it so badly needed.

Since its inception the Corps had occupied a peculiar position. As neither a land-based organization like the Army nor an entirely sea-based one like the Navy, the Corps' missions overlapped with both institutions. A mission can be understood as the tasks and roles—the function, the raison d'être—assigned to an institution that usually constitute its justification for existence. Usually an institution's mission or missions reveal its functional purpose. Whereas armies and navies can each claim their own domains, marines tend to have more varied missions and ad hoc responsibilities that overlap with both the land and the maritime domains. The institution most similar to the U.S. Marines—the British Royal Marines—transitioned from a light infantry and landing force into more of a specialized commando force in the twentieth century, for example.[11] This was not the case for the U.S. Marine Corps, which did not follow a predetermined path.

Yet often the Corps is viewed as doing just that. Jack Shulimson, for example, hunts for the roots of the Corps' expeditionary mission in the late nineteenth century. Marine officers, however, struggled to identify or justify a particular mission. The Spanish-American War marked an important point in the Corps' transition from a participant in transitory landing parties to more intensive expeditionary service, though not because the Corps proactively sought to make this change. This pattern only becomes clear in hindsight. Yet historians have stressed the shift to this expeditionary mission and the subsequent transition toward an amphibious mission in the interwar period.[12]

In the years between the Civil War and the Spanish-American War, the Navy and the Marine Corps participated in a significant number of landing operations around the world that the Corps might have seized upon more proactively to claim a unique mission. Generally transient raids, these operations aimed to protect American lives and property in response to unstable situations in other nations. Increasingly, the Navy used the Corps as a flexible force in readiness to be used whenever needed around the world. The Navy appreciated Marines because it maintained more control over them, unlike the Army.[13] The Navy could also use the Corps to acquire advanced bases to provide it with a more secure means to coal its vessels and launch operations when necessary.

To focus too much on this new mission, however, camouflages the extent to which Marines loathed losing any traditional roles. After all, if the Corps ceded its most traditional duties, as many in the Navy hoped—namely, guarding naval officers and naval vessels from unruly enlisted personnel—no guarantee existed that it might not resemble the Army. Even the development of an expeditionary role could not fully resolve the Corps' insecurities about what purpose it served.

The Corps' service in the Spanish-American War and subsequent imperial wars strengthened the institution's external image and its members' institutional identification. Subsequently, the Corps, along with a small handful of government agencies, helped to spearhead publicity in the government at the beginning of the twentieth century.[14] By around 1907 the Corps' foundation myths coalesced into coherent narrative as the institution began to think more creatively about recruiting. It institutionalized these ideas by establishing the Recruiting Publicity Bureau in 1912, which created a vehicle for disseminating the Corps' image to every corner of the nation.[15] Moreover, the combined focus on recruiting and publicity, and the concomitant emphasis on both external image and internal identity, enabled the Corps to provide more consistent and more powerful messaging. Internally, the bureau worked to increase the extent to which each recruit affiliated with his institution upon completion of training. Externally, the Corps acquired the means of flooding newspapers across the country with positive news of Marines and their accomplishments, while the bureau worked aggressively to end public ignorance and confusion surrounding Marines.

The bureau's existence testifies to the importance the Corps attached to this pursuit. Despite being the smallest service in the U.S. military, the Corps pioneered a powerful melding of history, publicity, identity, and image. Far more secure in its existence, by contrast, the Navy did not establish a news bureau until 1917, which provided only limited services; similarly, the Army's public relations' efforts originated in 1918 from within its Military Intelligence Division.[16] Neither felt compelled to create anything like the Corps' Recruiting Publicity Bureau until the end of World War I.

The bureau devoted itself to making it mean something to be a Marine. One recruiting pamphlet cover emblazoned with the words "Who Am I?" epitomized the Corps' central dilemma in educating the public about what purpose it served (see fig. 1). As the accompanying written material in the 1916 pamphlet explained, "I am a rover. I am the United States Marine." Fighting, and fighting well, became the Corps' mission, so to speak. Rather than seek to resolve the Corps' traditional insecurity regarding what mission it should fill, the bureau created a flexible image of an elite fighter capable of any and all missions. Claims to elitism and a sense of affiliation with a distinctive organization are central to group identity. An effective way to distinguish one's own organization is to show how it differs from "what is closest, against that which represents the greatest threat."[17]

This characteristic explains much of the tension between the Corps and the Navy. Historians overemphasize mission at the expense of a much longer battle between the Navy and the Marine Corps that centered on the identity of a sailor vis-à-vis a Marine, a conflict that originated at the beginning of the nineteenth century. Many naval officers vehemently opposed the presence of Marines on board naval vessels because they believed it hindered the creation of a strong naval culture. Naval officers lamented that the presence of Marines harmed morale, and they finally found favor with President Theodore Roosevelt, who removed Marines from naval vessels in 1908.[18]

Central to the Corps' self-definition, then, were comparisons to its sister institutions, the Army and the Navy, which shifted depending on the institution's needs. Given the incorporation of both the Army and the Marine Corps into the American Expeditionary Force in World War I, for example, the Corps had to refine its image to avoid appearing to

Fig. 1. "Who Am I?" *Paul Woyshner Papers, MCHD, 1916*

be a redundant land army. Elite forces, by contrast, appeared as "color-ful remnants of a different world" to the public. Similarly, the idea of "shock troops" that could be used to break the stalemate of trench war-fare appealed to the imagination.[19] As opposed to mass armies, shock troops showcased their "speed" and "mobility."[20]

   In actuality, the way Marines fought differed little from U.S. soldiers. In his study of World War II Marines, Craig Cameron argues that the Corps' traditional insecurities about its existence and its need to differ-entiate itself from the Army led it to favor "quick, decisive assaults" over the Army's more methodical campaigns. The Corps paid a heavy price for this doctrine, Cameron asserts, with greater casualties and combat trauma. Cameron traces the origins of this approach back to the Battle of Belleau Wood, where he believes the Corps learned to view "battle as a test of cultural mettle and institutional reputation."[21]

How Marines fought at the battle had far more to do with the doctrine of the American Expeditionary Force (AEF) than it did with the Corps' warfighting culture. Still, understanding how the bureau connected Marines to elite shock troops before Belleau Wood suggests how and why the Corps manipulated its image and how this publicity worked just as powerfully as the Corps' actions in France. The idea of Marines serving as special troops suggested that the Corps did not simply duplicate the role of the doughboy but provided something distinctive. By creating a flexible image, the bureau could attach itself to those missions that appealed to the public imagination.

This work argues not only that the Corps could not lay claim to a particular mission but that it did not want to choose one because even its most traditional mission of policing naval vessels always had been under threat. The process by which a maligned group of postbellum nineteenth-century naval policemen began to consider themselves elite warriors particularly benefited from Marine officers' active engagement with the Corps' historical record as justification for their branch's very being. Rather than look forward and actively seek out a mission that could secure their existence, late nineteenth-century Marines looked backward and embraced the past. They began to justify their existence by invoking their institutional traditions, their many martial engagements, and their claim to be the nation's oldest and proudest military institution.

It received an additional boost from its combat during the Spanish-American War and the prospect of exotic imperial service after it. Increasingly arguing that they could perform any mission, some Marine officers pointedly suggested the institution undertook tasks other services either did not want or could not complete successfully.[22] Individuals increasingly crafted stronger, more powerful images that demonstrated an increased identification with their institution while drawing on the public acclaim they received for fighting against all odds in imperial conflicts. Simultaneously, the Corps marginalized the participation of sailors in combat during and after the Spanish-American War. Marines depicted themselves as fighters as opposed to sailors, who purportedly embraced a more passive role in support of the Marines as the rowers of fighters to shore. Both at sea in manning a variety of naval guns and on land in fighting, the measure of one's masculinity—as defined by Marines—was the extent to which one willingly risked one's body in combat.

Recruiters conveyed these images to journalists while progressively institutionalizing this identity, particularly by instilling it within their recruits. They sought to establish an emotional connection with the public, to include recruits, echoing the transformation of advertising in the United States after the Civil War in motivating consumers to purchase products. Achieving this connection required both internal and external components that increased the attachment of Marines themselves to their institution as well as the public. The creation of the Recruiting Publicity Bureau enabled Marines to be more creative with the flexible image that the institution had normalized by this period. The bureau reinforced Marines' growing sense of eliteness. Individual recruiters increasingly recognized important psychological benefits to individuals by empowering them and enhancing their sense of self-worth.[23] The Corps maneuvered this image as necessary to deal with a number of challenges, including its evolving relationship with the Navy, the huge influx of recruits necessitated by World War I, and the addition of the first female Marines.

Most analogous to the Corps' experience in transforming its external image and gaining public acclaim is that of the French Foreign Legion, which created a powerful illusion that did not always match reality.[24] British officers similarly helped to reform the image of Scottish Highland troops from savage heathens to exotic, powerful warriors, which assisted their recruiting efforts.[25]

Even more challenging than tracing an evolving image can be understanding the internal process by which individuals choose to affiliate themselves with an organization. Scholars of organizational identity have suggested that individual identity has two components.[26] The first component is a sense of one's own traits and distinguishing characteristics, or a personal identity. The other component is the group or social identity, or the extent to which individuals find meaning in identifying themselves with various segments of society. Individuals may find meaning in any number of categories. How important each identity is depends on the individual.[27] For example, some individuals might gain a sense of belonging and empowerment by affiliating themselves with any number of categories, ranging from gender to ethnicity to religion. Of course, this identity can ebb and flow. In the case of World War I Marines, for example, an initial enthusiastic pride in the Corps during training probably diminished for many after experiencing the harsh realities of combat. Moreover, individuals could serve in the Corps without feeling any sense of attachment to the institution whatsoever.

Despite the general agreement by Marines and observers that the Corps has a uniquely strong and vibrant institutional culture and that its publicity efforts have been notable, few works examine these subjects in depth. Published in 1956, Robert Lindsay's *This High Name: Public Relations and the U.S. Marine Corps* is the only work focused solely on the institution's publicity efforts, yet it provides only a cursory examination of the subject with minimal archival research. But the Corps' efforts to improve its image and identity are not a historical side note or just a compelling story. Rather, they are the most important component to understanding the institution's historical evolution and its continued existence, and thus this work focuses on a critical yet understudied fifty-year span of its history.

A number of sources illuminate the Corps' increasing emphasis and reliance on image and identity. Especially valuable are the letters, histories, and articles produced by nineteenth-century Marine officers. The variety of available sources increases greatly in the twentieth century, providing a wider sample of voices, especially those of enlisted Marines. One of the greatest resources for understanding how the Recruiting Publicity Bureau expanded and strengthened an image while increasing the institution's group identity is its magazine, the *Recruiters' Bulletin*. Published monthly beginning in 1914, the *Bulletin* reveals how the Corps sought to attract recruits as well as strengthen the identity of current and former Marines.

Still, official sources like the *Bulletin* pose a challenge for the historian. On the one hand, it is tempting to view them as propaganda. Noted Marine historian Allan Millett, for example, characterizes the magazine as nothing more than "adventure stories designed to lure prospective recruits and entertain enlisted Marines."[28] This perspective misses the extent to which the publication actively worked to help convince individual Marines and the general public to connect emotionally with the institution in a manner consistent with changes in the advertising industry.

The individual contributors to the *Bulletin* also highlight the range of individuals across various ranks who contributed to this process. The historiography of how enlisted servicemen have shaped institutional culture is thin.[29] Some work, however, demonstrates the importance of taking enlisted subcultures seriously in examining identity formation.[30] Culture is not always imposed from above, even in extremely hierarchical institutions. In the case of the Recruiting Publicity Bureau, enlisted Marines had significant agency. As the *Bulletin*'s editor explained in 1916, the magazine's writings—including its editorials—were not "inspired by 'higher-ups,'" who did not even see the magazine until publication.[31] The Corps' image and identity developed far more from the efforts of the entire range of its ranks than it did from its commandants' individual efforts. As such, this work places less emphasis on well-known individuals who occupied more traditional positions of power and on influential decisions made outside of the Corps.

Together, enlisted Marines and officers helped to build on the Corps' historical record, which a cadre of late-nineteenth-century Marines officers had forged. Long before Marines began proclaiming their eliteness to anyone willing to listen, naval officers questioned their very existence. Chapter 1 explores the Corps' ambivalent relationship with the Navy throughout the nineteenth century. Despite fighting together during the War of 1812, many naval officers subsequently pushed for the Marines' removal from ships. As a result, the Corps only narrowly escaped being incorporated into the Army in the 1820s and 1830s. In the Civil War, the Corps saw limited service on land, spending most of its time on board naval vessels. Once again, it survived several calls for its abolition or assimilation into the Army. When the United States experienced economic difficulties in the 1870s, the Corps found itself even more vulnerable. Unable to find a mission to justify its existence, a small group of Marines worked to reshape the Corps' public image by creating a history asserting an unbroken continuum that could be traced as far back as the ancient Greeks.[32] Having also stressed controversially that it was the oldest military institution in the United States, the Corps began to find virtue in maintaining that it was the most traditional one as well. In an era of rapid change and dislocation, Marines hoped to use the Corps' deep roots in the past to provide an image of consistent service. Although the Corps made major strides in improving its image by the end of the nineteenth century, it still found itself in serious conflict with the Navy. As it fully transitioned to steam-powered vessels, the Navy intensified its attacks on the utility of Marines at sea. Although technological change helps to explain some of this tension, it does not go far enough; rather, it is the continuity of the cultural tension going back to the early nineteenth century that explains why some naval officers so vehemently opposed the presence of Marines. They felt it inhibited the development of the sailor's identity.

Chapter 2 examines how the Spanish-American War resolved some of the Corps' nineteenth-century challenges by providing it with more opportunities to receive public approval and intensify internal identification. During the war, Marines at sea served as gunners on the secondary batteries, where they did not receive much acclaim because the primary batteries proved more effective against the Spanish.[33] A battalion of about 650 Marines received significant attention during the first ground combat of the war when they landed in Cuba to set up an advanced base in a harbor the Navy wanted to use to recoal its vessels. Americans eagerly read about outnumbered Marines fighting in harrowing conditions. After the war, Marines stepped into the ready-made job of securing and policing imperial outposts, in part because the Navy wanted infantry it could control. The Corps' increased confidence

encouraged Marines to distinguish themselves as military elites in contrast to sailors and soldiers. As one young Marine officer remarked during the Spanish-American War, the "Marines are acknowledged to be
[the] best drilled and disciplined Corps in any Branch of our Services.
On board ship they out sailor the sailors, and on shore they beat the
Army in their own tactics."[34] This sort of hyperbole intensified in the
years after the Spanish-American War. Whether or not they could back
up such assertions, Marines boasted about their qualitative superiority
to the Army and the Navy.

Chapter 3 explores the Corps' early publicity experiments. Needing
to recruit thousands of men after the Spanish-American War, the Corps
began to experiment with new recruiting practices and commercial
advertising agencies. Most notably, in 1906 it shifted away from a heavy
reliance on help-wanted ads to using advertising disguised as regular
newspaper articles. These articles depended on emotional appeals to
attract recruits. While the Navy happily emulated the Corps' innovative
recruiting practices, it continued to seek the removal of Marines from
its ships and succeeded, albeit temporarily, in 1908. Marine officers
pushed back by drawing on aspects of the Corps' image, worried that
ceding one of their most traditional missions might result in the Corps'
absorption into the Army.

Having survived another existential crisis, the Corps established
a Recruiting Publicity Bureau in 1912. The bureau provided an official mechanism for drawing on, elaborating, and disseminating some
aspects of the Corps' image and identity that individuals had been per-
petuating since the nineteenth century. Chapter 4 examines the aggressive methods the bureau used to obtain recruits as it sought to ensure
that every household knew what it meant to be a Marine. Given that
a mission-based definition was problematic for the Corps, the bureau
preferred to stress that the Marine was simply a superior, elite soldier
capable of any task.[35] Looking for inspiration to some commercial
advertising practices, Marines created trademarks and slogans that they
hoped every American might recognize. By the outbreak of World War
I, the bureau had attached meaning and significance to these symbols to
reinforce the Marine's identification with his institution.

The remaining chapters focus on the years after the Recruiting Publicity Bureau was established to clarify how the Corps deployed and maneuvered its flexible image in response to various developments and challenges. Chapter 5 explores the continuing battle over identity between the Navy and the Marine Corps. Whereas sailors and Marines had fought side by side in nineteenth-century landing parties, twentieth-century Marines assumed greater responsibility for more complex landing operations requiring increased training and coordination. Simultaneously, the Corps began to construct a narrative of itself as the most masculine military institution, one that offered the surest path to becoming a "real" man. Even the basic rowboat—one of the oldest pieces of naval technology, if one can call it that—became a gendered site of contestation because it allowed one service to claim it was more masculine than another.

Marines of varying ranks increasingly celebrated their service in the Corps, and now the bureau sought not only to find recruits but to bond them to the institution during training, as chapter 6 argues. In concert with recruit training, the bureau attempted to inculcate the Corps' spirit into its recruits during initial training. To aid in this process, the Corps created an aristocracy based not on a recruit's social class but on his ability to prove himself worthy of belonging to the Corps' brotherhood. This emphasis on brotherhood is one manifestation of the bureau's attempts to strengthen group identity by encouraging the sense of belonging to something special while appealing to larger democratic tendencies within the United States.[36] It also rewarded its enlisted Marines by offering a viable path for enlisted Marines to become officers and celebrating close relations between its officers and enlisted men.[37]

The Corps did not succeed entirely with this approach, especially internally, as can be seen in the postwar accounts of Marines who fought in World War I. Many argue that the Corps' participation in World War I helped to intensify the Marines' sense of distinction from the Navy and the Army. But Marines who fought in France largely self-identified as soldiers, with their wartime mission overwhelming the meaning the bureau sought to impose. In fact, the bureau's rhetoric showed its limits in France when enlisted Marines' experiences did not live up to the expectations the Corps had created. The Corps' aggressive rhetoric also collided with the Army, which was furious at the Corps' overzealous publicity efforts at its expense. Subsequently, the Corps reined in some of its assertive publicity.

Finally, chapter 7 addresses the bureau's efforts to hypermasculinize its institutional culture. The enlistment of the first female Marines in 1918 ironically enabled the strengthening of this process. Mirroring society, the Corps transitioned from celebrating a restrained manliness in the nineteenth century to a more aggressive, virile masculinity at the beginning of the twentieth century. The admission of women Marines in 1918 challenged the Corps' identity temporarily, yet the bureau adroitly used this influx of new Marines to strengthen its claims to masculinity. It did this by regendering its division of labor. Now, it proclaimed, those male Marines who had served as clerks—an occupation increasingly seen as a feminine—had been freed to fight in France.

The Corps' successes in France brought it public acclaim, greatly improving its external image even as the war and the resulting expansion of the Corps challenged its identity. As one *Bulletin* cover attests, Marines increasingly felt appreciated by their nation (see fig. 2). Still, as the smallest military service, the Corps could tailor a more specific image and adjust it as needed. To handle its most pressing challenges, the Corps deliberately crafted in less than fifty years an image of a hero that finally made it mean something special to be a Marine.

NOTICE TO READERS.—*When you finish reading this magazine place a one-cent stamp on this notice, hand same to any postal employee and it will be placed in the hands of our soldiers or sailors at the front. No wrapping—No address.* A. S. BURLESON, *Postmaster General.*

The Recruiters' Bulletin

Published Monthly in the Interests of the Recruiting Service of the U. S. Marine Corps.

Volume 4. NEW YORK, NOVEMBER, 1917. Number 1.

Fig. 2. Uncle Sam: "My, how you've grown, sonny! Each year I am more thankful for you." *Cover*, Recruiters' Bulletin, *Nov. 1917*

PART I

CRAFTING THE CORPS' IDENTITY

Chapter One

Inspiration and Articulation
Othering the Navy

I n 1829 the U.S. Navy broke with tradition as the USS *Erie* sailed proudly out to sea. To the delight of its full complement of Navy officers, not a single Marine was on board. This event highlights an early point in the Corps' history, when one of its most traditional responsibilities came under threat. This trend continued throughout the nineteenth century as the Navy transitioned from the age of sail into the age of steam. Having difficulty claiming a unique mission, Marines responded by seeking to improve their image and strengthen their identity.

A few decades before, the Navy had been in a similar situation. The Navy of the American Revolution had been characterized by weakness and fragmentation. And even after its reestablishment in 1798, the Navy faced the challenge of convincing the public that such an institution was necessary. The young nation's naval victories during the War of 1812 greatly helped to cement the public's belief in the need for a Navy and improve its external image.[1]

But these events did not fully create a distinctive naval identity. Christopher McKee's *A Gentlemanly and Honorable Profession* richly illuminates the social history of early naval officers but shies away from deeply examining the Navy's culture. He states, for example, that "internal élan" came to characterize the institution soon after its founding without showing how or why that process occurred.[2] Nor does he explore how the Navy's exploits during the War of 1812 helped establish its distinct organizational and cultural identity by allowing it to settle debates about what kind of institution it should be. Pro- and anti-navalists had long dominated these arguments—would the United States use a navy more for coastal defense, a kind of naval version of its militia, or would it create something more akin to the British Navy to defend its commerce around the globe?[3] The Navy's victories in the War of 1812 provided naval officers with more agency to answer these questions and shape their institution. Indeed, Congress believed that the Navy did so well in the war that it authorized a significant construction program in 1816 almost as a reward. Approving nine ships of the line, Congress sharply veered away from a navy built for coastal defense.[4]

While the War of 1812 resolved some of the Navy's institutional challenges, it did not do so for the Marines, whose responsibilities and missions had been inchoate since its inception. When Congress established the Continental Marines on November 10, 1775, it had hoped to attack British war matériel and strongholds in Nova Scotia.[5] To do so, it believed it needed to seek "good seamen" to fill two battalions of Marines within the Continental Army.[6] The resolution contained the seeds of the perennial confusion regarding the institution. Congress only vaguely spelled out what duties it intended Marines to fill and further complicated matters by expecting Marines to have experience at sea while considering them part of the Army.[7]

During the American Revolution, Marines primarily served as soldiers at sea. As such, they served as marksmen in ship-to-ship combat, to include sniping from the ship's rigging and participating in boarding parties. They could also be used during amphibious landings in conjunction with sailors to capture forts or other military targets, as first seen in April 1776.[8] Capt. Samuel Nicholas, about two hundred Marines, and fifty sailors seized a fort on New Providence, Bahamas, without encountering much opposition. Capturing a significant amount of British war matériel, the Marines had fulfilled the kind of interdiction mission Congress had contemplated in the proposed raid in Nova Scotia. They also functioned as naval policemen, a duty that required them to protect ships and their officers from mutinies, desertion, theft, and other threats. The Navy's limited contributions during the American Revolution, however, prevented many opportunities for the Corps.

Within a decade, however, the United States reestablished the Navy to provide protection for its shipping, which had been plagued by pirates of the Barbary States in the Atlantic Ocean and the Mediterranean Sea. The subsequent passage of the Frigate Act of 1794 allowed one Marine officer and about fifty enlisted Marines to be placed on each frigate.[9] Ships with forty-four guns had one lieutenant, one sergeant, one corporal, and about fifty enlisted Marines. Ships of thirty-six guns received ten fewer enlisted Marines. This number aligned with the Royal Marine practice of assigning one Marine to each gun of a Royal Navy vessel.[10] In 1798 Congress authorized a fleet of thirty-six naval vessels that fell under the auspices of the new Department of the Navy. It also passed legislation specifically pertaining to the Corps on July 11, 1798, with an act for "establishing and organizing" a Marine Corps. The act allowed the Corps to be ordered to serve on shore at the president's request, including at forts and garrisons, in which case the Army's regulations governed them. Once again, though, it did not spell out the Marines' duties.[11]

As a result, ship captains exercised significant latitude in choosing how to use their Marine detachments. This leeway caused considerable consternation among Marine officers. Some felt naval officers tasked them with extraneous duties that impeded them from fulfilling their main responsibilities. For example, being ordered to participate in cleaning naval vessels, Marines argued, made it almost impossible for Marines to maintain the appearance of their uniforms as required to stand sentry duty when in foreign ports.[12] Similarly, Marine officers resented being subordinate to naval officers even if they technically held superior rank. The Department of the Navy tried unsuccessfully to resolve these tensions, sending a letter to naval captains intended to restrict the duties they could impose on Marine officers while clarifying the limited authority of Marine officers on board naval vessels.[13]

The Marines' presence at sea collided with heated wartime rhetoric during the War of 1812, as the U.S. Navy's ships sailed with flags briskly proclaiming "free trade and sailors' rights." In a war waged between a newly democratic nation and an aristocratic foe, rhetoric suffused descriptions of combat between the two navies. One American victory purportedly "made manifest that our tars (if fairly met) in defence of 'free trade and sailors' rights,' are invincible." The haughtiness and empty words of the British contrasted with a young America that had right and justice on its side.[14]

The ending of the war at the Treaty of Ghent affirmed these sensibilities. Naval officers increasingly understood their navy to be a uniquely American one. But one legacy of the Royal Navy aggravated and tested the patience of many naval officers to no end: the presence of Marines on board ship.[15] They argued that sailors could just as easily provide orderlies and sentries while afloat, guarding various areas of the ship such as the officers' quarters.[16] They also suggested that sailors could be trained to fulfill Marines' other tasks, including participating in landing parties and providing marksmanship.

The issue of British impressment during the War of 1812 had a disproportionate impact on the thinking of U.S. naval officers, given the limited number of sailors who experienced it.[17] But, having freed their men from the threat of British impressment, some naval officers determined upon a new mission: free their men of unnecessary Marine oversight.[18] They envisioned a ship that did not remove Marines from the same "situation" as sailors and then make them "invested with authority over" them. This unnatural elevation of Marines over sailors—despite their shared social origins—represented nothing more than a relic of the Royal Navy. After all, U.S. sailors enlisted voluntarily, so they would not seek to mutiny, or so some officers argued. This upsetting of the natural social order at the expense of their sailors made some naval officers nothing short of apoplectic.

Naval officers such as Isaac Hull who had fought alongside Marines during the War of 1812 now viewed their presence at sea dubiously. In 1812 Hull remarked how the Marines' conduct at sea in combat had "annoyed the enemy very much."[19] Even his British opponent conceded that he had lost too many of his own men because of the Marines' accurate marksmanship. In 1830, though, Hull made no mention of their combat efficiency. Rather, he argued that landsmen should replace Marines because the "sailor looks with a jealous eye upon men taken from the same station with himself." Similarly, MCmdt. Lewis Warrington proclaimed gratefully in 1814 that every "officer, seaman and marine did his duty, which is the highest compliment I can pay them."[20]

In 1830 now-captain Warrington had a different opinion, proclaiming that he had decided as early as 1810 that Marines were "superfluous" and that his opinion had only intensified since then. Despite his efforts to enforce good behavior as set forth in a detailed set of rules for his ship during the War of 1812, MCmdt. William M. Crane made no mention of sailors' behavior when considering whether Marines should be removed from ship. Rather, he argued that sailors could be used instead of Marines on board ship because of Americans' innate ability for marksmanship. In this way, he integrated a strong thread of American national identity—bound up in ideas about frontiersmen—with those serving at sea. This idea also reflected the sentiment that a sailor could act as a soldier, but not the reverse.[21]

Personnel issues, closely connected with identity, best help to explain this shift in opinion because they overshadowed other developments during the decades between the War of 1812 and the Civil War. Although the Navy did make some important administrative improvements, an economic recession limited the amount of new ships Congress had authorized in 1816. Technologically, the world was on the brink of a revolution in steam, but the U.S. Navy lagged behind other nations in its pursuit of this technology, with no steamship in its inventory at the time of the *Erie*'s sailing. The most consistent issue in its control that the Navy worked to improve was the quality of its personnel.[22] In particular, the Navy hoped to increase the number of citizens serving at a time when the merchant marine offered higher wages than the military. The sailing of the USS *Erie* in 1829 represented one experiment in personnel improvement that failed to fulfill its intended purpose. As the lowest-ranking sailors, landsmen possessed neither extensive knowledge of the sea nor much instruction in marksmanship, unlike their Marine counterparts, who trained to serve as sharpshooters from the rigging. One observer even described landsmen as fulfilling the least "honorable services" at sea.[23]

But in a decade of relative peace, such details could be overlooked. Without an opponent to occupy naval officers, Christopher McKee has suggested they turned their aggressive instincts inward on their institution. One symptom was the focus on the Navy at the expense of the

Corps. Thus, despite the limited experience and skills of the landsmen, naval officers found this experiment to be a successful one. "Disorderly conduct" purportedly decreased. The absence of Marines, Lt. J. M. Keever noted, "always seemed to impart increased ardor and good conduct."[24] A more homogeneous corporate culture at sea facilitated better behavior because sailors supposedly resented being policed by members of another military branch. This development outweighed the presence of more experienced and better trained men.

With the USS *Erie*'s return to port, the debates on the Marines' utility continued, but seemingly pragmatic discussions about the best way to man naval vessels veiled the deeper, underlying tensions over identity. A variety of opinions on this subject emerged in 1830 after Secretary of the Navy John Branch canvassed senior naval officers for their opinion on the need for Marines at sea. Of the sixteen officers who wrote to him, seven sought to remove Marines and nine hoped to keep them.[25]

How naval officers viewed sailors influenced their opinion of whether Marines should serve at sea. Some believed sailors to be incapable of undertaking the military, or soldierly, duties of Marines.[26] A sailor's identity was too disparate from a Marine's. As one observer explained so picturesquely even after the Civil War, sailors had a "swagger incompatible with the noble stiffness of a true marine."[27] These images suggested that sailors valued their independence too much to accept the strong discipline required of soldiers. To be a sailor in the U.S. Navy was to be free—almost an idealized version of what it meant to be a U.S. citizen.[28]

While anti-Marine naval officers suggested the Marines' presence hurt morale, one pro-Marine officer argued that ridding Marines from vessels actually undermined sailors' corporate identity. Capt. Thomas Jones found the idea of replacing the Marine Guard with sailors ludicrous because it diluted their identity. They lacked a "fixed or certain character" and "thus metamorphosed, would feel themselves disgraced in their *borrowed character*."[29] Jones grasped the presence of an other in facilitating identity formation, or the idea that close contact with another organization promotes deeper thinking about the nature of one's own institution by highlighting the contrasts between the two.

The continuing legacy of the War of 1812 also impacted these debates, particularly regarding impressment, as seen in a letter submitted with only the name of "Justice": "A comparison of our last naval regulations promulgated in the year 1815, will shew a most servile and discreditable imitation in our customs with the very worst feature of the English system: the peculiar characteristic of that service is the practice of impressment: to that feature chiefly is to be traced the necessity of a Marine Corps." Begging his readers to think critically, the author suggested that the Navy declare its independence fully from the British system by merging the Corps with the Army.[30] In looking back to the War of 1812, the author purposefully drew on the notion of justice by linking his sentiments to ones that had animated broader thinking about the very purpose of the war.

Journalists added their voices to the debate, including one who denounced the Corps in no uncertain terms. The Corps represented the Navy's most substandard part, which interfered with naval vessels' "efficiency and harmony." Marines were "of no use for the ordinary duties of the ship, or else, in becoming useful, they lose entirely their distinctive character, and cease to be more of soldiers than the seamen among whom they become mingled."[31] The Corps might continue to guard naval yards or be integrated into the Army, but it had no place on board naval vessels. In urging the Corps' "abolition," the journalist set out the heart of the institution's difficulties: it had to subsume its identity into the Navy's in order to be valuable, at which point Marines would no longer be soldiers.

By contrast, New York City's *Evening Post* settled on Cdr. Charles Stewart's letter as the most compelling of the sixteen letters for its "accuracy." Marines did provide some help sailing the ship. But the opposite could not be true. Sailors were "unfit" to be "infantry soldiers" because of their "ideas and general habits." Also, the argument that the Corps had no responsibilities "except for idle parades" needed to be challenged. In part, Commander Stewart argued that these kinds of trappings had even more importance in a "republican" government than in a monarchy because they helped to maintain order and "discipline" among citizens. Wary of too much democracy, Stewart valued the kind of ceremony epitomized by Marines' service at sea to remind the sailor of his correct place, just as he did for the average American.[32]

Commander Stewart's elitist vision did not resonate in popular fiction, which preferred to perpetuate naval officers' dismissive opinion of Marines. Authors used terms suggesting the naïveté and ignorance of Marines regarding nautical matters. The term "horse marine," for example, signaled the sailor's "contempt" for Marines.[33] It suggested an "awkward, lubberly person" who was "out of place" at sea.[34] Sailors also used the term "dead Marine" to describe an empty bottle, singling out Marine officers as being particularly worthless at sea.[35] As one nineteenth-century dictionary explained, the term "doubtless [arose] from the jealousy, dashed with a slight flavour of contempt" with which sailors viewed Marines.[36]

Marines rarely claimed to be sailors; indeed, Marines defined themselves as soldiers. The terms were virtually synonymous in their writing.[37] As such, they struggled to respond to naval officers' accusations that they did not contribute enough. In one instance, 1st Lt. Edward Reynolds took offense when a naval officer asked a sailor scrubbing the deck, "'Do you want any assistance? [I]f so, there's a marine *loafing* in the gangway,' pointing to a Corp[oral] *in belts* on *guard*." In taking issue with the naval officer's words, Reynolds hoped to establish once and for all the limits of how Marines could be tasked.[38]

Describing Marines as "lazy" was not a new development. Scholar Christopher McKee re-created the midshipman's first response on setting foot on board a naval vessel: "Almost certainly the first person he met when he came on board was the marine sentinel in full uniform marching back and forth at the gangway with his musket." The especially observant midshipman would even see the "well-drilled sergeant's guard, resplendent in their dress uniforms, now lounging more or less in idleness, but ready to turn out" instantly.[39]

Capt. John Broome complained of a situation similar to First Lieutenant Reynolds' after the *Hartford*'s executive officer ordered Marines to "scrape the gun carriages." Broome vehemently objected to doing what was "not part of the duty of a Soldier of the Marine Corps."[40] Defining a Marine as a soldier, Broome clearly delineated between Marines' duties as soldiers and sailors' responsibilities to maintain all aspects of the ship. Some enlisted Marines also embraced this demarcation. During the traditional "Neptune Celebration" that baptized those crossing the equator for the first time, Marines avoided participating.[41] Corp. Miles Oviatt, serving on board the USS *Brooklyn* during the Civil War, noted the Marines' refusal to participate in the proceedings, describing how "the lances['] men wer[e] all shaved, the[n] the Darks afterwards. They thought to Shave the Marines, but as they had not taken any part in the proceedings, they strongly objected. . . . Some few knocks wer[e] rec'd by the bluejackets. About this time, Mr. Daniels and Mr. Parker made their appearance and quieted the row. Mr. D then went to the captain to know if he could, by main force, take us up and put us through the process, which he did not think advisable to undertake. So they left us alone."[42] In this case, Corporal Oviatt and his fellow Marines set themselves apart from a cherished naval tradition. Despite being outnumbered by sailors, they felt secure in their power on board ship. They had no desire to participate in a ceremony that allowed sailors to upset traditional naval hierarchy and undercut their position at sea.

Being part of the Navy and yet distinct complicated the question of identity for Marines. Even Marines who jealously guarded their prerogatives on board ship could refer to their "service in the Navy," as Captain Broome did. Family ties also bound the two services together.[43] Perhaps most important for officers, some naval vessels sailed with only one Marine officer on tours that lasted multiple years. Whatever the bickering between the two services, their officers had to choose between companionship and loneliness.

Despite the friendships that formed at sea, the image many naval officers maintained of Marines as worthless supernumeraries had ramifications in Washington. Although Congress had decided against incorporating the Corps into the Army in 1830, it did clarify its relationship with the Navy in June of 1834. Members of Congress hoped to ease some of the tensions between officers of the two services that arose because their "rights and duties" had not been set out with exactness.[44] In "an act for the better reorganization of the United States' 'Marine Corps,'" Congress put the Corps under naval laws and regulations except when the president ordered Marines to serve with the Army.[45] It further clarified that Marine officers could not command navy yards or vessels and set the rank and pay of Marine officers to align with Army officers.

If Congress had intended legislation to end organizational problems, it was seriously mistaken. In December of 1835, the Navy Department issued regulations that put Marine detachments at naval yards more closely under the command of naval officers. The change infuriated Marine officers. One letter writer described how these regulations "brand[ed] them with degradation as a Corps" because they "destroy[ed] their identity as a body under military organization, and impeach[ed] their fidelity and trustworthiness as a guard, by imperatively requiring them to submit to the naval commandant of the yard, all orders."[46]

Issues of identity suffused matters of organization and hierarchy in the relationship between the two branches, whether at sea or not. From the Corps' perspective, the regulations severed the links between headquarters and the Marine Guard at the Navy Yard, putting the guard under the yard's ranking naval officer. This change threatened the soldierly character of the institution's corporate identity. Marines resented being forced to ask naval officers for approval every time they wanted to make an administrative decision ashore, such as temporarily removing a Marine from duty for misbehavior. President Andrew Jackson promptly moved to settle the matter, ordering Marines to remain under the control of the Corps' commandant, its highest-ranking officer, as set forth in an 1818 regulation. In seeking to provide the Corps with some physical distance from the Navy, some suggested building Marine barracks outside the navy yards to provide the Corps with more independence.[47] Such tensions characterized Navy–Marine Corps relations for the next decade. In 1847 one frustrated Marine officer explained how naval officers sought to denigrate his institution to members of Congress by describing Marines as fancy waiters.[48]

However much the Corps might have preferred greater distance from the Navy, it remained closely bound to it. Some Marines found this reality troubling during the Civil War because of the Navy's responsibility for blockade duty.[49] Primarily stationed on board naval vessels blockading Confederate ports along the Atlantic Ocean and

Gulf Coast, many Marines spent the war chasing the proverbial pot of gold, hoping for their share of prize money from captured vessels. The experience of Marines on board the *Vanderbilt* was representative of that of many Civil War enlistees. That vessel spent its time fruitlessly chasing infamous Confederate blockade-runner Raphael Semmes back and forth across the Atlantic.[50] Toward the end of the war, Marines also supported the Navy in short-lived landing operations, particularly the assault of Confederate strongholds protecting port cities.

During one of the greatest upheavals in U.S. history, the collective experience of Marines could largely be summed up as tedious.[51] As one Marine wrote in his journal, "even in these stirring times, the life of a marine is very monotonous, and judging from this, it must be next to unbearable in time of peace."[52] Many enlisted Marines found the lack of military opportunities during the war disheartening and hoped to transfer to a different service in order to gain glory or higher rank. Lawrence Carpenter wanted to take advantage of "great opportunities" for advancement in rank offered by the volunteers and "make a handsome thing of it."[53] Henry Meredith sought a discharge to escape the "position to which [he had] fallen." Having enlisted in the Corps because of reduced social status, he hoped his relatives, who held commissions in the U.S. Army, could help him with his "ambitions to succeed in life." He also worried that the Corps' current "state" precluded "the glories and terrors of an engagement with the enemy."[54] The missions Meredith had anticipated the Corps would fill during the war failed to fulfill his dreams of martial glory. While some sought the commandant's permission to be discharged, others simply deserted.[55] Marines might be considered soldiers, but their service during the war was distinct from their Army counterparts', who fought in significant land battles.[56] Even Marine officers contemplated leaving the Corps; 1st Lt. James Forney, for example, "chaf[ed] for want of active service." As late as 1865, Capt. Robert Huntington hoped he might transfer to the Army. Bored at sea in Asia, he hoped to find someone from the Army "foolish enough" to transfer to the Marine Corps in his place.[57]

Because the Corps could not recruit enough men to reach its authorized strength of 87 officers and 3,773 enlistees until the close of the war, many vessels lacked Marine detachments. As a result, the government turned elsewhere to find troops capable of accomplishing tasks normally performed by Marines. When the Corps could not meet the Navy's request to man boats on the Mississippi River, the Army established the Mississippi River Marine Brigade in 1862 and recruited soldiers to fill it. The brigade duplicated the military role Marines typically filled on naval vessels, such as conducting short landing operations ashore.[58] Additionally, naval vessels without Marines did not experience mutinies.

Historically, mutiny has been largely nonexistent in the U.S. Navy, especially in the traditional sense of sailors' physically removing or restraining their officers and seizing command of the ship themselves. American naval officers generally acted on suspicions of the intent to mutiny. But that does not mean naval officers did not fear the prospect, including during the Civil War, when they worried about low morale resulting from blockade duty. Some had suggested that the very presence of Marines helped to prevent mutiny in the first place by quick responses. Others, who had a more favorable impression of sailors, used the lack of mutiny during the Civil War to question continuing the employment of Marines as naval policemen.[59]

In seeking to resolve the challenge of filling its ranks, the Corps showed little creativity, largely because the military had yet to embrace the kind of public relations tactics that were beginning to dominate the commercial world.[60] The Corps focused most of its efforts on formulaic classified ads. Not only did the Army's and the Corps' ads appear in close proximity, they often appeared to be interchangeable. In 1861 the Army sought "able-bodied unmarried MEN, of good character." By contrast, the Corps sought "able-bodied MEN, for Sea and Land Service." Other than mentioning more variety in its service, this advertisement did not hold out any other inducement in regard to pay or benefits. Other recruiters mentioned various duties of Marines in a haphazard manner. One ad sought recruits for "service at our Navy Yards and on board our national vessels of war," while another just mentioned service at sea.[61] Some recruiting officers did change the tone of their ads over the course of the Civil War. Capt. James Lewis

Fig. 3. "Prize Money! Prize Money!" *Collection of the New-York Historical Society*

sought to lure recruits with promises of "varied and exciting" service as well as a "comfortable home" at sea.[62] These haphazard efforts reveal that the Corps had not crafted a master narrative to guide its recruiting efforts.

Similarly, two recruiting posters from during and immediately after the Civil War represent the Corps' typical appeals for much of the nineteenth century (see figs. 3 and 4). One poster sought to attract recruits with bounty money, then held out a more patriotic inducement to serve one's country. With war's end, another poster stressed the prospect of foreign travel. Still, it did not use the word "Marine" but rather "soldier." Many posters included a large chart outlining pay.

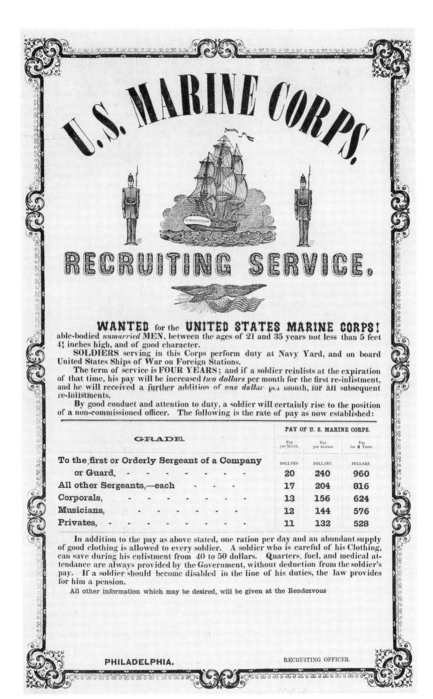

Fig. 4. "Wanted for the United States Marine Corps!" *Collection of the New-York Historical Society*

The reference to "soldiers" rather than "Marines" reflected the Corps' nineteenth-century practice of self-identifying first as soldiers. It also bears similarities in appearance and in wording to what is considered to be the Corps' oldest-known poster, which dates from the 1850s and shows a consistent approach.[63] More unconventionally, though, the poster appealed to those recruits who might obtain the rank of sergeant and thus receive "independent command" of Marine Guards on smaller naval vessels.

Another recruiting challenge owed much to the fact that the Navy and the Corps received far less public attention than the Army. While the public gloried in the achievements and heroics of its volunteer soldiers, it viewed those serving in the Navy as cowards, if it thought of them at all. The Navy's image also had been scarred by the antiflogging campaigns of the 1850s. The suggestion that sailors endured conditions reminiscent of slavery kept many from pursuing service in the Navy and marked a dramatic change from the images that emerged in the War of 1812.[64] The fact that the Navy and the Corps ran some of their classified ads together suggests that the Navy's image might have tarred the Corps' as well.[65]

Practical matters also made the Corps less attractive than other branches. Congress did not authorize the Corps to begin offering bounties until 1864.[66] Second, it required a longer enlistment term than the volunteers did.[67] Even though the Union received enough volunteers at the start of the war, it began offering monetary inducement. Also provided at the state level, these bounties motivated enough men that the government did not have to institute a draft until 1863. Sgt. B. W. Hopper's recruiting experience gives an idea of the competition the Corps faced. Having opened a recruiting office in the mining community of Pottsville, Pennsylvania, he described his office's location amid "some twelve others now recruiting" for the regular Army and the volunteers. Hooper did not know how he could get recruits when the Corps did not offer "superior inducement."[68]

By the end of the war, however, some of the Corps' recruiting woes ended thanks to four years of destructive combat. As Gerald Linderman has argued, romanticized ideas about war quickly faded for many who experienced combat. Where those seeking battle might have wanted to avoid the Corps in 1861, the opposite was more the case at the war's end. Indeed, Michael Bennett concludes that many men enlisted in the Navy to avoid the blood and gore of the battlefield.[69]

A notable exception to the Marines' wartime tedium occurred in January of 1865. Sailors and Marines acted as diversionary forces for the Army's main assault on well-fortified Fort Fisher, which protected the important port of Wilmington, North Carolina. A landing party comprised of 1,600 sailors and 400 Marines met with disaster after it received what some historians have characterized as confusing and unrealistic orders from Adm. David Porter. High-ranking naval officers generally appreciated Marines because they came directly under their command, unlike soldiers. In 1863, for example, Porter had requested Marines because he considered the militia troops on whom he was forced to rely to be "broken reeds."[70] His earlier apparent preference did not stop Porter from scapegoating the Marines, though, after Fort Fisher. He blamed the failure of the attack on the Marines' inability to maintain a "steady fire."[71] By contrast, Adm. George Dewey retrospectively characterized the operation as "sheer, murderous madness." He explained how sailors were armed with "only cutlasses and revolvers, which evidently were chosen with the idea that storming the face of the strongest work in the Civil War was the same sort of operation as boarding a frigate in 1812."[72]

Marines differed on the validity of Porter's critiques. Capt. L. L. Dawson decried these attacks as a "manifest injustice." Dawson found it "strange that the admiral attribute[d] the want of success alone to the 350 marines not clearing the parapet of a garrison 2,200 strong, which [Porter] admits was 'much stronger than he had considered.'" But in an anonymous letter purportedly written by Marines in 1866 regarding the Corps' future, one writer urged the Corps' integration into the Army. He admitted that his institution had "lost [its] prestige" at Fort Fisher but blamed the failure on cowardly Marine officers.[73] Becoming part of the Army, he reflected, offered the opportunity to improve the officers' acquaintance with tactics. One Marine responded in the pages of the *Army and Navy Journal*, explaining that the previous letter writer— who had signed his letter as "One Thousand and One Marines"—more fittingly should have signed it as "One Subordinate Marine." This writer suggested the Corps was "superior to any military body in our service," explaining that it was "certainly the best uniformed and equipped, and most attentive to the minute duties of the soldier."[74] The solution to these tensions, as many officers believed, was to make the Corps more soldierly. Marine Capt. P. C. Pope, who believed that sailors could not keep up with Marines in landing parties, hoped to polish the martial skills of Marines. Because he had limited knowledge of "bayonet drill," he requested a well-versed sergeant who could instruct his men. In a slightly different vein, Maj. John G. Reynolds hoped to make the Marine Corps more independent of the Navy on board ships for practical reasons, such as matters of pay.[75]

Cmdt. John Harris, however, found many Marine officers too desirous of shedding their connections to the Navy. He chided Maj. Augustus Garland, for example, for seeking to become more independent. Garland replied that he was not "unwilling to be associated with the Navy," but he thought the Corps should be more self-reliant. He described the institution as a "separate and distinct Corps, both from the Army and Navy, and is older than the Navy itself. The object of having such a Corps, was to have a body of Troops, under a military organization and discipline." Garland failed to point to any specific mission; rather, he emphasized general qualities typically found in armies. Harris found such opinions dangerous and believed they had resulted in some Congress members' suggesting the Army absorb the Corps. He explained that the Corps was "of the Navy" and had "nothing in common with the Army." The commandant's concerns were well founded. In 1862, for example, Congress had again considered making the Corps an Army regiment, severing its ties with the Navy.[76]

The Corps' participation in the Civil War did little to improve its reputation or public image, in part because few voices spoke powerfully for the Corps. In his naval history of the Civil War, Rear Adm. Henry Walker bemoaned that "other branches [had] their zealous champions . . . [but] how seldom we see an elaborate eulogy of the Corps."[77] Yet Walker only devoted two pages to the Corps in his four-hundred-page account of the war, expressing his "regret" at being unable to provide a "full estimate of the merits due to our marine corps." Rather than detailing aspects of their Civil War service, he quoted a long paragraph describing how Royal Marines had been unappreciated, believing the same could be said of the U.S. Marines.[78] Falling under the "ostensible protection of the admiralty, their interests are so subordinated to those of the fleet, that they have no status worthy of the name."[79] The Corps had difficulty changing its public image because it rarely received individual recognition for its actions; moreover, it had no one to speak for it on the national stage except as an afterthought.

After the Civil War, the Corps appeared to slumber through the 1870s and 1880s. As during the Civil War, Congress again considered incorporating the Corps into the Army and introducing budgetary reductions. Of course, other services faced the possibility of spending cutbacks, but they did not have to deal with speculation regarding their institution's abolition or absorption.[80] If the majority of the commandant's correspondence can be taken as an indication, the Corps existed to provide residents of Washington, D.C., with martial music through the auspices of its celebrated Marine Band.[81]

As a result, the image perpetuated by many naval officers since the 1820s of the Corps as replete with well-dressed but useless officers existed far beyond Washington, D.C. When the Corps offered to help the Army subdue the Sioux in 1876, a Michigan paper described how the "gorgeous" Corps sought to head west and go into the "hair business."[82] The article implicitly contrasted the Marines' interest in appearance with the stereotype that Native Americans practiced scalping. Another article published in an Ohio paper described Marine officers as "gingermen gentlemen" who preoccupied themselves with appearances first and martial duties second. The journalist advocated abolishing the Corps because only a few of its officers could be considered competent. If the Corps had received limited attention during the Civil War, at least it had not received much negative attention. A military institution of dubious usefulness serving a nation at peace and facing economic difficulties, however, was fair game for journalists.[83]

Considering the Corps to be an ossified institution, observers altered the Corps' acronym, USMC, to jokingly characterize its officers as "useless sons made comfortable." In a series of articles suggesting how the nation could achieve a more efficient military, the *Washington Post* singled out the Marine Corps for the most scathing remarks.[84] Written in the context of the economic crisis of 1877, the *Post* article unsurprisingly called for a reduction in spending by reducing the number of Marine officers. After all, it argued, the Corps was simply a repository for politically connected officers unable to find employment elsewhere.[85] Two months later, the *Post* went on the offensive again. An editorial entitled "Absolute Inutility" characterized the Marine Corps as an "amphibious hermaphrodite" that served only to provide "useless idlers" with income. The use of the word "hermaphrodite" epitomized the Corps' continuing dilemma: it could not carve out a unique claim to a mission because it overlapped with both the Army and the Navy.[86] Six months later, the *Post* attacked the Corps for its undemocratic practices.[87] At a time when society tended to view enlisted personnel negatively, this journalist suggested that the Corps' enlisted Marines actually merited respect, unlike its well-connected yet incompetent officers.[88] The journalist recounted his interview with an impressive-looking enlisted Marine, who represented the most "intelligent" type of service member.[89] He suggested the Corps should promote officers from the ranks rather than continuing to rely on patronage and influence in appointing commissions.[90]

The most vocal proponents of reform within the Corps embraced these negative representations as support for the organizational changes they wanted to see implemented. Viewing these attacks as an effective way to motivate the Corps' leadership to reform, 1st Lt. Henry Cochrane asked one newspaper editor why he did not describe the Corps' flaws more harshly. Cochrane believed that the medium of print provided the most effective means of "stir[ring] the ancient Marine foundations" because the Corps' leaders were "more afraid of newspapers than they are of the devil."[91]

Conscious of journalism's influence, Cochrane also considered the Corps' image in terms of recruiting. As a result, he interjected different themes into his classified advertisements than did his fellow Marine recruiters. One 1872 ad, for example, enjoined recruits to join the "favorite" branch of the service. Another described the Corps as the "oldest" military service that only accepted the "best," meaning it was "justly regarded as a 'crack' organization."[92] Cochrane's ads presaged the power of prestige intrinsic to the Corps' twentieth-century recruiting appeals.

By October of 1875, Cochrane proposed to resolve the Corps' negative image. In the past, Marines often had responded to critiques by publishing pamphlets containing naval officers' letters of support.[93] Cochrane wanted to try a different approach. In a confidential pamphlet entitled "A Resuscitation or a Funeral," Cochrane immediately tackled the Corps' troubling image, arguing that there was a "deep seated and wide spread antipathy toward the Marine Corps only the blind and imbecile can doubt." The press had been "hounding" the Corps in recent years. He summed up many of the negative nicknames used to describe the Corps as follows: "'Captain Jinkses,' 'carpet knights,' 'parlor warriors,' 'horse marines,' 'sea sogers,' *undergraduates* of the national schools,' . . . [and] 'shoulder-strapped Adonises.'"[94] In short, the Corps had acquired an image of being "neither respected nor respectable." It had "fail[ed] to cultivate that public opinion, or *esprit*."[95] Cochrane found this negative image to be the most pressing issue for the Corps because he recognized the importance of winning public approbation.

By contrast, the matter of what the Corps should do received far less attention. The pamphlet touched on the prospect of a new mission for the Corps in a section entitled "The United States Naval Artillery."[96] The section heading suggested that Cochrane found this new name to be the solution, but the section's content contained little more than an acknowledgment of how difficult it was to identify a mission. Cochrane contradictorily explained that the Corps had a "wide field for usefulness, and while I express myself dolefully as to what it is, I yield to no one in conception and conviction as to what it might be. A few short years of vigorous and wise administration would make us the American standard of military perfection and efficiency, and place us where our value would never be questioned." Despite the thought Cochrane gave to reorganizing the Corps, he failed to make a case for the Corps becoming a naval artillery.[97] Instead, he relied on a general quality of service to silence the institution's critics. Traits like perfection and efficiency echoed Garland's suggestion about ensuring the Corps' military traits.

Other Marines joined the chorus in the coming years, echoing the refrain that the Corps needed to improve its external image. As an anonymous Marine explained to readers of the *Army and Navy Journal*, "Interviews with enemies of the Marine Corps have shown in nearly every known instance that their opposition was based on misconception, or ignorance, of its history, and its multifarious functions ashore and afloat."[98] To improve public opinion, the Corps needed to ensure that its history and its numerous contributions were well known.

Historians have found little positive to say about officers in this era, suggesting that officers occupied themselves excessively with securing more pay and faster promotions. Others have characterized the few successful reforms of the period—such as enabling the direct commissioning of Naval Academy graduates—as "legislative flukes." Perhaps most damning, other historians charge that the Corps failed to match the Navy's "intellectual ferment" of the 1880s.[99]

Marine officers might not have participated in the technical aspects of professional debates to the same extent as their Army and Navy counterparts, who argued about everything from homing pigeons to electricity.[100] Yet with fewer than eighty officers for most of the 1870s and 1880s, the Marine Corps did well to have even a handful of officers actively engaged in seeking reform. Their interests moreover do not differ dramatically from their Army counterpart who discussed similar issues, to include promotion opportunities. One historian even characterizes Army officers' efforts as consisting more of sending anonymous letters to the *Army and Navy Journal* than writing detailed articles.[101]

Moreover, these characterizations rest on definitions of professionalization that privilege technical debates. When definitions of professionalization include identity, however, the Corps' efforts can be appreciated better. In connecting the Navy's professionalism to the Naval War College's establishment, for example, Ronald Spector defines professionalization as not only emphasizing the acquisition of technical knowledge but also gaining a "heightened feeling of group identity." The establishment of associations and journals did more than simply pro-vide forums for the dissemination of technical knowledge.[102]

Other officers pursued unique avenues to improve the Corps' iden-tity and image. In 1875 Richard Collum published the first of three edi-tions of *History of the United States Marine Corps.* By comparison, the Army did not receive similar attention until 1924, when William Ganoe published *The History of the United States Army.*[103]

Consistent with many of his counterparts, Collum looked to craft a military identity more than a naval one for the Corps. For example, he envisioned his institution's officers being educated at West Point rather than the Naval Academy. He believed that the future Marine officer's education *"must be military"* rather than *"half sailor and half soldier."*[104] While early twentieth-century Marines stressed the Corps' duties on sea and land, Collum emphasized the importance of forming soldiers first and foremost.[105] This education served to protect the Corps' "dis-tinctive character" to better "ensure its efficiency." Until Marine officers could be educated at West Point, he hoped that the Corps could expand its new officers' education beyond "infantry tactics" into other areas such as artillery.[106]

Collum began researching his study sometime around 1873. His knowledge of history presumably more impressive than his ability to condense, his publisher gave journalist M. Almy Aldrich the task of cull-ing the work, even publishing the work under his name.[107] Unhappy with Aldrich's version, Collum revised the work in 1890 and again in 1903.[108]

Jack Shulimson, the foremost expert on the late nineteenth-century Marine Corps, characterizes Collum's work as "rather undistinguished, consisting largely of a description of Marine battle exploits and large excerpts from the annual reports of the secretary of the Navy and the commandant of the Marine Corps." By today's standards, Collum's his-tory seems best suited to cure insomnia. Yet Collum's approach reflected the Victorian sensibilities of the time. He considered it inappropriate to boast of his Corps because such blatant self-promotion might undercut his efforts. Rather, he sought to provide a "fair book for the perusal of the public." This approach reflected his belief that an "unbiased report" of Marines offered the best chance of maintaining the Corps' reputation.[109]

Collum's opinion overlapped with naval officers, who generally distrusted commercial business practices. Even if they had viewed them more positively, their isolation from society due to their profession provided limited opportunities to observe how more aggressive marketing practices were beginning to dominate commercial practices.[110] In short, Collum's *History* is a product of its time.

In personal correspondence, by contrast, Collum willingly celebrated the Corps when writing to fellow officers. For example, when on duty surrounded by a variety of different units from various services, Collum exclaimed, "none of them can compare with our Battalion."[111] If the kind of pride that characterizes twentieth-century writing by Marines is absent from his public writings, it is not because he lacked those sentiments but because he found them distasteful for public consumption. In another letter to Cochrane, he cut short his comments praising the Corps, promising to not "annoy [him] further with my remarks on the Corps, because I might be guilty of egotism which, you know, should always be avoided; but I will say that our Corps should be the organization 'par excellence' of the service." Collum envisioned the Corps becoming an elite institution, but he chose to be far more subtle in writing for public consumption. He eagerly hoped that Marines would add "fresh laurels" to the institution's "reputation." And, even if he might be frustrated with his men while drilling them, in public a "certain 'esprit-de-corps'" was evident, and their appearance and execution of drill could not be "excelled" by others.[112]

Publicly, though, Collum focused on history to make more subtle claims to improve the Corps' image. History, one scholar explains, constitutes that "view of the past which looks to tradition to confer a permanent structure on experience." The common thread that linked the Corps' histories together—an emphasis on the length of the institution's existence, purportedly even antedating the Navy—typifies the approach often taken by peripheral or marginalized groups. The production of history is a key element of this process because it enables authors to impose an artificial "continuity" that links an "ancient" past to the present that can help to create a sense of stability in periods of crisis.[113] The Corps sought to benefit from the idea that long-established institutions had validity because of their age, just as businesses announce how long they have been in existence to demonstrate their products' continuing value and solid track record.

Taken together, Marine officers responded to their institution's continued state of crisis by looking back as far as the Classical Age.[114] Collum received assistance from well-known naval officer, reformer, and proponent of history Adm. Stephen B. Luce in his efforts. In contributing the work's second chapter, Luce created a symbolic chain linking the history of the first Greek marines to the Royal Marines to the U.S. Marines. He concluded that Marines had "well sustained the high reputation for steadfast courage and loyalty which has been handed down to it from the days of Themistocles."[115] An emphasis on Greek marines lent a timeless aura to any justification for the Corps' existence. It was much easier to create a sense of a "yearning for a lost golden age" than articulate a new mission.[116] Rather than have its history imposed on it by outsiders, such as naval officers who gave only secondary thought to Marines, the Corps began to construct its own narratives.

Collum's work also stressed the Corps' longtime existence in the United States, even purportedly antedating the Navy. He explained that the Corps "came into existence before the organization of the Regular Navy" and also before a "single vessel of the Navy was sent to sea."[117] In the tradition of Marine officers who sought to legitimize the institution by emphasizing its military virtues independent of fulfilling necessarily maritime missions, Collum suggested that the Corps did not need the Navy to justify its existence.

Collum's interpretation was not novel; rather, he drew upon the institution's existing identity.[118] As early as 1838, long-serving commandant Archibald Henderson had thanked his Marines for their service during a campaign in Florida, praising them for their role in "elevat[ing] their Ancient Corps in the estimation of the Country." Some naval officers even used the same wording to describe the Corps. In the 1850s Commo. Joshua Sands commented on the "*esprit* that has so long characterized the Old Corps." As has been seen, however, this kind of pride had a tenuous foothold among some officers by the 1870s and represented even more of a disconnect from the Corps' troubling external image. The Corps had not yet institutionalized these threads so that they could provide continuity amid changes in leadership, and Collum's work greatly aided this process.[119]

In addition to creating a historical record, Marines revisited many of the Corps' traditions. Historian Eric Hobsbawm has emphasized how nations or groups invent traditions when threatened. Often these traditions depend on recurring allusions to the past that can act as validating forces for an institution.[120] As a result, many Marines sought to focus on improving outward appearances and symbols. Debates about uniforms, the Corps' motto, whether the Corps should commission graduates from West Point or the Naval Academy, and a host of other concerns all help to reveal the different ways Marines envisioned their organization and wanted to reshape its image.

Beginning in 1872, First Lieutenant Cochrane launched a two-year campaign to change the Corps' uniform.[121] After soliciting his fellow officers for suggestions, Cochrane received more than sixty responses to his written inquiries, of which only four opposed change.[122] This represented an overwhelming response, as there were only ninety-five officers in the Corps. Some observers challenged the Corps' preoccupation with uniforms, given the more substantial problems facing the Corps. As Scott Hughes Myerly has argued, however, uniform changes help to renew a military institution's image. Unlike the Army and the Navy, both of which had made recent updates, the Corps had made few changes to its uniform for fifteen years.[123] Cochrane hoped to change the uniform to better convey a sense of the unique and wide-ranging missions of the Corps. The Corps' close relationship with the Navy also likely inspired his opinion that Marines needed to appear in stark contrast to sailors as the most "solid, soldierly, warlike looking body of infantry."[124]

Cochrane received diverging opinions as to what should influence the Corps' uniform, many of which reflected borrowed inspiration. One officer wrote "most emphatically" to make a number of suggestions. Some were practical—such as using the same coat for full dress and undress. Others sought to ape the uniform of others, including the 7th Regiment's hats. For example, 1st Lt. Charles Williams preferred almost anything to "this d—d brass foundry" that the Corps required its officers to wear.[125] Others believed changes should not be made if they were out of fashion with European armies. Another, 1st Lt. C. L. Sherman, preferred copying European units while also reverting to some of the Corps' traditions; he hoped to see changes made that would preserve the "proper" traditions of the Corps.[126] Ultimately, the Corps adopted and revised its uniforms to align more with British and German uniforms. Cochrane described the revised uniform adopted in 1876 as "varied and elaborate." While the Corps' most ornate dress uniform verged on being "rather gaudy," in his opinion the rest appeared "neat and in good taste."[127] The range of responses and the varied changes suggest Marine officers looked to any number of sources in seeking to craft their public representation. They did not yet have a compass to guide them in shaping their public image.[128]

Similarly, officers could not agree whether or not to readopt the Corps' traditional Mameluke sword. The Corps officially had adopted the sword in 1825, almost two decades after the Tripoli War's most memorable event for the Corps, when 1st Lt. Presley O'Bannon made a colorful trek across the northern parts of the Sahara Desert from Egypt to Tripoli with seven enlisted Marines and an assortment of native mercenaries to restore a deposed Tripolitan to his throne. As a result, a grateful Hamet Karamanli presented O'Bannon with his own Mameluke sword, striking because of its white hilt. By 1859, however, the Corps had discarded the sword for the Army's more efficient model.[129] The Corps had yet to embrace fully the importance of tradition in providing the institution with distinguishing symbols.

Despite the sword's history and the distinct impression it provided, Marine officers did not agree on whether the Mameluke sword should be readopted. One officer described it as ugly. Capt. George Collier, on the other hand, hoped to restore the traditional "old 'Mameluke'" sword in order to appear distinct from the Army, though he suggested minor changes in the metal used to make the scabbard.[130] Capt. Richard Collum also wanted to return to the previous sword to provide Marines a more "soldierly appearance, and in accordance with the progressive spirit of the age."[131] The reversion to the Mameluke sword in 1875 reflected a return to tradition over military efficiency. Still, officers did not agree unanimously on this change, further demonstrating the institution's weak corporate identity.

Importantly in terms of symbolic meaning, the Corps also decided to change its motto.[132] It had borrowed a new motto from the British Royal Marines in 1858, but now it chose to invent one of its own. Sometime in the 1880s the Corps changed its motto from *Par mare, par terrum* to *Semper fidelis*. The new motto emphasized one's attachment to the institution over a more mission-focused motto characterizing the Corps' ability to fight on land or at sea. It also stressed an aspect of the institution's corporate identity: the belief that it could be relied upon in all situations because of its discipline. Finally, it reinforced its role as policemen, reminding those who heard the motto that the Marines had never participated in a mutiny.[133]

Akin to how Marines conveyed their identification to the Corps by referring to it as old, the belief that Marines could be relied upon in all circumstances did not materialize out of thin air. It reflected how they felt they differed from sailors, in part due to their role as ship guards. During the Civil War, for example, Pvt. Phillip O'Neill had written that there was "more to be expected from the trained fidelity of the Marine."[134] In the 1870s, then, individual Marines seized upon bits and pieces of the Corps' cultural fabric, seeking to weave them together into a more integrated and cohesive internal identity.

The dissemination of the institution's new motto, however, was uneven. The institution's headquarters might promulgate symbols and history; however, it had yet to develop a cohesive and coherent way to inculcate these developments into individual Marines. As late as 1889, for example, Maj. James Forney erroneously noted that the Corps' motto was By Sea and by Land.[135] Despite the inability of some Marines to remember the new motto, it marked an important departure as the Corps began to stress and create its own traditions independent of its British counterparts.

These efforts, however, failed to head off the tenor of anti-Marine attacks that revived in the 1880s and 1890s amid great technological and institutional changes. Although American Robert Fulton had developed the first steamship, European navies began to adopt steam-powered vessels in significant numbers well before the United States. To Congress the expense of coal and the inefficiency and unreliability of early steam engines discouraged the use of steamships in a fleet responsible for showing the flag and protecting commerce around the world.

The birth of the so-called New Navy in 1882, when Congress finally agreed to fund three new cruisers and a dispatch ship, marked the beginning of significant changes in the Navy. Ardent proponents of navalism such as Alfred Thayer Mahan began to argue for a more aggressive overseas policy. Rather than relying on a largely defensive position, the Navy built a first-rate battleship fleet. Embracing this new navy required dealing with difficult manning questions, including the composition of its enlistees.[136]

In 1879 the prize-winning essay in the Naval Institute's publication *Proceedings* surprisingly stressed the importance of Marines at sea because they "enhance[d] the Navy's efficiency," and that opinion received much support in the ensuing discussion.[137] Increasingly in the 1880s and 1890s, however, naval officers believed that relying too much on Marines for protection inhibited the development of leadership among officers and of discipline within the ranks. Others insisted they could not retain the highly trained sailors to maintain steam vessels because the presence of Marines as guards made sailors feel like children. They believed the Marines' presence hindered the kind of homogeneous enlisted force it sought of native-born, English-speaking sailors.[138] Even as naval officers wrestled with the adoption of new technology, they verbalized arguments similar to those that their predecessors had made for more than fifty years.[139] The presence of Marines on ships, Lt. H. S. Knapp opined, was an "un-American practice."[140]

Although naval officers repeated earlier arguments, they also developed new ones that revealed how they wanted to tailor sailors' identities. For Marines to be useful at sea, naval officer Lt. John F. Meigs argued, they needed to expand their duties on board ship, at which point they might as well be made into sailors.[141] Others envisioned sailors increasingly resembling soldiers, with one lieutenant stressing the "new style" of "turn[ing] sailors into soldiers," which, of course, threatened to undercut the traditional role of Marines on board naval vessels.[142] Naval officers perceived the "New Navy" to be an "army afloat."[143] Not only should sailors learn some of the skills of Marines but they also must be infused with the kind of esprit de corps that they perceived in Marines. Others revisited the traditional image of Marines as lazy and worthless at sea. As Capt. W. S. Schley scathingly wrote, Marines were "a privileged class who ma[d]e dirt, but [were] not cleaners, as every man on board ship ought to be."[144] That the Corps did not fully participate only lessened the vessel's efficiency by failing to promote the solidarity that resulted from sharing the same duties and tasks, or so some naval officers believed.

Amid invigorated debate regarding the Marines' usefulness, Richard Collum turned more closely to the history of the Royal Marines when he revised and updated *History of the United States Marine Corps* in 1890, inspired by their ability to survive a similar crisis with the Royal Navy beginning in the 1870s.[145] Collum borrowed heavily from Lt. Paul Nicolas' *Historical Record of the Royal Marine Forces*, plagiarizing segments and copying the artwork in the frontispiece, simply exchanging the U.S. Marine Corps' symbols for those of the Royal Marines.[146] Marines frequently looked to the Royal Marines for inspiration, and borrowing their symbols worked to reinforce the legitimacy of its American counterpart.[147] It was also easier to borrow ready-made symbols from an institution in a similar situation than to devise a unique approach.

Collum did not simply update his history to incorporate events after the first edition. He also extended the origins of the American Marines to even before the American Revolution, describing the actions of Marines in the American colonies between 1740 and the Revolutionary War.[148] This enhanced the Corps' claim to be "ancient," which had emerged as one of the most distinctive aspects of its identity. The emphasis on the Corps as the oldest branch caused some disturbance. Although one naval officer admitted that the histories of the Navy and the Marine Corps were almost "inseparable," he disagreed with Collum's conclusion that the Corps antedated the Navy. Less critical reviewers, however, accepted Collum's point. The *Army Navy Journal* called the Marines a "historical body of troops, whatever may be the final determination as to the role they are to play on sea or land."[149] Precisely because of the continued difficulty of claiming a unique mission,

Collum invoked his institution's length of history and the multiplicity of its contributions to validate its existence.

Other Marine writers followed suit. In 1889, for example, Maj. James Forney detailed the daily lives of Marines on the heels of similar articles by Navy and Army officers in the *United Service*. He devoted less than one-third of his article, however, to his avowed purpose of describing life at his Marine post. Instead, he immediately began discussing the Corps' origins. He repeated the tradition emphasized by Collum and others, highlighting the indignity that the nation's "oldest" military service was the least well known.[150]

Having established the Corps' age, Forney struggled to describe a Marine to his military audience. He expressed the "general notion that the marines are of an amphibious nature; that they are neither fish, flesh, nor fowl."[151] Although he reasoned that people understood that the Corps served with the Navy at times and at other times with the Army, he also believed that they knew that the Corps was "independent" of both. Still, he insisted that Marines could fulfill any duty. He defined a Marine as a soldier whose duties were "entirely military" while also claiming that Marines were also "good sailors" who "knew every rope in the ship."[152] In this way he claimed that Marines could do any job while working to correct the lingering image of Marines as lazy at sea.

In seeking to improve the Corps' image, Forney took a different approach toward the Royal Marines than Collum had in his revised *History*. Forney emphasized the need to celebrate the Corps' own history as distinct from that of the Royal Marines. He feared that the reputedly tarnished image of their British brethren might hurt the U.S. Marines. Forney explained that the British public had developed an illogical "prejudice" against Marines, which the U.S. Marines had inherited. This image could be corrected, however, only if people acquired a "clear understanding in regard to the history of the Corps." Although Forney disagreed with Collum regarding the extent to which the U.S. Marines should look to the Royal Marines for emulation, he certainly appreciated the ability of history to improve image.[153]

The expression "tell it to the Marines" particularly epitomized the kind of image the Royal Marines had acquired and that Forney wanted to avoid.[154] Forney explained how the phrase had originated from a British naval officer who had made a rude comment about Marines, which he had reputedly backed away from when challenged. Over time, this expression had acquired various meanings and origin stories. As used by sailors, the expression typically belittled Marines by depicting them as ignorant fools. One nineteenth-century naval historian explained that this phrase epitomized the tensions between sailors and Marines, arguing that Marines "considered themselves two or three degrees better than the seamen, while the latter regarded the marines with supreme contempt as being no better than landlubbers, and anybody making a particularly stupid remark was told to 'Go tell it to the marines.'"[155] This explanation highlighted the traditional perspective of naval officers, who did not hesitate to point out the irony of the Marines' elevation given their ignorance of ships. The same year Forney published his article, the *New York Times* enlightened its readers that "from time immemorial it has been Jack's saying in response to all doubtful stories, 'Tell that to the marines,' for . . . the hearty contempt in which they hold the marines is sufficient to incite the firing of a volley of epithets at the latter on the slightest provocation." Sailors perennially joked that you could "tell anything" to the Marines; their gullibility knew no bounds. Sympathetically, the journalist addressed the Corps' negative image, explaining that no one had "come in for a greater share of contumely and received less praise than have the marines of the United States Navy."[156] However sympathetic, the journalist's confused idea of the relationship between the Corps and the Navy demonstrated the perennial and lingering confusion surrounding Marines.

The article represented the calm before the storm as attacks against the Corps intensified. An 1891 *New York Times* headline claimed that the presence of Marines "crippled" the Navy. Unless the Navy replaced Marines with bluejackets, it would not have enough "fighting men" at sea. It described Marines as idlers who ranked with "servants and non-combatants." By contrast, sailors composed the most "vital part of the ship's complements, namely, the combatant force." However admirable they might be, the Corps' duties at sea were "limited, except in a few instances, to sharpshooter work in the time of battle." Even then, sailors proved themselves to be even more effective marksmen than Marines, or so the article claimed. To make matters worse, bluejackets suffered while coaling the ship as Marines lay "about the decks off duty." A month later the *New York Times* proclaimed in another headline, "Everyone Should Work." Largely echoing the previous article, it also explained that sailors could be turned into soldiers. After all, the "Turoos in Africa, the sepoys in India, the blacks in the Congo . . . and now the Indians on our plains have been made into soldiers." This wording reflected the belief of many naval officers that sailors could become soldiers relatively easily but not vice versa.[157]

Naval officers followed up on these articles with letters to the editors. As they had in the years during and after the War of 1812, naval officers again called for justice for their sailors. One unnamed writer demanded that sailors' "rights" be upheld, given that they did "all the work and [bore] the brunt of the fighting."[158] Another letter published in 1892 similarly called for "Justice for Bluejackets" and described "Their Good Record, as Compared with Marines." The writer, who called himself "Fair Play," argued that people "constantly made" statements to keep Marines at sea that spoke "disparagingly" of sailors. The author attempted to demonstrate the better discipline of sailors as compared to Marines by proving that the latter were more than three times as likely to desert. He closed by challenging the reader to consider what such high desertion rates said about the validity of the Corps' motto of *Semper fidelis*.[159]

In addition to challenging Marines' faithfulness to their institution, naval officers questioned their work ethic. Observers considered the issue of the Marines' participation in coaling the ship to be the "great bugaboo on which line officers base their opposition to the marines on ship." The Corps' adoption of a coaling uniform in 1892 did not resolve the latest round of tension between Marines and sailors.[160] After all, on some ships Marines continued to be excused from coaling duty. In one instance, the number of excused men included the vessel's fifty-six Marines, half of whom were "doing nothing" and "the other half of whom [were] engaged in duty that is mere form or show," in accordance with a naval tradition should have been at work.[161] The author referred to the tradition of Marines standing smartly on deck in case foreign dignitaries arrived. Naval officers largely viewed Marines as an outdated relic of the age of sail in an era of modern ships; and, increasingly, naval officers questioned traditions as the Corps embraced them.

The historical work of Collum and other nineteenth-century Marines established a pattern and precedent that shaped the Corps' future use of history and traditions, reinforcing its tendency to look to the past in times of crisis. Amid the loss of traditional military symbols due to the industrialization of war, one Marine lieutenant celebrated the Corps' singular decision to maintain the drum for field music in 1897. Fortunately, as he explained, of "all the regular organizations in the United States service, the Marine Corps, the oldest, last retains the drum."[162] The article continued the importance attached to emphasizing the Corps' age, but it incorrectly stated that the Corps alone retained drums.[163] That was immaterial to the larger point implied by the article—the Corps cherished and held fast to its heritage amid greater societal change.

Marines did not concoct an image in isolation, though. Major Forney might have wanted to keep his Marines distinct from his British counterparts, but that proved impossible after the publication in April 1895 of Rudyard Kipling's poem about Royal Marines in *McClure's Magazine*. Entitled "Soldier an' Sailor Too," the poem described an overworked man capable of any task and caught between the Army and the Navy.[164] Told from a soldier's perspective, it stressed how the Marine could be relied upon to support the Army when required. Kipling began the poem by explaining how the soldier caught sight of a man on board a ship who, though dressed more in the style of a soldier, busily scraped paint. This setting thus depicted a Marine engaged in duties characteristic of sailors, namely, maintaining the appearance of vessels. In this way, Kipling challenged the Marine's general image as lazy or failing to contribute to the ship. As a soldier and a sailor, the Marine was something of a "giddy harumfordite" and a "bloomin' cosmopolouse." The Marine knew how to handle just about any job, but he did not really fit in with the Navy.[165]

Kipling's work quickly became inseparable from the American Marine's image. Pieces of the poem "Soldier an' Sailor, Too" filtered into

an article that the *New York Sun* ran and multiple newspapers subsequently reprinted in August of 1896.[166] Entitled "Pfeifer's Triumph," the
article described a Marine sergeant who had previously served in the
German army as well as the U.S. Navy after immigrating to the United
States. His past status as a noncommissioned officer in the German
army, however, made his new lot as a low-ranking sailor intolerable so
he enlisted in the Corps. As a Marine sergeant, he received the responsibility of command as the highest-ranking Marine at sea because the
Corps "had no superfluous officers." In and of itself, this depiction of a
pruned Marine officer corps represented a notable departure from the
1870s. As Pfeifer's cruise drew to an end, the ship was decommissioned,
requiring a ceremony in which Marines played the most important
part. In undertaking the ceremony, though, a mere sergeant upstaged
and embarrassed a naval officer because he had a greater knowledge
of such matters. The story overlapped with the increasing tendency of
Marines to appreciate and uphold naval traditions and ceremonies in
contrast to naval officers, who embraced a more forward-looking perspective.[167] And, to many naval officers, Marines constituted the most
outdated naval tradition of all.

Chapter Two

Internalization

Image and Identity in Imperial Wars, 1898–1905

I n an era of limited combat during the late nineteenth century, the Corps had acquired a reputation for its Marine Band, particularly under the leadership of its renowned band leader John Philip Sousa. The most famous Marine of the nineteenth century, Sousa believed that the Corps always upheld its best traditions. Learning in 1902 of the acquittal of Lt. Col. Littleton Waller, who had been charged with ordering eleven Filipino porters to be summarily executed, he sent off a terse telegram of congratulations to the Corps' commandant, insisting, "A marine always fights fair." Sousa served at a time when the institution could bask in acclaim for its band performances instead of wrestling with ethical challenges.[1]

The Corps' involvement in America's early twentieth-century impe-rial wars challenged Marines even as it provided new directions for the institution's developing image. In many ways, imperialism tested the culture of chivalrous manliness that had characterized the late nineteenth-century Navy and Marine Corps, as epitomized by Cap-tain Collum's restrained *History of the United States Marine Corps*. And Waller's court-martial served as a stark reminder of the differ-ence between the short landing parties of the nineteenth century and the complexities of fighting imperial wars, posing the possibility of besmirching the Corps' evolving and improving image.

America's imperialism sparked a rising public interest in all things military.[2] No longer did the American public consider the military something fit only for the dregs of society. The public eagerly embraced and celebrated the heroic exploits of Adm. George Dewey and the sail-ors who seemed to win the Battle of Manila Bay so effortlessly during the Spanish-American War. With the rise of yellow journalism, popular curiosity about exotic foreign cultures, and more frequent and better-publicized engagements abroad, the Marine Corps became the subject of greater interest.[3] Well-known journalists and novelists, including Stephen Crane and Richard Harding Davis, brought the ostensible glamor of military adventure into the homes of Americans, and Marines eagerly internalized these heroic images.[4]

An examination of the Corps' participation in the Spanish-American War, the China Relief Expedition, and the Philippine-American War reveals imperialism's lasting imprint on the Corps' image and identity. In some ways imperial wars provided significant challenges to the Corps' sense of self, but on the other hand these events bound Marines of all ranks more closely together internally while externally cementing an image of elite fighters. Additionally, many participants subsequently served as recruiters, and they conveyed these new responsibilities and experiences to journalists and members of the public.

As such, another solution to the Corps' image problem began to emerge after the Spanish American War. Increasingly, the Corps sought less to explain its missions and more to make romanticized appeals to the public based on its willingness to fight and, more specifically, to fight better than its counterparts. For example, it stressed various firsts as evidence of its readiness, which distinguished the Corps from the Army's need for time to mobilize and deploy. As one journalist explained, the Corps tended to be "'first among the foremost' when any fighting is to be done." This responsibility for fighting also highlighted the difference between Marines and sailors. In a headline that proclaimed, "Uncle Sam's Marines Are True Heroes," an article reinforced what the public purportedly already recognized: "as everybody knows, the marines are the fighting men on board Uncle Sam's ships, as against the blue jackets, who 'man, sail and steer.'"[5] Ignoring the naval victories that had occurred two years before, the journalist defined Marines as fighters and sailors as ship operators. He then recounted the Corps' "glorious" history and traditions before explaining the Marine Corps' recruiting process. Informing the journalist, though, was Marine Col. F. H. Harrington of "Guantanamo fame." A combat veteran now detailed to recruiting duty and buoyed by the success of his Corps' recent endeavors, Harrington had conversed with the journalist, detailing the Corps' recent successes while drawing on the Corps' late nineteenth-century historical record and traditions.

Some Corps historians view the contributions of Colonel Harrington and other Marines during the Spanish-American War as largely securing the institution's existence in providing the institution with an expeditionary mission.[6] The reality, however, is more complex. The silencing of guns at the end of the Spanish-American War failed to determine the role of Marines on board ship, especially regarding naval gunnery. Still, its image improved because of its well-publicized battle at Guantánamo.

The public had been paying close attention to Cuba as early as the *Maine*'s destruction in February of 1898 in the harbor of Havana, and it subsequently clamored for the United States to declare war on Spain, believing the *Maine*'s loss to have resulted from Spanish foul play. The articles building up to the war provided far more favorable coverage of the Corps than the institution had experienced at the beginning of the decade. One journalist described the Corps as "picturesque" and "attractive." Citing the traditional ignorance of the institution, the journalist decried that the Corps had not received credit for its "peerless efficiency."[7] Another hyperbolized that some even believed the Corps to be the "finest body of soldiers in the world," again reflecting an idea that had been suggested increasingly since the 1890s.[8] Still, ignorance about the Corps' purpose remained. One article recounted how the unexpected presence of soldiers on board ship intrigued a young woman visitor. Alas, her guide faced the typical "trouble" of having to "explain what a Marine was."[9] The Spanish-American War brought more media attention to the Corps, but it did not resolve the public's confusion about the institution.

Although the majority of Marines served on board naval vessels during the Spanish-American War, the most powerful image of Marines to emerge from the war celebrated the Corps' combat ashore. The Corps conveniently had an opportunity to test its soldiering skills even before the Army had departed from its staging camps in the

United States, for which it received extensive press coverage. In early June 1898, as U.S. forces sought to wrest control of Cuba from Spain, the Navy ordered Marines to capture a base at Guantánamo to provide a sheltered harbor during hurricane season and allow for the resupply of its vessels.[10] Located about forty miles away from Santiago, where naval vessels had established a blockade of Spanish naval vessels in May, Guantánamo provided an excellent natural harbor. Arriving at the beach at the upper reaches of the harbor, naval guns from vessels offshore easily destroyed a Spanish camp. The *Marblehead*'s guard of about forty Marines then landed in case the Spanish returned, and on the afternoon of June 10, the *Marblehead*'s captain, Cdr. Bowman McCalla, ordered Lt. Col. Robert Huntington's battalion of more than 650 Marines ashore.

The Marines had arrived on a recently commissioned naval transport, the *Panther*. Commanding the *Panther* was Cdr. George C. Reiter, who resented the unglamorous job of transporting Marines from one location to another. He took out his frustration on the Marines, particularly the unfortunate Marine found "gambling," whom he punished with double irons for ten days.[11] Marines on board the *Panther* then happily disembarked from the *Panther* on June 10. They began establishing a camp of their own without challenge until the night of June 11, when a small group of Spanish soldiers killed two men on patrol before opening fire on the main camp area.

In what Maj. Henry Cochrane dubbed "the 100 hours war," Marines came under fire for three nights. Exhausted, they determined to seek out the Spanish inland to end the constant attacks. The arrival of Cuban reinforcements helped with this decision. A Cuban officer suggested attacking the Spanish base at Cuzco Well, the only source of clean drinking water for miles, located about two miles away from the Marines' position. On June 14 Capt. George F. Elliott and about 160 Marines and 50 Cubans advanced on the Spanish position. Although they faced a larger force of about 500 Spaniards, they quickly made it to high ground, despite losing the element of surprise. A separate, smaller detachment of Marines provided additional firepower, flanking the Spanish to prevent their retreat. When the USS *Dolphin* added its

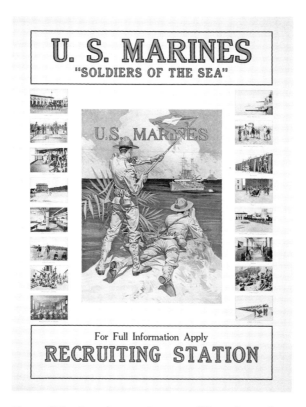

Fig. 5. "The Signaling at Cuzco Well." *Paul Woyshner Papers, MCHD*

naval gunnery to the battle, it accidentally fired on the smaller detachment of Marines. The Marines desperately needed volunteers to signal the ship to cease firing (see fig. 5). With the naval gunfire successfully redirected, the Spanish retreated after four hours.

Witnessing the Battle of Cuzco Well was journalist Stephen Crane, who published his account with the headline, "The Red Badge of Courage Was His Wig-Wag Flag." In the *New York World* article, the novelist elaborated upon his famous Civil War novel to describe Sgt. John Quick's signaling to the *Dolphin*. As he stood exposed to Spanish fire so that the *Dolphin* could read his signals, Quick exemplified "tranquility in occupation. He stood there amid the animal-like babble of the Cubans . . . and the whistling snarl of the bullets, and wig-wagged whatever he had to wig-wag without heeding anything but his business."[12] Crane's depiction drew clarity from his racialized depictions of the Cubans even as it marginalized the valuable intelligence they provided to the Marines. Cubans could not control themselves in battle, at least in Crane's vignette. By contrast, Quick displayed only the briefest hint of emotion, then only irritation when the flag caught on a cactus. With this portrayal Crane dramatically ended his report, heightening the sense of Quick's bravery as being something so extraordinary that no practical details, such as whether the Marines carried the day against the Spanish, were needed. How could they not carry the day, Crane implied, with warriors like Quick? Crane provided a far more romanticized account of war than he had in his novel about the Civil War. That this event became memorialized through an art piece depicting Quick's bravery only helped reinforce its importance in the Corps' historical narrative, with the institution continuing to use the image until World War I.[13]

Unlike the sailors who had provided naval gunnery from a safe distance offshore, the Marines had faced overwhelming odds, or so it appeared. When Spanish soldiers surprised two Marines on outpost duty, Spanish bullets did such damage to the Marines that it appeared that the Spanish had used machetes to kill them. As a result, the press initially reported that the Spaniards had mutilated the Marines in an egregious breach of international law. Continued accounts of the so-called Hundred Hours War depicted a gallant band of Marines fighting against overwhelming odds.[14] Accolades now showered the Corps, with one enthusiastic writer informing readers that Marines more eagerly defeated their opponent than other American men and hoped to use the war to "capture and occupy a page of history" for their institution. Another raved that they had exemplified "peerless heroism . . . in the face of almost overwhelming odds at Guantanamo."[15]

The Corps' success at Guantánamo, however, did not help to rectify the perennial confusion surrounding the Corps.[16] One article featured the misspelled headline "The Mariners." Another inaccurate correspondent reported that Congressman Thomas Butler's son had been commissioned in the Navy when in fact he had become a Marine officer. Another newspaper published the letters of Marine Pvt. Patrick Ford, yet described his great love for the Navy rather than the Corps.[17]

Other journalists, increasingly finding their image of the Corps challenged, became sympathetic to the Corps' continuing struggle for attention. Having accepted the lingering nineteenth-century image, one journalist now surprised himself by recounting the fighting abilities of what he had previously considered to be "generally ornamental soldiers." Assuming his audience's ignorance, he provided readers with a brief history and description of the Corps: It was "a sort of amphibious corps that are not always rightly esteemed in time of peace. The army regards them as only a part of the decorative equipment of the navy, while the navy looks on them as landsmen who are of no use on shipboard."[18] The journalist accurately described the Corps' uncomfortable position between two services that had strong claims to unique missions. The Corps, by contrast, found itself limited to asserting that it had been at the forefront of fighting both on land and at sea.

This suggestion spilled over into popular culture. One song explained that Marines could neither replicate fully the duties of sailors or soldiers:

> We hear about the navy and naval heroes grand. . . .
> But not as often as we might about our brave marines. . . .
> They are not exactly soldiers like soldiers on the land. . . .
> They are not exactly sailors, and may not understand
> Just how to splice the main brace on a dark and stormy night,
> But at Guantanamo they've shown how they can fight.[19]

Conveying the sentiment that the Corps did not receive as much attention, the writer dismissed the Corps' odd situation between the Army and the Navy as irrelevant because Marines had proven they could "fight." They did not need to replicate sailors' nautical knowledge to be useful. That is not to say that they did not seek to excel at sea combat, however. Their best such claim occurred during the Battle of Santiago in July 1898, when they manned the secondary batteries for Adm. William T. Sampson's fleet. As opposed to larger naval guns that targeted the ship itself, secondary batteries consisted of smaller naval gunnery and rapid-fire guns that targeted the personnel of the opposing vessels.[20] As seen by 1st Lt. Henry Cochrane's suggestion that the Corps become a body of naval artillerists in 1874, Marines had sought to acquire a naval gunnery role for decades.[21] Of course many naval officers opposed this, but in 1896 Secretary of the Navy Hilary A. Herbert officially assigned Marines to the secondary battery.

How to divvy up responsibilities between sailors and Marines had long been a source of controversy. The Marines' determination to take on new responsibilities had thrown them into increased competition with sailors. During most of the nineteenth century, Navy and Marine duties on board ship differed.[22] Sailors ran the ship and fired its main guns while Marines served as sharpshooters, firing small arms onto the decks of enemy vessels and boarding and repelling boarders when required. In some ways the transition from sharpshooting to manning the secondary batteries was a natural one for Marines, but it reinvigorated old rivalries. The Navy considered its gunners to be its elite sailors, chosen only from the best. Naval gunnery thus became a highly contested ground that spurred some Marine antagonism. During the 1890s, for example, Capt. Robert Meade directly challenged naval gunners' reputations when he alleged that they had scaled the walls of the Navy Yard to avoid having their alcohol confiscated by Marines, thus highlighting the sailors' purported indiscipline. Meade's diatribe on discipline went deeper, influenced by a century of tension between the two institutions. In contrast to the image of Marines as idlers, Meade suggested that Marines actively sought out new duties on board naval vessels and even worked longer hours than sailors.[23] Meade's argument, however biased, epitomized the approach Marines took to convince others they could and would do anything.

Unsurprisingly, then, Marines took every opportunity to stress their contributions in the Battle of Santiago. Cmdt. Charles Heywood felt vindicated by his decision to push the Navy Department to allow Marines to man the secondary batteries. He believed this decision demonstrated how the Corps had adapted to technological change, referring to Spanish officers' reports showing that the secondary guns had caused the most damage. Now retired, Maj. Richard Collum supplemented the official view, revising and updating his *History of the*

United States Marine Corps for the third time in 1903.[24] Collum propounded the view that Spanish battle wreckage clearly demonstrated
that the Marines' secondary batteries caused more destruction than
the "heavy guns" manned by sailors.[25] This was so self-evident, Collum
believed, that "no further comment on the skill and endurance of the
Marines [was] required."[26] In this way, Collum continued his pattern of
reticence as he subtly sought to bring attention to his beloved Corps.

Collum also drew on individual after-action reports that supported
this opinion. Capt. Littleton Waller—who lacked Collum's self-restraint—
enthusiastically reported that the *Indiana*'s commanding officer had
informed him that he viewed Waller's men as the best in the squadron.
Waller's account of the report differed from the naval officer's, who had
more circumspectly noted that Marines only "equaled in excellence" the
Indiana's sailors. Similar to Waller, Marine Capt. R. Dickins noted his
Marines maintained their bearing throughout the entire engagement
despite "occupy[ing] the most exposed position." Dickins implicitly contrasted the sailors' positions at the main guns behind turrets with the
exposed position of the seemingly braver Marines, and at least one journalist borrowed this distinction.[27]

Others made more sweeping claims for the Corps. Robert Meade,
now a major, who had argued for the undisciplined habits of sailors in
the 1890s, now launched into a new tirade. Meade noted that there was
"no work the marine cannot do," exemplifying the way Marines justified
themselves in terms of the variety of roles they could fill.[28] Rather than
restricting himself to arguing for a few roles, Meade sweepingly claimed
that Marines' quality and pugnaciousness enabled them to meet any
task. Meade emphasized not only that Marines in the Spanish-American
War "formed a large proportion of the fighting force of every ship"
but that the purportedly heavy casualties suffered by the Marines in
combat at sea in comparison to the rest of the services provided "evidence that the marines were well at the front." Given some journalists'
depictions in the early 1890s of sailors as combatants and Marines as
idle noncombatants, it is not surprising that individual Marines determined to counter this image rhetorically after being tested in battle. Yet
these interpretations required some creative accounting. The Navy had

ten sailors killed in battle as opposed to six in the Corps. And the two suffered a similar proportion of nonfatal wounds: forty-seven sailors compared to twenty-one Marines.[29]

Naval officers, however, stressed the irrelevance of the secondary batteries. Lt. F. K. Hill dismissed them as only important "accidentally" and implied that the battery would have been ineffective if the U.S. Navy had faced a viable opponent. Some historians have also questioned the significance of the Marines' contributions to naval gunnery, but contemporary Marine officers did not concern themselves too much with the niceties of their record. They assimilated the accolades as part of their evolving identity.[30] To be a Marine was to be a "good deal more of a man." Whereas steel armor protected sailors at their posts in the gun turrets, the Marine claimed there was "nothing between him and eternity" but his uniform shirt to protect him.[31] A masculine ideal of courage distinguished the Marine from the sailor, at least in this particular Marine's opinion.

At times, journalists made similar distinctions ranging from the slightly tempered to extremely sympathetic to Marines. One article distinguished the fighting characteristics of sailors and Marines by drawing on the prevailing image of sailors as brave yet impetuous figures who, as such, could not endure sustained conflicts because they lacked discipline.[32] This account thus challenged naval officers' claims that sailors could be just as disciplined as Marines. The journalist even suggested that the Marine Corps had been established during the American Revolution precisely because the Navy needed a reliable force of fighters. In an article explaining how Marines differed from sailors, a more enthusiastic journalist even suggested that the Navy sought to hold back Marines. He characterized the Marine as the "most competent of the fighting force on shipboard whenever he [was] allowed to compete on equal terms with his sailor shipmate, and in target practice is without a rival."[33] He lamented the ignorant person he referred to as "Mr. Landlubber" who spoke of the sailors' "desperate fighting" at Guantánamo, when in fact the Marines had done the desperate fighting. Similarly, well-regarded journalist J. S. Van Antwerp claimed in July of 1898 that Marines had been ignored since Guantánamo and even accused naval officers of failing to praise Marines in their reports.[34] Van Antwerp might have been a little impatient in his lament; the Department of the Navy released the reports in August. Another wrote that the Corps' recent activities had "disarmed" its critics, especially those within the Navy Department who had opposed increasing the Corps' size or missions.[35] Another journalist reworked the phrase "tell it to the Marines." The phrase traditionally had signaled a sailor's dislike or disrespect for the Corps. Now, however, one journalist joked that one planning to "tell it to the Marines" do so "politely" because the institution was a "fighting corps." Those who persisted in viewing the Corps as solely a ceremonial service failed to understand, he argued, that Marines were "fighters from 'way back.'"[36]

Although in some ways the war created a clear mission for the Corps in securing advanced bases, the Corps' leadership did not clamor to stress new responsibilities.[37] Still, the war temporarily quelled much discussion about whether the nation needed a Marine Corps. The Army had been subject to almost constant critiques during the Spanish-American War, but the Marine Corps had deployed efficiently and suffered few casualties from disease.[38] Congress responded to the Corps' war efforts by approving personnel increases, nearly doubling the force to more than six thousand men.[39]

Similarly, the Spanish-American War and the passage of the Naval Personnel Bill of 1900 brought an influx of new officers. Unlike Marine officers commissioned between 1884 and 1897, few of these officers attended the Naval Academy. As Peter Karsten has shown, the Navy sought to create a homogeneous officer corps, a practice that began at the Naval Academy. The cadre of Marines baptized in imperial wars thus escaped the Navy's four-year indoctrination program. And many wrote home enthusiastically to share their pride in being Marines rather than soldiers or sailors. William Upshur, first lieutenant and cousin of well-known Marine officer Littleton Waller, addressed a negative article about the Corps early in his career. In a letter to his parents, he challenged imagery of Marine officers that persisted in some journalists' accounts, specifically one journalist who suggested that the Corps "offered a *refuge* to many men who were out of employment and who *were not fitted* to *enter the Navy!*"[40] Upshur disagreed vehemently, believing that a Marine was "just as intelligent, was more matured, had better physique, and was cleaner and had far better discipline than a blue jacket—furthermore that in nine ships out of ten in the Atlantic fleet—it would be found that the Marine Guard, could take on board more coal . . . could out pull any divisional boat crew—and could and did make as good or better scores at target practice than any blue jacket division." Marines, Upshur suggested, were equal if not outright superior to sailors at all their duties, even in coaling ships. In another letter he reminded his mother—who remained unconvinced—that she erred in believing that Marines played "a very poor second fiddle."[41] In the case of the Upshur family, their son's identification with the Corps was more powerful than the family's sense of the Corps' image.

Having spent two years as an enlisted Marine, newly commissioned second lieutenant Earl Ellis found himself surrounded by more soldiers than sailors while traveling to and serving in the Philippines. As a result, he defined the Corps in opposition to the Army. Traveling on board a transport with about 800 soldiers and 150 Marines afforded Ellis an opportunity to compare the two services. In a long letter written while sailing to the Philippines, he expressed his happiness that he was "going to soldier at last." Even if his job might resemble that of someone in the Army, he found plenty of room to belittle the Army's less favorable appearance and discipline as compared to those of Marines. Summing up his thoughts, he exclaimed, "the more I see of the other branches of the service the better satisfied I am with the Marine Corps—'small but mighty.'" In another letter describing his first post, he expressed his happiness at "being a Marine," a sentiment he claimed to share with a fellow officer who believed that they belonged to "a chosen few."[42]

Enlisted accounts reflected similar attitudes. Disappointed in his search for work, Frank Keeler enlisted in the Marine Corps because the uniforms of sailors and Marines impressed him. Keeler's initial image, then, did not distinguish between sailors and Marines. Just as service in the Philippines provided Ellis with the opportunity to distinguish between Marines and soldiers, however, Keeler's service in Cuba led him to notice institutional differences. When commanded to attack Manzanillo, Cuba, he remarked: "The idea that 650 Marines could take a powerful built fort where 20,000 men had failed was preposterous. There were times, however, when I thought that a hundred marines would and could do as much as [a] thousand Army Men." Although Keeler tempered his comment by crediting the Corps' superior rifles, his identification with the Corps helped him endure naval officers' whims, including one who ordered Marines to do the sailors' "work of scrubbing." He consoled himself with the thought that Marines were "all picked men." Keeler never expanded on what particular characteristics distinguished Marines from sailors and soldiers. Rather, he referred to Rudyard Kipling's poetry. Upon landing in Cuba, he wrote, Marines transformed themselves from "sea-dogs to land-lubbers as the novelist says, 'Soldier and Sailor too.'"[43] Kipling's work resonated enough with another Marine that he advised his parents to read his writing if they wanted to understand his experiences.[44]

Given the paucity of such accounts, it is difficult to determine how common these sentiments were. Many Marines who fought at Guantánamo had enlisted only a few days before stepping foot on a naval transport that took them to Florida for training before arriving in Cuba. In private letters to his son, Lt. Col. Robert Huntington explained that the troops under his command who left the United States in April 1898 had "little idea of obeying orders," though he had hopes they might improve.[45] Still, buoyed by more positive accounts in newspapers and the enthusiastic outpouring of support for the military, the Corps' image certainly improved, and individual Marines began discussing more openly their pride in their institution and their confidence in its superiority. The Corps' next military engagement reinforced the same sense of the few against many at Guantánamo, but this time they fought alongside westerners rather than Cubans.

With an American empire came added responsibilities for the Marine Corps. Many Marines sent to help garrison naval stations in the Philippines found themselves dispatched to China to help quell the Boxer Rebellion, a movement to free China of Western imperialism and Christianity. After early successes in the countryside, the Boxers gained momentum and swept toward Peking (today's Beijing), where they targeted the European legations.

Along with other U.S. soldiers who had been serving in the Philippines, the Marines helped to form part of the China Relief Expedition of 1900. As at Guantánamo, Marines faced what appeared to be harrowing odds and some rash allies, particularly the Russians.[46] The first contingent of fewer than fifty Marines on the USS *Newark* arrived at the harbor of Tangku on May 28. The first of the allies, they anxiously awaited a train for Peking, where they protected the Westerners holed up in the city's Legation Quarter against the vast "horde" of Boxers outside.[47] It quickly became apparent that the Legation Quarter needed reinforcements. Although the Boxers had destroyed segments of the railroad from Tientsin to Peking, a U.S. sailor made enough repairs to the lines to move within twenty-five miles of the city, where they encountered significant Boxer resistance.

Reinforcements under Maj. Littleton Waller arrived in June, and later that month the Legation Quarter came under attack after Westerners ignored a Chinese ultimatum to leave Peking in twenty-four hours. Troops supporting the quarter immediately began strengthening their defenses as Boxers probed and attacked weaknesses, including the substantial "Tartar Wall" manned by Marines. They held on until a relief force of more than 18,000 troops arrived in the middle of August. After a ten-day march from Tientsin, this force easily cleared Peking of opposition. The Marines' defense of the Legation Quarter furthered the image of a small, beleaguered group of brave and determined fighters. Newspaper articles published during the siege questioned whether Marines were even alive, creating an air of heightened suspense.[48]

Most of the Marines did survive and began comparing themselves to their allies.[49] Marines disparaged French troops, whom they described as dirty and undisciplined, unlike the more impressive appearance of Japanese and British Indian troops.[50] While informally ranking the other troops with whom they came in contact, Marines expressed their confidence that they were "as good" as the others.[51] Others celebrated the praise they received from even their opponents. Pvt. Oscar Upham recorded in his journal the following encounter with Chinese troops: "They keep up their sniping all day but we have taught them to respect us (during the truce a Chinese Colonel in command on the wall was holding conversation with our officers; he eagerly asked who those men were that wore the big hats? On being told they were American Marines, he shook his head and said, 'I don't understand them at all; they don't shoot very often, but when they do I lose a man; my men are afraid of them')."[52]

Upham prided himself on Marines' behavior in combat, as characterized by their carefully controlled and precise marksmanship, which echoed journalist Stephen Crane's characterization of Sgt. John Quick.[53] Sgt. George Herbert also celebrated his combat experience in reasserting foreign control over Tientsin, writing, "We are Russians, French, Germans, Italians, Britishers and last but not least 10 American Marines and we have been into every-thing so far and lost but 5 men. I don't know how long I shall be here, but as long as I stay I'm going where these Yankee Marines go. They are daisies!"[54] Perhaps the use of the third person represented a lingering sense of restrained Victorian manliness that did not seek to boast of oneself. Lt. H. J. Hirshinger, by contrast, characterized his fellow Marines as heroic warriors, recounting in a letter home how the "indomitable American Marine" had "rescue[d]" some Russian troops.[55]

The Marines felt the closest affinity with British troops.[56] While serving together in defending Peking's Legation Quarter, Marine Capt. John T. Myers led both U.S Marines and Royal Marines in what some hailed as the "bravest and the most successful event of the whole siege." During this decisive moment, about sixty British and U.S. Marines and fifteen Russian sailors attacked Chinese forces in one of the few successful offensive attacks in defense of the quarter.[57] Myers' success strengthened the allies' defensive position significantly. The U.S. Marine Corps forged similar ties to other British troops, especially the Royal Welch Fusiliers. Serving side by side for more than four months during the China Relief Expedition, the two forces sometimes merged their troops.[58] Before leaving, the Royal Welch commemorated their relationship by gifting a loving cup, for two people to drink from, to the Marines.[59]

Still, Americans prided themselves on retaining their more democratic instincts in comparison to the British. One correspondent noted the differences between British officers, who dined on gourmet fare served by Indian servants, and American officers, who helped themselves to the same food their troops ate.[60] He wrote that the "American officer prides himself upon the fact that he lives exactly as do the men in the ranks." This had not been the experience of Marine officers while at sea, given the far more aristocratic habits of their naval counterparts.[61] Imperial service, then, helped Marine officers such as Lt. Smedley Butler to now highlight the more egalitarian tendencies of Americans. Butler, for example, described how the aristocratic British officers were "seated in state" while he and his fellow officers dined on a chicken that had "walked entirely too far in its life."[62] Americans applied the same perspective to the matter of uniforms. Nineteenth-century Marine officers had been derided for their elaborate dress uniforms. Their field uniforms, by contrast, appeared more muted, which suited Lt. H. J. Hirshinger because Marines had demonstrated the "mettle of which the American soldier is made, and that it was not necessary to put on fine feathers to make a soldier."[63]

Even though Marines identified as American soldiers, they still contrasted themselves with U.S. Army officers. As one Marine officer purportedly recalled, Maj. Littleton Waller's actions appeared in sharp contrast to those of U.S. Army officers, particularly Gen. Adna R. Chaffee: "Major Waller and his Marines camped on a filthy flat piled high with Chinese fertilizer. . . . A trim orderly came to the Major with the message, 'The General's compliments, sir, and he invites the major to move his bedding roll up the hill and spend the night there.' [The Major replied,] 'Present my compliments to the General and tell him that Major Waller will stay with his men.'"[64] Ignoring the privileges of rank, Waller remained with his men, suggesting he wanted to encourage his enlisted Marines by choosing to stay with them in unpleasant circumstances in a gesture designed to improve morale and esprit de corps. It is easy to view such an example cynically. However, there are a number of reasons to give this incident credence.[65] First, photographs from the Boxer Rebellion show Waller napping on the ground without any concern for privacy or rank. Moreover, the difficult conditions of the Boxer Rebellion—characterized by brutal heat and limited supplies, including food and water—helped to diminish distinctions of rank.[66] Finally, the Corps had a tradition of placing more trust in enlisted men than was the case in other services. Taken together, these characteristics bridged some of the divide between officers and enlisted men more than in other military services.[67] The passage of the Naval Personnel Act of 1900 formalized this shift, with Marines hoping to lure better recruits with the prospect of commissions.[68]

While in China, though, Marines competed alongside their allies, eagerly seeking to achieve various firsts to promote their reputations.[69] As one American noted, the various powers jostled to lead the march into Peking to rescue those Europeans trapped in the Legation Quarter. American naval officer Capt. Bowman McCalla urged on his sailors and Marines at "the double-quick" to ensure they arrived first at the Legation Quarter. Unfortunately for his ambition, Sikh troops beat them there.[70]

Others emphasized the Marines' claim to be the first Westerners to open the gates to the Forbidden City. Reading an issue of *Leslie's Weekly* that credited the U.S. Army for arriving first in China incensed Maj. Thomas Wood. Finding such information to be "manifestly false and misleading," he demanded that the publication issue a correction to receive just as much attention as the original article. When *Leslie's Weekly* failed to issue a correction quickly enough, Wood sent another letter threatening to discredit the magazine in the service newspapers.[71] The forthcoming correction heaped encomiums on the Corps, hyperbolizing that "American marines were first in the fighting in China; they will ever be first wherever they can have their own way."[72] The phrase "hav[ing] their own way" suggested that perhaps *Leslie's Weekly* considered Wood's demanding letters somewhat childish. Wood, though, found it to be of utmost importance to keep the Army from taking credit for the Corps' accomplishments.

The Boxer Rebellion had provided a small and largely unknown institution with frequent headlines for months. Journalists had recounted the daring and courageous acts of a small contingent of Marines within Peking's Legation Quarter, as well as the exploits of Marines in concert with other troops on the march to Peking. In some ways, participation in the China Relief Expedition fueled the Corps' sense that it was something special. Marines believed themselves to be equal to many of the imperial soldiers with whom they fought, even as they celebrated their sense of being different. Awash with a sense of patriotism and nationalism stoked by victories during the Spanish-American War, Marines readily embraced their imperial mission in China. As Waller remarked about the Marines with whom he served in China, "They have made history, marked with blood. . . . They were the first in the field, and, please God, they will remain until the last man, woman and child is relieved from the toils of these barbarians."[73] Unlike their far more controversial mission in the Philippines, these Marines had few qualms as to whether their mission justified the sacrifices they made.

If the Spanish-American War and the Boxer Rebellion provided the Marine Corps with mostly positive experiences, the Philippine-American War proved at times to be a depressing contrast.[74] Instead of rescuing Europeans and Americans from what they perceived to be Asian barbarity, Marines had to be rescued from themselves in the Philippines.

It also marked the first time a significant number of Marines experienced long-term occupation duty. By 1901 one-third of the Corps could be found in the Philippines, a total of 64 officers and 1,934 men. The Navy scattered the Marines around sixteen naval stations, including the large bases of Cavite and Olongapo, where they guarded naval property and carried out some pacification duties. This latter mission allowed the Navy to nudge the Army gradually out of the area, thus preserving its sphere of authority.[75]

Over time, the Corps received additional duties, which individual Marines eagerly embraced. The Navy sent Marines to Samar in the fall of 1901 to support Gen. Jacob H. Smith's 6th Separate Brigade after insurgents killed a number of soldiers. While much of the Philippines had been pacified, the island of Samar remained populated with insurgents led by General Vicente Lukbán Rilles. The son of a wealthy family, Lukbán had arrived in Samar at the end of 1899 accompanied by one hundred soldiers. Declaring himself to be the Philippine Republic's governor of Samar, he formed an alliance with a local group. When American troops arrived in Samar, Lukbán and his supporters took refuge in the jungles.

Pacifying Samar became a top priority for Maj. Gen. Adna R. Chaffee after the so-called Massacre of Balangiga. On the morning of September 28, 1901, townspeople and insurgents in Balangiga attacked and killed forty-eight of seventy-four 9th Infantry soldiers as they ate breakfast. As a result, the commanding naval officer in the Philippines offered three hundred Marines to Chaffee, who welcomed their assistance. One Marine recalled his surprise upon learning the Marines had been ordered to Samar, as he considered pacification to be the Army's work.[76]

Upon arrival, the Marines' commanding officer, Maj. Littleton Waller, met with Smith. Smith shared Waller's short stature and his reputation for being a fighter who did not have much patience with insurgents' tactics. Smith purportedly informed Waller that he should kill every person over the age of ten, regardless of sex, with the goal of turning Samar into a "howling wilderness." Returning to his Marines, Waller reportedly conveyed a far more tempered message to one of his officers, Capt. David Porter: he should only target males capable of being armed. Still, Marines eagerly sought the chance to avenge the 9th Infantry, with whom they had served during the Boxer Rebellion.[77] Reflecting the Corps' increasingly assertive image, Marines also enthusiastically served under Waller because, as Sgt. Harry Glenn explained, he was a "born fighter" whom Marines "loved."[78]

Marines did not find much fighting at first. Carrying out operations along the coastal areas gave insurgents advance warning to flee. Frustrated, Waller learned of an important insurgent base deep in the jungle at Sojoton, which he understood to be a "last rallying point."[79] The Marines' reconnaissance up a river to a base perched atop a seemingly unassailable cliff once again alerted the insurgents to their arrival. When the main body of Marines arrived at the now-reinforced base, they began to attack the complex of cliffs and camps that insurgents had spent more than three years constructing. This time caught by surprise, insurgents could not destroy the bamboo ladders they used to reach the base.

Waller celebrated the "heroic" march, exaggerating the scaling of cliffs hundreds of feet tall "as a new feature of warfare." He also believed the successful mission sent the message to the insurgents that there was no place the Marines could not reach.[80] Congratulations flowed in from others serving in the Philippines. Major General Chaffee begged Waller to give each Marine his "high appreciation of the manly heart and soldierly spirit which makes light of obstacles and is never daunted." Journalists echoed these accolades, suggesting Marines could manage with ease not only counterinsurgency but "anything anywhere."[81] This kind of praise better served the Corps' needs since it did not tie Marines to a single mission.

Buoyed by his success, Waller's subsequent actions seemed to correlate with the Corps' intensifying determination to show it could accomplish anything. Waller set off on a new mission on December 28, 1901, to determine if a telegraph cable could be placed across the interior of the island along the Sojoton trail. Two Army officers had just returned from an unsuccessful twelve-day attempt to do this, but Waller ignored their warnings not to repeat the mission and set off with more than fifty Marines and thirty-five Filipino scouts and porters.[82] Dangerous river rapids forced the expedition to discard its boats and continue on foot. Constant wading through the river quickly took its toll on the Marines. By January 3 rations had been reduced severely, and they had lost the trail. Waller then split the expedition into two groups. He and those Marines in the best condition returned as quickly as possible to send a relief party. Within a few hours the group fortuitously found a clearing with crops. Waller sent a porter back to inform the party, but the porter returned without delivering the message, stating that he feared insurgent attacks. By January 6 Waller and his party arrived back at their original position, having found an inhabited clearing with natives able to guide them back to their base.

In the meantime, the rest of the Marines under Lt. Alexander S. Williams desperately tried to reach safety, but they struggled to walk more than three miles a day. Ten Marine stragglers died where they fell, and three of the native porters attempted to murder Williams and also allegedly withheld food from the Marines. The survivors among Williams' party were finally rescued on January 18. They had marched about 180 miles. Almost immediately after their return, Waller ordered ten porters executed for treachery. Later, Waller would be court-martialed and subsequently acquitted, with eleven favoring this decision and two opposing it.

Opinions on Waller's disastrous expedition have run the gamut from highly critical to forgiving. In the school of military historiography that seeks out lessons from victories and failures, many historians have focused on whether or not Waller used sound judgment in undertaking this operation.[83] Brian Linn, for example, argues that Waller "consistently relied on physical courage and endurance to make up for deficiencies in planning and judgment." To support this interpretation, he cites an offensive operation against overwhelming numbers Waller participated in during the China Relief Expedition that resulted in the abandonment of ten dead Marines on the battlefield.[84] In assuming that certain ahistorical constants affect planning and judgment, Linn characterizes Waller's choices as bad judgment.

Two cultural forces, however, provide greater insight into Waller's decision. First, he and other Marines increasingly claimed and acted on the belief that they could succeed at anything. Second, they found it more challenging to differentiate themselves from soldiers—who had similar duties in the Philippines—than from sailors. Epitomizing this approach almost a year after this expedition, 2nd Lt. Earl Ellis relished that the Army was "exceedingly jealous" of the Corps' ability to cover far more territory with fewer men. The Marine Corps, moreover, purportedly finished jobs the Army could not. Ellis would not settle for defeat at the Army's hands, even at sports. He ensured that Marines skilled at baseball received orders to his post to dominate Manila's baseball league. Similarly, the Corps' future commandant George Elliott claimed in an official report to the current commandant that Marines could capture and hold any coastal city, unlike the Army, which always "publish[ed] the point of attack to the natives." Waller himself joked in subsequent years about competition with the Army, noting in 1910 regarding the purchase of a humble vacuum cleaner, "I know you don't want the Army to get ahead of us on a thing like this."[85] The Corps' nagging self-doubt and constant need to prove itself hurt its reputation among its counterparts in the Philippines.[86] And its inability to claim a single unique mission forced it into laying claim to the most difficult

and challenging missions. Men died in Samar because of this intensifying culture.

Imperial culture also shaped Waller's decision. As Craig Cameron
has suggested, war's strategy and tactics are indivisible from the cultures that produce them. Cameron stresses that military historians
have made a false dichotomy between a study of tactics and doctrine—
viewed as rational and scientific—and a study of myth and imagery.
A better method, he argues, begins with the premise that doctrine
itself is a cultural construction. Cameron might overstate the extent to
which "practical developments were usually secondary to imagination
in shaping ground combat," but his approach helps provide a path to
understanding why Marines and soldiers often acted as they did.[87]

Culture shaped how Marines conceived of and acted on their
responsibilities during imperial wars.[88] Must a Marine always fight fair
if his opponent did not know or refused to accept Western rules of war?
Waller's pejorative view of insurgents' tactics helped him justify the rules
that dominated Western warfare. He was not alone; a similar way of
thinking about what Westerners considered "small wars" pervaded both
American and British military mind-sets.[89] The belief that his opponents
were savages who avoided direct confrontation dominated Waller's perspective. How Marines viewed insurgents was characterized by frustration with their treachery and their refusal to fight on an open battlefield.
In describing the clothing belonging to insurgents he had found in a boat,
Waller began detailing the "uniform of an insurgent officer" before cor-
recting himself, continuing, "I mean a coat with four pockets and a pleat
or band around the wrist." Waller revised his use of military terminology to avoid labeling the insurgents as legitimate opponents. Similarly,
Waller testified that during one expedition, his Marines encountered
natives who had "swarmed on the beach with their bolos waiting for the
[Marines] to land. There was no doubt about their intention to slaughter these men."[90] Rather than describe what many would consider to be
some kind of an ambush, Waller used the wording of "slaughter" to suggest something more akin to murder than military-sanctioned killing.

Scholarship about the relationship between imperialism and masculinity sheds some light on the Marines' mentality in Samar.[91] Gail

Bederman has emphasized the shift from a Victorian culture of civilized manliness to one of primitive masculinity during the late 1890s and early 1900s. Men like Theodore Roosevelt, she argues, exemplify these changes. The wealthy easterner could have spent his life in a luxurious setting, but instead he sought out war and adventure. For a time, these traits of civilized manliness and primitive masculinity coexisted, which helps to explain the culture that shaped Waller. While in the jungle of Samar, these self-proclaimed fighters expected the Filipinos to care for them. In describing the Samar expedition to the *Wide World Magazine*, Sgt. Harry Glenn depicted both Waller's civilized manliness and his more assertive masculinity.[92] He could be a masterful fighter, but he could also be a caring father figure. Describing the exhausted band of Marines searching for a way out of the jungle, Glenn explained that Waller had overcome his exhaustion to stay awake with the sentry. The same situation occurred the next night. This time, however, one of his captains slept with his head in Waller's lap.[93]

Warwick Anderson has challenged the idea of a confident colonial overlord, suggesting that the "white masculine gaze was often more a nervous glance than a commanding stare." At an early point in their imperial careers, Marines certainly evidenced a certain hopelessness that contrasts with their behavior in other settings. Waiting for rescue to arrive, frustrated Marines wondered about the behavior of their Filipino porters, who "became sulky, practically refusing assistance to the white man." While Marines suffered from the constant rain and lack of food and passively waited for the porters' assistance, the porters busily constructed temporary shanties and procured additional food due to their knowledge of plants, which they refused to share. Eventually, Marines began to worry that the porters would turn on them. As one naval officer reported, the "time came when no white man could carry a rifle, and those not lost were in the hands of the natives; under the altered condition, it required considerable diplomacy" to manage the porters.[94] The contrast between the Marines' experience in the jungle and that of the porters is striking. Far from being the tough fighters of lore, these Marines could not even carry their own weapons. As one Army general ironically pointed out in the fall-out from the expedition, even more Marines probably would have died without the porters' assistance.[95]

Samar demonstrated that imperialism was not a "pleasure trip," as one newspaper headline suggested. As this reality set in and some became more cynical about their role in the Philippines, some Marines turned to the British model of handling recalcitrant natives. Indeed, Waller defended his actions in ordering the porters executed by arguing that he had seen the British deal with native "treachery" similarly in Egypt.[96] Waller argued "he had every right to believe that his acts were approved, so far as the American forces were concerned. He knew they were approved by those of other nations." He stated emphatically that "neither my people nor the world will believe me to be a murderer." Marines rallied around Waller, finding his execution of the porters a necessary solution that civilians back at home could not appreciate because they had not witnessed Filipino treachery.[97]

Brian Linn has questioned why Marines would have chosen to cele-brate Samar. Indeed, it seems obvious from a modern perspective that the killing of eleven porters might have significant repercussions on coun-terinsurgency efforts. Furthermore, Linn suggested that by any measur-able military definition of success, such as distance or enemy opposition, Waller's mission in no way equaled more "epic marches." Still, individual Marines sought to memorialize Samar in ways that became engrained in the institution, whether or not officially sanctioned.[98]

The experience both officers and men shared—strengthened by defining themselves against the "savage" other—led to a diminish-ing sense of the distance between officer and enlisted.[99] One Marine described the lasting bonds between enlisted Marines and their officers forged on Samar: "There were several famous officers of the Marines who knew the survivors by the marks the jungles and the horror had left [on] the enlisted survivors. These officers' headquarters were always open and perhaps the quarters were crowded with other officers, and [when] an enlisted man or a former enlisted man with haunted eyes came softly in, the word passed gently like a whisper, 'Stand gentlemen, this man served in Samar.'"[100] The distance between enlisted and officer already had begun to diminish, and in a small institution bound together by this seminal event, barriers broke down faster and faster.[101] This was not just a one-sided occurrence in which officers behaved paternalistically, though that may have been a factor. Some enlisted Marines noted that the expedition had reduced distinctions between the ranks as they struggled to remain alive.[102]

While a great deal has been written on how nations remember war, less scholarship has explored how soldiers themselves recall their experiences.[103] The 1857 Indian Mutiny, once more commonly called the Sepoy Mutiny, offers some parallels, at least in the extent to which the British felt betrayed by an indigenous population. In this instance, Hindu and Muslim soldiers mutinied in widespread violence that lasted more than a year, in part for what they considered to be British insensitivity to their religious and cultural practices. In remembering their losses, especially those of women and children, the British used physical markers such as tombs and memorials.[104] Marines might not have established physical markers, but they used other physical acts, such as standing when a veteran of Samar entered the room, and writing to memorialize their service and the service of those comrades who had died in Samar. As one Marine wrote two decades later while giving an overview of the Corps' history, Samar was a "wild" place where "no white troops had ever before been, filled with hostile savages, and much cut up by streams and jungle. They were misled by their native guides, were lost in the wilderness, and suffered untold privations. A number of men died on that march, but Waller brought his battalion through, marching clear across the island." Rather than challenging Waller's decisions, Marines blamed the environment and especially their guides' treachery.[105]

With the mostly negative public attention they received from Samar, some considered the implications of imperial warfare more carefully. They had stressed good sportsmanship and gentlemanly actions during the Spanish-American War, but the Spanish had played by the same rules.[106] Arriving in the wake of Waller's acquittal, Ellis cynically remarked that the British knew the best way to handle the natives. In his opinion, American citizens could not appreciate what was required to wage this type of warfare.[107]

In adapting to imperial warfare, Marines looked more directly to the British example for inspiration, adding new accouterments such as swagger sticks. Benedict Anderson has contrasted colonial armies, which he characterizes as glamorized forces interested in "glory, epaulettes, personal heroism, polo, and an archaizing courtliness among its officers," to militaries maintained for the protection of the nation-state, concerned with professionalism, discipline, and technology.[108] For an institution already drawn to tradition, it would be an easy step to adopt traits of the former.

Well-known poet and journalist Damon Runyon's "The Marine," published in 1904, summarized some important aspects of the Marines' evolving identity since the Spanish-American War. Separate stanzas of the poem connected the Marine's job to the duties of both the Navy and the Army. The poet reiterated the Corps' belief that Marines furnished the most critical naval gunnery, as reflected in the reports of Marine officers during and after the Spanish-American War. The next stanza focused on the Corps' recent imperial conflicts:

Guantanamo to Samar, on the Chinamen's heathen ground,
He's left his dead as with steady tread he fought the world around.
Horse and foot and guns, he one and all combines,
As he backs the ships' big guns, or charges the enemy's lines.
No flowers for his grave.[109]

Guantánamo, Samar, and Peking had left their imprint on the Corps. Not only did the poet emphasize the ability of the Marine to fulfill any mission, but he also suggested the Marines' consistent steadiness. Finally, with the mention of the barren grave, the poet continued to echo generations of previous Marines who lamented their unappreciated institution. Of all the elements that suggested the greatest progression in the Corps' identity, however, most prominent was the idea that Marines could carry out any mission. It would be easy to discount this confidence as bombast, and such a conclusion would be correct in terms of the institution's mission capabilities. This piece of doggerel, however, reflected the Corps' idealized vision of itself and perhaps even what it *needed* to be to resolve the perennial question of why it was necessary.

The Spanish-American War appeared to offer a temporary respite for the Marine Corps after the Marines had faced a severe crisis in the 1890s when naval officers attacked the utility of Marines on board ships. Almost overlapping involvement in the Spanish-American War, the Boxer Rebellion, and the Philippine-American War, however, progressively challenged the Corps to adapt to new forms of warfare. At the same time, it threw the institution into close contact with U.S. soldiers and the troops of other nations in a way that convinced some Marines they were better able to fulfill the missions of both soldiers and sailors.

Still, the early efforts of nineteenth-century Marines like Henry Cochrane and Richard Collum began to bear fruit at the beginning of the twentieth century. And the same men who fought at battles such as Guantánamo subsequently joined the battle for recruits to man a growing Corps. This was the case for Capt. A. S. McLemore, who received orders to head the Corps' recruiting efforts on the west coast in 1899.[110] By World War I, McLemore led the Corps' recruiting and publicity efforts. As both recruiters and "fighters," men like McLemore increasingly took every opportunity to propagate the Corps' intensifying imagery as recruiting moved front and center in the institution.

Chapter Three

———————————◆———————————

Refinement and Elaboration

The Navy's Impact on the Corps' Early Publicity Efforts

n August of 1907, Corporal Murtaugh opened a new recruiting office in Logansport, Indiana. Raising one of the office's windows, he proudly hung an American flag out, only to draw the ire of the local police captain. In the ensuing confrontation, the policeman informed him that flying flags from windows violated local ordinances. Murtaugh responded by pulling out his six-shooter and suggesting the policeman drop the issue. After all, flying the flag from federal property was excluded from local ordinances. A group of Civil War veterans quickly formed in support of Murtaugh, and an Army recruiter eagerly emulated Murtaugh's example in hopes of drawing similar attention.[1] Murtaugh's aggressiveness and assertiveness attracted the attention of newspapers around the nation.

Corporal Murtaugh's commanding officer praised his actions, and the public clamored around him, even stopping outside of his office during a Labor Day parade to honor now-sergeant Murtaugh, the promotion due to his stubborn defense of Old Glory, or so one journalist suggested. Multiple newspapers around the nation reprinted the story, some viewing the incident as emblematic of the continued tension over states' rights. None of this, however, helped Murtaugh find recruits. The same article that celebrated his promotion expressed his frustrations: "Soldier Life Evidently Does Not Appeal Just Now."[2] The headline also revealed that it did not yet mean something self-explanatory to be a Marine, as the journalist connected Murtaugh's service with soldiering in general rather than with the Marine Corps.

The journalist also sympathetically detailed the creative recruiting efforts that all of the military branches had been taking, which ranged from "movie pictures" to skilled lithography, a departure from the trends of the previous fifty years. Since the late nineteenth century, the Corps in particular had sought personnel in an ad hoc manner with mostly formulaic recruiting materials that rarely considered creative approaches. It used temporary recruiting stations, and few formalized rules or regulations governed their operations. In their correspondence recruiting officers primarily focused on seeking waivers from the commandant for the recruits they did manage to snag, not on improving recruiting as a whole.[3]

Slowly, though, this limited approach began to change in all of the military services, and the thoughts of one Marine recruiting officer offer insights into this shift. In considering how to obtain the desired quantity and quality of recruits, Capt. James Breckenridge convinced his commanding officer, Maj. L. J. Magill, that advertising in streetcars was the "only practicable way of reaching the better class of men." Breckenridge also suggested that new recruits be encouraged to write to friends about their enlistment in hopes of motivating them to join as well, and Magill promised to provide him some mimeographed statements to include with these letters.[4]

Breckenridge focused not only on the quality of the recruits he wanted but also on the value of the men with whom he already worked, hoping to see two of his enlisted Marines be promoted. Magill agreed with his subordinate regarding the importance of these promotions, noting he wished they occurred far more frequently. The Corps, he contended, should "have only the best men on recruiting duty." In seeking these improvements, both men still took comfort in their belief that they had better men than the Navy, demonstrating the increasing tendency of Marines to compare themselves to the Navy, only to find the latter lacking. This shared awareness of another branch's recruiting practices—enabled by the Corps' coexistence with the Navy under the Navy Department's umbrella—also helped both branches evaluate and improve their own efforts.

Breckenridge's ideas epitomized how imaginative recruiting practices intersected with the Corps' late nineteenth-century historical narrative and its intensifying sense of self between about 1905 and 1910.

The Corps began to discard the recruiting practices it had used since at least the Civil War, including formulaic help-wanted ads that made few distinguishing remarks about the Corps. It experimented with forms of publicity that sought to inform the public not only of its existence but also of its distinctiveness. It did not do this with much centralized direction; rather, individual Marines came up with new ideas for representing themselves internally and externally.

To the public, service in the Marines could not often be distinguished from service in other military branches; to Marines themselves, however, that distinction was becoming increasingly clear. As Marines refined and elaborated on their identity, they did so in close service with the Navy. This relationship would be tested once again, however, when long-simmering identity clashes between the two services erupted in 1908. As a result, President Theodore Roosevelt ordered Marines off ships in 1909, threatening the permanent loss of the Corps' most traditional mission. The Corps would weather this storm; indeed, it relied on its evolving image to endure the greatest existential crisis it had faced since Capt. Henry Cochrane first bemoaned the Corps' poor image in the 1870s.

Although the Corps' image had improved greatly since the 1870s, its recruiting practices had not. The Corps largely relied on print media, particularly formulaic newspaper ads placed in the help-wanted section that emphasized pay and occasionally travel. These ads had limited visual appeal, with little to differentiate them from any other ad. A popular help-wanted ad after the Spanish-American War read: "Wanted—For the U.S. Marine Corps, unmarried men between the ages of 21 and 35, able-bodied, of good character and temperate habits, citizens of the United States, or who have legally declared their intention to become such; must speak, read and write English; marines serve at sea on men-of-war in all parts of the world, on land in our island possessions and at navy yards in the United States. Recruits desiring service in the Philippine Islands may be enlisted accordingly."[5]

Only after exhaustively setting out its requirements for a recruit did the Corps explain what a Marine might do. The Army also used similar, albeit terser, wording for almost a decade: "Wanted for U.S.

Army—able-bodied unmarried men between ages of 21 and 35, citizens of the United States, of good character and temperate habits; must speak, read and write English."[6] The Army's ads often ran next to or close to the Corps', and little distinguished them except the actual locale one might expect to perform his duties. Early in 1906 the Corps switched to a shorter ad that stressed only the opportunity for travel and asked the reader to visit the recruiting office or write for more information. It also limited its emphasis on requirements, stating only that recruits must be between twenty-one and thirty-five years old.[7] The Corps continued to use variations of these formulaic ads well into 1910, even as it also began to innovate with more creative ways to attract newspaper readers.[8] These approaches overlapped with the civilian world's understanding of advertising as more an announcement of a product's introduction or availability than an active attempt to sway a viewer's interest. As companies consolidated and grew larger, this practice shifted focus away from the local market to the national one. Increasing competition then forced more creative product differentiation that appealed to buyers' feelings and desires, including an impression of stature. Mass media reflected this shift, as the number of pages in magazines devoted to advertisements increased at astronomical rates. Readers in the 1880s could expect to see about ten pages with advertising in a typical publication; their counterparts just after the turn of the century saw about one hundred.[9]

At the end of the nineteenth century, a few individual recruiters had departed from this long trend of formulaic help-wanted ads in a way that overlapped with broader transformations in advertising. These new ads reflected a strong desire to benefit from the Navy's image based on recruiters' recognition that the public did not understand what a Marine was. One ad, for example, characterized the Corps as an "important branch of the Naval Service."[10] A California recruiter had devised this phrase as early as 1889, and subsequent recruiters continued to use this wording at least until 1896, in spite of exploding coverage in other newspaper sections of the rising tension between the two branches about the role of Marines on steamships. A 1901 classified ad in a Philadelphia paper made even closer connections between the two services

in calling for "Marine Corps U.S. Navy Recruits."[11] Recruiters also highlighted the attractive prospect of serving on the Navy's ships. Indeed,
a prospective recruit entering a Marine Corps recruiting office might
see a large sign emblazoned with the words "U.S. Marine Corps; U.S.
Navy Recruiting Office."[12] For recruiting purposes, the Corps sought to
emphasize the close links between the two branches.

The Corps' largest pieces of advertising—including recruiting posters and billboards—made similar connections to the Navy. An 1898
recruiting poster, for example, described the Corps as being an "important branch" of the Navy. The poster had much in common with the
heavy emphasis on textual information and pay charts evident in Civil
War–era recruiting posters.[13] During this period, recruiting publications
lacked the striking artwork that dominated all branches' advertisements
by World War I. Billboards also made connections to the Navy. A popular one featured a uniformed Marine standing in front of the battleship
USS *Kearsarge*. Navy recruiters used this image as well, even though it
pictured a Marine.[14] Taken together, the various practices suggest that no
branch gave careful thought to crafting a powerful message to reach its
desired audience. The need to be creative or offer an emotional appeal
did not yet dominate recruiters' thinking, perhaps because military
officers distrusted the business world's advertising practices. The transformation that occurred over the course of the late nineteenth and early
twentieth centuries led to society's general acceptance of a practice that
many had viewed as troubling, possibly even immoral, given the aggran-
dized claims advertisers made about their products.[15]

Still, as early as 1904, the Corps had realized it needed larger posters
to attract attention, but printing them required congressional approval.[16]
Although the Corps had yet to consider using professional advertisers
to shape its imaging, it had no objections to hiring businesses to place
its ads on billboards, fences, and elsewhere. It also experimented with
the Gunning System of advertising, which placed large "painted bulle-
tins" on popular roads. Like the Army, however, the Corps discontinued
the practice because of cost.[17] The actual content of the posters slowly
began to change as well, as all branches increased their use of striking
visuals while reducing their wording.[18] Again, this echoed larger shifts

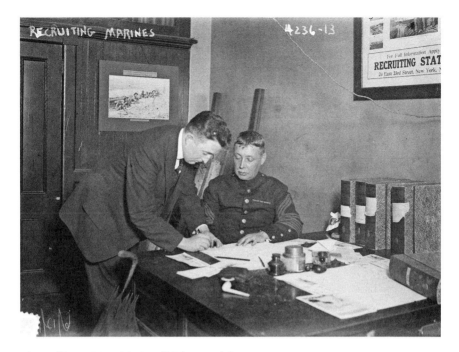

Fig. 6. "Recruiting Marines." *Library of Congress*

that were gaining significant traction over the course of the early twentieth century; visual imagery increasingly communicated "normative overtones" through the medium of advertising, creating a kind of fantasy world.[19] Over the next decade, the Corps better learned to craft and manipulate such images to appeal to potential recruits.

Despite making some improvements to its recruiting material, the Corps found it challenging to meet its manpower requirements in the wake of the Spanish-American War, struggling to almost quadruple in size from 2,500 men to more than 9,000 by 1908.[20] The Corps experienced periods of success interspersed with more difficult times, largely related to shifting economic conditions. In November of 1906, for example, Cmdt. George Elliott informed the New York City recruiting officer to be selective, as there was no "haste."[21] A few months later, however, Elliott seemed to be approaching something near panic.

The Corps began planning to experiment with a revolutionary form of advertising at the end of 1906 amid relative plenty, demonstrating the commandant's receptiveness to innovative recruiting approaches.

In November of that year, several advertising companies had tried to convince the commandant to contract out the Corps' recruiting advertisements and switch from classified ads to what was called diversified, or display, advertising. Diversified advertising consisted of large, splashy visual imagery accompanied by text that blended in with surrounding articles rather than being restricted to the paper's help-wanted section. The commandant looked favorably upon this suggestion; after all, it was not so dissimilar to contracting out billboards, which he had considered in 1904.[22] The Corps ultimately selected the Charles H. Fuller Company and urged the experiment be conducted as soon as possible.[23]

It soon became apparent that the experiment entailed more than using a different section of the newspaper. In a notable departure from past practice that aligned with trends in civilian advertising, the articles' rhetoric made powerful appeals to the reader.[24] The commandant and the Charles H. Fuller Company collaborated with the recruiting officer in Chicago, Capt. Carl Gamborg-Andresen, in planning the experiment. Gamborg-Andresen sought to put the brakes on some of the commandant's enthusiasm, worried that he could not plan adequately with matters moving so quickly. He needed not only to help with the articles but also to plan a tour of the local area in hopes of capitalizing on the expected enthusiasm of newspaper readers for joining the Corps. The commandant gave him permission on December 13 to postpone the experiment and promised to provide additional enlisted recruiters from Iowa on temporary duty and an additional officer if one could be found.[25]

Rather than focusing on the obvious city of Chicago, from which the Corps had been garnering a significant percentage of its recruits since 1903, the advertising company selected four Illinois towns for the experiment: Danville, Peoria, Springfield, and Rockford. In these small, thriving Illinois towns, labor was in high demand and well paid, thus providing a significant test of the new approach. The company placed smaller ads on alternating days a week before the arrival of the recruiting party and then ran much larger ads each of the six days the recruiting party was in town. The largest ads reached ninety inches and spanned six columns.[26] One ad screamed, "YOUNG MAN! YOU ARE WANTED!" The headline promised "Light Work, Short Hours and Plenty of Time Off on Land"

and opened with the almost habitual explanation that the public knew much about the Army but little of the Corps. Unlike future bureau releases that set forth the prospect of challenge, however, the advertising company characterized the Marines' duties as generally being "very light." After extolling all of the Corps' benefits, the writer concluded hyperbolically that it was "doubtful if there exists today any more desirable, pleasant and honorable occupation" than that of a Marine.[27] A larger ad published two days later included a large image of a Marine and proclaimed a similar message of a well-paid, relatively easy occupation that still enabled a recruit to achieve the highest form of manhood. A Marine could "enjoy [himself] and be a man among men."[28] The normative appeals in these advertisements appealed to potential recruits' desire for prestige and reputation and set forth the prospect of a life of relative ease in a manner consistent with trends in the civilian world.

Display advertising resulted in follow-on free publicity when the recruiting party arrived in town. One newspaper ran an article celebrating recruiting officer Gamborg-Andresen's rise from private to commissioned officer.[29] Certainly, this reinforced the kind of status the newspaper ads had held out enticingly. But Gamborg-Andresen departed from the advertising firm's approach to speak more forthrightly, particularly in regard to the nature of service life. While he still maintained that the government sought to do "everything in its power to make pleasant the life" of a Marine, he also admitted that the service required "strict discipline." Still, Gamborg-Andresen made a similar appeal to a potential recruit's sense of masculine identity, arguing that this discipline "makes men."[30] Even as he collaborated with professional advertisers, he refused to parrot all of their messaging. But he did share their willingness to hold out the promise of attaining normative ideals of masculinity through service in the Corps.

Like other recruiting officers such as Capt. A. S. McLemore, Gamborg-Andresen had fought in some of the Corps' key battles, including the Battle of Santiago and the Boxer Rebellion, where some had celebrated the Corps' masculinity at the expense of the Navy's.[31] Their increasing identification with the Corps forged through these battles emanated through the information they now assertively provided to journalists.

These new advertising methods had the potential to save the government money. Procuring manpower is not only challenging but expensive. The Corps had paid $2,748.68 for the experiment, with $1,278.08 of that amount covering the advertising agency's ads. The bulk of the remaining funds covered the recruiters' lodging expenses. In conducting the experiment, Gamborg-Andresen stressed that the recruiters needed to be on the best of terms with everyone they encountered, including tipping bell-boys well. Despite the expense of procuring goodwill, the average cost of obtaining a recruit had dropped to $50.58, from $64.46 in November 1906 and $83.29 in December that year.[32] Captain Gamborg-Andresen believed future experiments could use less extensive advertising and still be more efficient than traditional advertising methods.

The experiment not only introduced many to the Corps but also reached what Gamborg-Andresen considered a far better quality of recruit, especially in smaller towns. In the town of Danville, for example, Gamborg-Andresen encountered recruits of a quality rarely seen, including ten farmers who "knew absolutely nothing about the Marine Corps" before reading the advertisements.[33] Peoria had a population three times greater than Danville's 35,000. In Peoria Gamborg-Andresen saw the kind of "undesirable" recruits more typical of Chicago, and the recruiting party struggled to attract much interest. Gamborg-Andresen met an Army recruiter in Peoria who admitted his own recruiting frustrations. In Springfield, for example, he had obtained only 120 recruits in an entire year.

By contrast, the recruiting party in visiting a handful of towns spoke with 334 individuals, of whom 140 applied to join the Corps. Gamborg-Andresen approved 66 of those, of whom the surgeon medically rejected 15 for a total enlistment of 50 Marines and 1 apprentice. He had recruited them in only 24 business days; by contrast, he had obtained only 31 recruits in the three previous months. Of Gamborg-Andresen's 51 new recruits, 19 came from cities and 32 from the countryside. He felt sure he could have acquired far greater numbers of farmers had severe weather not kept them from visiting.[34]

In addition to delineating between urban and rural recruits, Gamborg-Andresen investigated how potential recruits learned of the Corps. He found that a preponderance of the men had responded to the advertisements. Only five had much prior knowledge of military service—two were veterans themselves and three had friends in the service. Display advertising thus seemed to hold the promise of reaching largely untapped numbers of high-quality recruits because it reached a broader number of readers. The traditional placement of help-wanted advertisements tended to limit readership to those seeking employment. Also, the advertisements reached more potential recruits in the countryside, rather than attracting what recruiters referred to disparagingly as the cities' "floating population" of itinerants. In considering how to employ display advertising in the future, Gamborg-Andresen recommended eliminating "all superfluous reading matter," leaving just enough information to "attract attention and excite" potential recruits to seek out more information from a recruiter.[35]

He also took the important step of seeking to understand what motivated recruits to enlist and how they responded emotionally to advertising. Did they enlist to see the world, to better themselves, or to be soldiers? Twenty-eight replied that they wanted to improve themselves, thirty-nine that they wanted to become soldiers.[36] Even Gamborg-Andresen's use of the word "soldier" is revealing in that he felt compelled to conduct his survey by using the word Marines had most often used to describe themselves since the nineteenth century.

After its first display advertising experiment, the Corps eagerly sought to implement it on a larger scale, given increasingly challenging recruiting conditions. By the end of February 1907, the commandant worried how he would recruit the 500 men he needed to meet his quota of 8,779 men. The Corps now believed it needed to take "unusual efforts" to recruit them. Some of these efforts entailed shifting recruiters' geographical focus away from the eastern part of the country, where people were more familiar with the Corps. By 1907 the Corps recognized it must get its name out in the West, Northwest, and Southwest. But a year later it had only thirteen recruiting officers, who controlled various substations scattered around the central office. In 1908 these included offices located in Buffalo, Atlanta, Chicago, Boston, Detroit, Saint Paul, Saint Louis, New York, Toledo, Philadelphia, Pittsburgh,

Cincinnati, and Seattle.[37] Recruiting stations could shift relatively quickly if they failed to bring in enough recruits, but many geographical areas of the United States simply did not receive coverage.[38] Prospective recruits from those neglected areas who wrote to the commandant were informed of the nearest recruiting location and sometimes, if supplies allowed, were mailed a booklet that described "life in the Marine Corps." The fact that potential recruits from Texas learned they had to travel to St. Louis to enlist, however, shows the limits of the Corps' recruiting net.[39] With cost a key issue in recruiting, the Corps focused on what it deemed promising population centers rather than on dispersing its meager resources throughout the nation.

As had the commandant, acting Secretary of the Navy Truman Newberry increasingly concerned himself with recruiting. Just a little more than a month after the experiment's conclusion, he began requesting that both the Navy and the Marine Corps provide him with monthly reports of recruiting expenditures detailing rent, travel, and printing expenses. Such oversight benefited both branches because it familiarized them with different approaches and practices. After the secretary approved the Corps' request for display newspaper advertising, for example, the Navy conducted its own test of display advertising that same month, with similarly successful results.[40]

The secretary of the Navy's requests for the two services' monthly expenses brought to light the Corps' seemingly excessive spending. Most of the costs associated with recruiting, resulted from the recruiters' needs to visit various towns overnight and to transport recruits to their new posts. In May of 1907, the Corps reported it spent $13,053.05 to obtain 322 recruits, an average cost of $40.54 per recruit. Of that, it spent about 44 percent on traveling expenses for its recruiting officers and recruits, 33 percent on transporting recruits to their duty stations, 10 percent on renting offices, 7 percent on newspaper advertising, 3 percent on medical exams, 2 percent on the posting of recruiting posters, and 1 percent on assorted expenses.[41]

After the secretary of the Navy demanded an explanation for why the Corps needed $41.90 to obtain a recruit but the Navy needed only $11.92, the commandant revealed his familiarity with the Navy's recruiting efforts.[42] Questioning the Navy's accounting, he found its advertising figures far too low, given the Navy's "expensive items of newspaper display advertising, pamphlets, circulars, biography pictures and theatre program advertising." The Navy also paid its sailors better, making recruiting more challenging for the Corps. The Corps' frustrated quartermaster similarly commented that if "any discrepancy in favor of the Navy should be found it is believed that it can be accounted for by the higher pay and lower standard as to age maintained by the Navy." Over the course of five months, the Corps had accepted only 1,636 of 9,430 applicants, an acceptance rate of 17 percent.[43] Such high standards also illuminated differences in the Navy's and Corps' recruiting costs, or so Marines argued.

Still, the commandant admitted his dissatisfaction with the Corps' current recruiting practices. He eagerly sought to increase its efficiency, though he found some of the Navy's recruiting practices "excessive" and thus impracticable for the Corps.[44] The Navy's greater size and resources enabled it to cast a wider and deeper net with greater variety in recruiting materials. The fact that the Navy Department oversaw two services, however, spurred creativity and experimentation because it enabled the department to glean greater insights into the most effective recruiting practices and adopt or adapt them when feasible.

By May 1907 the commandant urged the secretary of the Navy for permission to expand on the Chicago experiment. Now under strength by 610 men, the commandant argued he required the use of "more modern methods of newspaper advertising." He considered traditional methods no longer "adequate," and, of the "various systems" tried, he believed display advertising to be most successful.[45] Pointing to the Navy's implementation of the same concept in the wake of the Corps' experiment, the Corps begged to be "put on the same footing" as the Navy and included an example of the Navy's display advertising. The commandant admitted—perhaps still trying to avoid the Corps' reputation for spending too much money—that the Corps' experiment in January had been a bit overzealous.[46] The secretary found the commandant overwrought, informing him that the Navy's Bureau of Navigation, which managed recruiting, had no special permission that the Corps did not. Although not quite sold on display advertising's efficacy, he informed the commandant he only need submit for approval any kind of display advertising he wanted to publish.[47]

Even as the Corps integrated commercial business practices, individual Marines worked to develop new traditions for the Corps that celebrated its intensifying institutional identity. The unofficial motto, Once a Marine, Always a Marine, the invention of recruiting officer Lt. L. P. Pinkston, appeared in a handful of newspapers by 1907.[48] In many ways, this motto overlapped greatly with the Corps' official motto of *Semper fidelis*. Still, it more pointedly suggested that emotional ties bound Marines to their Corps even after contractual ties had expired. Given that a recruiting officer coined the phrase, it also indicated the hope that former Marines would act as unofficial ambassadors after leaving the service in a way that might stimulate recruiting.

By the end of 1907, the Corps heaved a collective sigh of relief that it had met its recruiting quota, even ceasing to run classified advertisements. The efforts of creative recruiting officers like Lieutenant Pinkston had been instrumental. He alone had convinced 531 men to enlist in eighteen months. That November the Corps had its best recruiting month in history, despite Marines' substantially lower pay than sailors'.[49] One newspaper article bragged that the Marine Corps had so many recruits that it allowed Army and Navy recruiters to enlist its potential recruits.[50] Still, the commandant did not take his eye off ways to keep improving the appealing nature of the Corps' recruiting material. Continuing the increasing emphasis on visual imagery, he sent a circular letter suggesting that the Corps use postcards featuring "pictures of men in action" or "local objects of interest" to better inform the public about the Corps.[51]

Individual recruiters made their own innovations, and their ideas spread quickly throughout the Corps. Ordered to the Chicago recruiting office in 1907, Capt. William Harllee devised the idea of communicating with Marine barracks to keep in touch with new recruits. Recruiters thus acquired insights into the best sort of men on whom to focus, just as Gamborg-Andresen had sought to understand recruits' motives for enlisting. Harllee also wanted to provide local newspapers with interesting accounts of former residents' accomplishments. This practice would help his recruiting office "get much valuable advertising" while also "stimulat[ing] public interest in the Marine Corps in general." A Pittsburgh recruiting officer adopted Harllee's practice promptly, requesting additional details from the commandant. He shared his own interest in following through with recruits to determine how well they had "adapted to the life of a soldier, particularly whether he has been disappointed in his selection of the branch of the service."[52] Increasingly, recruiters wanted to understand recruits' motives and the extent to which they affiliated with their chosen institutions, and they eagerly shared their ideas through informal networks.

Recruiters also worked to ingratiate themselves with local journalists, assisted by the fact that display advertising offered more opportunities than the old method of buying classified space to interact with them. Even if they could not always pay for large, compelling advertisements, they could provide information to journalists that would motivate them to write favorable articles. In the process, Marines conveyed a number of sentiments that emphasized the Corps' changing relationship to the Navy as well as romanticized imagery of colonial service. Sgt. Joseph Gallagher believed that the Corps had been "lost" in the Navy until the Spanish-American War, when it finally received the recognition it deserved. Still, though, he thought the public maintained an image of the Marine as simply serving at sea to serve as a repository for the "longest and most importable of the sailors['] yarns." Rather than celebrating the Marines' accomplishments, then, the public's outdated image of the Corps better reflected the nineteenth-century relationship between the two branches, as epitomized by the old mantra of "telling it to the Marines." Gallagher could not understand why the Corps had been ignored for so many years, especially considering the "picturesque nature of its duties." Other newspaper articles similarly emphasized the multiple places Marines traveled, sometimes coupling these descriptions with stories of men who reenlisted, having quickly tired of civilian life.[53]

With a secretary of the Navy asking the Corps to account for its spending, a commandant eager to experiment with new recruiting strategies, and Marine recruiters increasingly communicating with journalists and each other, the Corps refined and strengthened its narrative, built on the foundation of the Marine officers who had crafted a historical narrative now internalized in its members' memory. It was so strong that sailors noticed it, occasionally mocking Marines' reverence for their historical bent. One sailor described the arrival of his ship in Guantánamo Bay toward the end of the Spanish-American War and questioned how the Marines established a base there at the war's beginning, which resulted in a discussion with his fellow sailors about the Corps' history, including its motto and its claim to be the oldest institution. That they were joking became apparent when one of the sailors "produced an ancient book from his ditty box, and proceeded to read . . . in a loud, sonorous voice" the legislation creating the Corps in November of 1775.[54] Pointing to the Corps' origins in 1775, as Collum had, rather than 1798 demonstrated the extent to which this narrative dominated popular understandings among the naval service.

Newspapers repeated these claims, with one Idaho newspaper citing the now-familiar claim that the Corps was the nation's oldest military service. This 1909 article even expanded this claim to argue that the Corps had been in "continuous existence" since its establishment in 1775, unlike the Army or the Navy. In hyperbole that would become the norm in less than a decade, the article informed readers that the nation had lacked an army or a navy in the nation's early years. At that time, the fate of the entire nation supposedly had rested on a "faithful corps [that] was its only defense." Similarly, the reader learned how the Corps upheld its motto of *Semper fidelis*.[55] And, reflecting the emphases of late nineteenth-century Marines, no other service had "richer traditions." The article also held out the inducement of becoming a noncommissioned officer to lower-ranking Marines. Scattered throughout the world at imperial outposts, sergeants were "monarchs of all they survey[ed]." Advancement in rank, then, came with the allure of great power, consistent with the trend in advertising to attract customers with the promise of prestige.

The few historians who have analyzed the Corps' burgeoning publicity efforts have pointed to the establishment of the Recruiting Publicity Bureau in 1912 as pivotal.[56] Yet this 1909 article includes many of the same rhetorical flourishes that are so common to the bureau. A clear line can be traced from the article's appearance and wording to the yearly recruiting pamphlets the bureau began publishing in 1912. Six illustrations accompanied the article, as well as a large box of text summarizing "Duties, Experiences, Opportunities, Pay." These words also headlined the Corps' recruiting pamphlets, including one Cmdt. George Elliott had asked Maj. Charles McCawley to write in 1908.[57] The bureau's establishment certainly helped the Corps increase its ability to reach Americans, but the kind of messages the Corps disseminated largely were crafted amid the shift to diversified advertising while building on the Corps' nineteenth-century historical narrative. At a time when manning issues encouraged the Corps to be increasingly creative, the institution made great gains in refining its image and convincing outsiders to echo its evolving narrative. But an intensifying image could not save it from yet another clash of identity with the Navy. As already seen, naval officers had attempted to remove Marines from ships at several points since 1829. These efforts had intensified in the nineteenth century's last decades as the Navy began building battleships and other new ships.

These tensions had not been resolved, even after Marines received orders to participate more fully in maintaining these new ships. In 1895 Capt. Robley D. Evans had argued that his newly launched battleship *Indiana* simply did not have room for Marines. Secretary of the Navy Hilary A. Herbert did not agree, but he did subsequently require Marines to participate in all duties, including coaling. The Marines' additional duties did not satisfy many naval officers. Navy Cdr. C. H. Davis Jr. wrote in 1896 that the word "Marine" was a "synonym for idleness, worthlessness, and vacuity of intellect." Another naval officer questioned the Marines' strategy of embracing as many duties as possible, suggesting it might backfire. He continued to believe they should be replaced with sailors. Naval officers resented the Corps' efforts to expand its duties even if they could no longer claim that Marines received special treatment.[58] Now appearing eager to volunteer for anything, the Corps refined its image to claim to be jacks of all trades.[59]

Unhappy naval officers finally found a receptive ear in President Theodore Roosevelt, who removed the Marines in November 1908. Having served as assistant secretary of the Navy in 1897–98, Roosevelt was familiar with debates about Marines' usefulness at sea. The same year as his appointment, Roosevelt had even presided over a board that discussed, among other matters, whether Marine officers should be absorbed into the Navy.[60] He also believed that the Corps had far more influence in Washington, D.C., political circles than it should. His opinions coincided with that of the most ardent anti-Marine naval officer, Cdr. William Fullam, who had spent more than fifteen years seeking the Marines' removal.[61]

Roosevelt accepted naval officers' arguments that Marines took up valuable space on board ship. They could be used more efficiently if stationed permanently on land, where they could be dispatched more quickly to international hot spots.[62] As set forth in Executive Order 969 in November of 1908, the Corps' duties would now entail 1) garrisoning navy yards and naval stations, 2) serving as the first defenders for naval stations outside the continental United States, 3) manning whatever types of other defenses might be erected outside the continental United States, 4) garrisoning the Panama Canal, and 5) providing expeditionary forces on land. Marines lost both their newest duties at sea on the new battleships and their most traditional ones as preservers of order at sea.

Upon learning of Roosevelt's order, many Marine officers reacted strongly to the news, believing that the order "doomed" the Corps to extinction.[63] Writing to a local newspaper, 1st Lt. J. J. Meade explained that the Corps' history was replete with "deeds of valor and patriotism, probably more than any other branch of the service, because of the mobility of action and the esprit de corps, which can be called 'worship.'"[64] In words that echoed Collum's and Cochrane's private correspondence, Meade stressed the Corps' unique history, which could be understood with reference to its corporate identity, or esprit de corps. Meade elucidated the strength of these feelings; they were so strong that they approached something resembling a spiritual experience. Men felt so fervent about their institution in part because it offered "exceptional" opportunities to the man who could enlist and in time rise as far as the office of commandant.

This existential crisis allowed Marines to articulate their increasing identification with their institution in the previous several decades.

Unlike Meade, the Corps' commandant demonstrated little angst over the new order at first. Elliott had heard rumors of this change as early as 1906. He had even written a draft of the Corps' duties on shore at Roosevelt's insistence. Believing that the Corps risked overextension, Elliott either agreed with Roosevelt's plan or at the very least acquiesced to it. It was not the "death knell" that the Corps' other officers considered it to be. Elliott refused to watch his Corps "die by the slow method of tuberculosis." He and his fellow Marines would not be passive; if necessary, they "would do so with our boots on and leave the ships entirely." Elliott's opinion changed dramatically, however, when rumors began to circulate that the Army might absorb his institution. The news that the Army would be sending troops to Hawaii in a role similar to one traditionally filled by Marines infuriated him even more. With the removal of Marines from naval vessels, it appeared possible that Marines' duties might overlap dangerously with those of soldiers.[65]

The short-term effects of Roosevelt's order profoundly challenged the Corps' identity. Observers suggested that the Marine Corps would do well to consider a name change. If Corps members were to be stationed on shore, one journalist mused, the "name marines had best be dropped," and they might as well become part of the Army.[66] According to another journalist, the severance of the traditional ties between the Navy and the Corps turned Marines into "humble infantrymen." The powerful image of the Marine as a "soldier an' sailor too"— Rudyard Kipling's description of Royal Marines that was quickly adopted for American Marines—would be another casualty of Executive Order 969.[67] Marines would simply be soldiers from then on if Executive Order 969 remained in effect. They would lose many of the distinctive qualities they had begun to embrace. Similarly, recruiters doubted they could inveigle recruits with the prospect of serving as glorified "watchmen" on shore at naval stations.[68] The chance to see much of the world also appeared less likely without sea service.[69] As a result, the Corps worried it might lose its recruiting "edge" against the Army. The *New York Times* noted that recruits suddenly were "scarce."

Recruiting officers, though, busily followed orders to strike out all references to sea service in their recruiting pamphlets and other material.[70]

Finding the implications of Executive Order 969 upsetting, other Marine officers sought to voice their opinions.[71] Commandant Elliott, however, moved quickly to forbid Marines from commenting on the president's order. He similarly prohibited them from seeking legislation to restore the Corps to its sea duties, informing them that "'Semper Fidelis' would be but a meaningless term if it shone only on the sunny side of life or duty."[72] Prohibited from speaking, Marine officers expressed their displeasure in more creative ways. Among his many progressive efforts to improve the military, Roosevelt had instituted more stringent physical tests for service members in 1908.[73] Officers had three days to walk fifty miles, ride ninety miles on horseback, or cycle one hundred miles. Many military officers, especially more elderly ones, resented this decision. Some Marine officers, however, embraced it. The month after Roosevelt issued Executive Order 969, five Marine officers determined to complete the test in one day, and this trend continued until the commandant put an end to it in May, after Col. Littleton Waller rode on horseback and Maj. Harry Leonard and 1st Lt. E. L. Bigler accomplished the "feat" on foot.[74] If Elliott forbade them from speaking publicly, determined Marine officers sought to make their point in other ways. Not only were they prepared to carry out their duties, Marine officers suggested, but they were ready to do so in an exceptional manner. These kinds of determined, aggressive responses helped to counter any lingering remnants of the stereotypical nineteenth-century lazy Marine, an image the Corps had worked increasingly to erase in the 1880s and the 1890s.[75]

In retrospect, some viewed Executive Order 969 as a positive step for the Corps.[76] Because some naval officers suggested that Marines provide an expeditionary service similar to the Corps' current duties, it is easy to view this incident as a logical progression toward the current paradigm.[77] This aspect of the debate, however, was ancillary to the larger argument about why Marines needed to be removed.[78] The executive order and the battles surrounding it had less to do with the Corps' duties and more to do with clashing identities, as seen in testimony before the House Naval Affairs Committee in January of 1909.

In questioning the soundness of Executive Order 969, officers of both services at times discussed practical implications of the Corps' removal. Marines argued that it would be costly to replace Marines with sailors because sailors received more pay, among other reasons. Cdr. William Fullam, however, considered cost to be irrelevant. It was more important to put an end to the Corps' favored position over the Navy, as naval officers had been attempting to do for almost a century. Fullam believed that the role of orderly on board ship unfairly rewarded Marines with the "most honorable station" possible. As a result, they were "looked up to as the elite corps aboard ship, and that has been the secret of their success in a way—that they have insisted upon their being the elite corps."[79] This tendency was amplified because Marine officers created the impression that Marines were superior to sailors.[80] The presence of a sort of "foreign detachment" impinged on the homogeneity of the Navy, thus threatening its corporate identity.[81]

The long-standing tension between the Navy and the Corps had flared again, this time aggravated by the Corps' increasing success at defining itself as an elite institution and disseminating that message to the public. Maddened by their accomplishment, Fullam suggested that naval officers who supported the Corps should be removed from the Navy. Only those "willing to make the American blue jacket the equal of any soldier in the world" should be allowed to serve.[82] Importantly, Fullam's vision did not focus on the relationship of the American sailor to other nations' sailors but to soldiers, which put them more directly in competition with Marines.

The battle over the Marines' role can best be understood as a cultural war over institutional identity rather than as a mission- and role-driven debate.[83] Considering that some naval officers had spent more than twenty years trying to rid battleships of Marines, those who testified had a remarkably hazy conception as to what Marines should do when placed ashore.[84] When questioned by committee members, for example, Rear Adm. John E. Pillsbury admitted he had given little thought to what would be done with the Marines once they were moved to the shore.[85] If the primary purpose of removing the Marines was to task them with a different mission, then this was a startling oversight.[86]

The public fight between Marine and naval officers did not work out as the Navy intended. Congress pushed back against what it considered to be executive overreach and decreed that a ship's personnel had to include at least 8 percent Marines. Nor did it unfold as planned in the papers. Some articles avowed that Marines had been put ashore because sailors envied them, which epitomized the way the Corps had reworked the traditional relationship between sailors and Marines.[87] Marines had often been the butt of sailors' jokes. Now, though, sailors sought to become more like soldiers. Marines intensified this rhetoric by arguing they provided the true fighting force of the Navy Department. The Corps became increasingly vocal in this regard in the coming decade, drawing upon new organizational resources to sell itself. By contrast, the Navy remained wary of what it considered to be propaganda, choosing to embrace a strategy that stressed facts and accurate information.[88]

Restored to its duties at sea, the Corps did not have to reinvent itself. Still, it continued to revisit its recruiting practices. After touring forty different recruiting offices in 1911, for example, the officer in charge of recruiting, A. S. McLemore proposed various changes based on a reassessment of the efficacy of the Corps' newspaper advertising and its recruiting personnel.[89] Like advertising in general, McLemore believed recruiters needed to "bring home to the individual in the most forceful manner the matter which is advertised" and the best way to be "forceful" was to identify and target individual prospects. Newspaper advertising had cost the Corps $19,513.10 the previous year, which averaged about $11.75 per recruit.[90] Now-promoted Major McLemore suggested incentivizing recruiters with a reward of two dollars per enlistment, balancing the institution's increasing expectation that an individual identify with the Corps with more pragmatic inducements. Ultimately, the commandant sent the plan forward only to have the secretary of the Navy reject it. Recruiters were "selected men" in the first place, and as such he believed they should be expected to discharge their duty faithfully without extra monetary inducement.

The Corps soon found itself forced to make other adjustments to its recruiting and publicity efforts. Having learned of the Navy Department's display advertising practices, the Treasury Department declared it had no authority to use an advertising company on April 25, 1912. The Navy Department retrospectively summed up the value of these developments when imploring the chairman of the House of Representatives' naval committee to approve the continuation of these practices: "Recruiting for the Navy for the past five years has been recognized as a success, both in the service and among commercial advertisers, who have shown great interest in the methods employed. Prejudices against the naval service have been broken down, and an ideal, thought a few years ago to be visionary—that the department could pick and choose among the best young men in the land, and that it would be considered an honor for any many to be accepted has been abundantly realized."[91]

Display advertising had transformed the type of powerful images that both the Navy and the Marine Corps conveyed to the public. Events like being forced off ships in 1908–9 forced the Corps to think more carefully about its image and what it meant to be a Marine. Moreover, because of the Treasury Department's decision, it had to disseminate its image to the public without the assistance of commercial advertisers.[92] That it had an image in the first place, though, owed much to the creativity of individual recruiters who had built on the legacy of late nineteenth-century Marines, buoyed by their increasing confidence in their imperial wars. Corporal Murtaugh had communicated his message from behind a gun when he sought to fly the American flag from an Indiana building in a way that connected with his audience. Subsequent recruiters increasingly aimed for recruits' emotions and then sought to ensure they tied those emotions to recruits' sense of service during training. The Recruiting Publicity Bureau supported these efforts by providing a centralized organizing point for refining and disseminating the Corps' increasingly emotional appeals for external and internal consumption.

Chapter Four

Intensification and Dissemination

The Recruiting Publicity Bureau's Influence on the Corps' Image and Identity

Visiting his local library in 1916, Sgt. Frank Stubbe discovered he was the first person to borrow Richard Collum's *History of the United States Marine Corps* since 1904. The difficulty the librarians experienced in simply locating the tome epitomized to Stubbe the key challenge facing recruiters: the public's ignorance about the Corps. Stubbe concluded from his experience that the "public does not know we really are a branch of the U.S. service," much less a "good" one.[1]

Writing four years after the Corps' establishment of its Recruiting Publicity Bureau in 1912, Stubbe and his fellow recruiters still faced the challenge of selling a small military service to all corners of the nation, despite the significant advances the Corps had made in previous years. The bureau's establishment, however, had enabled the Corps to increase its messaging as it developed recruiting from a localized art to a more centralized and industrialized process. As such, the Corps refined and intensified its image, with a noted increase in its rhetorical hyperbole. Countless newspaper articles, for example, eagerly proclaimed the variety of tasks Marines could accomplish, with one headline asserting, "There's Nothing a Marine Can't Do."[2] Between the establishment of the Recruiting Publicity Bureau in 1912 and World War I, the Corps did everything it could think of to reach the public. A journalist at the time might have summarized the bureau's activities with the headline, "There's Nothing the Publicity Bureau Won't Try."

Despite an increase in creative approaches, the bureau relied on rhetoric consistent with that used before its establishment, as can be seen in its recruiting pamphlets. In 1912 the Corps issued the second edition of *U.S. Marines: Duties, Experiences, Opportunities, Pay*, a book-let for potential recruits that continued the practice that Cmdt. George Elliott had instituted in 1908.[3] The 1912 version set forth the Corps' perennial problem: Marines believed the public had only a vague idea of what Marines did. The actual roles filled by the Marines, it continued, were largely irrelevant since people recognized the Marine "as being a man who is thoroughly onto the job, and lets it go at that."[4] Rather than seeking to convey to the public the precise mission it fulfilled, the Corps proferred gendered references to the quality of service it provided and its ability to complete any assignment. These sentiments echoed the kind of rhetoric Capt. Carl Gamborg-Andresen had used in the 1906–7 publicity experiment.

The 1913 edition did not differ dramatically, though the changes the bureau did make showed how it continued to evaluate and tinker with the Corps' image.[5] The format remained much the same: each edition began with a general summary of the institution's duties, then moved on to dis-cuss practical benefits, typical duties, and other relevant aspects of mil-itary life. Early editions had reprised Collum's techniques of linking the service to the ancient Greeks and the Royal Marines. The bureau omit-ted these paragraphs from subsequent editions of recruiting pamphlets, believing some found this information tiresome.[6] By contrast, Rudyard Kipling's colorful descriptions of the British Royal Marines remained:

> An' after I met 'im all over the world, a doin' all kinds of things
> Like landin' 'isself with a Gatlin' gun to talk to them 'eathen kings;
> 'E sleeps in an 'ammick instead of a cot, an' 'e drills with the deck on
>   a slew. . . .
> 'E's a sort of bloomin' cosmopolouse soldier and sailor too.[7]

U.S. Marines appropriated the Royal Marines' experience to point out the Corps' increased global responsibilities. The poem also highlighted some unique aspects of naval life, such as the hammock that charac-terized sleeping accommodations at sea as opposed to the cots found ashore. These details reminded the reader that the Marine was more than a soldier while also reinforcing the bureau's preferred description of Marines as "soldiers of the sea." This nickname allowed the Corps to distinguish itself from the Army and the Navy while stressing its diverse duties. The bureau buttressed this theme with the concept of "two-in-one" service, which it hoped appealed to those seeking adventure.[8]

Landings of the type mentioned in the Kipling poem also increasingly graced the pamphlet covers. One Marine described one cover illustration as picturing "four stalwart Marines charging over a Robinson Crusoe island, with their rifles all set. A palm tree or two swayed in the breeze. Beyond was the blue sea, with a grim battleship riding at anchor."[9] This romanticized depiction of the Marines stressed the inducement of glamorous travel and masculine exploits.

In addition to producing recruiting pamphlets, the bureau served as a central clearinghouse for the production of posters, press releases, and other recruiting materials.[10] Once established, the bureau regularly issued press releases, often accompanied by photographs, to thousands of newspapers across the United States multiple times each week.[11] The bureau had begun with little fanfare. Its first Marine, Captain Harold Snyder, arrived in New York in October of 1912, although he almost immediately received orders to temporary expeditionary duty.[12] By February of 1913 1st Lt. Otto Becker Jr. took charge in Snyder's absence of the thirteen enlisted Marines now stationed at the bureau, to include one gunnery sergeant, two sergeants, two corporals, and seven privates.[13] In the sections detailing the Corps' recruiting in his annual reports to the secretary of the Navy, the commandant did not even mention the bureau in 1912 or 1913.[14] After all, the Corps did not do anything terribly different than it had in the previous year; rather, it had just internalized its recruiting practices of more than five years. Progress became more notable after that. Quickly outgrowing its first location, by 1915 the bureau moved to a building affording nine thousand square feet, twice the amount it had previously occupied. And by 1917 it had one active-duty officer, thirty-three enlisted men, and thirteen reservists.[15]

One of the more important achievements occurred in November 1914, when the bureau released the first edition of the *Recruiters' Bulletin*. As the Corps' first magazine, the *Bulletin* provided an invaluable forum for recruiters to share best practices. Sgt. C. J. Lohmiller,

"Gee! It must be great to be a Marine and travel all over instead o' stayin' home and hoeing corn."

Fig. 7. Sgt. C. J. Lohmiller, "What's a Good Title for This?" *Recruiters' Bulletin, October 1916, 17*

for example, wrestled with how to create glamorous imagery that suggested the Corps offered an escape from the drudgery of farming (see fig. 7). That the recruiters used the *Bulletin* as a forum for discussion and debate becomes apparent in the blunt title of the image he submitted, "What's a Good Title for This?" Other concerns of the *Bulletin* dealt with practical recruiting matters, such as tips about how to form a favorable impression with recruits and how to select quality candidates. The *Bulletin* also provided insights into the Corps' history and military operations in hopes of providing more fodder for securing recruits.

Even as the *Bulletin* helped recruiters consider how to improve the Corps' external image, it had a complementary internal focus in that it also provided a forum for nurturing and disseminating the Corps' identity. Every recruiter received a copy of the *Bulletin*, and the bureau mailed out copies to one in twenty Marines, with the assumption that recipients shared the magazine with their comrades.[16]

The *Bulletin* also provided a forum for recruiters, who functioned as an elite within the Corps' enlisted ranks, to discuss their lives, families, and feelings about the Corps.[17] A recruiter's experience differed in many respects from that of most Marines. The average enlisted recruiter could and did often spend years in one location, and many feared the prospect of losing the stability they had acquired after years of more itinerant service. The bureau held up recruiters' lifestyle as a model for what a recruit could achieve by serving in the Corps. One press release highlighted Sgt. Maj. James Deaver's accumulation of a significant fortune as an example of how a Marine could enter the service with "no capital" and make something of himself through his "own efforts." The suggestion that the Corps could make a man better reinforced the sense of belonging to an elite institution even while offering a recruit the sense that the Corps provided a road to self-improvement.[18] It, along with the bureau's rhetoric of domesticity, resonated with those Americans seeking a way to rise to the middle class. The Corps similarly stressed how it offered a viable path for enlisted Marines to be commissioned as officers.[19]

The bureau matched some of this rhetoric with its own practices, breaking down some of the traditional hierarchical divide between officers and enlisted men. Historically, enlisted recruiters—often in charge of their own subrecruiting districts, just as they had been of Marines on smaller ships—had greater latitude than other enlisted Marines. They also contributed their recruiting experiences and ideas to the *Bulletin* and, in the process, helped mold the Corps' identity in a forum largely free from the influence of the commandant and headquarters.[20] Sgt. Norman Shaw, for example, felt secure enough that he wrote an article for the *Bulletin* that faulted officers for suggesting uniform changes that he believed erased important aspects of the Corps' history. He also praised those Marines who refused to "slavishly" copy the Army's uniform changes. Occasionally, the *Bulletin*'s editor, Maj. A. S. McLemore, interjected a dissenting opinion. Even the critical comments of the editor and a commentator could not deter one sergeant, however, from writing a second article elaborating on his ideas for improving the Corps' uniform.[21] And other officers sometimes supported an enlisted Marine's idea in opposition to McLemore. In another debate, a major backed Sgt. Louie W. Putnam's suggestion to add current news articles to signs outside recruiting offices.[22] Other officers took the time to commend enlisted Marines for the ideas they contributed to the *Bulletin*.[23]

Thus men from a working-class background played a critical role in the Corps' early publicity efforts. The fact that the Corps did not rely on advertising executives with privileged backgrounds could explain some of the institution's recruiting successes. Just as enlisted recruiters made important contributions to debates within the bureau, they had some initiative in conveying the Corps' image to the public. The bureau encouraged recruiters to reach out to journalists in their communities and to elaborate on the bureau's articles by adding a "local connection." These efforts often enabled the Corps to secure free, favorable publicity. In a five-month span, one sergeant's efforts to win publicity for the Corps resulted in the publication of sixteen articles in his small Missouri town newspaper.[24] Such efforts afforded recruiters an opportunity to end the perennial confusion about what purpose a Marine served, though they did not have complete success immediately.[25]

Recruiters expressed their frustration with the ignorance they experienced. In the kind of exaggerated and lighthearted humor that characterized the bureau's efforts to intrigue the American public, one recruiter described meeting a potential recruit who had announced contradictorily that he "want[ed] to be a soldier" and yet sought more to "be a submarine than anything else."[26] The Corps made sure to stress the variety of missions it engaged in, but this recruit's interests clearly pushed the boundaries of the possible. The missing logic, though, interested the Corps less than the play on words, which the bureau hoped to use to capture the reader's interest.

Like those advertisers trying to "create acceptance and demand" for "new products," the bureau also used the *Bulletin* to help determine the best way to make every household familiar with the Corps. And recruiters unleashed a wealth of creative ideas to bring their institution into the limelight, with some verging on the outlandish. On one occasion, a party of Marines set out with journalists in tow to rid the New

Jersey coast of sharks, which had been terrorizing swimmers.[27] The outing did not result in any shark deaths. Nevertheless, the Associated Press' wire account of the excursion reached North Carolina, where one recruiter found himself besieged with questions by local residents. The residents also welcomed the Corps' recruiting material, particularly a picture depicting two Marines raising a flag that was proving so popular that he expected "every home" in the town soon to have one hanging somewhere. Another recruiter ignited a debate throughout Boston after hearing a Civil War veteran bemoan the public's ignorance of the national anthem. The recruiter subsequently asked a Boston journalist if he could write an article to rectify the situation. When the article's publication prompted further discussion, the recruiter took advantage of public interest to pass out five thousand small cards with the anthem's lyrics on the front and an abbreviated history of the Corps on the back. Marines distributed all of the cards in less than an hour. Moreover, these efforts led to additional newspaper articles with little effort on the part of recruiters required.[28]

To persuade the public of the Corps' merits, the bureau launched a "comprehensive" campaign designed to ensure that people became as familiar with the Corps as they were with the Army and the Navy. The bureau sent press releases to thousands of newspapers, "embroidered" just enough to entice newspapers to publish them.[29] When it came to releasing articles to newspapers, the bureau also attempted to spark pride in local residents. After the Corps issued a list of Marines who had obtained an expert marksmanship rating, for example, the bureau released a skeleton article for recruiters to edit as they saw fit to include names of local Marines.[30] One article cited the "many interesting experiences and adventures" of Oral R. Marvel, who was stationed in China. His officers considered his qualifying as a marksman as "little short of marvelous," given that he was "scarcely more than a recruit." In the future, they "expect[ed] him to break many marksmanship records." That two other Marines located in different cities received almost identical commendations in print, however, suggested that Marvel's actions were not as exceptional as the article claimed.[31] Other articles mentioned local Marines' relatives, seeking to rectify the traditionally negative images of enlisted men by demonstrating their hometown ties to presumably respectable citizens. The bureau referred to these articles as "flimsies," designed to allow individual recruiters to "hang a local connection to them."[32]

National newspapers and magazines as well as smaller ones reprinted the bureau's releases, including the *New York Herald*, the *New York Tribune*, and the *New York Journal*.[33] The articles appeared in duplicate form across the country, with often the only difference being the headline's wording.[34] Most editors who were queried for their opinion of the articles' quality responded favorably, with only a few expressing concerns about the propriety of taking the Marine Corps' accounts at face value. The city editor of Washington, D.C.'s *The Star*, for example, pointed out that the element of "propaganda" evident in some stories tended to undercut the "good human interest" of the releases.[35]

The Corps ignored these detractors, wanting to convey the message that "every old Tom, Dick, and Harry isn't eligible to enter its ranks." Historian James D. Norris has identified the use of superlatives as a common tendency among advertisers struggling to determine how to distinguish their products from their competitors' goods. By 1916 the Corps had determined it needed to home in on the precise message it wanted to convey. Cognizant of those changes, Sgt. Clarance Proctor noted that successful businesses focused less on "giv[ing] notice" and more on shaping public opinion.[36] The Corps could achieve this goal most effectively through product differentiation.[37] It had to demonstrate its superiority not only to its primary competitors, the Army and Navy, but also to civilian employers.[38]

Like professional advertisers, the bureau began seeking a trademark, or what might today be considered "branding," to make Marines easily recognizable.[39] One recruiter believed that the public needed to latch onto a standard image associated with the Corps. He suggested the figure of the "Hiker," which, to him, seemed "emblematic of an ideal Marine—attractive, rough and ready, prepared, and commanding respect."[40] The term "hiker" had gained popularity during the Corps' service in the Philippines because of the distances Marines had to cover on foot while searching for insurgents.[41] This recruiter's vision of the model Marine, however, linked the institution to its more recent expeditionary service on shore rather than its longer tradition of sea service. Others considered broader appeals to the "prospective warrior" that made no mention of any specific mission. Unlike some of its individual recruiters scattered throughout the nation, however, the bureau preferred the phrase "soldiers of the sea." More sensitive to the Corps' larger organizational concerns, the bureau preferred a trademark that allowed the Corps to distinguish itself from the Army and the Navy while stressing the versatile nature of its duties. It hoped the idea of double service appealed to those seeking adventure. From the bureau's perspective, it was "much more satisfactory to be a Marine than a bluejacket" because one was always "charging gallantly into something or other, and the papers at home talk about you."[42] Of course, newspapers mentioned the Marines so frequently in part because of the bureau's success in disseminating its articles.

While many of the bureau's practices coincided with the emergence of modern advertising in the United States, the Corps stopped short of fully adopting Madison Avenue's commercial advertising practices. In fact, civilian advertisers did not contribute to the *Bulletin* until December 1916, when the first civilian "expert" discussed advertising in conjunction with a proposal his firm had submitted. The proposal focused less on obtaining recruits and more on selling the Corps to the general population in accordance with the way advertising had transformed countless aspects of American society. To do so required "commanding attention, stimulating interest, then creating desire, then conviction. *Selling the Marine Corps* to the people of the United States is no less than that." If they had not contemplated such an approach before, the *Bulletin*'s readers now received a blueprint for the kind of advertising campaigns already underway in the United States that had the potential to transform not only the public's knowledge of the Corps' existence and its purpose but its feelings and emotions. Readers did not accept the suggestions unthinkingly, however, particularly the expert's advice to deemphasize the possibilities of war and focus on "opportunity" instead.[43] His suggestions troubled Sgt. George Kneller in particular, who expressed his distaste for what he saw as misrepresentation.[44]

While Kneller had no problem pointing to the practical applications of the Corps' training in an incidental way, he opposed the advertiser's suggestion to avoid any mention of the "cannon and the uniform." Kneller believed this approach required recruiters to "practice a form of hypocrisy and resort to subterfuge."[45]

His opinion coincided with the rhetoric among recruiters that honesty profited the Corps in the long run. Recruiters stated their preference for obtaining a smaller number of top-quality men more likely to complete training over wasting limited resources on unlikely candidates.[46] As the *Bulletin*'s editor argued, Marine recruiters should have little difficulty in meeting with success due to their "superior article."[47] Contributors to the *Bulletin* repeatedly stressed the value of being straightforward with candidates to ensure that recruits understood what military service entailed.[48]

They also deliberately held out the lure of challenge. As one Marine wrote, life in the Corps was "not a bed of roses."[49] Still, one recruiter—in taking this increasingly common analogy one step further—argued that at least the Corps had fewer "thorns" than any other branch. Becoming a Marine might not be easy, recruiters suggested, but overcoming the challenges the institution offered provided the recruit with long-term benefits. Faced with impending quotas, no doubt some recruiters eschewed the *Bulletin*'s approach. Overall, though, the discourse of challenge helped reinforce the Corps' claims to being an elite military institution. As such, it strongly resisted any suggestions that it was designed to reform reprobate characters or provide a last resort for the unemployed.[50]

An emotional rather than a rational appeal became the hallmark of American advertisers in the first decades of the twentieth century, and the bureau's practices increasingly exemplified this approach. A "crack military body" was no "dumping ground for incorrigibles," one headline screamed at its readers. The article sought to counter the notion that the Corps accepted moral delinquents.[51] The Corps did not just seek bodies; it sought those invested in maintaining the Corps' first-rate reputation. Recruiters, Sgt. Louis F. Zanzig argued, had a responsibility to ensure they selected the recruits most likely to identify with the Corps. Given its "wonderful" history, it could "afford to be particular."[52]

Recruiters not only influenced the Corps' recruiting and publicity efforts, but their ideas helped to shape the institution, especially its practices and ceremonies. Sgt. Edward Callan suggested that Marines render salutes to Civil War veterans. Other ideas worked more particularly to ensure that Marines remained connected to their institution. The commandant adopted a proposal to celebrate Marine retirements with more "ceremony." The Corps also efficiently implemented Sgt. Leslie C. McLaughlin's suggestion that all honorably discharged Marines be presented with a pin upon leaving the service.[53] Recruiters believed that ensuring the goodwill of retiring Marines helped to secure future recruits in their home communities. Others suggested the formation of a national organization for those with prior service in the Corps.[54]

Contributors also developed traditions that highlighted Marines' distinctiveness from other branches. Capt. Frank Evans, for example, celebrated that only the Corps had its own song, but he decried the fact that so many different versions of the song circulated among Marines. The tendency of Marines to add to the song after each expedition, he claimed, only aggravated the problem. In hoping to "standardize" the song, known as "The Halls of Montezuma," Evans suggested purging those verses containing "undignified or bombastic wording."[55] Thus Evans hoped to institutionalize a form of the song, showing how Marines of all ranks worked to regulate and normalize what had been more inchoate expressions of identity before the bureau's establishment. Another development occurred as the song gradually became referred to as a hymn, suggesting the deep and almost sacred bonds between individual Marines and their institution consistent with the bureau's intensifying emotional appeal.[56]

As much as the bureau encouraged new ideas, it also retained some of the foundation established by Collum and others, especially in stressing the institution's legacy. In seeking to "force" journalists to include Marines when they wrote about soldiers and sailors, one bureau member hoped to end the "utter exclusion of the oldest branch of the service" as was so typical. His emphasis on the Corps as the "oldest" military branch reflected Collum's legacy of stressing its lineage to justify its existence.[57] Still, some began rethinking the traditional dependence on discussing the origins of ancient Marines. As late as 1914, favorable articles continued to stress the institution's roots in the "days of the Phoenician galleys."[58] By 1916 the *Bulletin*'s editor no longer believed that beginning articles with such distant references assured favorable reception.[59]

The *Bulletin* provided a forum not only for discussing how to obtain recruits but also for fostering the Corps' identity and affording Marines with a creative outlet. Doggerel had been a popular pastime for Marines for decades, but now they had a place to showcase their efforts.[60] Stationed on board the USS *Mayflower*, Pvt. K. A. Painter sent an illustration depicting his interpretation of how Latin American nations "recruited" their troops, implicitly contrasting the involuntary enlistment of troops in Caribbean nations to those of Marines.[61]

One ramification of the *Bulletin*'s success and the doggerel of Marines such as Private Painter was the realization of the need for additional service magazines, including one for new recruits.[62] One sergeant expressed his approval, noting he was tired of reading national military publications only to find the Corps relegated to a small section. Suggestions poured in for the new magazine's title. Corp. Thomas W. Dench looked to the Royal Marines' publication, *Globe and Laurel*, and suggested *Hemisphere and Eagle*. Sgt. James Taite believed that "no more appropriate name could be given than 'Semper Fidelis,' the motto of [the] grand old Corps."[63] Taite's selection of adjectives helped reveal his respect and admiration for his institution.

Similarly, the Corps' officers sought to reestablish an association that could spur increased institutional affinities. In 1911 Col. Littleton Waller and some Marine officers serving in Cuba had established the Corps' first association, but it proved short-lived.[64] Again in Cuba in 1913, a handful of officers—most notably then–Lt. Col. John A. Lejeune —reconstituted the Marine Corps Association. Lejeune received enthusiastic support from Capt. Harold C. Snyder, who had established the Publicity Bureau in the previous months.[65]

If the Corps led the Navy and the Army in creating a Recruiting Publicity Bureau, it had lagged greatly in creating associations, though this delay is perhaps understandable due to the Corps' small size.[66] But after the association was created a second time, it took root. By the fall of 1915, almost half of the institution's current and retired Marine officers had joined. And by 1916, 200 of 344 active-duty officers had joined.[67]

Among other goals, the association dedicated itself to documenting and circulating the Corps' history. Of course, this approach coincided with Marine officers' interest in history, which dated from the nineteenth century. To disseminate such discussions, it began publishing the *Marine Corps Gazette* in 1916. The *Gazette* served as a forum to discuss the "aims, purposes and deeds of the Corps" and helped to promote different ideas to improve the Corps. The focus of today's *Gazette* on tactical subjects might suggest the magazine exists largely as a forum to discuss professional matters. By contrast, the *Gazette* in its early years focused more on "increase[ing] its esprit, disseminat[ing] information on professional subjects and plac[ing] in permanent form historical data that now lacks that form." This approach replicated the Corps' late nineteenth-century approach to professionalism.[68]

History had been important to individual nineteenth-century Marine officers, but now a group of officers had formally dedicated themselves to establishing and propagating the Corps' history. The association also shared the bureau's desire to capture human interest, as epitomized by its fictional work. If history had been at the core of some nineteenth-century Marine officers' interests, fictional stories and romanticized nonfiction also seized the imaginations of many twentieth-century Marines. They tended to highlight their "varied service" in a way that stressed the multiplicity of the Corps' duties rather than focusing on any one mission.[69]

Although the *Gazette* and *Bulletin* had different purposes, they both ultimately worked to further the Corps' identity while reinforcing each other's messages. Marines who served in the bureau made many contributions to the *Gazette*. Capt. Frank Evans, who played an integral role at the bureau, served as the *Gazette*'s first editor.[70] Evans' articles helped to glamorize expeditionary service. In a 1917 *Gazette* article, Evans noted that the public might consider the years after the Spanish-American War as uneventful, but Marines certainly would not agree. These years had turned the Corps into a "veteran body of seasoned officers and men to whom the seizing of coast towns, the razing of supposedly impregnable native strongholds, and the secrets of bush fighting and street fighting in tropical countries became an open book." The glamorized image of the Marine as the hardened fighter permeated the *Gazette*. In one article Capt. Walter N. Hill drew on the purportedly exotic culture of Haiti. Searching for a translator, Hill almost wanted to give up until two natives led him "towards an old, white-haired Negro. Up from the crowd rose the exclamation: 'Here comes the Englishman!' Bewildered at the confusion, the old man stood still until I laid my hand on his arm and said: 'I am the white man, Captain Hill, the white captain. Can you understand me?'"[71]

The atmosphere of acclamation with which he was reputedly greeted and his repeated reference to his whiteness presaged the fictional descriptions of Marine authors that flourished in the 1920s. While the *Gazette* did publish technical articles, its inclusion of writing about the Corps' history embroidered the bureau's and individual Marines' suggestion that they, as picked men, could handle any task. A military member who had once been a virtual unknown was now a larger-than-life swaggering Marine.

An article in the inaugural issue of the *Gazette*, "How the Marine Corps Recalls Sergeant John P. Poe, Jr.," depicted the ideal masculine Marine who sought nothing more than the opportunity to fight.[72] Poe served in the U.S. Army, various militias, and the Marine Corps. Desperate to see even more intense combat, he joined the British Army, dying in World War I. Although he had served in Panama for just three months in 1904, Poe had somehow made such an impression that the Corps felt his death with a "peculiar force." A graduate of Princeton University and a noted football player, Poe refused a commission as a second lieutenant because, as he explained, "nobody expects anything of a second lieutenant. They do of a sergeant."[73] Poe's purported words—if recalled correctly twelve years later—suggested the idealized rhetorical place noncommissioned officers like sergeants occupied in the Corps. Imperial service heightened this tendency because enlisted Marines became officers within the constabularies of native troops, thus allowing for a rise in their status.[74] As did the *Bulletin*, the *Gazette* sought to strengthen the institution's corporate identity, in part by col-lapsing some class differences.

The Corps' increasing concern for publicity and the loyalty individ-ual Marines had for their institution began to spread more thoroughly through the ranks. In a condolence letter to a Marine's father, 1st Sgt. Francis Fisk cautioned the father not to share his letter with any pub-lication. He clarified that he was not "ashamed of what I have said." Rather, "we (the U.S. Marines) don't care for publicity of that sort."[75] Fisk did not elaborate, but to include such an appeal in a condolence letter suggested the extent to which he considered the Corps' reputa-tion sacred. Fisk's letter also represents the extent to which individual Marines believed the public still remained ignorant of the Corps. Fisk felt it necessary to explain what a Marine was even to a family member. As a result, Fisk specified in his letter to the father that his "son was a mighty fine Marine (soldier)." Marines recognized the confusion that attached to their ambiguous military role. And although Fisk might have identified as a Marine, he lacked confidence that the father could translate what exactly it meant to be a Marine so he explained it for him, summing it up with one word: "soldier."

As late as 1916, some of the Corps' members still assumed the term "Marine" was not yet self-explanatory, despite the bureau's best efforts. Still, the Corps had refined and expanded its publicity efforts in seek-ing to become known to the public at large. At the same time, it con-tinued to contrast itself with other services. The establishment of the Recruiting Publicity Bureau had enabled the Corps to consider more carefully how to hone its image to reach the public. It had not needed to create this imagery out of whole cloth, as an increasing number of individual Marines increasingly demonstrated their love for the insti-tution they served.

Part II

Deploying the Corps' Identity

Chapter Five

Differentiation

How the Marine Corps Engendered Landing Parties, 1908–1918

While interviewing Col. John A. Lejeune after the joint Navy–Marine Corps landing at Veracruz in 1914, a journalist asked him if "there was anything the marine could not do." Lejeune's response perfectly complemented the bureau's message, his words equaling any script the bureau could have supplied. Lejeune replied in the affirmative that indeed there was something the Marine could not do. The reader's interest perhaps piqued, the journalist then explained how Lejeune escorted the reporter over to look at the variety of duties occupying his Marines. Lejeune subsequently pointed out that the one thing Marines could not do was to be idle.[1]

At first glance, this kind of hyperbolic rhetoric suggests that perhaps the bureau interviewed Lejeune and then released it to newspapers across the country. On the contrary, however, a journalist named J. S. Stewart Richardson wrote the article while working as a "[s]pecial correspondent of the *Philadelphia Inquirer* and *New York Herald*." Despite complementing the bureau's message so seamlessly, Lejeune did not have recruiting experience. Nor had he been stationed at the bureau, and the *Recruiters' Bulletin* had yet to be published. Lejeune's wording and that of his fellow officers suggests the extent to which the Corps' small officer corps shared a vision that existed before the bureau's establishment. Those officers who interacted with journalists only corroborated the bureau's image, and now journalists such as Richardson increasingly accepted the Corps' message.

Recalling his time in the Corps, Lejeune noted that he viewed the institution's successes in Veracruz as "crucial" to its future.[2] But what made a two-day military operation, followed up by a relatively short and easy military occupation, so important? After all, Lejeune commanded the American Expeditionary Force's 2nd Division in World War I. His reasons for touting Veracruz remain obscure unless considered in context with other sources written during or after the Veracruz Incident. Marines magnified the kind of rhetoric they had begun embracing around the time of the Spanish-American War to demonstrate their superiority to sailors. Not only did individual Marines represent themselves as capable of undertaking landing operations, they did so in a way that portrayed sailors as being passive or even incompetent. The Recruiting Publicity Bureau amplified the voices of individual Marines, seizing on favorable articles to reinforce its improving and strengthening image. If the 1908–9 ship guard crisis gave the Marines a chance to continue serving in their traditional role at sea, the Veracruz Incident of 1914 allowed the bureau and Marines in general to make good, rhetorically at least, on the competition for elite status that underlay the ship guard crisis.

The Recruiting Publicity Bureau's establishment had enabled the Corps to flood American newspapers with stories touting Marines' exploits. When it had the chance, the bureau similarly seized upon joint naval operations to refine its image at the Navy's expense. If the Corps had waged its battle against the Navy during the ship guard crisis of 1908–9, it had done so largely from a position of weakness, with Congress as its greatest weapon. Now, however, the Corps had a powerful asset that helped it to vocalize its message anonymously in newspapers across the United States. By the time of the Veracruz Incident of 1914, the bureau had become more vocal in claiming that it formed the "backbone" of landing parties rather than serving more equally in conjunction with sailors.[3]

Increasingly, the Corps argued that it provided society's true fighters. The Navy simply transported the Corps to combat. From the establishment of the Continental Navy and Marines, their men had fought at close quarters nearby each other. In the nineteenth century and early twentieth century, naval combat increasingly became characterized by distance. It is much harder psychologically to kill at close quarters than it is at a distance.[4] To storm a ship in the nineteenth century and kill one's opponent was the apogee of demonstrating one's manliness. At the end of the nineteenth century, however, naval weaponry changed greatly, which resulted in tensions between Navy and Marine officers over who fired what weapons at sea. In the end, sailors generally fired their weapons from the primary batteries behind a protective barrier in the age of the battleship, just as they had done in the age of the frigate. By contrast, the Marines exposed their bodies to fire at the secondary batteries.

Those acts of courage and feats of daring reflect aspects of what some have characterized as hegemonic masculinity, or the achievement of what society considers to be the most idealized notions of masculinity. The concept of hegemonic masculinity has come under fire from scholars who contend that it cannot account for individuals' fractured gendered identities.[5] While it is true that hegemonic masculinity has lost its stranglehold on U.S. society, it is also true that acts reinforcing such idealized notions of masculinity occur every time a little boy is told to "stop crying like a girl." The understanding is that boys need to be raised to be tougher and stronger. More importantly in regard to the Corps' relationship to the Navy, hegemonic masculinity helps to explain "gendered power relations among men," or the way individuals or institutions make gendered claims—such as what makes real men—in a way that empowers some while weakening others. The Corps seized upon society's idealized notions of masculinity by claiming its Marines epitomized what it meant to be fighters. They played a "leading role in the drama of war." The Corps accepted only "the cream of manhood." Marines even had to be reprimanded for their "reckless disregard of death in battle."[6]

The bureau refined and strengthened this image by erasing or marginalizing the Navy's contributions. Some of the most striking of these images centered on the humble rowboat. One of the oldest pieces of naval technology, the rowboat became a gendered site of contestation because it allowed one service to claim it was more masculine than another. For centuries, the rowboat allowed the transport of sailors, serving as temporary soldiers, and Marines to move from ship to shore to engage in small skirmishes as members of landing parties. Because a normal contingent of Marines on a large frigate tended to number around 50 as opposed to about 200 to 250 sailors, sailors constituted the majority of these landing parties.[7] At the beginning of the twentieth century, however, Marines commenced seeking to marginalize the participation of sailors in these skirmishes. Marines depicted themselves as fighters in contrast to sailors, who purportedly found themselves relegated to the more passive role of rowing Marine fighters to shore. Both at sea in manning a variety of naval guns and on land in fighting, the measure of one's masculinity—at least as Marines defined it—was the extent to which one was willing to put one's body at risk in combat. Marines seized upon the ultimate weapon—hegemonic masculinity—because it did not require significant financial expenditure or bureaucratic approval. It also resonated with larger societal undercurrents as men struggled to adapt to the significant repercussions of the Industrial Revolution and other societal changes.[8]

The only research on the gendered identity of the Marines during this period argues unsurprisingly that military service affirmed the Marines' masculine identity. The imperial service of Marines in a position of increased power, Mary Renda contends, furthered an "ethos of male rivalry based on competitive claims to toughness and physical prowess."[9] This competition found its deepest expression in a battle over a rowboat, as the Marine Corps sought to expand its mission to provide infantry on land at the expense of the Navy. In an era when naval technology and the vastness of the ship and its naval guns almost dwarfed the individuals who operated them, the rowboat enabled the Marine to channel a rawer form of masculinity that still permeates the relationship between members of the Corps and the Navy today.

At the same time, the Corps perpetuated more consistent masculine and martial imagery than the Navy's often individualistic and varied depictions of sailors, which found their roots in the nineteenth-century image of a jolly sailor. A 1909 Navy recruiting pamphlet, for example, depicted "an Apollo-like youth in white trousers and a blouse waving a colored flag to another ship from the deck of his own. . . . Inside the possible recruit sees sailors boxing or playing checkers on the deck with many of his mates around." These kinds of descriptions shied away from combat, depicting something more akin to a lark.[10] In short, some naval officers maintained a more Victorian masculinity even as Marine officers embraced a more assertive, primitive masculinity reinforced by their imperial service.

Ironically, though, the number of sailors participating in landing parties increased after the Spanish-American War. The landing at Guantánamo in 1898 was an early exception. Marines and sailors served in similar numbers in landing parties well up to World War I. In 1912, 1,030 sailors landed, as opposed to 1,272 Marines, in Nicaragua, with both coming under fire as they participated in several assaults against rebels. Sailors outnumbered Marines in the landing and occupation of Veracruz. And again during the

1915 occupation of Port-au-Prince, Haiti, 215 sailors landed, as opposed to 162 Marines, and held the city in "unsettled conditions."[11]

Regardless of the landing parties' composition, the writing and imagery that Marines and outsiders produced increasingly celebrated the bravery and willingness of Marines to risk their bodies in combat. In 1908 one journalist had sought to explain the Corps' newfound appeal by suggesting that the public viewed Marines as "first on the firing line" after they were "row[ed] . . . to shore" by sailors.[12] The journalist distinguished the martial abilities of Marines from those of sailors, who simply provided a means of transportation. One cartoon made an even more mocking contrast. It depicted a sailor reading an advertisement encouraging sailors to enlist in the Corps for service in Cuba. The sailor amused himself at the prospect of convincing one of his friends to transfer from the Navy to the Corps, noting that when he received orders to Cuba, he would be "scared to death." Another scene in the cartoon juxtaposed the same sailor busy scrubbing the deck with a Marine idling away his time at sea. The cartoon implicitly excused the Marines' "idling" because now the Navy had the "soft" or easy service in contrast to the Marine's "hard" duty on land.[13] Another newspaper cartoon showed boats full of Marines in the act of landing in Haiti. Sailors acted more passively, with a naval officer observing the landing from the ship's bow and a group of sailors throwing an anchor overboard.[14]

Marines themselves gladly echoed this rhetoric, with one professing that sailors "play[ed] but a small part in time of war." The Marine, he suggested, was the true "fighting man" on board naval vessels. Because of his discipline, the Marine could be "called upon for everything" during the heat of battle. Even a popular civilian writer, Damon Runyon, in a collection of poems about soldiers published in 1912, found room to praise Marines at the Navy's expense. The outsider characterized Marines as fulfilling the most important role at sea, rhyming that a Marine stood "at the back of the gun 'till the battle's won, the bulwark of the fleet."[15] This wording put Marines at the heart of a ship's martial efforts.

In 1914, however, the Marine Corps and the Navy shared the spotlight during the Veracruz Incident, with both contributing similar numbers of troops. The Mexican Revolution, which had begun in 1910, had tested the patience of President Woodrow Wilson. After General Victoriano Huerta orchestrated the murder of President Francisco I. Madero and then succeeded him, Wilson called for Huerta to resign. Tensions increased during the Tampico Affair of April 9, 1914. The Navy had been sitting offshore in the Gulf of Mexico in case it needed to intervene to protect American lives and property. When Mexican troops ordered a handful of U.S. sailors on a supply run off a small vessel at gunpoint and subsequently detained them, Navy Rear Adm. Henry T. Mayo demanded a twenty-one-gun salute as a formal apology. The Mexican government demurred, arguing that the arrest had been a regrettable mistake. Mexican troops had assumed the sailors were prorevolutionary troops. They had detained the Americans for less than an hour until higher-ranking officers could overcome a language barrier to resolve the situation.

Wilson supported Mayo's demand. Perhaps conveniently, he viewed the arrest in light of similar incidents, suggesting the Mexican government did not respect American rights.[16] Wilson received the excuse to use military force that he had been looking for upon learning that a German ship planned to arrive in Veracruz on April 21. The ship carried weapons for Huerta, thus breaking the U.S.-imposed arms embargo on Mexico.[17] Wilson therefore resolved to land troops to stop the shipment's arrival. Because the Navy did not want to disrespect German sovereignty by seizing the weapons from the German ship, it decided to violate Mexican sovereignty instead. The Navy determined to capture the customshouse to prevent the ship from unloading its cargo.

Despite expecting little resistance, naval officers wanted as many men as they could get. Threatening weather, however, compelled Rear Adm. Frank F. Fletcher, the highest-ranking naval officer at Veracruz, to begin the invasion without the desired reinforcements. Beginning the morning of April 21 about 11 a.m., the Naval Brigade commanded by Capt. W. R. Rush began landing. The Naval Brigade consisted of the 1st Marine Regiment, commanded by Marine Lt. Col. Wendell C. Neville, and the 1st Seaman Regiment under Navy Lt. Cdr. Allen Buchanan. The 1st Marine Regiment had 22 officers and 578 Marines, while the 1st Seaman Regiment had 30 officers and 570 sailors. Of those troops, 502 Marines and 285 sailors participated in the initial landing. Sailors received orders to secure the primary objective, the customshouse.[18] Within the hour the landing party had established a headquarters, captured the post office and telegraph station, and set up a post for signaling messages to ships in the harbor. Marines focused on securing the train station to prevent the arrival of Mexican reinforcements.

The Mexican government had ordered regular troops to withdraw, making the initial landing easy. Mexican army officer Gen. Gustov Mass, however, had armed local militia troops and prisoners to resist the U.S. landing. By noon these and other Mexicans began shooting at the landing party. A sailor signaling atop a rooftop to a ship in the harbor quickly fell dead, the first American casualty. Americans would not capture any additional ground that day.[19] Despite this resistance, the United States gained control of the town in two days, aided by the landing of additional troops early the next morning. Going house to house, they had control of the city before noon that day.

Some historians have suggested that the Marines handled the resistance they encountered relatively easily, while sailors faced more difficulties. According to Marine historian Allan Millett, Marines "fought ashore with more skill and fewer casualties than the seamen's regiments."[20] Indeed, the Navy suffered fifty-nine wounded compared to thirteen Marines, and fifteen sailors died compared to four Marines.

U.S. sailors took many of their losses from the steep resistance they encountered at the Mexican Naval Academy, where cadets ambushed them. In the best argument for naval incompetence, Navy Capt. E. A. Anderson ordered his sailors to march up the streets on April 22 in perfect formation, much to the dismay of his younger officers. In doing so, Anderson ignored the more cautious advice of Capt. W. R. Rush regarding the best way of proceeding through the streets. It could be argued, then, that the Navy's most costly blunder during the Veracruz Incident demonstrated faulty and inexperienced leadership rather than the sailors' inability to fight. Despite more than three decades in the Navy, Anderson had never experienced ground combat. Other sailors performed far more admirably. One sailor, for example, drew sniper fire in his small vessel, enabling naval gunners on ships to identify and destroy the snipers' positions.[21]

In the only monograph on the subject, Robert Quirk suggests similarly to Millett that the Navy fought "crudely and ineptly—if with valor."[22] One of his sources for this conclusion, though, is *Old Gimlet Eye*, Smedley Butler's memoir, cowritten with journalist Lowell Thomas. Not only did

Thomas and Butler publish the work almost twenty years after the invasion, but Butler had a reputation for loathing the Navy.[23] Historians, then, have bought into the Corps' argument that Marines fought better than sailors.

Marines in Veracruz certainly took this rhetorical approach in comparing their service to that of sailors. They depicted an image consistent with the Recruiting Publicity Bureau not only because some of the bureau's Marines received orders to Veracruz but also because this process was mutually reinforcing. Marines' identification with their Corps in documents not meant for publication suggests the extent to which officers had already internalized the Corps' flourishing identity. In normally formulaic after-action reports, Marines praised their own efforts but found the Navy's performance lacking. Capt. William Harllee's report exemplified this tendency. He noted how the "only case of excessive drinking was by a man re-enlisted from another service." Suggesting that men of other military services could not meet the Corps' high disciplinary standards, Harllee recommended that the Corps stop recruiting men who had previously served in the Army or Navy.[24] Although Harllee had not been stationed at the Recruiting Publicity Bureau, he had contributed to the Corps' recruiting practices in a formative period while stationed in Chicago in 1907 and 1908. He also captained the Corps' rifle team, which the institution prided itself on as a way to demonstrate evidence of its superior military capabilities.[25] In this case, his military experience and his recruiting perspective melded, shaping his interpretation of this joint operation through the lens of his identification with the Corps.

Harllee's insistence that Marines had the highest standards of discipline does not seem to have mirrored reality. Despite the Navy's being much larger than the Corps, more Marines than sailors were brought to trial for a number of offenses in 1914. These offenses included assaulting or threatening to assault an officer, disobeying an officer's order, and drunkenness while on duty. During 1913 fifteen sailors received courts-martial for drunkenness compared to twenty-four Marines. Likewise, in 1914 the judge advocate general reported that it had court-martialed an equal number of Marines and sailors for drunkenness.[26] These figures suggest that Harllee's comments represented some wishful thinking on his part.

Whether or not Marines actually behaved better than sailors, Marines expressed the belief that the Corps produced the best-disciplined soldiers.

Like Harllee, Col. John Lejeune noted in a private letter to Cmdt. George Barnett that so "far as I can learn there was not one case of over-excitement or nervousness, or anything resembling nervousness on the part of a single individual. All officers and men were perfectly cool, deliberate, and courageous."[27] Even in private correspondence, officers portrayed Marines in hyperbolic rhetoric that simply did not bear out the realities of combat experience. From their perspective, Marines acquired these traits through better training and marksmanship. One Marine officer recollected that the sailors just "rush[ed] through the streets" while Marines drew on their "training in Indian warfare," going through houses with pickaxes rather than exposing themselves in the streets. Marines did not have actual experience fighting this way; rather, they appropriated what they perceived to be Native Americans' "natural" propensity for fighting to intensify their claim to be superior to sailors.[28] Marines also stressed the Navy's poor marksmanship. After sailors erroneously fired on Marines, a number of officers recommended that sailors be put back on board ship as soon as possible.[29] Similar occurrences elsewhere in the Caribbean reinforced this belief. Smedley Butler regretted what he considered the Navy's undisciplined fire in Haiti, noting that the sailors had been "shooting at everything that walks."[30] Butler relished the opportunity to criticize the Navy, especially if it made the Corps look better. Butler believed that these sailors could improve, however, simply by serving closely with Marines and thereby acquiring some of their attributes.

Marines' interpretation of their performance at Veracruz reinforced the argument that sailors should focus on their nautical duties rather than seeking to become more soldierly. While from today's vantage point it might seem natural that Marines would be tasked with ground combat more often than sailors, this development was not inevitable. To argue that technology dictated these developments is to miss the extent to which naval officers sought to create a more cohesive institutional culture for the Navy.

These arguments prompted Marines to respond by suggesting that they could outfight sailors. Lt. Col. Wendell Neville, who had commanded the 1st Marine Regiment at Veracruz, hoped to see increased numbers of Marines on board ships so that sailors would not have to be landed ashore during military operations. Neville believed that naval officers would surely agree. Rather than limiting Marines to transports, Neville argued that

Veracruz demonstrated the need to augment the Corps' traditional roles at sea.[31] Drawing on the institution's success at Veracruz, Neville sought to augment Marines' roles on board naval vessels in a way that harkened back to more recent debates surrounding the ship guard crisis of 1908–9.

The bureau amplified the internal documents that Marines produced. Articles published in the *Bulletin* regarding Veracruz exemplified this approach, as well as the tendency of some Marines to suggest exaggerated interpretations of their contributions. Sgt. A. S. Campbell explained how Marines landed first at Veracruz, demonstrating their unique training as a "mobile, straight-shooting expeditionary force." His account ignored the reality that sailors and Marines had participated in the same landing party. It represented the way Marines bombastically sought to erase sailors from the record or make claims that improved the Corps' image at the Navy's expense.[32] Campbell suggested that Marines' actions had "paved the way" for sailors and made naval participation in the occupation virtually irrelevant. During the initial phase of the occupation, moreover, Marines "had the situation so well in hand that the bluejackets had been returned to their ships." Similarly, the bureau's Capt. Frank Evans made soldiers appear almost superfluous. He noted that Marines left little for the soldiers who arrived to assist with the occupation but to "police and clean" the streets of Veracruz. Campbell and Evans conveyed the same attitude as Neville and other Marines, arguing that Marines could take care of matters without assistance from sailors. In reality, though, the removal of sailors had nothing to do with the Marines' accomplishments and everything to do with the fact that naval officers needed the sailors back on board their vessels to maintain readiness.[33]

Journalists increasingly, albeit not universally, bought into the Corps' image as fighters as opposed to sailors. Allan Millett argues that newspaper correspondents largely focused on the Corps' exploits even though there were more sailors than Marines by the second day of operations at Veracruz.[34] Perhaps it is more accurate to state that Veracruz represents a tipping point, showing how the bureau had convinced more Americans of the Corps' value than not. Certainly, numerous newspaper headlines printed before the landing at Veracruz indicated that Marines were sent to the fleet without mentioning sailors.[35] Some of these articles suggested, as discussed earlier, that journalists assumed Marines would be at the forefront of such military operations. Others simply pointed to more general troop movements. Newspaper articles covering the actual landing rarely singled Marines out at the expense of sailors, but a careful reader could note the increased attention given to Marines.[36] Still, few articles stated the precise number of representatives from each service.[37] Others specifically praised the bluejackets' courage and marksmanship.[38]

The Corps did not leave its exploits from Veracruz fully in the hands of journalists. Published in 1914, *The U.S. Marines in Rhyme, Prose, and Cartoon* demonstrates one of the bureau's more subtle approaches to capitalizing on the Veracruz Incident in a way that Richard Collum would have appreciated.[39] Page after page sung the praises of the Corps' achievements, its long history, and its unique service to the nation. Nothing appeared to be written by a Marine except for the obvious exception of the institution's hymn. As a result, a reader might have been more inclined to accept the sentiments expressed in the pamphlet as produced by supposedly unbiased journalists than he or she might have if Marines had written the articles. One editorial in particular attempted to show how the Corps had "borne the brunt of the fighting" throughout the nation's "naval history." The editorial thus legitimized the Corps' claim to be "always fightin' men" at the Navy's expense.[40]

Marines might have felt justified in this interpretation because they believed they deserved more recognition. Indeed, the editorials reprinted in the *Marines in Rhyme* submitted this view. They also suggested the public should appreciate the Corps even if the Navy and the Army would not.[41] Marines, one editorial proclaimed, deserved "special distinction." The other services "look[ed] upon the Marines as the hewers of wood and the drawers of water."[42] This comment suggested the Corps was engaged in the more laborious tasks that other services might want to avoid. Sailors had depicted Marines as idlers who had escaped unpleasant tasks, such as coaling, in the nineteenth century. Now, however, Marines countered this image, presenting themselves as eager to undertake any job, no matter how laborious.

Various articles written after Veracruz praised Marines in ways that erased sailors' contributions. One article explained how nearly 3,500 Marines had captured Veracruz in four hours, inaccurately reporting the time it took to subjugate the city as well as ignoring sailors' presence altogether. Marines became increasingly ambitious in their attempts to rewrite their own narrative. A June issue of the *World's Work* featured multiple photographs depicting the "taking of Vera Cruz by American Marines."[43] The issue did not include similar photographs of sailors.

Other articles rewrote earlier incidents in the Corps' history to highlight Marines' contributions while expunging sailors from the historical record. Well-known war correspondents James F. J. Archibald and Berton Braley wrote an article entitled "Soldiers and Sailors, Too" that *Collier's* published a month after the capture of Veracruz. Only briefly mentioning Veracruz, it recounted a number of the Corps' historical contributions. In a way that complemented Lejeune's interview at Veracruz, Archibald and Braley explained how Marines could handle any military duties. Like those Marines who submitted articles to the *Bulletin* making claims that Marines had landed first, this article stressed the achievements of Marines while downplaying those of sailors. The authors then suggested that the Marines had "won entirely" the Navy's "first battle" in the Bahamas in 1776, ignoring the presence of fifty sailors.[44] By claiming the Corps had won the nation's first as well as its most recent battle, the authors implied that the Corps must have been significant in any other number of battles as well. These historical representations helped to counter the lingering belief maintained by some people that, as one Marine sergeant quoted in the article explained, Marines were "supernumeraries—kind of ornamental decorations around a ship."

The Corps interpreted its performance in Veracruz as further proof of the institution's importance, especially in light of the sailors' purportedly poor martial skills. The Corps used this incident to buttress its argument not only that Marines could do anything but that sailors should leave the fighting to Marines. Published in 1917, the third edition of *Marines in Rhyme, Prose, and Cartoon* adopted the approach of Archibald and Braley. In a new addition to the pamphlet, a section entitled "Historical Sketch" proclaimed New Providence to be the "first battle of the American Navy" which "was fought and won by the Marines."[45]

However much the Marines publicly declared sailors to be incompetent or irrelevant in Veracruz and much earlier battles, the reality continued to be that Marines and sailors largely served side by side. The Navy's doctrine even showed an intensified focus on landing operations. In 1918 it published the first edition of its 553-page *Landing Force Manual*, which had been overseen by a board consisting of three naval officers and one Marine officer. This manual avowedly patterned itself on the practices of the U.S. Army. A 1921 version grew to 760 pages. The first half of the manual detailed general practices of land warfare, and the second half focused more narrowly on the tactical application of those practices. Interestingly, the number of naval officers that participated increased to six even as no Marine officer now contributed.[46] By contrast, the Marine Corps did not produce a similar manual independently until 1934. The extension of the Navy's doctrine and the Marine officer's removal suggest that the Navy was not ready to surrender to the Corps' onslaught of publicity related to landing parties. It sought to refine the best military practices to improve its landing party capabilities.

Meanwhile, the bureau continued its fight with the Navy in recruiting posters, with the rowboat becoming an iconic symbol of the Corps' service as fighters and the Navy's as the rowers of the fighters. In many ways, the Navy and the Marine Corps increasingly drew upon the same type of crisp modern imagery, which in some ways represented a divergence from a general tendency around World War I to use more Victorian imagery.[47] The Corps, unlike the Navy, however, increasingly put the viewer face-to-face with a Marine in the act of leaving a rowboat and starting to fight, as if challenging him or her to somehow resist this onslaught of masculine bravery (see fig. 8). The rowboat became the symbol of what enabled Marines to do their job—combat. By contrast, the Navy did not see the need to put the martial act of combat at the center of its recruiting imagery. In "Pull Together Men," for example, the only martial aspect of the poster is the ominous red sky that suggests a looming threat (see fig. 9 shown in b/w). Those threatened simply continue to row as a naval officer tries to ascertain the nature of the threat through his binoculars. The sailors just needed to be in unison as a team to succeed.

A similar poster for the Marine Corps, on the other hand, embraces the actual combat itself (see fig. 10). As naval guns fire in the background, the Marine in the bow of the rowboat appears ready and eager to begin fighting even before the ship has touched the shore. He stands confident and assertive, willing to risk his body without fear. There is no time for observation, as in the naval poster, only action.

Fig. 8. J. C. Leyendecker, U.S. Marines, "Soldiers of the Sea"; Good pay—foreign travel—congenial employment. *Library of Congress*

Fig. 9. Paul R. Boomhower, "Pull together men—the Navy needs us." *Library of Congress*

Fig. 10. Sidney H. Risenberg, "Democracy's Vanguard." *Library of Congress*

Nineteenth-century Marine and naval officers had more common-alities than differences, particularly in regard to their notions of late nineteenth-century Victorian manliness. And they both sought for their men to become part of an elite. With great technological changes, some naval officers seized upon the opportunity to remake the identity of the sailor into something much closer to a Marine. Marine officers and even some enlisted Marines pushed back at this. As a weaker institution that faced perennial insecurity, it latched onto the same hegemonic masculinity that some naval officers sought to infuse into the Navy. But the Navy, with its need for greater recruiting numbers, needed to reach a broader number of potential male recruits, whom it preferred to lure with an emphasis on practical benefits, such as training, and personal benefits, such as exciting travel opportunities.

After the declaration of war against Germany in 1917, the Corps would continue to depict itself as a martial institution in opposition to the Navy. In the bureau's first release announcing the arrival of Marines in France, it contrasted the cool, businesslike departure of Marines for war as they marched to their transport with an image of sailors practicing for a baseball game. The Marines "slipped away so quietly that the ball players did not know until afterward that they had missed seeing the departure of a regiment of 2,700 men bound for the battle front."[48] Sailors played on as men marched off to war, rhetorically bound together by peculiar bonds of comradeship.

Chapter Six

Democratization

From Boot Straps to Shoulder Straps, 1914–1918

I n 1906 one Marine officer's actions made headlines after he ordered the band of the USS *Wisconsin* to play a popular jingo, "Always in the Way," at a sailor's funeral. An infuriated enlisted Marine responded to the incident by rhyming, "Yes—ye, we'll salute ye, and we'll all say 'yes, sir', too, / But we salute the shoulder straps—we wouldn't speak to you. / Ye're farther down beneath us than a dog a beggar owns."[1] In this way the anonymous enlisted Marine challenged the officer's disrespect for an enlisted service member (of a different service no less) by challenging the typical assumption that the officer was a gentleman.[2]

In some ways, certain aspects of the Corps had made this kind of episode rarer than in the Army and the Navy. Yet the possibility of similar occurrences lingered under the surface, and it took central place in the fictional work *The Wall Between*, a novel published by Ralph D. Paine in 1914.[3] In this way, the Corps' publicity efforts attracted scrutiny and interest from all elements of society, which resulted in other depictions of it that the Corps did not necessarily control.

This chapter explores a variety of externally and internally created representations of the Corps, all centering on the extent to which the Corps lacked or epitomized a democratic institution. Over time, the Corps more fervently stressed that many of the hierarchical links between officers and enlisted men had been broken down. Much of the motivation for this change came from the bureau's need to recruit more men after the United States entered World War I. To meet this challenge, the Corps sought to sell Americans on its democratic nature and then immerse its recruits even more fully in this culture once they had decided to enlist. As such, in initial training, recruits became involved in this democratic culture and other aspects of the Corps' identity. But this democratic identity had its limits, which can be seen in the experiences of Marines who fought in World War I, when many perceived a disconnect between the Corps' democratic rhetoric and their own wartime experience. Enlisted Marines had been so indoctrinated in the Corps' culture that they expected their officers to live up to democratic ideals. Those officers who failed to epitomize this culture, especially ones commissioned during the war, bore the brunt of enlisted Marines' antipathy accordingly. This disconnect led some Marines to reject the Corps' identity, tellingly described by one Marine novelist as a "Peculiar Spirit."[4]

About two decades before, journalist Ralph Paine had observed the Navy, and thus presumably the Corps, during the Spanish-American War and the Boxer Rebellion. During the Boxer Rebellion, some Marines had highlighted their institution's democratic culture, epitomized by the way officers and enlisted Marines shared similar living conditions, unlike the British army. Like the anonymous enlisted Marine poet expressing his furor at an officer in 1906, though, Paine's novel challenged this democratic culture by critiquing the reality of the wide social distance between officers and enlisted men.[5]

The novel centered on the competition between two Marines, Lt. Thomas Burkett and Sgt. John Kendall, for the affections of Edith Farris, the niece of their stern commanding officer, Col. Percival Dickenson. The author starkly contrasted the young, wealthy Lieutenant Burkett with the enlisted Sergeant Kendall. Having acquired his commission due to political connections, Lieutenant Burkett proved to be cowardly in combat. His depiction contrasted greatly with the author's portrayal of the brave, diligent Sergeant Kendall. Kendall epitomized one of military fiction's tropes—the "gentleman ranker," or that person of distinguished family who had enlisted in the military because he had no other options after making grave mistakes in the civilian world. As such, the fictional Kendall stood out from his fellow enlistees, most of whom tended to communicate in the novel through heavy Scottish and Irish accents as opposed to the far better-educated Kendall, who spoke more formal English.

Despite his negative portrayal of Lieutenant Burkett, Paine did not set out to attack all Marine officers; in fact, he depicted many of them in a positive light. But he had a harsher indictment for what he described as the entire military's undemocratic, hierarchical "caste system." Paine explained how the "social distinctions, the personal stigma branded upon the soul of the enlisted man, no matter what his grade, were archaic degradations."[6] However hyperbolic, such beliefs could prove daunting to overcome for a nation seeking to increase the size of its military, especially for a nation relying on democratic rhetoric to mobilize its populace to fight against Germany.

The publication of *The Wall Between* challenged the limits of the Corps Recruiting Publicity Bureau's democratic leanings.[7] An anonymous reviewer in the *Bulletin* unintentionally confirmed the chasm between enlisted Marines and officers, stating that the "story itself was far from a true picture of everyday service life, for only in fiction does a quartermaster sergeant aspire to the hand of his commanding officer's daughter in marriage."[8] The reviewer not only found the possibility of such fraternization virtually unthinkable, but he also worried that the novel would be bad advertising for the Corps because "unthinking people will make much of the 'Wall Between' and its cow-eyed hero."[9] In 1916, then, the reviewer's primary stated objection to the novel centered upon Sergeant Kendall's flaunting of social hierarchies—this from an institution that prided itself on offering the opportunity to rise from the ranks![10] Moreover, Kendall's "cow-eyed" tendencies perhaps challenged the bureau's image of the assertive, aggressive man.

Americans did not concern themselves too much with the social status of men like Sergeant Kendall in 1914, but as World War I intensified, they became more troubled by the dissonance between a democratic nation and a seemingly undemocratic military hierarchy. As such, the U.S. military gave more thought to the rhetoric of democracy to expand and reach more Americans. Because of its smaller size, its familiarity with democratic rhetoric, and the early lead it took in public relations compared to the Army and the Navy, the Marine Corps most successfully worked to collapse its military hierarchy while simultaneously strengthening its institutional culture before troops arrived in France.[11]

Practically speaking, the Corps benefited from its smaller size because it could resist the draft and enlist more selectively, thus raising the quality of the average Marine—at least rhetorically—above that of the average soldier. An elite institution demanded only the best candidates to ensure the institution's versatility. The Corps suggested it had to find recruits that were "just a little bit better."[12] As early as 1916, one recruiter claimed that the Corps had such a difficult admission test that recruits who passed could "readily enter the Army or the Navy." "Quality not quantity" was the order of the day for Marine recruiters, at least ideally.[13] Despite its rapid increase from 10,346 to 33,076 men between 1916 and 1917, the Corps secured recruits relatively easily. The Corps did not even lower its standards in 1917, when it nearly tripled in size over the course of less than one year.[14] The difficulty of becoming a Marine continued after the declaration of war on April 6, 1917, with the Marines accepting only one in four recruits. And Marine enlistees such as Gerald Clark prided themselves on this; Clark made sure to inform his family that Marines were better than sailors and soldiers because they passed a more exacting physical examination. By April 28 Cmdt. George Barnett announced the Corps had reached its full strength of 17,100. Barnett assured "red-blooded men" that they would not have long to wait to be "first to fight."[15] Even when Congress approved the Corps' expansion by 30,000 in May of 1917, the Corps insisted it would not lower its standards. Rather, it would increase them.

The Corps' rhetoric, however, overstates the extent to which the Corps upheld more exacting physical standards than the other services. The Army found 70.41 percent of the more than 3 million men it examined to be fully qualified for service. This 30 percent rejection rate did not differ too dramatically from the Corps' rejection rate of 25.2 percent. And it did not differ greatly from the Navy's and Corps' combined prewar rejection rate of 30.18 percent.[16]

Recruiters relied on a creative interpretation of rejection rates to argue that the Corps demonstrated far higher standards than the other branches. They also continued to depend on contacts with journalists established in previous years and on the quality of Corps recruiting material to help meet increased manpower requirements with relative ease, at least in the early enthusiasm after the declaration of war.[17] The Corps worked to personalize its communications as much as possible. It reached out to various newspapers and organizations around the country via telegraph and other means, thanking the papers by name in articles tailored to each newspaper, which many subsequently printed.[18]

The Corps' recruiting successes impressed outsiders. Surprised by the Corps' ease in exceeding its required numbers by two thousand, one newspaper editor described the changing perception of Marines: "Up to a short time ago the Marine Corps was the most unpopular branch of the armed forces. Its members were neither sailors nor soldiers. The jackies regarded them with mild contempt because of the Marines' duty on shipboard, which was mostly police work. Soldiers looked upon them as half baked sailors. As fighting men the Marines were highly regarded on all hands."[19] Dismissed by both sailors and soldiers, the editor still contended that Marines had earned the respect of both for their ability to fight.[20] While the editorial's reasoning left something to be desired, it did illustrate how some journalists accepted the Corps' primary justification for its existence. The editorial reflected the idea promoted during Veracruz of Marines as "fightin' men." The bureau found it easier and more compelling to win the public's approval by focusing on its battle prowess rather than defining its precise role vis-à-vis sailors and soldiers.

This assertive imagery contrasted with the Navy's more sedate recruiting style. Three weeks after the declaration of war against Germany in April 1917, the Navy focused its recruiting efforts on reaching out to citizens with connections to potential recruits. To facilitate this practical approach, it released a circular letter that guided citizens on how they could find recruits for the Navy. Highly progressive in approach, the letter suggested forming a committee of teachers, doctors, YMCA representatives, and the like raising funds, printing copies of recruiting material; and then getting chauffeured vehicles to take recruits to the recruiting stations.[21]

Whereas the Navy used more subtle recruiting efforts because it worried that blatant self-promotion would backfire, the Corps had few such qualms. The Corps' commandant, George Barnett, envisioned

"Marine Week" to help get four thousand recruits during the week of June 10–16.[22] The Corps planned a flood of publicity in newspapers and magazines. Because all branches sought to recruit men at this time, the Corps could not as easily obtain newspaper articles focused exclusively on it. Still, the praise heaped on the Marines mirrored the bureau's own wording. An Arizona newspaper, for example, commended the 1st Arizona as consisting of "Arizonans of the best type," suggesting it would see service before the National Army. Even more superlatively, however, it characterized the Corps as consisting of "picked men." It was the "most romantic branch of the service . . . the most adventurous." Crafted and refined by recruiters, the Corps' image had taken root in the public imagination. But the Recruiting Publicity Bureau continued to believe it had more work to do. One of Marine Week's "principal aims" was to help the public understand the difference between a sailor and a Marine. Amid congressional debates about conscription, the Corps also sought to encourage volunteerism. It coined a new slogan just for Marine Week proclaiming it wanted only "real recruits—no slackers!"[23]

As such, the Corps did not rest on its image. It took creative measures during Marine Week in keeping with its overzealous tendencies. The Corps envisioned attention-catching efforts like launching a gigantic kite over the Empire State Building. The Corps also planned to screen *The Star-Spangled Banner*, the first commercial film to feature the Corps, during Marine Week. Ministers pleaded from the pulpit for recruits after a committee in Philadelphia asked five hundred churches to hang up the Corps' recruiting posters. One recruiter sought out and received permission to mount posters on every streetcar in Raleigh, North Carolina.[24]

This approach, of course, continued the bureau's general trend of using creativity to ensure it kept the Corps in the public eye. Recruiters shared their ideas regarding how to do this in a new section in the *Bulletin* entitled "Keeping Our Corps in the Limelight." The title implied that the bureau's efforts already had captured significant public notice. This segment generally featured more than a dozen ways that recruiters had secured attention, such as using daredevil stuntmen dressed as Marines doing headstands on office building ledges.[25]

The Corps sought to undertake similarly uncanny feats in the realm of more military pursuits as well. The Corps reinforced the idea that it could achieve the impossible in a wide array of assignments. One Marine officer attempted a "feat" that naval aviators had considered "impossible": making not just one but two loops in a seaplane.[26] The Corps happily seized any opportunity to one-up the Navy. As the base paper of the Corps' overseas training camp in Quantico, Virginia, joked, "the only thing a marine could not do or was not expected to do was to perform the services of a deck hand on a submarine" because such a feat really was impossible.[27] The same kind of rhetoric that the bureau used for external communication with the public also could be seen in a newspaper designed for internal consumption by new recruits bound for France.

Journalists also showcased the Marines' initiative and creativity of local recruiters.[28] In articles describing the progress recruiters made for all branches, the Corps' determination to stand out emerged. One recruiter, for example, planned to exhibit the gun he had used to become the nation's "champion marksman." At an Atlanta station, recruits enthusiastically piled into a truck and rode through the streets yelling, "Rickety, Rickety, Russ; come on and go with us! We're going to win for Uncle Sam; with the U.S. Marines or Bust." Eschewing sophomoric antics, a more circumspect group of Marines began a sixteen-city tour to get support from city mayors in preparation for Marine Week.[29]

Despite the extent to which the Corps perpetuated hyperbolic rhetoric and some recruits gladly internalized that rhetoric, whether the Corps met its full goal is unknown. The Corps had prepared citizens for Marine Week with a flood of publicity. Yet in the aftermath of Marine Week, the Corps remained silent about its success at the national level.[30] At the local level, a few signs of the Week's limited success emerge. One sergeant in Durham, North Carolina, ruefully announced that he had recruited only five of the fifteen recruits he had expected to enlist. Only twenty men had even visited his office. Initial enthusiasm for joining in the fight in France had waned quickly. The Corps did receive its highest number of applicants that month for the year of 1917, but numbers increased by only about four hundred over the previous month. The writing are believed to be of little value at the present time."

District of New York: "In the opinion of this office the only posters worth retaining are Recruiting No. 28 and Recruiting No. 30. All the other posters are either too out of date, having been used long before the war; or, the few new ones, such as the *Punch Poster* have not a sufficient body of color to put across the message. Notwithstanding the fact that Recruiting No. 28 is old, it has the necessary color and is most attractive and gets the desired results. Some of the older posters are printed on such heavy paper that the billposters find it impossible to use them, and they are confined to the use of "A" signs."

Other districts made equally pertinent suggestions regarding the utility of present day posters, all of which are summarized in the detailed report, from Lieut.-Col. Evans furnished to the Officer in Charge of Recruiting and the Officer in Charge of the Publicity Bureau.

This synopsis will be of great assistance to the Bureau in the preparation of new posters to replace those which have outlived their usefulness. At present suggestions are requested for a new poster with a strong economic appeal. It is believed that a poster showing how the average man would be better off financially in the service than he would be in civilian life is a particularly timely subject.

POLICE REMOVE POSTERS
IN NEW ENGLAND TOWN.

The unwarranted destruction of Marine Corps posters by the police of Manchester, N. H., caused Major W. T. Hoadley, officer in charge of the District of New England, to write a letter of protest to the sheriff of the county referring to the drastic action of the authorities.

According to press dispatches from Manchester officers of the Marine Corps called upon Mayor Verette to obtain permission to place posters on the fence about the city yard, which is passed by hundreds each day and was considered by the officers as an advantageous place. Permission was also obtained from the trolley company and private individuals to put up posters on their property.

Taking advantage of a city ordnance, which reads, "Advertisements, notices and signs shall not be displayed on or attached to any barricade or fence in any highway," the chief of police proceeded to have the posters removed. They were replaced and again removed by the police, despite the fact that the posters were government property.

Following the protest made by Major Hoadley, the mayor and board of aldermen granted the Marines the privilege of posting their literature on fences owned by the city, according to an item in the Portland *Express-Advertiser*. Incidentally Manchester, a new station, has already secured two recruits.

NOTICE TO NEXT OF KIN.

Mr W. L. Mann of the firm of Mann and Landry, commercial photographers, 325 North Howard Street, Baltimore, Maryland, has photographs of several hundred individual graves of Marines buried in the cemetery near Belleau Wood and at Romaine cemetery. He has not the names of every man buried, but has the section numbers and grave numbers.

It may be possible for the next of kin of men buried in the two above mentioned cemeteries to get photographs of the graves from Mr. Mann by sending to him the section and grave number and cemetery in France in which their relatives are buried.

VETERAN REACHES GUAM.

The first of the veterans of Marine activities during the past war to arrive in Guam was Sergeant George M. Murphree, U. S. Marine Corps, who arrived on the army transport *Sheridan*, says the *Guam News Letter*. He is one of the old-timers of the Corps who ship over every four years or so because they like the life, and this is his second advent in Guam.

Sergeant Murphree saw service aboard the U. S. S. *Louisiana*, was in an engagement in Santo Domingo, and later on was with the A. E. F. in France, during his last enlistment. The *Guam News Letter* gives Murphree's story in detail in a recent issue.

The truck shown above, standing in front of the Depot of Supplies, Philadelphia, toured several cities in the interest of Marine Corps recruiting. The photo was forwarded to the *Bulletin* by Colonel Radford, officer in charge of the Depot of Supplies.

Fig. 11. "Preparing for the Tour." Recruiters' Bulletin, *4*

Corps may have found more success through traditional advertising, as it received almost five thousand requests for additional information in response to the ads it published in the *Saturday Evening Post*.[31]

The full-page ad the Corps ran in the *Post* contained many appeals that the institution had stressed increasingly over the previous decades.

Fig. 12. Advertisement. Saturday Evening Post, *May 1917, 30*

Even with the declaration of war, the Corps maintained much of its standard approach to seeking recruits. It emphasized its ties to the Navy as well to the variety of possible service. Marines were the "master of any situation." The article referred to its purported glorious past but did not rest on it. Indeed, it stressed above all else the promise of action (see fig. 12).[32]

Despite great consistency in its message, especially before the Corps knew it would go to France, the institution did make some changes to its messaging. With the entry of the United States into the war, the *Bulletin* had encouraged recruiters to jettison more conventional benefits of service such as pay, travel, or adventure. Now Marines stressed patriotism. After quickly issuing "rally round the flag" posters on the day that the United States declared war, the bureau began holding out the lure of being the "first to fight."[33] Some commented that the Corps, alone of the branches, had devised a slogan that resonated among so many. And Maj. A. S. McLemore, the head of the Recruiting Publicity Bureau, received credit for the idea, though he had borrowed the wording from the Marine Corps hymn.[34] The Corps had plenty of precedent to support its claim, given its traditional participation in landing parties, which ensured it would often be first to the fighting. As has been seen, moreover, individual Marines had worked hard in the preceding years to emphasize the Corps' firsts.[35]

Still, the use of this slogan after the declaration of war held some risk in that the Marine Corps could not guarantee service in France. Cmdt. George Barnett made it clear how the Corps' "morale . . . would seriously be affected and the personnel offended" if the institution did not see combat. Glad to have "delivered the advertising 'goods,'" the bureau released a collective sigh of relief in a June 1917 editorial when it announced that a regiment of Marines would be among the first American troops to arrive in France.[36]

In conjunction with its patriotic appeal, the Corps once again stressed its historical origins. The popular "spirit of 1917" poster epitomized this approach. Drawing on the precedent established by nineteenth-century Marines, the poster made connections back to the "spirit of 1776" that emphasized the length of the Corps' service to the nation. In the same vein, the Corps described the Marines as the "minute men" of 1917, connecting their tradition of readiness back to those iconic volunteers who had fought for America's freedom. The Corps wanted to avoid any sense of association with draftees, whom some disdained for not choosing freely to serve their nation.[37]

It also assertively bragged that it was an elite institution. By 1918 the Marine Corps announced its relation to other military services on the first page of its recruiting pamphlet: "U.S. Marines are often confused with sailors of the Navy. They are not sailors—they are soldiers! When you see a soldier with a globe, anchor and eagle on his hat, cap or helmet you may know that he's a U.S. Marine. That's the distinguishing badge—the trade mark of his service! It means that particular soldier belongs to an organization that is almost always mentioned in the same breath with the Foreign Legion . . . and the famous Texas Rangers."[38] Now Marines were soldiers, but soldiers set apart by their corporate identity, in this case symbolized by the emblem of the Corps in modern wording: the eagle, globe, and anchor.[39] The bureau used the wording as a way to distinguish the "Soldier of the Navy" from the "soldier of the army," beginning a few months after the declaration of war.[40] The Corps continued to feel compelled to explain just what exactly it meant to be a Marine.

Despite the institution's desire—even desperation—to see service in France, it did not discard its traditional sea service heritage on posters, which referenced both land and sea. In April of 1917, amid the early enthusiasm for war, the bureau informed its recruiters that the Marine was first and foremost a "soldier—not a sailor—and [would] not spend his entire enlistment on the ocean wave." Still, he should be prepared to spend some time on the "torpedo guns." Multiple recruiters continued to stress the prospect of naval service, demonstrating how the Corps had not forgotten Executive Order 969, when its Marines had been removed from naval vessels.[41] Praising the Corps' colorful, attractive images, observers noticed how the Corps highlighted the range of its duties. The popular phrases "sea soldiers" and "soldiers of the sea" suggested the variety of responsibilities that Marines could expect to encounter, more so than just simply serving as basic infantrymen.[42] As one outsider noted, Marines were "more than soldiers and more than sailors." They were, in fact, "sailor soldiers," which purportedly enabled them to fulfill more missions. As a result, no troops could "strike more telling blows," or so the Corps informed the American public.[43]

Scholars have tended to emphasize the "search for a mission" that purportedly shaped the Corps' historical trajectory. They have periodized eras into types of warfare, such as expeditionary or amphibious.[44] While this approach helps to grasp large changes in focus, it conceals the extent to which Marines themselves sought to avoid whittling down the institution's role to just one mission. Even as the possibility of involvement in a major land war loomed in front of them, the Corps did not forget its history of existential crises; after all, it had endured them even in times of war.

To suit its purpose of not focusing on any particular mission, the bureau interpreted the variety of the Marine Corps' missions as proof of the service's superiority. By focusing on the quality of the service it provided, Marines escaped the traditional muddle it faced as being neither sailor nor soldier. Unlike others in an "age of specialization," Marines argued they functioned as one of the "few surviving jacks-of-all trades."[45] As such, Lt. Charles Cushing—who had served as a journalist before joining the Corps—argued that the Corps was a "large fighting force so completely equipped in all branches that it can act as an independent army." Cushing was not alone in this argument. Such a vision proved to be wishful thinking, as the American Expeditionary Force subsumed parts of the Corps. A few weeks earlier, a journalist had pronounced that the Corps constituted a "complete army—infantry[,] artillery, cavalry, aviation, signalmen, etc, fully equipped in all branches to get right on the job."[46] Given that Congress had considered merging the Marine Corps into the Army during the Civil War, the Recruiting Publicity Bureau's decision to emphasize its ability to fulfill these roles appears risky. By emphasizing its elite fighting capabilities, however, individual Marines celebrated their claims to be essential to the nation.

The Corps also increasingly emphasized the extent to which it reflected the nation's democratic spirit. Congress slowly began to tear down the wall between enlisted servicemen and officers as early as the Spanish-American War, and this trend intensified in the years before World War I. In advising recruiters of new possibilities for enlistees to be commissioned, the Recruiting Publicity Bureau pointed out that "recent legislation ha[d] done so much to remove 'The Wall Between.'"

The title of the novel that had alienated the bureau in 1916 had now been appropriated as emblematic of a new social order within the institution. Another *Bulletin* article pointed to the "exceptional opportunities afforded the worthy enlisted man to win an officer's spurs." Individual recruiters expressed these sentiments at a more personal level as well. Writing to a worried mother living in Sheltonville, Idaho, a recruiter reassured her that there was "no closed portal, no gulf the young man may not bridge, he may reach the highest rank—a proof of the democracy of our service."[47]

In some ways, this rhetoric coincided with shifts in legislation and the commandant's recommendations. In 1914 Cmdt. George Barnett had urged that the secretary of the Navy commission officers only from the Naval Academy or from the noncommissioned officer ranks, as the long custom of giving commissions to civilians who had passed examinations was resulting in too many officers developing physical ailments. The Naval Academy, Barnett believed, served as not only a mental testing ground but a physical one as well. Also, the number of men the Secretary of the Navy could appoint to the Naval Academy increased from fifteen to twenty-five after the August 29, 1916, passage of the Naval Appropriations Act.[48] Eighteen noncommissioned officers received the opportunity to take the examination to receive a commission, and twelve passed. While this number seems small, the Corps only had about 340 officers in 1916. By 1917 Barnett had succeeded in civilian applications for officer commissions, moving instead to grant them to enlisted Marines.[49]

Due to these changes, some Marine officers argued that their institution was far more democratic than the Army or the Navy, providing another avenue to distinguish the Corps from the other branches. Two years after raising its eyebrows at *The Wall Between*, now the Recruiting Publicity Bureau relished these rhetorical tendencies. The "cast[e] system" so prevalent in the Army and the Navy potentially explained why they, unlike the Marines, struggled to obtain recruits.[50] Advocating the benefits of volunteers over draftees, Maj. William Harllee testified before Congress in 1917 that the "caste system" purportedly preferred by the Army did not provide enough opportunity for the enlisted man and "deleteriously forb[ade]" him from "associ[ating] with his superiors."[51] Syndicated articles that appeared representative of the bureau's press releases similarly pointed to the "democratic fellowship" that ostensibly existed between enlisted Marines and officers even at social functions.[52]

The stress the Corps placed on becoming more democratic also influenced its recruiting slogans. Over time, the Corps shifted some of its emphasis away from the "first to fight" slogan toward a slogan that stressed the possibility of rising from the ranks to receive an officer's commission. The phrase "Climb to the Shoulder Straps," referring to the shoulder straps on officers' uniforms, spoke to the institution's decision to find officers from within the ranks rather than from qualified civilians.[53] The Corps even published a pamphlet explaining this climb through the ranks (see fig. 13). On the last page, the bureau held out the prospect to an individual of emulating this trajectory, stating in bold capital letters, "During the period of the war all commissions in the United States Marine Corps will be given to worthy enlisted men. If you would reach the tree of promotion in Uncle Sam's 'First to Fight' branch, you'd better enlist today. It may mean a brilliant career for you." Missing from the brochure was any corresponding mention of enlisted ranks, thereby hinting at the likelihood of Marines to be promoted from the ranks. Regardless of the possibilities for promotion, this change in rhetoric infiltrated deeply into institutional culture. Whether or not most enlisted Marines fully accepted this discourse, the Corps broke down some barriers by insisting that all Marines belonged to a special brotherhood. This approach was consonant with those military institutions seeking to be considered as elite, a key preoccupation of the bureau at the time.[54]

The Corps hoped this process strengthened recruits' loyalty to the institution, with some believing that this bridging between the ranks helped create an esprit de corps second to none. This process began at the institution's "recruit training camps," where the Corps sought to induct Marines into a mystical brotherhood.[55] To construct a brotherhood required the Corps to stress how the hierarchy of class disappeared within its enlisted ranks. In this vein, the Corps emphasized how many recruits deliberately chose enlistment over a commission,

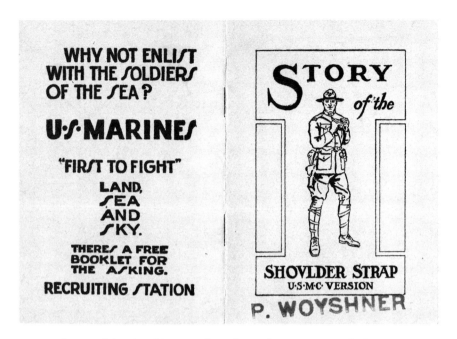

Fig. 13. "Story of the Shoulder Strap." *Paul Woyshner Papers, MCHD*

including the son of Secretary of the Navy Josephus Daniels. Perhaps most conspicuous was former congressman and future secretary of the Navy Edwin Denby, who proclaimed that he had enlisted because all could not "begin as officers."[56] And the bureau had already published articles about Marines who had made this transition. One *Recruiters' Bulletin* cover story detailed the rise of a Norwegian immigrant from private to lieutenant colonel.[57] Whereas the bureau had proclaimed a colonel's niece to be off-limits to Paine's Sergeant Kendall in 1916, now it suggested that the enlisted recruit could himself become a colonel.

These themes emerge in the first two movies that featured the Corps. Produced by Edison Studios, both films explored relationships forged across and in spite of class differences. In 1917 the studio adapted a Mary Raymond Shipman Andrews novelette, *The Star-Spangled Banner*.[58] And in 1918 it released *The Unbeliever*, another adaptation of an Andrews story, *The Three Things: The Forge in Which the Soul of a Man Was Tested*. Neither novelette mentioned Marines, unlike both movie adaptations. Rather, *The Star-Spangled Banner* featured a U.S. Army officer, and *Three Things* was about a young man who joined the British

Expeditionary Force. The author might not have chosen to write about the Marine Corps, but Hollywood did, showing an increasing appreciation for profiting from the Corps' improving image.

Analyzing the differences between the civilian novelette *Three Things* and the movie made with the full cooperation of the Marine Corps' Publicity Bureau reveals insights into what the institution hoped to convey to the public. Historiographically, scholars have explored these films within the larger context of developments in American war movies and propaganda. Lawrence H. Suid, for example, considers *The Unbeliever* and *The Star-Spangled Banner* to be seminal war movies not because of what they reveal distinctively about the Corps but because they created the "images that have evolved into clichés" that now inform most U.S. war movies.[59]

Although the Corps could not control the film's content, it certainly sought to influence *The Unbeliever*'s producers to reinforce its claim to be able to unify the best male Americans—as determined not by their social status but by their abilities—into a true brotherhood of Marines. This theme replicated a similar emphasis in *The Star-Spangled Banner*, whose release the Corps timed to correspond with a recruiting drive. In the novelette version, an American woman remained in England after her husband's death. Her son thus had grown up considering himself English rather than American. Many years later the woman met and married a U.S. Army colonel in London. In the movie, by contrast, she marries a Marine colonel. But the officer is not the focus of this movie; rather, this connection just provides the opportunity for the new stepfather to introduce his stepson to an enlisted Marine. It is the heroic first sergeant—notable for his ability to "grasp situations and act promptly and intelligently"—who inculcates the boy with true American patriotism.[60] An upper-class boy who sees himself as English thus transforms into a true American through the auspices of an enlisted Marine rather than the officer, class differences notwithstanding.

This same brotherhood brought the two heroes of *The Unbeliever* together, as the pride of serving in the Corps quickly erased class differences. Soon after the release of *The Star-Spangled Banner*, the Edison Corporation requested permission to make another two films about Marines and began adapting *Three Things.* The novel showcased the transformation of a twenty-three-year-old upper-class young man, Philip Landicutt, who was a consummate snob, an atheist, and a hater of all things German. Stirred by patriotism, he decided to enlist in the British Expeditionary Force to help free Belgium because the United States had yet to declare war. In the Expeditionary Force, he overcame much of his snobbery. Within a few months in the trenches, he found himself becoming friends with a lower-class British soldier who had previously worked as an aristocrat's chauffeur.[61]

Similarly, the movie highlights the impressive mansion Landicutt occupies with his mother while adding an uncle and highlighting his U.S. Civil War service. Philip spends his days loafing around a golf course rather than laboring. As a superficial representative of the best of American society, Landicutt's background seems to befit him for a commission. But Landicutt—in keeping with the novelette's democratic rhetoric—enlists. It is this act that enables him to fulfill his potential.

The bureau influenced *The Unbeliever* through several avenues. The movie drew the largest number of Marines for its drill scenes from the 6th Marines, which soon departed for France. However, of the named roles filled by Marines, all but one featured Marines assigned to the Recruiting Publicity Bureau.[62] Some scenes were filmed in Quantico, Virginia, because the Corps had training trenches there.

The assistance of the Rivoli, the prominent New York City movie theater that first released the movie, was equally important. The version of *The Unbeliever* finally screened before the public departed from today's practice in that the Rivoli's manager paid for the rights to edit the movie as he wanted, which could entail condensing the movie reels or adding "new intertitles" between scenes. And that manager happened to be a former Marine named Samuel Rothafel.[63] Rothafel enlisted five months after his mother's death in 1902, when he worried about earning a living. Although he had served in the Corps after the Spanish-American War in a period of relative peace, by 1911 he wove a tale to journalists and others about the combat he had seen in the Boxer Rebellion.[64] Today, Rothafel's actions might be considered "stolen valor"; at the time, though, his actions complemented the Corps' efforts to equate a Marine with a fighter. Rothafel may not have fought during his time in the Corps, but he had spent the last years of his service recruiting. This firsthand experience attuned him to the best ways to attract men to the Corps.

Rothafel's sentimental attachment to the Corps also reflected the bureau's increasing dissemination of the message that a Marine should not only serve his institution but also love it. Accounts described Rothafel as openly crying at the first showing of the *The Unbeliever*. No doubt some of this could be dismissed as theatrics; after all, Rothafel was a master of publicity. Yet his own experience as a Marine in many ways mirrored the story the bureau sought to tell about the power of enlisting in the Corps. Rothafel had been born in Germany and emigrated to the United States when he was four years old. While he sought to erase his suspect links to Germany during World War I by claiming he had been born in Minnesota, he more openly prided himself on being only the third Jew to receive promotion to corporal.[65] This promotion did not enable him immediately to occupy the kind of "distinctive" position the bureau promised in 1917—after all, he sold encyclopedias after leaving the Corps. Still, by 1917 he had become one of America's most prosperous theater owners. Despite his success in the theater industry, the "one outstanding feature of his successful career—in his own estimation—is the fact that he once served with U.S. Marines," or so the Recruiting Publicity Bureau reported.[66] *The Unbeliever*'s emphasis on the equality based on their talents more than their class or ethnic background, then, probably resonated with Rothafel because it echoed his own personal experience. A man who had been promoted in spite of his religion and had become a success without a college education likely could relate to a film that showed a deep friendship bridging an enormous social gap.

In recruiting to fight a war for democracy, the Corps deployed rhetoric to argue that one could "see the bank president's son toting the same rifle as the file leader who may be the son of the village blacksmith."[67] That this wording appeared in the *Quantico Leatherneck* rather than the *Bulletin* shows the extent to which the bureau's rhetoric had spread, suffusing the training process. In *The Unbeliever* Philip Landicutt appeared as a stand-in for the bank president's son, while the chauffeur stood in for the village blacksmith. The movie erased any class differences by virtue of both men's decision to serve their country.

In this way, while the Corps offered recruits the plum of a commission, it simultaneously informed them that even enlistment offered the path to elite status. Philip Landicutt's background is so apropos because his enlistment subtly demonstrated that members of America's elite could find a place in the rank and file of the Corps. In *Three Things* Landicutt's determination to enlist is not given much explanation or specificity other than that he hates Germans. The story simply begins with his telling his mother he is determined to fight. In *The Unbeliever*, by contrast, the key moment occurs on a golf course where male and female friends surround him. As they watch one friend take a shot, Philip gets distracted as he notices Marines marching in perfect formation several hundred yards away. With an enormous smile on his face, he turns to his friends, who are similarly excited for a moment or two before boredom and disinterest in the war creep in quickly. But argument quickly eclipses the group's more positive excitement, with Philip in vehement disagreement with his friends. At one point his friends stare at him with serious expressions, except one woman, who smiles more charitably—or condescendingly, if one is a cynic. The general sentiment the producers seek to convey becomes more apparent as words flash upon the screen, with Philip voicing his belief that "it is our fight." In response, a few of his friends look even more disgusted at his newfound patriotism. From that point on, Philip's facial expressions alternate between grimaces at his friends to sheer excitement as he looks back to the Marines. The group breaks up as one friend proclaims his thankfulness to be at the "end of the draft." Even if he were to be drafted, his "tango toes" precluded his service.[68] A hobby, it is suggested, is enough to exempt the military service of America's upper classes. In marked contrast to his friends, Philip walks over to the Marines. There, he realizes he knows one of them because the Marine used to chauffeur his friends around before enlisting. Someone who is decidedly not Philip's social better has done the "right" thing first, and Philip rides home determined that he must enlist as well.

Philip's primary motive to serve is not to kill Germans. Rather, as he explains to his mother in the film, it is the fact that the nation's "best men are going. . . . I must do my share." By contrast, in the novelette he explains to his mother, "If the country won't fight, I will! I'll do my share as a gentleman ought."[69] It is his class allegiance—his status as a gentleman—that necessitates his service in the novelette. In the movie, he might have been born into the highest class, but he must join the rest of the nation's best through service to the Corps.

This word "best" likely reflects Samuel Rothafel's editing or the bureau's influence.[70] Similarly, Philip's words in *The Unbeliever* contradict the class snobbery so integral to the novelette *Three Things*. In the novelette, battlefield camaraderie slowly broke down walls between Philip and his new friend. Only after months in the trenches can Philip even begin to admit that there could be such a creature as a "low-bred man with well-bred qualities." But even then he considers the chauffeur an outlier—someone no more than a "'sport' example, like a puppy with points in a litter of mongrels." Philip's snobbery even prevents him from telling the chauffeur that they are cousins. Philip convinces himself that acknowledging their familiar relationship risks destroying their "comradeship" because neither knew how to act around the other without their respective class identifications.[71] By contrast, the Corps' rhetoric sought to erase those class distinctions in the first place. Service in the Corps—with its careful selection process and high standards—created a distinct class of Marines regardless of social class.

Military service erased class differences much more quickly and completely in the film *The Unbeliever* than in *Three Things*. Philip and the former chauffeur, Lefty, appear inseparable from their introduction to combat when German soldiers send a note to Marines attached to an inert grenade. The note states, "Leather-Necks—Give us a bombardment in five minutes, The Lieut-Colonel is coming to inspect us and we want to discourage him from doing it again. Auf Widershen, Fritz." With Lefty and Philip surrounded by their laughing comrades, Lefty holds the grenade while Philip holds the note, whose rhetoric unites all of the soldiers, regardless of national origin, into a unified team that pokes fun at officers. The movie then takes a more serious turn, with Philip and Lefty volunteering together for a dangerous mission to locate German mining efforts. The two then take matters into their own hands, taking dynamite without permission to attack German soldiers. After they return from that mission, their lieutenant scolds them, stating: "Do you realize your assumption of authority in taking that dynamite might mean court-martial?" Because the Corps' rhetoric minimized the distance between officer and enlisted man, the transgression did not necessitate punishment, as evidenced by the use of the word "might." The Corps, the movie seemed to suggest, need not be populated by military martinets to maintain strict and unnecessary order as in the German army. After all, it had the best recruits.

As the Corps projected a democratized vision of itself, it also promoted the social benefits of this egalitarianism. Less than a week after the declaration of war, the *Washington Evening Star* printed an article angled for potential recruits with the promise not only of combat and adventure but also a path to improved social status. Although to a lesser extent than the Navy, the Corps did seek to attract recruits with the promise that their training had relevance after leaving the service. But now the Corps did something different. It did not emphasize practical job training, rather, it promised to prepare its recruits to "occupy distinctive positions in civil life."[72] The article substantiated this enticement with reference to two men who purportedly had done just that after leaving the Corps. It also cited the case of fifty officers who had been promoted out of the enlisted ranks. Furthermore, the article suggested that the "brotherly feeling" that existed between officers and enlisted Marines made this transition far more natural in the Corps than it might be in other branches.

To some extent, this reflected the reality of officer-enlisted relations at the Publicity Bureau. The rise of Thomas Sterrett from private to major epitomizes the possibilities for talented enlisted Marines to contribute significantly to the bureau and, ultimately, to the Corps. Figure 14 demonstrates the interactions between Marines of a variety of ranks at a farewell meal. The bureau's Marines, however, sought to expand this rhetoric to encompass the entire Corps. Being the smallest military branch further enhanced the institution's sense of brotherhood. Marines, Sgt. B. J. Rutzen explained, were the "aristocrats" of all the U.S. military branches.[73]

A. W. McRener speeds the parting Marine guest, (Q. M. Sergeant Gould), at Guffanti's Restaurant, New York City, April 13, just before the popular Publicity Bureau sergeant left for the Officers' School at Quantico.

BITS OF CURRENT HUMOR.

What men will say for a few days off:

"I request that I be given five days' furlough in order that I may visit my father who is sixty years old."

"It is requested that I be granted four days' leave that I may go home and be the *best* man at my sister's wedding."

Sergeant Canavan to one of his "own" who answered to the name of Cohen. "Now listen here you; if you don't snap out of it pretty quick, I'll—I'll—I—I'll tell the rabbi on you."

"No. You'll never make a Marine," said the worried drill sergeant to the bow-legged recruit. "Look at ye. The bottom half of yer legs is standing to attention, while the top half is standing at ease."—*Tit Bits.*

SOMEWHAT MISCALLED.

"Any complaints, corporal?" asked the colonel, making a personal inspection one morning.

"Yes, sir. Taste that, sir," said the corporal.

"Why," the colonel said, "that's the best soup I ever tasted."

"Yes, sir," said the corporal, "and the cook wants to call it coffee."

HE'S A SPRINTER.

Green recruit—Do you think we'll ever get back?
Scared one—I don't know about you, but if the first shot doesn't hit me the rest are going to fall short.

A SURE SIGN.

Omar—I understand that Paul Baylor got caught in the draft.

Aroma—Well, if that's the case, the war ought to be over soon. He never held a job more than three months in his life.—*Judge.*

HIS FINANCIAL MEASURE.

Lady (entering bank, very businesslike)—"I wish to get a Liberty Loan bond for my husband."

Clerk—"What size, please?"

Lady—"Why, I don't believe I know, exactly, but he wears a fifteen shirt."—*Indianapolis Star.*

ANSWERING HIS COUNTRY'S CALL.

Last summer, when every young man's thoughts were on the war, a wealthy lumberman from Seattle arrived in New York on a business trip. His business having been attended to, he was a guest at a dinner given one evening by an officer in the United States Marine Corps. As the hours and the flowing bowl passed, speeches became more and more frequent, everybody was wrought up, and there was no man so base as to say that he would not go to the front for his country.

Early the next morning the Seattle man started back home.

A few days later the officer of Marines received this telegram from him:

"Did I enlist that night? If so, instruct me when and where to report."—*Popular Magazine.*

Fig. 14. Farewell Dinner. Recruiters' Bulletin, *April 1918, 25*

These forces worked to strengthen the institution's esprit de corps.[74] In his work on esprit de corps among Civil War soldiers, Mark Dunkelman defines the term as a sense of shared community that inspires fervor and fidelity to the unit or institution. He argues that esprit de corps initially arose from the Army's recruiting practices of creating regiments from the same geographical areas. These local ties strengthened on the battlefield because of the regiment's shared experiences that fostered "camaraderie."[75] The Corps chose not to replicate units based on geography as the Army did at the division level, but it could expand the reach of the bureau not only to attract recruits but also to initiate them into the Corps' group identity during training.

As such, joining the Corps became something akin to belonging to nobility, albeit one not determined by social class. A newspaper article entitled "Join the Marines If You Would Be a Military Nobleman" stressed the appeal of joining the Corps.[76] Using adjectives commonly associated with medieval knights, one recruiting poster challenged men to live up to the standards set by other Marine fighters. Like knights of old, Marines were "stalwart, square, and valorous" (see fig. 15).[77]

One joined this knighthood not by virtue of one's social class, however. Once again, the *Quantico Leatherneck* chimed in to amplify the bureau's message. Local residents, it claimed, had come to view all Marines as "gentlemen." In an inspired fit of progressivism, the Corps sought to make more than "citizens."[78] With just a bit of training, common Marines could become something akin to their officer counterparts. Marine training not only turned a recruit into a man, but it also enabled the acquisition of "gentle" traits to form a complete gentleman.[79]

Despite the bureau's intensifying emphasis on hypermasculinity, it also stressed a more sensitive, manly attachment to the institution, in keeping with the rhetoric of the gentleman. A special supplement to one *Bulletin* edition revealed the consensus among recruiters that successful recruiting required a strong attachment to the institution. This focus on "love" drew on one of the key aspects of chivalry, but it substituted a romanticized view of an institution for the idealized

Fig. 15. "Man Wanted—To Fit This Hat." *L. S. Rose Papers, MCHD*

worship of women.[80] Sgt. Clarence Barry found it difficult to express his feelings for the Corps because he had never experienced a "love affair in real earnest." Perhaps only the Legion of Honor, he claimed, might have such a "spirit of fellowship" as existed in the Corps. By looking to an institution created by Napoleon Bonaparte to reward merit with chivalric symbolism, Sergeant Barry highlighted the Corps' emphasis on a brotherhood of knights. As another recruiter noted, this trait distinguished the Corps' "aristocracy" from the other military branches.[81] One Sergeant Chamberlain had the appearance of a highly masculine man, as evident in the way a journalist described him as "ability and forcefulness," yet he did not hesitate to make known his feelings. He was "thoroughly in love with [his] branch." Capt. D. W. Blake elaborated on these feelings, describing recruiters in religious imagery. The recruiter served as the "Father of the Corps" as well as the "Son," and as such he "Loves, Honors, and Obeys. He knows the Corps, its history and traditions."[82] This view put recruiters at the center of the Corps' institutional culture as caretakers of the Corps' distinctive identity, which meant some recruiters felt they had to act on the Corps' claim to be an institution of fighters. Sgt. Frank Stubbe, an enthusiastic contributor to the *Bulletin*, felt his "conscience" no longer allowed him to remain on recruiting duty. He had served for ten years without seeing real action, and the stories he had heard from those he had recruited motivated him to ship over to France.[83]

The bureau's efforts to promote a love for the Corps did not cease once recruits had been sworn in. The bureau encouraged the indoctrination of trainees with the same "spirit" and love of the Corps it expected its recruiters to manifest.[84] Some at the bureau believed the acquisition of this spirit to be the "most important acquirement" for Marines, thus implicitly outweighing the importance of traditional military traits like marksmanship or discipline.[85] The Corps used a prominent new enlistee to inculcate these sentiments in new recruits: Edwin Denby, who had been an avid proponent of preparedness. A naval reservist during the Spanish-American War, Denby enlisted in the Corps after the declaration of war. Given his relatively advanced age of fifty-eight years old, Denby found himself responsible for opening recruits' "eyes to the significance of membership in the historic Corps." Denby viewed this process as a "vital step in the making of a Marine, the value of which can hardly be overestimated." One officer concluded that no one was better equipped to "flood the minds and hearts of his hearers with the spirit of the Marines."[86] At times, the Corps rhetorically attached more importance to a recruit's affiliation with the institution than it did to learning how to aim a rifle or march in formation.

This trend persisted after initial training. The commander of Quantico, Virginia's Overseas Training Camp, noted that Marines did not just receive practical military instruction because officers worked to fill young Marines "full to bursting with the spirit of the Corps." Similarly, a young officer eagerly reflected on how the Corps sought to turn recruits into "Marines for life" in a way that celebrated the Corps' 1907 motto, "Once a Marine, Always a Marine."[87] A number of enlisted recruits internalized this rhetoric. The *Bulletin*, for example, reprinted Pvt. Julian Carlisle's letter, which stressed the importance of the "Good Old Marine Spirit."[88]

The bureau also increased its emphasis on the "globe, eagle, and anchor" as the symbol of that spirit and reinforced it through publicity and training. Before the war, Marines had debated the best trademark for the institution. Known for decades as the eagle, globe, and anchor, the Corps borrowed this symbol from the British Royal Marines, adopting it in 1868 with minor modifications. Recruiters sought to keep the device "constantly" in the public eye, in part because they still believed that the public's perennial inability to recognize a Marine had not been fully resolved.[89] One *Bulletin* cartoon highlighted these difficulties, pointing to the failure of many citizens to recognize Marines. One observer asked a confused citizen, "Don't you see that thing on his cap?" The requirement of the American Expeditionary Force (AEF) for Marines to wear the Army uniform while in France only intensified this approach in the bureau's eyes.[90] The uniform might change, but the device remained as the "one unchanging mark by which we may be identified." Evaluating the Corps' use of this symbol, one commercial advertiser noted that this symbol represented the institution's "service on land, on sea and in the sky. And if anybody makes his trade-mark good at all times and under all conditions," it was a Marine.[91] In this way, the symbol epitomized the Corps' image of a jack of all trades, which it had honed since the end of the nineteenth century. The Corps may have borrowed the symbol from the Royal Marines, but it gained meaning of its own through Marines' purported willingness to take on any task. By World War I, the symbol had become increasingly romanticized. The bureau stressed that all Marines belonged to the "great order" of the Globe, Anchor, and Eagle, now capitalizing the symbol's name to signify the reverence with which one should view it.[92] And to gain entrance to this order was not easy.

During recruit training, future Marines learned that to wear the globe, anchor, and eagle was the "greatest honor in the world bestowed on a man. The men get this spirit drilled into them."[93]

Similarly, the Corps made it mean something to be a Marine by amplifying the Recruiting Publicity Bureau's rhetoric of challenge in its recruiting messages. Marines recalled how the Corps challenged potential recruits to "Join the Marines 'IF' you can!"[94] It promised "more romance and red blooded adventure" than "any other group of fighting men in the world." Prospective recruits, it explained, could still join despite the draft's implementation, but only "'IF' the Marines will accept you." This acceptance demonstrated that a recruit was "100 per cent. MAN, too, if you get by. TRY." Recruits such as Arthur Davis felt compelled to join, given the challenge the Corps offered as well as its reputation for training and instilling discipline.[95]

During training, the Corps continued disseminating similar messages that many recruits embraced at the time.[96] One recruit remarked, "It seems as difficult to become a marine as to be elected to office or make a million $." To complete training and become, as one recruit phrased it, a "full fledged" Marine held enormous significance. As recruits neared the completion of training, many expressed their great pride in the Corps.[97] Initially attracted by the "First to Fight" recruiting posters, Mel Krulewitch later reflected that as the end of recruit training neared, "the miracle of the Marines broke through. . . . There quickened in the march that first hint of assurance, that swagger."[98] Likewise, a proud Marine father described to Cmdt. George Barnett how the Corps had transformed his son. Indoctrination into the institution's esprit de corps had "permeated his system with the feeling that the most important and capable branch of the service is the Marines." Other Marines connected their pride in their new institution to other historically elite warriors, such as the newly minted Marine who believed that his training had made him the "greatest thing since Caesar's legions."[99]

Not only did the Corps stress that it was the finest military institution, it continued to do so by envisioning an inferior other, the Army and the Navy. As Marine novelist John Thomason remarked, esprit

de corps could be "defined as esteeming your own corps and looking down on all the other corps." Recruits were taught, for example,
that enlisted Marines ranked far above Army officers when it came
to their soldiering ability. Victor Sparks noted that he and his fellow
recruits "sustained our morale by believing that a Marine private
was superior to an Army Lieutenant and a Marine N.C.O. superior
to an Army Captain."[100] Arthur Davis imbibed these lessons so well
that he reminded his relatives of the differences between soldiers and
Marines in four separate letters between June and September of 1918.
In one letter, he emphatically stated, "for Heaven's sake, don't address
me as 'Corporal.' I repeat, that I am not in the National Army and the
Marines don't make men 'Corporals' in a few weeks." Davis stressed
the challenge of being promoted in the Corps, suggesting it signified
a far greater achievement than in the Army. In another letter Davis
wrote, "You must remember I am not in the National Army; that is
a picnic compared to what we get." Davis expressed his pride in the
Corps because of the obstacles he had to overcome. One of his friends
who had enlisted in 1917 wrote to Davis from Cuba to share similar
sentiments, telling him that he would not "swap for any branch of
the service. . . . When you get in the Marines you can look any mili-
tia-man, National Guards-man, draft-man, Officers or privates, in the
eye and know in almost every instance that you have something on
them."[101] Davis' friend made no mention of sailors, tending to compare the Corps to other soldiers.

Many historians similarly have worked to illuminate the Corps' purportedly qualitative uniqueness. Peter Owen, for example, has stressed
how the institution's successful recruitment of droves of athletic, college-
educated young men made a difference on the battlefield. At a time
when only one in thirty young men attended college, a Marine company might consist of 66 percent college students. Owen focuses particularly on the 2nd Battalion, 6th Marines, to understand its Marines'
"readiness and resilience." He claims that their "unit cohesion" helped
them to endure poor doctrine and tactics, such as an excessive emphasis on the individual rifleman's firepower. Measuring unit cohesion is a
challenging task, but Owen claims that more U.S. soldiers than Marines

deserted. However, he presents little evidence to justify the Marines' distinctiveness other than that they received more thorough training, particularly instruction in marksmanship. It is also an implicitly classist argument because what appears to be unique about the Marines is that so many came from relatively privileged backgrounds that could afford the chance to attend college.[102]

Historians also assume that the Corps' rhetoric significantly motivated the Marines who fought in France, and that the fact that the AEF attempted to subsume the Corps into the numerically superior Army only intensified this tendency. Although numerous Marines continued to serve with the Navy during World War I, it was those Marines who served alongside the Army who received the most popular attention. A popular apocryphal story from the war epitomizes the purported identity of Marines during and after World War I: "They tell the story of some distinguished visitors who were passing along the cots in a military hospital in France. On one of these cots lay a man quite still, with his face buried in the pillow. Something about him caused one of the visitors to remark, 'I think this must be an American soldier.' From the depths of the pillow came a muffled voice—'Hell, no; I'm a Marine!' "[103] Not only did this Marine assertively clarify his military affiliation amid his suffering, he did so in a manner that assumed his audience's familiarity with a Marine, which had rarely been true for much of the nation's existence. Nineteenth-century Marines might have been content to describe themselves as soldiers. In World War I, it clearly meant something to be a Marine, at least to the bureau and to those recruits who internalized its rhetoric.

The Corps certainly sought to inculcate recruits with its culture, including an offensive spirit. In reality, though, these actions did little to motivate or sustain Marines in combat unless their officers' actions matched institutional rhetoric. Especially after the Spanish-American War, the Corps' rhetoric had been characterized by its increasing bombastic and assertive tone. In particular, its recruiters fervently sought to convey the Corps' superiority to convince men to enlist in accordance with the inspiration recruiters received from the pages of the *Recruiters' Bulletin*.[104]

The Corps' lore stresses how Marines sought to retain their distinctiveness while being absorbed within the Army-centric American Expeditionary Force.[105] And scholars have shown how the presence of an other often works to stimulate identity formation. Indeed, some of the letters discussed in the previous chapter conform to these expectations, especially those written at the beginning of individuals' military service. For the most part, though, institutional differences between Marines and soldiers appeared to be of limited importance except to those wounded Marines recovering in French hospitals who had the luxury of contemplation. Contrary to the bureau's claims that it "meant something to be a Marine," for most Marines who fought in France it meant little more than to be a soldier. Marines' identification with their Corps generally did not increase in France. Perhaps if Belleau Wood had been their first and last battle, they might have sounded more like their counterparts at the Recruiting Publicity Bureau. But what they endured was too terrible. What mattered to combat Marines was serving under officers who upheld the Corps' rhetoric of a democratic brotherhood of professional soldiers.

In June 1918 the Marine Corps faced the biggest battle of its history to that point at the Battle of Belleau Wood. With Russia's surrender, Germany had hoped to transfer its troops from the eastern to the western front for a spring offensive designed to defeat the Allies before Americans could fully join the war. As the French retreated before the German offensive, Marines and soldiers found themselves rushed to the front in a desperate attempt to halt the German advance. From June 1 to June 5, the 6th Marine Regiment and 9th Infantry Regiment held the line they had established on the road between Château-Thierry and Paris, less than ninety miles away. On June 6 these units staged a counterattack that led to what one scholar has described as a "futile bloodbath of inexperienced Marines."[106] These enormous casualties occurred in large part because Marine and Army officers embraced the tenets of open warfare, an untested doctrinal approach to combat that rested on assumptions about American exceptionalism and marksmanship.

After Belleau Wood until the armistice in November of 1918, Marines bled and died at horrific rates as their officers struggled to adapt their tactics and train replacements. They spent almost a month fighting at Belleau Wood, a battle that dragged on so long that the AEF removed Marines for a five-day rest before putting them back into the fight. Less than a month later, they found themselves rushed to the battlefield of Soissons, arriving exhausted and still unprepared for the kind of battle they faced. That battle taught the Corps to hold 20 percent of men in reserve to avoid the annihilation of entire units.[107] They rested for almost two months before returning to the battlefield at Saint-Mihiel in September of 1918. At the end of the month, they participated in a draining weeklong battle at Blanc Mont, which further reduced the Marines. Finally, the war came to an end in November of 1918, the Marines having endured about five months of intense combat.

To what extent did the imprint of recruit training remain consistent, especially for those Marines who fought in France? The answer is difficult to ascertain, in large part because of the limited number and the nature of sources written during and after war. Sources written during the war, such as letters, had to be censored. As a result, Marines such as Warren Jackson revealed little to their families while in France, in part because he wanted to be more optimistic to his loved ones but also because his company officer censored his letters, thus giving him little privacy in making forthright comments in the first place. Jackson's letters at times echo the Recruiting Publicity Bureau's rhetoric. In a letter he wrote home on June 19, just after being relieved from the Battle of Belleau Wood, for example, he exclaims: "You should have heard the boys who relieved us talk about the Marines! They say the Marines were all they had heard for a week."[108] This kind of rhetoric, however, cannot be reconciled with the horrors that comprise the majority of his account.

On the other hand, far harsher accounts written after the war might reflect how attitudes about the purposes for which the war was fought might have grown more cynical as the ideas of the so-called lost generation took hold. One of the most popular novels written by a Marine about World War I certainly fits this mode. Thomas Boyd, who wrote *Through the Wheat*, received inspiration and ideas from his acquaintance with prominent authors of the lost generation, including F. Scott

Fitzgerald and Sinclair Lewis. Thomas Boyd first saw combat at Belleau Wood, and he later died from the effects of the gassing he received there. Published in 1923, *Through the Wheat* is one of the more prominent accounts of a World War I Marine because of its literary style; it was also one of the earliest.[109] Boyd's title highlights the wheat field Marines naïvely crossed when beginning their offensive at Belleau, having no idea of the difficult terrain and heavy fortification they faced in the forest beyond the field.

Although it is a fictional work, many of the main characters' names differ only slightly from their nonfictional counterparts. Scholars largely agree that the main character Pvt. William Hicks is Boyd's "alter ego"; as such, experiences will be viewed as largely reflecting Boyd's own thoughts and experiences. Scholars tend to read *Through the Wheat* as an antiwar novel.[110] Such a reading misses the extent to which Boyd expresses his military identity, which centers on his disillusionment with the Corps and those individual Marines who failed to uphold the best of the institution's rhetoric. He wants their actions to match his idealized vision of what an authentic soldier should be.

In the novel, the future private William Hicks cannot resist the lure of the Corps' recruiting efforts after the United States declares war against Germany, as epitomized by a "bespangled sergeant" who promises him "real action." The "rich brogue and campaign ribbons that the sergeant professionally wore" capture his "heart."[111] His decision to join centers less on a desire to enlist in a particular branch of the military and more on the promise of combat and the perceived glamor of a professional soldier's life.

Quickly disillusioned by the motives of those surrounding him, Hicks singles out the classism of his noncommissioned officer for his strongest vitriol.[112] While Peter Owen celebrated the bevy of college students enlisting, Hicks reserves his strongest contempt for Sgt. Kerfoot Harriman, who carries "with proud satisfaction the learning and culture he had acquired" during three years at college. Harriman's refinement only results in feet too tender to "stand the heavy hobnails issued to the soldier." He views himself as anything but a "common" soldier, disdaining to sleep among lower-ranking enlisted Marines. Throwing all of his gear on the supply cart with Lieutenant Bedford, he "gaily" leads heavily burdened Marines on a march.[113] In some ways, Harriman's enlistment upsets the social norms of Boyd's company. Before World War I, non-commissioned officers typically shared their men's class origins before being promoted to positions of greater responsibility. Harriman's social rank, by contrast, ensures he identifies more with officers, which makes it difficult for him to share in the common experiences of the rank-and-file soldier. Ultimately, Harriman reveals himself to be the worst sort of soldier when he chooses self over service, pitifully shooting himself in the foot after his fiancée informs him that she is considering marrying someone else. The sergeant's determination to return home immediately to stop her backfires when he realizes amid sniveling that his actions will result only in "disgrace."[114]

Hicks' officers offend him less, but he marvels at their determination to uphold the Corps' culture amid the mud and misery of France. He characterizes them as "white-collared fighters for democracy" preoccupied with the platoon's "spirts, its 'morale.'" They worry about how to integrate fully all of the replacements for those killed or wounded. After one battle, the officers eagerly observe their men joking and playing cards. In response, the officers "smiled and told each other that [the men] were not only recovering their morale, but were imbuing the new men with that spirit peculiar to the Marine Corps."[115] Hicks' officers believe something special distinguishes the Corps' culture from other institutions and that it is powerful enough to be worth instilling while in France. They also assume their Marines will inculcate it in the replacements. In actuality, exhausted enlisted Marines had little patience for the trappings of institutional culture. When a Marine from the rear brings Hicks' platoon hot chow at the front, the frontline visitor belts out, singing:

> Oh, the infantry and the cavalry
> And the dirty engineers,
> They couldn't lick the leathernecks
> In a hundred thousand years.[116]

This kind of ditty reflects the Corps' "peculiar spirit" with its hyperbolic praise for the Marine at the expense of other soldiers. Shattered after battle, however, Hicks' best friend just looks at the singer "sourly," scornfully informing him that he would not be singing if he had been in combat the previous night. It is possible that Boyd exaggerates this experience by drawing upon the trope of the rear echelon soldier. Even so, the scene strengthens the importance Hicks attaches to his idealized vision of an authentic fighter, which is all that matters to him in France.

Regardless of his disillusionment with the Corps' culture, Boyd demonstrates his military identity by measuring other individuals by the extent to which they act like "real" soldiers. This sentiment emerges most clearly in his description of Maj. John R. Adams, who represents two different individuals, Maj. John A. Hughes and Capt. Robert E. Adams. Major Adams, he explains, "belonged to that type of officer each of which you meet with the feeling that he is the sole survivor of the school of regular soldiers. . . . He wore his campaign hat adeptly. He limped as he walked, from an unhealed gunshot wound received in the Philippines. Campaign ribbons were strung across his breast. With him authority was as impersonal as the fourth dimension. He was adored and held in awe by half of the battalion."[117] In some ways, this characterization shares much with Hicks' recruiter, whose campaign ribbons similarly reveal his combat experience. But, unlike his recruiter, Hicks observes Adams in action, sharing a combat experience that enables him to verify his authenticity. In one scene, Adams returns from the hospital after recovering from a wound, only to find most of his battalion has been wounded or killed in a recent battle. The exhausted unit springs to life, "smartly" saluting at his return in a way that pays tribute to Adams' leadership qualities. Adams' return unites all varieties of soldiers: "tired, worn-out, hungry soldiers; the dirty, blood-smeared, lousy soldiers . . . the stupid, yellow, cowardly soldiers; the pompous, authoritative corporals; the dreamy, valiant, faithful soldiers."[118] Adams reestablishes his rapport quickly with the troops, sarcastically informing them, "This is not a battalion, it's a platoon. That was a hell of a way to let a bunch of Germans treat you." Then Adams buys all of the men beer, forcing the battalion's mess sergeant to be "deprived [of] his safe dugout far in the rear. . . . for a few hours." Again, Boyd draws on the rear echelon trope to contrast the mess sergeant forced to bring beer with the men with whom he serves. Still, Hicks has no idealized sense of his fellow Marines' individual identities. All that matters is their shared experience of combat and their mutual respect for Adams, who has led them before and will lead them again in combat.

By contrast, the Corps' newest officers preoccupy themselves with romanticized notions of war and their newfound rank. Hicks disparages them for having acquired their knowledge of "modern warfare from the books supplied by the nearest officers' training camp." They "learned how to order men about, that he was an officer and a gentleman" but only "felt a slight interest in the men of his command."[119] They repel Hicks because what attracts him to enlist in the first place is the lived experience of the Corps' fighters. To characterize *Through the Wheat* simply as an antiwar novel misses the extent to which Boyd loves his majors because he perceives them as doing more than playing at being soldiers.

Boyd's frustration with those officers who failed to uphold the Corps' democratic rhetoric is not unique. Nor is his identification of himself more as a soldier than a Marine, which is characteristic of most Marines who published accounts during this time.[120] This account highlights that the bureau's difficult task of making it mean something to be a Marine had yet to fully succeed.

But those Marines who did show the most identification with the Corps in their memoirs of the war had the best experience with their officers. In his memoir, Elton Mackin valued the willingness of his officers and noncommissioned officers to "get out in front of their own men." To be truly equal requires all Marines to potentially sacrifice themselves in combat. Recounting an apocryphal story of an officer who has a runner executed for not relaying a message quickly enough, Mackin explains that he must have been one of the "older military school, whose kind has largely gone, and rightly so. He rated common soldiers far below common dogs. . . . The fostered spirit of America will not submit to anything but honest leadership in soldiering."[121] This was not Mackin's experience. Rather, rhetoric and reality intersect for Mackin, in part because of the number of his officers commissioned from the ranks. As he explains,

> Following men like these is what makes tradition for the fighting men. In the Marine Corps, for the most part, we followed real soldiers. There are a few advantages in serving with the marines in time of trouble, most of them having to do with the type of men you soldier with and take orders from. The vast majority of our line officers come from the ranks. They understood the soldier kind because in their day, their time, they had worn the harness and felt the lash—the harness being the burden of the pack equipment carried, the lash being the harsh discipline meted out and the unquestioning response expected. . . . But the man in the ranks has the advantage of knowing that, rich or poor, gentleman or otherwise, the man who leads him out to die, for the most part has a code of his own—a part of the tradition that says he shall not send men where he dares not go himself.[122]

For the professional soldier, the experience of combat shapes one's identity so profoundly that differences such as class can become trivial as long as officers willingly sacrifice themselves alongside those enlisted Marines ordered to do so. Mackin credits his officers' inclination to do this to their own experience in the enlisted ranks, and he thrives under strong officers who give him few reasons to challenge the nation's or the Corps' rhetoric, which explains his stronger identification with the Corps in addition to his sense of being a soldier.

As head of the Recruiting Publicity Bureau, Col. A. S. McLemore, who had overseen the Corps' participation in *Unbeliever*'s filming, explained in 1919: "The Marine Corps has always stood for justice in its service to the country and in its attitude toward the enlisted man. In no organization on earth is there a closer relationship between officer and men; a straighter, cleaner, finer attitude of man to man."[123] McLemore's words match few of the published accounts of enlisted

Marines' experiences in World War I. It is possible that these accounts represented outliers motivated by frustration with their experience, but because they manage to find some positives in their experiences, their motives appear more complex. While some officers certainly demonstrated exemplary leadership, they tended to be long-serving officers with combat experience. Flooded with new and inexperienced officers in France, the Corps' utopian rhetoric often outran reality. The Corps' propaganda, then, set up unreal expectations that often caused disappointment and frustration.

The Corps had done much to overcome the kind of hierarchical distances Ralph Paine portrayed in *The Wall Between*, not only through the narratives it crafted but through real steps taken to promote its noncommissioned officers into the ranks of its commissioned officers. But Paine's work is also important because, as the Corps acquired more visibility, it sometimes received more attention than it could control. While the Corps found itself reacting to Paine, it drove the messaging more in other mediums. With the increasing importance of film, the bureau quickly embraced opportunities to work with filmmakers to help influence public depictions of itself. It also increasingly refined and intensified its internal emphasis, particularly in recruit training. It expected its recruits not just to join the Corps but also to love it. And its external focus, particularly its strong relationship with journalists, helped it attract enough recruits to expand for the war, though perhaps not as successfully as it would have liked, given its few comments regarding the success of Marine Week despite its most creative efforts.

But the limits of the Corps' propaganda efforts were most noticeable among the survivors. As Marines had since the nineteenth century, many of them continued to identify most distinctly as soldiers and only secondarily with the Corps. It did not yet mean something to be a Marine for many of them. Of course, there are exceptions. Some individuals did accept the Corps' culture and even thrived in doing so. Accounts written decades after the war, moreover, sometimes show a more decided identification with the Corps that suggests the extent to which it managed to institutionalize this culture more deeply in its training after World War I.[124] In the meantime, though, the Recruiting

Publicity Bureau's Marines continued to refine and strengthen the Corps' highly masculine identity in order to answer new challenges to the institution's image at home, no matter how odd that image seemed to some Marines fighting in France.

Chapter Seven

Hypermasculinization

Every Male a Rifleman, Every Female a Clerk

Pvt. Martha Wilchinski might as well have written a Dear John letter.[1] Indeed, she joked that he could have his ring back. The letter she wrote to her fiancé, Corp. Bill Smith, included everything a Marine fighting in France in 1918 did not want to hear. After informing Smith that she had enlisted, Wilchinski warned him not to be surprised if she received a croix de guerre, a medal awarded to those who displayed heroism during combat. She spoke condescendingly of his knowledge of military rank, suggesting that a mere corporal might not understand what a colonel was (despite the fact that she was a private, a rank below her fiancé). She even questioned why she had not received the helmet of the German soldier he had claimed to kill, wondering if he had really "got the fellow." From her safe location in New York, she undermined his pride and challenged his manhood, overtly through the matter of the missing helmet and more subtly through mentions of military hierarchy. Her words could be expected to fuel the misogyny often present during wars. Wilchinski's words epitomize what Stephen J. Ducat refers to as the "castrating" female whose actions are "powerful and self-authorizing."[2] By empowering herself through enlistment in the Marine Corps, threatening to make similar achievements, and questioning some of his, Wilchinski pushed Smith to confront deep-seated male anxieties, including irrelevance, cowardice, and shame. Wilchinski's letter could have encouraged her fiancé to further the division between female Marines and "real" Marines (i.e., those fighting in France) because of its provocative content. Wilchinski's fiancé, Corp. Bill Smith—with his nondescript, common English surname—stood in for all Marines who had a duty to prove themselves in combat to the females supporting them from home.

Wilchinski intended her fictional letter for public consumption, and the *Recruiters' Bulletin* published it in September 1918, a month after the first female Marines' enlistments. Of the 305 females who served during World War I, five received orders to the Corps' Recruiting Publicity Bureau located in New York City, including Wilchinski. Wilchinski's degree in journalism from New York University made her an ideal candidate for the bureau, with its responsibility to flood U.S. newspapers with positive descriptions of the Corps.[3]

Of the woman who served as the model for Rosie the Riveter, Cynthia Enloe wonders whether she was "maneuvered or empowered—or both?" The same should be asked of Wilchinski.[4] It is instructive that the bureau quickly put Wilchinski to work not in composing the anonymous press releases so central to its daily work but rather in making the addition of female Marines readily apparent in the *Bulletin*.

Wilchinski and the other 304 women who served in the Marine Corps during World War I have yet to receive attention that reveals the complex institutional culture in which they served. Their story has been told solely from the perspective of women's history that glowingly portrays the many hurdles they overcame to serve. Female Marines have been celebrated as pioneers of military service in a way that often assumed an inevitable progression toward equality. Yet this interpretation does not accord fully with the Corps' rhetoric at the time.

An approach that draws on gender rather than women's history helps to reveal the incongruities and meanings with which the Corps wrestled as it incorporated women. While some feminists have assumed that the inclusion of women in the military marks a step toward equality, other feminist scholars such as Anne McClintock suggest that nations have "sanctioned . . . gender *difference.*" An emphasis on difference helped a highly gendered institution make room for women.[5] The presence of an other—female Marines—sharpened the identity of male Marines as fighters first and foremost. The ultimate significance of female Marines centered on boosting the identity of male Marines rather than ending a purported manpower crisis. The addition of female Marines symbolically created a division of labor based on gender, reinforcing the image of the male Marine as a fighter. At the same time, it incorporated women into the Corps in a manner consonant with its image as an elite institution. These dual purposes—both critical to maintaining and intensifying the Corps' institutional culture—explain some of the Corps' contradictory rhetoric. Even if the incorporation of women did not constitute the Corps' most pressing issue in 1918, it showcases the institution's adroit ability to reshape its imagery when required. The Corps needed to do less internal maneuvering, given that few male Marines interacted with their female counterparts. As with its emphasis on democratization, though, there were limits to how much the Corps sought to or even wanted to change and challenge deeply held ideas about gender. Externally, its efforts were more important, given the Corps' claims to hegemonic masculinity, or the way a society privileges certain traits, qualities, or characteristics as being the most worthy and valuable. In short, hegemonic masculinity is what a society generally believes to be the "approved way" of being a man.[6]

As such, the bureau emphasized something akin to physical perfection. Of course, all military institutions maintain certain physical requirements. Marine recruiters, however, linked the purportedly elite status of the Corps to the physical qualities it required. These traits drew on currents in larger society such as social Darwinism. As one sergeant rhymed, Marines were the "best of men / That Uncle Sam can get, / And if you're not perfect in eye and limb / You'll be rejected, you bet!" The importance the Corps placed on high standards reinforced its corporate identity as an elite institution while playing to society's image of the ideal man. After the Corps rejected a talented marksman because he was missing several fingers, a bureau press release explained the recruit's potential difficulty drilling as well as the displeasing appearance of the recruit's hand, which "look[ed] bad." Recruiters considered carefully the image the Corps had to maintain, and they relished seeing "exceptionally fine specimens of manhood," not just for practical purposes but for the impressive visual spectacle they provided.[7]

Marine posters had stated the desire to recruit "men" since the nineteenth century, but the addition of the word "real" in the twentieth century suggested the need for men to prove themselves. It spoke, ironically, to ideas about masculinity connected not to physical characteristics but to normative ones. The Corps did not just seek men but "real men."[8] The individual who embraced and fulfilled the challenges set forth by the institution could take pleasure in knowing he was not just a "man" but a "*man*."[9]

As such, recruiters determined which characteristics or qualities could be improved and which ones could not. They considered men with "artistic temperaments," for example, more likely to desert. Similarly, the *Bulletin* recounted how William James was about to be sworn into the Corps when he saw a cat and began screaming in fear.[10] James' subsequent rejection by the Marines helped to remind the reader that the Corps could afford to be selective. William James' irrational fear of a harmless cat demonstrated that he was not a "real man" and was thus unworthy of becoming a Marine.[11]

By contrast, recruiters devised more flexible solutions for applicants deficient in other areas. Minnesota recruiters even opened a "night school" for physically qualified recruits who had not received enough education.[12] But a recruit either met the desired standard of masculinity or was not fit to be a Marine. The Corps also encouraged "otherwise perfect men" not to linger too long in factories, where men stood for hours on end "wearing poorly made shoes, which led to flat feet, a defect that disqualified them for military service."[13]

In this way the Corps appealed to the enthusiasm for virile masculinity sweeping through society by challenging a recruit to see if he measured up to society's highest expectations.[14] The Corps channeled society's expectation of men emerging through a series of tests to prove their ability to meet gendered norms. Making his own signs for a recruiting drive, one sergeant enjoined potential recruits on the front of one sign, "Be a man. Join the Marines." The back stated: "If you're afraid to be in the thickest of the fight, don't join the Marines." While not every American male ascribed to the same idea of masculinity, the Corps' appeal to the highest normative ideas of masculinity resonated with a broad segment of society. The Recruiting Publicity Bureau also drew on male insecurities to draw some to the Corps as a means of demonstrating their understandings of manhood. For at least one recruiter, simply wearing the Corps' uniform served as "an outstanding insignia of perfect manhood" that could not be found in the other branches.[15]

Fig. 16. Howard Chandler Christy, "If You Want to Fight!
Join the Marines." *Library of Congress*

In what appears at first to undercut that mentality, the bureau also
used feminized imagery, disseminating an image of a female dressed in
a Marine uniform in 1915, two years before the United States entered
World War I (fig. 16). The famous poster of the "Christy girl," drawn
by well-known artist Howard Chandler Christy, enjoined the potential
recruit to "join the Marines" if he desired to fight. The colorful woman
towers over the fighting Marines. Scholars have noted the sexualized
imagery in Christy's posters as they sought to lure recruits with the
prospect of acquiring women. More deeply, however, the poster reveals
differences in institutional cultures as well as the threat of emasculation. While Christy clothed the men in combat uniforms, he dressed

the female in the Corps' most decorative, ceremonial uniform. This decision reinforced the stereotype of women as more vain and more concerned with appearance. Christy also drew on the stereotype of men as active and women as passive. Christy positioned the men facing the other direction, engaged in some sort of action suggestive of combat, thus delineating clearly between the place of men on the front lines and the place of women decidedly elsewhere. The woman appeared more passive, standing in fixed position, with her smile suggesting her role as cheerleader of the busy men. Arming her with a bayonet further distinguished her from the men, who carried rifles. On a battlefield characterized in 1915 by the dominance of the machine gun, the trench, and artillery so favorable to the defender, a bayonet had questionable utility. On a deeper level, however, the seemingly harmless woman in the Corps' ceremonial dress poses a far more significant threat because weapons, particularly bayonets, "act as fetishes of phallic power, security against the overwhelming castration anxiety brought about by war."[16] Even as she wielded a weapon, she did not menace the Marines placed well behind her. Rather, she affixed her gaze to the poster's viewer. It is he she threatened with emasculation if he did not enlist. This and other recruiting posters epitomize the Corps' ability to appeal to deep insecurities in a way that resonated with potential recruits.

Similar posters produced by Christy in 1917 for the Navy exchanged weapons for low necklines (fig. 17). By depicting a more martial female than appeared in the navy's posters, the Marine "Christy girl" poster worked to reinforce the Corps' sense of itself as more aggressive. By drawing upon hegemonic masculine ideals, the Corps sought to draw precisely those recruits necessary to maintain the institution's closer embrace of normative masculinity than the Navy. With much larger manpower needs, by contrast, the Navy needed to project a wider variety of masculine types. Even before the Corps began accepting a small number of women in August of 1918, some women worked alongside recruiters in a volunteer capacity. No doubt the Christy posters and other aspects of the preparedness movement functioned as the impetus for many women to want to assist the Corps' recruiting efforts. As early as 1916, twenty-year-old Edna Payne purportedly rented office space in

Fig. 17. Howard Chandler Christy, "Gee!! I wish I were a man . . ." *Library of Congress*

New York City, where she "'manfully' took her stand" next to a recruiting poster. As the first female "recruiting sergeant," albeit unofficially, Payne supposedly acquired more recruits "than any man ever stationed there."[17]

The depictions of women provided publicity for the Corps while relying on gender differences to shame men into joining.[18] Before declaring war against Germany, for example, one Marine recruiter encouraged males to enlist by dramatically claiming he had two women applicants for every male. The Corps was not alone in this approach. At one point, the Navy considered enlisting even one woman to highlight the urgent need for men.[19]

Dressed in uniforms similar to those of Marines, the Corps' female volunteers implored men to do their patriotic duty. In Ohio, for example, a Marine recruiter used Mildred Rahrig, nicknamed Sergeant Pep, as his last resort to convince men to join. Similarly, an Oklahoma woman known as "Sergeantlette" Fletcher, who prided herself on the service of her two Marine brothers in France, out-recruited the civilian men.[20]

Even as the Corps used women in a volunteer capacity, the Navy recruited women in an official capacity beginning in 1917. The decision to enlist women in the Navy originated at the highest levels of civilian leadership. Secretary of the Navy Josephus Daniels discovered that the Naval Act of 1916 had created a force of reserves referred to only as "persons." Army legislation, by contrast, specified that only "male persons" could enlist.[21] By March of 1917, Daniels decided to enlist women in the Navy. More than 11,000 women, known as yeowomen, enlisted to perform clerical and other similar duties. At its peak size of about 532,931 people, women represented 2.1 percent of the Navy's personnel.

Yeowomen caused some consternation to naval officials, who chastised them for various reasons, including wearing only selected parts of the uniform. The Navy's delay in making all components of the uniform available to women, however, explains the purported intransigence of the yeowomen. Shocked by seeing yeowomen wearing fur coats, one naval officer accused them of being "undemocratic." Naval officials also chastised yeowomen for their conduct within the office, citing instances of chewing gum, sitting on tabletops, and gossiping. No doubt male sailors broke similar rules, yet officials issued a separate code of regulations that dictated the expected conduct for women.[22] That the Navy needed to develop a different set of rules based on gender speaks to the way female participation enhanced the idea of multiple types of military service.

For unknown reasons the Corps did not immediately follow the Navy's lead in enlisting women. The standard argument suggests that the Corps decided to enlist women in order to compensate for the Corps' numerous casualties in France. In reality, though, the enlistment of 305 women could not offset the institution's casualties. In its first major battle, which lasted almost the entire month of June 1918, the Corps suffered more than 9,000 casualties.[23] Despite such tremendous casualties, the Corps continued to acquire male recruits relatively easily. The month before the Corps announced it was enlisting females it exceeded its previous recruiting record, enlisting 8,584 men. By August the Corps needed thousands of men to meet and maintain its authorized strength, not a few hundred women. And the Corps recruited a much smaller percentage of females than the Navy, even though four times as many Marines were killed in action. In contrast to 2 percent of the Navy, females comprised less than 0.5 percent of the Corps' overall strength.[24]

The Corps issued the call for women in the same month that active recruiting for males ceased and the United States began to rely more fully on the draft. Earlier that summer, the Corps had responded to a June request from Congress to know how many male service members held clerical roles in the United States. It took Cmdt. George Barnett about two months to reply that 202 Marines were on clerical duty in the United States and that the Corps had begun seeking females to replace any males capable of overseas service. The Corps assumed it needed three female Marines to do the clerical work formerly done by two male Marines.[25]

As Barnett explained to Congress, a large percentage of male Marines had received waivers to allow their enlistment in the first place and, as such, had been declared unfit for combat. Thus it is not surprising, given the conditions of their enlistment, that a photograph taken in October 1918 shows a large number of male clerks.[26] The first female Marines, then, did not free many, if any, male Marines to fight.

This reality, however, did not fit the bureau's discursive needs. According to the bureau, the recruitment of female clerks freed men who had been "chafing under the restraint of unactivity." The Corps purportedly had moved to enlist females in "response to appeals of men and officers" who wanted to "fight," releasing "devil dogs" who were "now irked by desk jobs."[27] No matter how valuable, clerical work was by nature too passive and stationary, the opposite of the sense of aggressive masculinity the Corps promoted.

Regardless of its reasons for enlisting women, the Corps received significant interest once it announced the new opportunity, with about a thousand women reporting to a New York City recruiting station in one day alone. Maintaining its image as an elite institution, the Corps proclaimed it refused to bend its standards for female Marines, which proved to be more of a rhetorical gesture than reality.[28] Female Marines did not complete the initial physical examination, nor did they receive the same training. Male Marines spent between eight and twelve weeks in basic military training.[29] Female Marines, by contrast, immediately entered the office.

Ironically, the incorporation of women simplified rather than threatened the gendered identity of male Marines. Women filled clerical positions that society increasingly gendered as female. As John Pettegrew explains in regard to football in a way that sheds light on female Marines' incorporation, the Corps "constructed a tightly wound homosocial universe that, rather than excluding women altogether, subordinated them to a spectatorial role, which, in turn, heightened the martial heroic element of the sport."[30] The Corps superficially welcomed women into the Corps' ranks as spectators to and supporters of male combat in France.

The Corps used contradictory discourse in explaining the kind of female Marines it wanted. On the one hand, it sought only women who made a favorable impression. This was not to say, as it proclaimed, that it wanted only "pretty girls." The Corps expected women to uphold the standards that male Marines maintained in terms of dress and bearing. It also emphasized that the Corps desired women around thirty years old who could be considered "real" women. The use of the word "real" corresponded with its emphasis on "real" men. The *Bulletin*'s editorials praised the women as "experienced business women" who had the "right of being addressed . . . as integral parts of the nation's fighting force." Marcia Bartle, for example, had been a telephone operator. In serving, she joined a sister in the Navy and three brothers-in-law in the Corps.[31]

Whatever their experience and their desired age, the bureau and journalists struggled not to refer to them as "girls." Early on, a bureau editorial informed readers that no nicknames should be applied to them. But, elsewhere in the same issue, the *Bulletin* more paternally noted that women must be "made to understand" that "their work was serious."[32]

The bureau's higher-ranking officers might have toed the official line on welcoming female Marines, but other members demonstrated emotions ranging from hesitation to resistance. In a reversal of the claim that enlisting women freed a man to fight, National Guardsmen teased Marine Raymond Stenback that the Corps could enlist women because it did not "do any fighting anyway." Interviewed for a story about the new enlistees, one Marine recruiter similarly conveyed his opposition to a receptive journalist. An article published about one week before Pvt. Opha M. Johnson's enlistment entitled "Charming Blonde Seeks to Enlist in the Marine Corps" depicted a woman who appeared to be anything but charming. The story explained how a loud, well-dressed female entered a recruiting office, determined to enlist in the Corps. While confidently stating her many qualifications, she also made it clear that what mattered most to her was the uniform. Her comments reinforced the stereotype of feminine vanity. She then succumbed to female competition when another woman entered the building. Rather than mention her credentials, the second woman sought to prove she was more qualified by acting in a "coy manner." At this point, the women's "interest in the marine corps was diminished and their interest in each [other] intensified." The recruiting sergeant George Kase finally intervened, yelling, "This is a man's office—nothing doing." Kase recounted the story of the females unable to suspend their vanity long enough to become Marines to make clear that women did not belong in the Corps. Their very presence, he believed, threatened his institution. "Barely able to make himself heard above the dim created by the chattering of the women and the laughter of the by-standers," Kase appeared to be on the verge of losing control of his own masculine space. In concluding the article, the journalist included the wishful thinking of some Marines: the two females left the office, having "decided it was time to go and that the marine corps was no place for them."[33] This article represents the extent to which local recruiters' individual autonomy undermined the Recruiting Publicity Bureau's ability to control fully the rhetoric surrounding the incorporation of women.

The women who spoke for the Corps, however, acted more consistently in ways that reinforced gendered assumptions. Pvt. Opha Mae Johnson, the first female to enlist on August 13, 1918, had previously worked for the Civil Service. She explained that in the Corps she had been tasked with convincing female prospects to join. The fact that women had deluged the recruiting offices seemed to make such a job superfluous. In expressing her sense of the particular challenges women faced in the Corps, she believed that "girls" struggled with the "word 'obey'" because they "want to talk and do things their own way"; she thought they struggled with the discipline inherent to military life.[34]

Regardless of purported female vanity, the Corps had to select a uniform for the new enlistees. Different institutions chose to send different messages about uniforms. As Carol Burke argues, military institutions must determine whether they will outfit women in uniforms that closely resemble the male uniform or whether they will provide a more feminine version. Most frequently they have chosen a more masculine uniform, as the Corps did.[35] Whereas the yeowomen had a slightly more feminine uniform, the Corps provided female Marines with a uniform closely modeled on the dark-green and khaki uniforms of their male counterparts.[36] They also received the same "overseas cap" worn by the men. This decision probably represented the desire to reinforce the institution's claim to be the most martial of the military services. When yeowomen and female Marines marched in the same parades, the Marines' uniform contrasted with the less military-looking white gloves and hats and blue uniforms of the female sailors.[37]

According to newspaper articles, the female Marines could barely contain their excitement over their uniforms. At an enlistment ceremony publicized by the Corps, the "girls" wanted nothing more than to discuss their anticipated uniform, and one new Marine immediately requested a mirror. Similarly, the Corps stressed male interest in the female uniform. Accompanied by pictures of three female privates wearing the new uniform, one article in the *Bulletin* made no mention of any duties. Rather, it sought to assuage men's curiosity about their new counterparts. The article wondered whether the recruits were "fair" or "dark" or "slender" . . . or "perhaps—perish the thought—they are not at all."[38] This emphasis on vanity undercut the practical expectations the Corps had of these women.

Still, the Corps expected its women to fulfill more military duties than the Navy did, even if outsiders wondered why. For example, the chair of the House Naval Affairs Committee, Congressman Thomas Butler, whose son was a Marine officer, wondered how women seemed to have time for "drilling and learning to play billiards."[39]

Befitting its more aggressive image, the Corps drilled female Marines as part of their duties in contrast to yeowomen, some of whom drilled during their free time. Drill has been a critical aspect of military service for centuries, instilling discipline and unity into military institutions with the ultimate purpose of improving combat effectiveness.[40] The decision to drill the women, even though such training did not improve their ability to serve as clerks, might have demonstrated the importance the Corps attached to inculcating a sense of belonging, as it worked so hard to do with its male recruits. It also represented the Corps' desire to project an image of a highly disciplined elite military institution to the public.

Yet the Corps drew the line at drilling with rifles. One article explained how the male Marines responsible for training the "girls" discovered this duty was not as distasteful as originally assumed. The speed at which the female Marines learned drill also impressed the male Marines, or so the bureau suggested. By contrast, female Marines remembered struggling to learn drill, as could be expected given they did not receive the basic training their male counterparts did.[41]

Still, differences between male and female Marines only heightened the masculinity of male Marines by virtue of their otherness. As one gender historian has argued, "war does not change but rather exacerbates the social and political order." This order became heightened in numerous ways. One journalist observing female Marines at drill, for example, described the palpable difference between the "husky, masculine" voice of a male Marine and the "high pitched" sounds of the female Marines.[42] In this case the emphasis on voices worked to "overfeminize" female Marines in a way that enhanced the male Marines' masculinity.[43] Those female Marines, who drilled without weapons, were distinct from male Marines who were now unified symbolically as fighters, consistent with the Christy Girl poster from 1915 in which the woman dressed as a Marine lacked a rifle.

The rhetoric and imagery of the *Bulletin* epitomizes the complex, convoluted, and contradictory ways that the Marine Corps sought to integrate women to reinforce its sense of being an elite institution as well as a hypermasculine one. "The Girl He Left Behind" poster (fig. 18) best fits the image the Corps sought to perpetuate of freeing a man to fight, even if only a rhetorical gesture. Here, a female clerk bids adieu to a male Marine, who holds a rifle as he prepares to live up to the words of the recruiting poster next to him and go to France. The woman's palm is raised in support, and she seems confident, ready to tackle any clerical work required of her.

Other illustrations, however, depicted female Marines as childish. In echoing the interest of female Marines in their uniforms, a cartoon featuring Martha Wilchinski in the *Bulletin* showed her deciding to become a Marine because the Corps had the "prettiest" uniform. The cartoon, drawn by a male Marine, echoed the traditional disconnect between the expectations and realities of military service. Some male Marines, for example, acknowledged how the appearance of the Corps' dress uniform swayed their decision to enlist. Yet the cartoon ultimately depicted an independent woman with a college degree as a helpless child wearing clothes far too big for her.[44]

Fig. 18. Cover, Recruiters' Bulletin, *September 1918*

If the cartoon depicted Wilchinski as a child, others showed a far more "sexualized femininity." Sonya Rose suggests how an emphasis on appearance is a "crucial component in the construction of gender difference."[45] In one illustration published in the *Bulletin*, a female Marine appears to be receiving military instruction from a Marine officer (fig. 19). That she needed instruction worked to reinforce the difference in status between her service and that of male Marines. In the background, enlisted Marines stand at attention, with inscrutable faces and question marks over their heads, thus speaking to the contrast between their outward military bearing and their inward questioning as to Wilchinski's presence. As the officer adjusts her belt with a smile on his face, she smiles as well, her hand either gesturing in a salute or fixing her hair. The officer's smile adds the element of sexualized femininity Rose speaks to into the image, raising the unlikely prospect of the officer smiling while adjusting his male Marines' uniforms. The *Bulletin*'s depiction of Wilchinski in repeated images borrowed from the imagery of the "Gibson Girl," made famous by artist Charles Dana Gibson, whose artwork symbolized ideal feminine beauty, and the "Christy Girl."

The feminine, softened image of Wilchinski differed greatly from her much plainer appearance as photographed in various guises in 1918.[46] The similarity in the image, however, was that once again Wilchinski was cast in the role of observer, touring various Marine posts to learn what "real" Marines did despite being a Marine herself. Similarly, a syndicated article depicted the female Marines' clerical responsibilities to take care of their male counterparts as highly physical acts in which the "fingers of the girl Marines are on every movement of every Regiment, Battalion, Company, man, at home, abroad, any time. And there is romance in it."[47]

While it seems certain male Marines at the Recruiting Publicity Bureau helped create sexualized images of women, they received help from women. Like Wilchinski, Lela Leibrand also worked in the bureau. With a background in writing Hollywood screenplays, Leibrand controlled the editorials of the *Leatherneck*, the Corps' magazine for enlisted Marines, for three months in 1918. Yet, like Wilchinski, she overly feminized her written contributions in a way that undermined

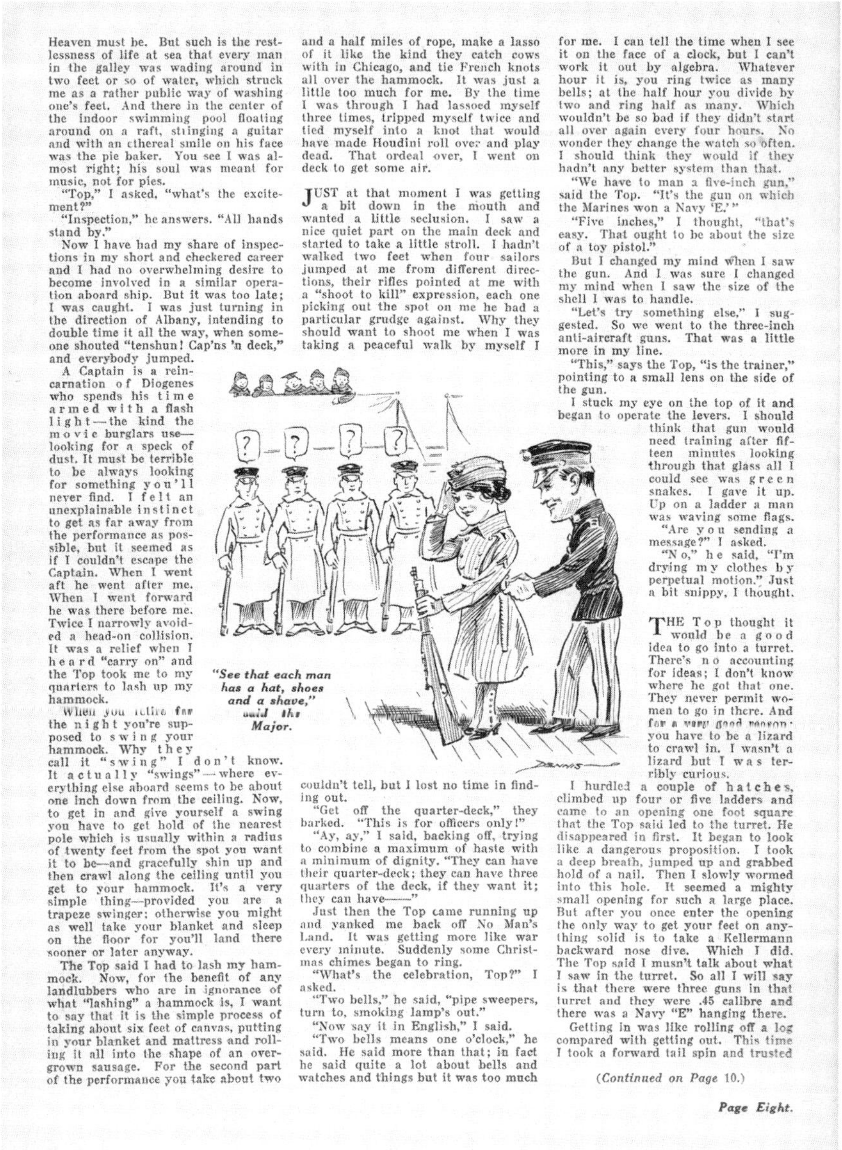

Fig. 19. "Hurdling the Hatches," *Recruiters' Bulletin, January 1919*, 8

any claims to equality. An article entitled "Fair Marine Tells of Flight in Hydroplane" stressed appearance from the first word of the headline. Similarly, Leibrand almost immediately expressed her desire to know "how she looked" while flying and then described one of the pilots who flew her as "deucedly handsome."[48] By commenting on the pilot's appearance, Leibrand hinted at a sexualized awareness of her male counterpart that undermined her interest in the Corps' military duties. Similar to Wilchinski's depictions, Leibrand's article suggests the role of the female Marine as a kind of perpetual sightseer in uniform rather than as a dedicated employee with serious responsibilities.

While the Corps worked diligently to shape its public image, it occasionally revealed more complex imagery. One *Bulletin* cover, for example, depicted a woman holding an issue of the *Bulletin* showing a Marine fighting in France. She appeared saddened, no doubt thinking of her boyfriend overseas, demonstrating her allegiance to the Corps with a large necklace consisting of the eagle, globe, and anchor, the Corps' symbol. With the passing of a month, however, she had enlisted, thus becoming symbolically united with the male Marine in service to country. Even as the male Marine saluted, though, his other arm inhibited her from saluting. Contradictorily, though, his left arm rested loosely upon her right arm in the more stereotypically feminine position. Given that the inclusion of women supposedly freed a man to fight, the image does not make sense if interpreted at face value. If her service had freed him to fight, they could not be standing next to each other. Although the war ended in the middle of November 1918, the same month of publication, it is highly unlikely that publication schedules allowed for the inclusion of the armistice. Indeed, the issue makes mention of it nowhere else.

The spatial ambiguity of the image can only be resolved with reference to the choice of uniform. Interestingly, the gendered assignment of uniform reverses that seen in the Christy recruiting poster. The male Marine now appears in the Corps' dress uniform while the female Marine wears the uniform of those in France. Their facial expressions, however, remain the same. The male has an impassive face befitting military bearing while she smiles, looking quite feminine. If the image shows the transformation of the woman from civilian into Marine, it also shows the Marine being removed from the battlefield and being put into a dress uniform. While the individual aspects of the drawing are difficult to interpret in isolation, taken together they suggest the incorporation of women into the Corps was fraught with

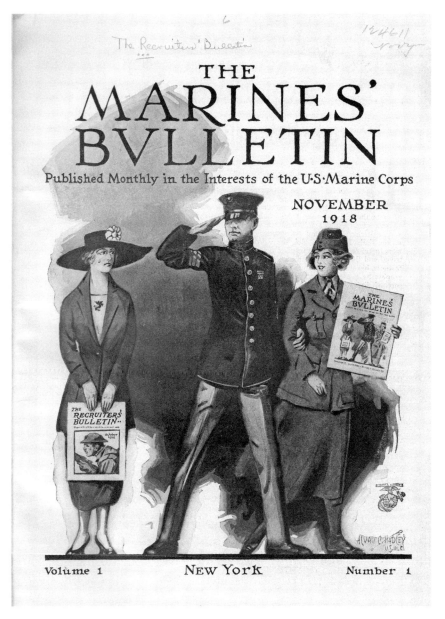

Fig. 20. Cover, Recruiters' Bulletin, *November 1918*

far more difficulties and complexities than traditional women's history has argued. At first glance, the male artist who drew the image portrays an image that seems to welcome female Marines (see fig. 20). On closer examination, though, is she the castrating female, so feared by men, who has reduced the male Marine in dress uniform to holding onto her arm? Interestingly, the commandant later instructed male and female Marines to stop "skylarking" about "arm in arm" on the streets of Washington, D.C. Many interpretations can be drawn from this image, but perhaps the final takeaway is how difficult it is for an institution to control the complete message it conveys on issues like gender that can be subtly manipulated or undermined. Given the variety of reactions to the incorporation of women, it is not too much to suggest that one Marine subtly wove his negative feelings about female Marines in his drawings, especially because he showed interest in gendered comparisons between the defeated Germans and the victorious Americans in other cartoons.[49]

Women also produced contradictory rhetoric, just as the male artist of the November 1918 *Bulletin* cover had. In her first month of service in the Corps, Pvt. Martha Wilchinski publicly proclaimed her "hunch that the Marines would realize the necessity of women some day." What did she mean? Superficially, at least, Marines did recognize women's necessity or Wilchinski would not have been given a role in publishing for one of the key conduits of institutional culture. Indeed, when summarizing the thoughts of her male commanding officer, she suggested his full approval of female Marines' efforts. She even quoted him as saying he believed female recruits filled clerical positions better than did male Marines.[50] In this regard, Wilchinski appears to be the model of the confident female Marine, simply biding her time for the military to recognize her ability to contribute to the war. Similarly, she signaled the importance she afforded her military service by putting her loyalty to the Corps before her fondness for her fiancé. In closing one letter, Wilchinski hoped to avoid offending Corporal Smith by her obligation to sign her name with her rank according to regulations rather than in a more "affectionate" manner as was her wont. Still, her contradictory rhetoric perhaps better epitomizes Cynthia Enloe's suggestion that military service simultaneously empowers and uses women. In a subsequent letter, Wilchinski appeared occupied with everything but the supposedly critical clerical work for which women had enlisted. Rather, Martha was cleaning and dusting in case an officer happened to drop by to inspect the offices, thus engaging in a decidedly feminine role. And in January of 1919, Martha appeared cast down by the challenges of wartime uniform requirements. Despite the horrific suffering that had ended for the Marines in November of 1918, the article jokingly suggested that the "cruel, cruel war" still continued for Martha, who feared buying a civilian hat, which she would not be able to wear until it was unfashionable due to the slow discharge rate of service members.[51] Finally, after providing a running discourse on her trip to Washington, D.C., and praising the attractive appearance of naval officers, Wilchinski came to the point. This missive was a real Dear John letter. Bill was "too slow" for her, content to take a girl to a movie and "hold her hand." And then she accused him of buying her a fake diamond ring. Again, Wilchinski's letter did nothing to highlight her own service except to send her on another sightseeing tour of a ship. The rest of the letter epitomized the most negative tropes surrounding women Marines' service on the home front.

The Corps made clear that female service was only a temporary aberration. This view fit with the social norms of the time, but what makes it worth pointing out is that the bureau believed it so necessary to articulate these sentiments, even though most female Marines simply moved from civilian workplaces to the Corps. As Sonya O. Rose has argued about British women during World War II, women could "participate" but they should not be "transformed by that participation." The bureau maintained this perspective, suggesting females should consider saving a portion of their income for a "hope-box" in light of the fact that their service as Marines was of a temporary nature. Service in the Corps represented a short-term exception justified by World War I. After the war, the Corps expected women to achieve their true goals through marriage. As one *Bulletin* article had pointed out, new female recruits had jokingly stated "I do" during their formal enlistment in a way that mirrored a wedding oath.[52]

By 1919 female Marines had been placed on inactive duty. As poet Corinne Rockwell Swain suggested, the "marinette" had done her duty patiently throughout the war but happily anticipated exchanging her uniform for more feminine finery, as Wilchinski had implied in her Dear John letter. Describing female Marines with words the Corps had purportedly discouraged use of in official guidance, Swain wrote: "Greeting you, dainty coquette / Fair as a rose after rain, / How can mere men-folk regret / Anne's in her 'civies' again?"[53] At last, the delicate female Marine could put aside her uniform and embrace her feminine appearance, a change both sexes supposedly embraced. With the war's end, the temporary disruption of gender norms had come to a close.

While it might be uplifting to celebrate the efforts and contributions of the first female Marines, it is more useful to understand how the addition of different societal subgroups can affect larger social dynamics within social institutions. Gender historians have focused much scholarship on the ramifications of gendered, militarized discourse in regard to larger questions of citizenship, yet there is more work to be done on how these ideas animate institutions. The Corps deftly manipulated ideas about gender to serve its larger institutional needs, ranging from recruiting to waging war, when forces outside its control forced a change upon it that some of its members disliked. Although the bureau gave some lip service to the importance of female Marines, the representations of females within its pages suggested a far greater reluctance to fully welcome them. Rather, female Marines' service rhetorically freed men to fight in a way that reinforced the image of the male Marine as a fighter who could now be replaced by three females doing the clerical work he and just one of his fellow male Marines had done. Although most female Marines had worked in the civilian world before enlisting and some, such as now-promoted Corporal Wilchinski, even had college degrees, those realities received little treatment in the pages of the *Bulletin*. Rather, even the women who wrote for the *Bulletin* upheld disfavorable tropes about women on the home front and showed themselves preoccupied with their appearance and their uniform, rather than with their real duties.

Epilogue

Anyone seeking to get a rise out of a Marine should try calling him or her a soldier. While polite Marines may bite their tongues, most will respond decidedly that they are not soldiers. This tendency has been characteristic of most twentieth-century Marines, but it was not the case for their nineteenth-century predecessors, who generally used the term "soldier" to describe themselves in both official and personal correspondence. This change is one example of how markedly the Corps transformed its external image and internal identity between 1874 and 1918. Essentially, the Corps made it mean something to be a Marine.

Many factors helped shape this process. Most importantly, the Corps' tenuous claims to a unique mission convinced Marines such as Richard Collum and Henry Cochrane that they needed to focus on image and identity. Although they flirted with missions like naval artillery, they realized that some of the Corps' oldest missions, such as providing security on board ship, had been tenuous since the beginning.

In large part, the Corps struggled to claim these missions because they interfered with the vision of naval officers to shape a distinctly American navy. This necessitated ending the British practice of using Marines to prevent mutiny. Moreover, the close relationship between the two services provided an other that sparked identity formation. The periods of greatest tension between the Corps and the Navy occurred when competing cultures clashed, such as at the end of the nineteenth century, when some naval officers wanted their sailors to more closely resemble elite soldiers. By contrast, Marine officers had been pursuing a similar vision for their personnel to improve institutional identity and public image since the Civil War. Establishing a historical record and reworking the institution's traditions and uniforms helped to serve these dual purposes.

As the Corps endured several crises with the Navy and gradually worked to improve its image, it also benefited from participation in numerous small wars, where it gained the reputation of fighting outnumbered in challenging circumstances. These small wars also necessitated a large increase in the number of recruits. Receptive to a trend known as diversified advertising in the civilian world, the Corps embraced the practice of selling itself to the public rather than simply providing notice of opportunities in help-wanted ads. Recruiters also appreciated the possibility of using this approach internally to increase all Marines' emotional attachment to their institution, including recruits and current and former Marines.

The Corps institutionalized these trends in 1912 with the establishment of the Recruiting Publicity Bureau. The new organization's name exemplified how closely the Corps had married its efforts to improve its external image and its internal identity. Although the bureau did not make drastic changes to the Corps' messaging, it greatly altered the volume of its efforts. Most noticeably, the Corps disseminated its desired image multiple times a week to thousands of American newspapers.

In selling itself not only to potential recruits but also intentionally to the general population, the Corps seized upon normative masculine ideals. For those seeking to become real men, the Corps claimed to offer the surest path to that goal. It established these claims in part at the Navy's expense, depicting Marines as fighters as opposed to sailors, whom it relegated to a far more supporting role.

The Corps also appealed to the public's sense of national identity, casting itself as a highly democratic institution. This democratic rhetoric epitomizes the Corps' receptiveness to larger trends in society and its ability to shift in response. Although the institution's hierarchical structure had differed to some extent from the other services in giving more responsibility to its noncommissioned officers, it now consciously stressed their unparalleled importance and took concrete steps to procure most of its officers from those ranks. While the Corps' democratic rhetoric greatly resonated with recruits, it had internal limits. Little frustrated enlisted Marines who served with the American Expeditionary Force more than when their officers failed to uphold the democratic messaging that they had heard so much of during recruitment and training. Enlisted Marines demonstrated less frustration with the Corps' experienced field-grade officers, whom they often adored for exemplifying the Corps' identity.

The Corps had to adapt after the first female Marines enlisted in 1918. Rhetorically, the Corps seized upon this change by claiming that employing women in clerical positions freed men to fight. In reality, most men in clerical positions already had been declared unfit for overseas service. Even as the bureau superficially professed to welcome female Marines as equals, moreover, it undercut any claims to equality or even to much utility in most of its representations of women in the *Bulletin*. The presence of female Marines ironically strengthened the image of the real Marine as the quintessential male fighter.

World War I provided the Corps with key opportunities to solidify its external image with the public. The Corps now believed the public knew it meant something to be a Marine. In a similar fashion, internally the Corps' members increasingly avoided using the word "Marine" synonymously with "soldier," as they had done so frequently throughout the institution's existence. Unlike the more general word "soldier," the moniker "Marine" epitomized a distinctive elite, capable of excellence in all things, in part due to his place atop the pantheon of American manhood. The Corps also realized that no single mission could provide its raison d'être. As such, it carefully pointed out that it had continued to fulfill a wide variety of responsibilities throughout the war.

After World War I and into the early twenty-first century, aspects of the Corps' image have remained relatively consistent, even as the institution has strengthened its training efforts and refined some of its traditions. Its image as an elite military institution has largely remained, and it still resists the perils of becoming too much like the Army. After repeated deployments to Iraq that mirrored the Army's contributions during Operation Iraqi Freedom, for example, Cmdt. James Conway believed the Corps had to stress its ties to the Navy. More specifically, he sought to return the Corps to its "expeditionary roots, which means shipborne operations in close-to-shore areas" around the world. The Corps has relied on Marine expeditionary units as the foundation for such operations.[1] These floating units of infantry, airpower, and logistics constitute an updated version of nineteenth-century landing parties. They represent the bifurcation in many ways between sailors who focus on the maintenance and operation of the ship and those who participate in combat. Only limited numbers of sailors, such as corpsmen, accompany Marines on shore in landing operations as they did at the beginning of the twentieth century. The fact that the nation has seen fit to keep Marines on ships similarly challenges the Navy's repeated, centuries-old arguments that the Corps could better serve the nation on shore. Having long sought to differentiate themselves from the Navy, Marines now confidently joke that they are the "men's department of the Navy," suggesting the Navy exists simply to transport them from one locale to the next.

To make these jokes, Marines had to reshape their relationship with sailors. During that long process, Marines began to view themselves as fighters and members of an elite institution with a proud history and traditions. This solution to the Corps' perennial existential crises began to take shape in the late nineteenth century thanks to the efforts of individual officers. In the first decades of the twentieth century, the Marine Corps increasingly drew on this historical foundation, particularly to reinforce its emergent identity and to help legitimize its service, especially by arguing it was the nation's oldest military institution. It finally institutionalized this historical bent in 1919. Cmdt. George Barnett determined to establish a historical section responsible for storing the Corps' historical records, developing a history of its contributions to World War I, and updating historical publications.[2]

Culture is never fixed, and thus the bureau's work was not fully complete. Still, it had made significant expansions and elaborations to the foundation of external image and internal identity developed by Collum, Cochrane, and others in the nineteenth century and then by recruiters and other individuals before World War I. Due to its continuing existential crises, it could not do this by linking its image and identity to a particular mission. Rather, it invoked a flexible and adaptable approach bound to the nation's normative ideals, including democracy and masculinity.

The continuity between Marines of the 1920s and Marines of the 1870s in terms of how they valued their institutional history emerged in a novel targeted at adolescent boys. For example, 1st Lt. Giles Bishop used prescriptive language to convey the change that occurred when Marines knew their history. Disturbed by his friend's hazy knowledge of the Corps' original duties, one boy urged him to read Collum's *History* because it was the "best thing to make you get the right kind of ginger into your work. It will make you proud of your job and proud to be a U.S. Marine." A knowledge of history infused the reader with esprit de corps, which "kept this outfit up to snuff." Bishop recognized the importance of historical knowledge in shaping and reinforcing the Corps' elite identity. Without this tradition, the Marine Corps knew that "no organized body of men could make a name for themselves."[3] Between 1874 and 1918 the Marines did just that, deliberately making a name for themselves in way that made it almost self-explanatory to any American just what it meant to be a Marine.

Notes

Preface

1. To understand these sentiments, see Karl Marlantes, *What It Is Like to Go to War* (New York: Grove Press, 2011), 10–12.

Introduction

1. Kemper Frey Cowing, comp., and Courtney Ryley Cooper, ed., *Dear Folks at Home: The Glorious Story of the United States Marines in France as Told by Their Letters from the Battlefield* (New York: Houghton Mifflin, 1919), 177. A sergeant was a fairly high-ranking enlisted position at this point in time. For the rank structure of the late nineteenth- and early twentieth-century Marine Corps, see Bernard Nalty, *Enlisted Ranks and Grades, U.S. Marine Corps, 1775–1958* (Washington, D.C.: Government Printing Office, 1970), 18 and 21; Mark Henry, *US Marine Corps in World War I, 1917–18* (Oxford: Osprey, 1999), n.p.

2. Cowing and Cooper, *Dear Folks at Home*, 172. The letter quoted one Marine amputee who had purportedly claimed, "The Boches may not have left me a leg to stand on, but I know I got three before they put me out of business. I plugged one, and got the other two with the bayonet." One story cited in the letter even mentioned a Marine who preferred the bayonet so much he had almost "forgotten he had ammunition" (Cowing and Cooper, 171, 177).

3. Cowing and Cooper, 172–73; U.S. House of Representatives, *Hearings before Committee on Naval Affairs of the House of Representatives on Estimates Submitted by the Secretary of the Navy* (Washington, D.C.: Government Printing Office, 1919), 810, 811.

4. U.S. House of Representatives, 810–11. The editors of *Dear Folks at Home*, however, merged the letters and added their own personal touches. None of the original letters, for example, mentioned German cowardice. See Cowing and Cooper, *Dear Folks at Home*, 172, for one example.

5. Henry Cochrane, "Reorganization of the Marine Corps," *Army and Navy Journal*, 20 Nov. 1875, 239; "A Corps of Frauds," *Saint Louis Post-Dispatch*, 17 Aug. 1875, 1; *Courier-Journal* (Louisville, KY), 21 Aug. 1875, 1. For the quartermaster scandal that precipitated some of these critiques, see "Washington: Some Particular Irregularities of the Quartermaster's Department of the Marines," *Courier-Journal* (Louisville, KY), 21 Aug. 1875, 1.

6. Jack Shulimson characterized these writings as simply a "fairly strenuous public relations campaign." See *The Marine Corps' Search for a Mission, 1880–1898* (Lawrence: University of Kansas Press, 1993), 16.

7. Edgar H. Schein, *Organizational Culture and Leadership*, 4th ed. (San Francisco: Jossey-Bass, 2010), 18.

8. Schein, *Organizational Culture and Leadership*, 74. Carol Reardon describes how the U.S. Army began stressing the importance of history around this period. However, Army officers used history as a tool to assist in the institution's professionalization. See *Soldiers and Scholars: The U.S. Army and the Uses of Military History, 1865–1920* (Lawrence: University Press of Kansas, 1990).

9. Carl H. Builder, *The Masks of War: American Military Styles in Strategy and Analysis* (Baltimore: Johns Hopkins University Press, 1989).

10. Mark R. Shulman, *Navalism and the Emergence of American Sea Power* (Annapolis, MD: Naval Institute Press, 1995), 2, 46. The classic work on "othering" is Edward Said's *Orientalism* (New York: Pantheon, 1978).

11. Works on the Royal Marines include Brian Edwards, *At the Turn of the Centuries: An Anniversary Portrait of the Marines in the Royal Navy of 1700, 1800, 1900 and After* (Portsmouth, UK: University of Portsmouth Printing Office, 2000); and Richard Brooks, *The Royal Marines, 1664 to the Present* (Annapolis, MD: Naval Institute Press, 2002).

12. Allan R. Millett, *Semper Fidelis: The History of the United States Marine Corps* (New York: Free Press, 1991), v–vi.

13. Jack Shulimson, "The Influence of the Spanish-American War on the U.S. Marine Corps," in *Theodore Roosevelt, the U.S. Navy, and the Spanish-American War*, ed. Edward J. Marolda (New York: Palgrave, 2001), 88.

14. See Mordecai Lee, *Congress vs. the Bureaucracy: Muzzling Agency Public Relations* (Norman: University of Oklahoma Press, 2012), 66–67.

15. "The Publicity Bureau: Its Equipment and Activities," *Recruiters' Bulletin* 3, no. 4 (Feb. 1917): 1 (hereafter *Bulletin*).

16. Some might argue whether the origin of the Navy's public relations can be found in the News Bureau or the Information Section, which evolved into today's Office of Information. Correspondence with Ryan Wadle, 22 Jun. 2017. For the impetus of World War I in this process, also see U.S. Navy, Navy Department, Bureau of Ordnance, *Navy Ordnance Activities, World War, 1917–1918* (Washington, D.C.: Government Printing Office, 1920), 218. It also points out the separation between the News Bureau and the Recruiting Bureau. Also see James B. Eller, "A Study of U.S. Fleet Operations Public Information Programs" (PhD diss., Boston University, 1965).

17. "Who Am I," Paul Woyshner Papers, Archives Branch, Marine Corps History Division (hereafter MCHD); David A. Whetten and Paul C. Godfrey, eds.,

Identity in Organizations: Building Theory through Conversations (Thousand Oaks, CA: SAGE Publications, 1998), 194; Pierre Bourdieu, *Distinction: A Social Critique of the Judgment of Taste*, trans. Richard Nice (London: Routledge, 2010), 481.

18. Bourdieu, 61.

19. Roger A. Beaumont, *Military Elites: Special Fighting Units in the Modern World* (Indianapolis: Bobbs-Merrill, 1974), 2, 16. For a historical overview of shock troops, see David C. Knight, *Shock Troops: The History of Elite Corps and Special Forces* (New York: Crescent, 1983). For more specific studies of World War I shock troops, see Tim Cook, *At the Sharp End: Canadians Fighting the Great War* (Toronto: Viking, 2007).

20. Wolfgang Schivelbusch, *The Culture of Defeat: On National Trauma, Mourning, and Recovery* (New York: Henry Holt, 2001), 255.

21. Craig M. Cameron, *American Samurai: Myth, Imagination, and the Conduct of Battle in the First Marine Division, 1941–1951* (New York: Cambridge University Press, 1994), 135, 23. He makes a convincing argument regarding the Battle of Peleliu that Marines sacrificed their troops needlessly, but has limited evidence for Belleau Wood.

22. Lowell Thomas, *Old Gimlet Eye: The Adventures of Smedley D. Butler as Told to Lowell Thomas* (New York: Farrar and Rinehart, 1933), 94.

23. In a letter written in 1912, for example, one officer discussed the merits of psychological tests in weeding out mentally deficient recruits, believing a careful selection process could improve esprit de corps and retention. Officer in Charge of Recruiting, Saint Paul, Minn. to Major General Commandant, 30 Apr. 1913, Robert Denig Papers, MCHD.

24. Douglas Porch, "The French Foreign Legion: The Mystique of Elitism," in *Elite Military Formations in War and Peace*, ed. Ion A. Hamish and Keith Neilson (Westport, CT: Praeger, 1986): 131. As Porch notes, it is "not important that the ideal does not always live up to the reality." It is the motive for service and the legion's status as "outcasts" rather than the service itself that the public finds compelling because it is tied to their image as "heroic desperados" (120). While many histories suggest the legion has always fought heroically, closer scrutiny reveals it was often on the verge of disaster. This was to be expected given its recruitment of desperate men. For historical comparisons to the legion, see "The U.S. Marine Corps Turns Out 'Two-Fisted' Chaps Who Can Use Their Heads," *Philadelphia Inquirer*, 5 Mar. 1920, 8.

25. Heather Streets, *Martial Races: The Military, Race, and Masculinity in British Imperial Culture, 1857–1914* (New York: Manchester University Press, 2004), 58, 59, and 157. For a similar argument, see Robert Clyde, *From Rebel to Hero: The Image of the Highlander, 1745–1830* (East Linton, SCT: Tuckwell Press, 1992), 157–59. Before the English subjugation of Scotland

in the eighteenth century, the English commonly depicted Highlanders as savage heathens. Streets has demonstrated how once the English had crushed military opposition and the Highlanders no longer posed a threat, the British no longer needed to other them as uncivilized brutes to justify the harsh measures the British had employed against them.

26. For a work that highlights important developments in the field of organizational theory, see Mary Jo Hatch and Majken Schultz, *Organizational Identity: A Reader* (New York: Oxford University Press, 2004).

27. Blake E. Ashforth and Fred Mael, "Social Identity Theory and the Organization," *Academy of Management Review* 14 (Jan. 1989): 21.

28. Millett, *Semper Fidelis*, 176.

29. For example, in her account of the Corps' occupation of Haiti, Mary Renda departed from previous works by focusing on the experiences of enlisted Marines. Yet, because Renda argues that the Corps co-opted enlisted Marines into serving the state in its imperial project, she does not ascribe much agency to enlisted Marines. See *Taking Haiti: Military Occupation and the Culture of U.S. Imperialism* (Chapel Hill: University of North Carolina Press, 2001), 12.

30. Peter Stanley, *White Mutiny: British Military Culture in India* (New York: New York University Press, 1998). The impetus for this change was the Indian Rebellion of 1857. While this mutiny has been treated as political history, it has not been fully studied from the perspective of ordinary soldiers. Government officials' decision to merge the two armies gave little thought to how these different military cultures might clash. While the British Army represented the old order in Great Britain, the East India Company Army offered more opportunity for officers and enlisted men alike, attracting those who sought to improve their standing in society. In regard to working-class culture, Stanley views the soldiers' responses as a "civil protest in a military setting," epitomizing the extent to which "civilian" influences shape the actions of service members. Stanley, 8, 12, 141, 162.

31. "Tis Not for Gold We're Here," *Bulletin*, Nov. 1916, 16.

32. Royal Marines began stressing these connections even earlier. See Marine Officer, "Economy of a Man of War," *Army and Navy Chronicle*, 19 Oct. 1837, 1.

33. Millett, *Semper Fidelis*, 130.

34. James Breckenridge to Mother, 8 May 1899, Breckenridge Papers, MCHD.

35. For the benefits of "mystique" in recruiting in other military institutions, see Dennis E. Showalter, "German Army Elites in World Wars I and II," in *Elite Military Formations in War and Peace*, ed. Ion A. Hamish and Keith Neilson (Westport, CT: Praeger, 1986), 154.

36. For uses of the word "brotherhood" by Marines, see Sgt. Harry Baldwin, "How Necessary is Love of the Corps to Successful Recruiting?," discussion

supplement, *Bulletin*, Feb. 1918, 2. He further explained that love "of the Corps is instilled in the heart of the newly enlisted recruit from the moment he enters the barracks as a 'rookie,' and it only ends at death."

37. By comparison, the Army allowed single soldiers under the age of thirty with two years' service to apply beginning in 1892. Edward M. Coffman, *The Regulars: The American Army, 1898–1941* (Cambridge, MA: Harvard University Press, 2004), 123. The Navy was slower to open the ranks. See "Let the Sailors Rise," *New York Times*, 31 Aug. 1897, 6. During World War I enlisted soldiers who had been commissioned constituted 8 percent of the Army's officer corps. See U.S. Senate, *Reorganization of the Army: Hearings before the Subcommittee of the Committee on Military Affairs*, 66th Cong., 1st sess., 4 Sep. 1919, 584. The Army commissioned far more soldiers from the ranks than the Navy. See Coffman, *Regulars*, 124. In the Navy 1,734 warrant officers and sailors received "temporary" commissions during World War I. See "Personnel," *Proceedings* 45 (1919): 1254. For one observer's opinion of the problems in the Army with encouraging the commissioning of enlisted soldiers, see William Harding Carter, *The American Army* (Indianapolis: Bobbs-Merrill, 1915), 228–31.

Chapter 1. Inspiration and Articulation

1. Christopher McKee, *A Gentlemanly and Honorable Profession: The Creation of the U.S. Naval Officer Corps, 1794–1815* (Annapolis, MD: Naval Institute Press, 1991), xiv, 65, 8.

2. McKee, xi.

3. Stephen Howarth, *To Shining Sea: A History of the United States Navy, 1775–1998* (Norman: University of Oklahoma Press, 1999), 55; Craig L. Symonds, "Defining an American Navy, 1783–1812," in *In Peace and War: Interpretations of American Naval History*, ed. Kenneth J. Hagan and Michael T. McMaster (Westport, CT: Praeger, 2008), 18–19.

4. Linda Maloney, "The War of 1812: What Role for Sea Power?," in *In Peace and War: Interpretations of American Naval History,* ed. Kenneth J. Hagan and Michael T. McMaster (Westport, CT: Praeger, 2008), 45–46; Howarth, *To Shining Sea,* 57; E. B. Potter, *Sea Power: A Naval History*, 2nd ed. (Annapolis, MD: Naval Institute Press, 1981), 109. A recession that occurred two years later had a significant impact on the ships' progress. See Harold D. Langley, "Protector of Commerce and Defender of the Nation: The U.S. Navy between Wars, 1815–1844," in *In Peace and War: Interpretations of American Naval History*, ed. Kenneth J. Hagan and Michael T. McMaster (Westport, CT: Praeger, 2008), 49.

5. By contrast, the Army was established on 14 Jun. 1775 and the Navy on 13 October 1775.

6. *Journals of the Continental Congress, 1774–1789*, vol. 3, ed. Worthington C. Ford (Washington, D.C.: Government Printing Office, 1905), 348. Allan Millett argues that the influence of the British Royal Marines can be seen in the fact that each of the individual state navies had marines as well. Millett, *Semper Fidelis*, 7–23. Naval officer Stephen Luce had a different interpretation of the Continental Congress, arguing that its emphasis on "good seamen" showed it had "little conception of the nature of a properly organized Marine Corps." Richard Collum, introduction to *History of the United States Marine Corps* (Philadelphia: L. R. Hamersly, 1890), 21.

7. For the struggle to create a Navy for men who knew little of these matters, see Sam Willis, *The Struggle for Sea Power: A Naval History of the American Revolution* (New York: W. W. Norton, 2016), 90–91.

8. For a detailed treatment of the Corps during this period, see Charles R. Smith, *Marines in the Revolution: A History of the Continental Marines in the American Revolution, 1775–1783* (Washington, D.C.: Government Printing Office, 1975). Millett states that Marines were a "bit more expert" in these landings than sailors, although he does not explain how he arrived at this conclusion. Millett, *Semper Fidelis*, 15.

9. For this period of the Corps' history, see A. B. C. Whipple, *To the Shores of Tripoli: The Birth of the U.S. Navy and Marines* (Annapolis, MD: Naval Institute Press, 2001). U.S. Congress, *Statutes at Large*, Vol. 1, Ch. 12, Section 1 (Approved 27 March 1794), 3rd Cong., 1st sess. (Boston: Charles C. Little and James Brown, 1850).

10. By comparison, the act called for five naval officers (one captain and four lieutenants) as well as a chaplain, a surgeon, and about 250 sailors of varying ranks. Paul H. Nicolas, *Historical Record of the Royal Marine Forces*, vol. 1 (London: Thomas and William Boone, 1845), x. This practice was not always followed, perhaps due to manning challenges. An 1813 act authorized only sixty Marines for a 74-gun vessel. Benjamin Homans, *Laws of the United States, in Relation to the Navy and the Marine Corps* (Washington, D.C.: J. and G. S. Gideon, 1841), 91.

11. U.S. Congress, *Statutes at Large*, Vol. 1, Ch. 72, Section 1 (Approved 11 Jul. 1798), 5th Cong., 2nd session. (Boston: Charles C. Little and James Brown, 1845), 595.

12. Millett, *Semper Fidelis*, 32–33, 42. For the Corps' ceremonial duties in port see *The Life of the Late General William Eaton* (Brookfield, MA: E. Merriam and Co., 1815), 384; and U.S. House of Representatives, *Hearings before the Subcommittee on Naval Academy and Marine Corps*, Committee on Naval Affairs, House of Representatives, on the Status of the Marine Corps, 61st Cong., 2nd sess., 7 Jan. 1909, 204.

13. Millett, *Semper Fidelis*, 36–37, 40.

14. *The Weekly Register*, "Events of the War," 18 Sept. 1813, 45.

15. For the British relationship, see Frederick Marryat, *Complete Works of Captain F. Marryatt*, vol. 1 (Philadelphia: Jesper Harding, 1850), 261. Marryat had served as an officer in the Royal Navy. Also see Nicolas, *Historical*, 252.

16. Millett, *Semper Fidelis*, 41–42; Lt. J. M. Keever, USN, to the Secretary of the Navy, 6 March 1830, appendix to Secretary of the Navy John Branch to the U.S. Senate, 23 March 1830, "On the Expediency of Dispensing with the Marine Corps as Part of the Armed Equipment of a Vessel-of-War," *American State Papers: Naval Affairs*, vol. 3 (Washington, D.C.: Gales and Seaton, 1960), 564.

17. McKee, *Gentlemanly and Honorable Profession*, 101. Embroiled in the Napoleonic Wars, the British desperately needed manpower to maintain their fleet. Moreover, the British government did not recognize naturalized U.S. citizens, believing that a citizen born in Britain could not renounce that citizenship to become a citizen of another nation. Sailors, preferring the better conditions of service in the U.S. Navy, loathed the threat of British impressment, some considering it akin to "slavery." Myra C. Glenn, *Jack Tar's Story: The Autobiographies and Memoirs of Sailors in Antebellum America* (New York: Cambridge University Press, 2010), 70.

18. See, for example, "Marine Corps," *National Gazette*, 13 March 1828, 3. For the stories ordinary seamen told about their experience in the War of 1812, see Glenn, *Jack Tar's Story*, 58 and 71. Also see Donald R. Hickey, *Don't Give Up the Ship! Myths of the War of 1812* (Urbana: University of Illinois Press, 2006).

19. John Brannan, *Official Letters of Military and Naval Officers of the United States during the War with Great Britain* (Washington City: Way and Gideon, 1823), 52. Hull also described the loss of one Marine officer, who had been leading his men in preparation to board the enemy, thus showing their use in combat, which naval officers later claimed had become irrelevant.

20. William M. Fowler Jr., *Jack Tars and Commodores: The American Navy, 1783–1815* (Boston: Houghton Mifflin, 1984), 174; Master Commandant to Lewis Warrington to the Secretary of the Navy, 6 March 1830, "On the Expediency," 561; Brannan, *Official Letters*, 330. Writing from New Orleans in 1815, Daniel L. Patterson made similar comments, grateful for the support of his Marine officer. Brannan, 463.

21. *American State Papers: Naval Affairs*, 3:561, 562; William S. Dudley, ed., *The Naval War of 1812: A Documentary History: 1813*, vol. 2 (Washington, D.C.: Government Printing Office, 1992), 616–19; McKee, *Gentlemanly and Honorable Profession*, 166. For the idea that manifest destiny occurred not only on land but at sea, see Brian Rouleau, *With Sails Whitening Every Sea* (Ithaca, N.Y.: Cornell University Press, 2014).

22. Potter, *Sea Power*, 117; Langley, "Protector of Commerce," 47 and 56.

23. For a derogatory description of landsmen or "green hands" published the same year the *Erie* sailed without Marines, see "A Civilian," *Sketches of Naval Life with Notices of Men, Manners and Scenery, on the Shores of the Mediterranean*, vol. 1 (New Haven, CT: Hezekiah Howe, 1829), 48.

24. McKee, *Gentlemanly and Honorable Profession*, xiv; Keever, "On the Expediency," 564.

25. Simultaneously, in 1829 President Andrew Jackson suggested incorporating the Corps into the Army as a means of "curing the many defects in its organization." U.S. Congress, *House Journal*, 21st Cong., 1st sess., 8 Dec. 1829. In 1829 the House of Representatives Committee on Military Affairs urged the consolidation of the Corps with the Army to resolve the Corps' "anomalous" position. Blaming the original Continental Congress for organizing the Corps almost accidentally, one commentator believed the best solution would be to make the Corps a part of the Army in the belief that soldiers would eagerly serve on board naval vessels for variety. "The Navy," *Military and Naval Magazine of the United States*, Sep. 1834, 15. For other examples see Alexander Slidell Mackenzie, *The Life of Commodore Oliver Hazard Perry*, vol. 2 (New York: Harper and Brothers, 1843), 135. Royal Marine officers reacted similarly, especially when they felt their institution was not being treated as well as the Royal Navy. See A Subaltern, "Promotion in the Corps of Marines," *United Service Journal and Naval and Military Magazine*, 1832, 538–39. The situation of both U.S. and Royal Marines was strikingly similar at times. Neither, for example, could serve in Navy courts-martial at sea. See *The Parliamentary Debates*, vol. 79 (London: Wyman and Sons, 1900), 1480–81; and McKee, *Gentlemanly and Honorable Profession*, 33.

26. A similar belief could be found in the Royal Navy. See William Nugent Glascock, *Naval Sketch-Book: The Service Afloat and Ashore*, vol. 1 (Philadelphia: E. L. Carey and A. Hart, 1835), 2 and 270.

27. George Alfred Townsend, *Washington, Outside and Inside* (Hartford, CT: James Betts, 1874), 384. For similar comments not put as rhetorically but from the same time period, see Harry Bluff, "Our Navy," *Southern Literary Messenger* 7 (May/Jun. 1841), 379.

28. See the recounting of U.S. sailors attacking Brazilian Marines framed in the traditional distrust of the sailor for the Marine as a sign of a growing "national or professional spirit." "Anecdote," *Long-Island Star*, 17 May 1827, 1.

29. Captain Thos. Ap Gatesby Jones to Hon. John Branch, 5 March 1830, "On the Expediency," 569. Emphasis in original.

30. Justice, "For the Evening Post," *Evening Post* (New York), 13 Jan. 1830, 2. For the extent to which the U.S. Navy absorbed much from the British Navy, see McKee, *Gentlemanly and Honorable Profession*, 215.

31. "Art. V. Report of the Secretary of the Navy to the President of the United States, December 1, 1829," *North American Review* 21 (April 1830): 386.

32. Charles Stewart to Secretary of the Navy John Branch, 8 March 1830, "On the Expediency," 565; "The Marine Corps," *Evening Post* (New York), 9 April 1830, 2. For this continuing trend in naval culture, see Peter Karsten, *The Naval Aristocracy: The Golden Age of Annapolis and the Emergence of Modern American Navalism* (Annapolis, MD: Naval Institute Press, 1972), 205–7.

33. Richard Henry Dana Jr., *Two Years before the Mast: A Personal Narrative* (Boston: Houghton Mifflin, 1911), 261, 270; Herman Melville, *White-Jacket or the World in a Man-of-War* (New York: United States Book Company, 1892), 377. Various explanations exist for the term's origins. Some said it developed from the nautical term "hawse" while others linked it to sea horses. William S. Walsh, *A Handy Book of Curious Information* (Philadelphia: J. P. Lippincott, 1913), 399. Others explored the impracticality of having cavalry at sea. Glascock, *Naval Sketch-Book*, 11–12. Marines appropriated these terms at the beginning of the twentieth century to celebrate their range of duties. See, for example, "The Secret Is Out: There Are Horse Marines," *Duluth News-Tribune*, 13 Jan. 1918, 2.

34. Samuel T. Fallows, *The Progressive Dictionary of the English Language* (Chicago: Progressive Publishing, 1885), 252. In his account Dana described how the term "Marine" was viewed as even worse than a mere "soldier." Dana, *Two Years before the Mast*, 253.

35. Pierce Egan, *Grose's Classical Dictionary of the Vulgar Tongue*, rev. and corrected (London: Sherwood, Neely, and Jones, 1823); Eric Partridge and Jacqueline Simpson, *The Routledge Dictionary of Historical Slang*, reprint (London: Routledge, 2000), 246. For an anecdote about the term's origins analogous to the phrase "tell it to the Marines" in that it purportedly originated from English royalty, see "A Story of William IV," *Tit-Bits: From All the Most Interesting Books, Periodicals and Newspapers in the World*, 18 March 1882, 3. For an example of the term's usage in nonmilitary contexts, see "The Hallroom Boys," *Fort Worth Star-Telegram*, 17 Dec. 1908, 3. In perhaps a similar manner, the institution's name was often spelled as "Marine Corpse." See W. P. Drury, *The Peradventures of Private Pagett* (London: Chapman and Hall, 1915), 68. For an explanation of this spelling's origin see Tristam, "Retirement of the Officers of Marines," *Colburn's United Service Magazine*, 1848, 31.

36. Charles G. Leland, ed., *A Dictionary of Slang, Jargon, and Cant* (New York: George Bell and Sons, 1897), 285. See also H. C. Johnson, "The Dead Marine," in *Voices from the Press: A Collection of Sketches, Essays, and Poems by Practical Printers*, ed. James G. Brenton (New York: Charles B. Norton, 1850), 163–66.

37. Marines often interchanged the term "Marine" with soldier. For example, see Capt. Charles McCawley to Col. Cmdt. John Harris, 5 Jul. 1862, Headquarters Marine Corps (hereafter HQMC), "LR, 1818–1915," Entry 42, Box 42, Record Group 127. For a detailed journal that does little to distinguish Marines from sailors, see Charles R. Smith, comp., *The Journals of Marine Second Lieutenant Henry Bulls Watson, 1845–1848* (Washington, D.C.: History and Museums Division, Headquarters, U.S. Marine Corps, 1990).

38. First Lieutenant Edward [?] Reynolds, USMC to Col. Cmdt. John Harris, 23 March 1861, HQMC, "LR, 1818–1915," Record Group 127, National Archives (hereafter cited as "LR, 1818–1915," RG 127). Emphasis in original. First Lieutenant Reynolds to Col. Cmdt. John Harris, 23 March 1861, "LR, 1818–1915," RG 127.

39. McKee, *A Gentlemanly and Honorable Profession*, 122.

40. Captain John Broome, USMC, to Captain Palmer, USN, copy sent to Col. Cmdt. John Harris, USMC, 11 Dec. 1862, "LR, 1818–1915," RG 127. The executive officer was the second in command of a naval vessel. A gun carriage was the mechanism required to use naval guns. See *A Naval Encyclopedia* (Philadelphia: L. R. Hamersly, 1880), 331. Also see Capt. Charles McCawley, USMC to Col. Cmdt. John Harris, USMC, 9 Jun. 1862, Office of the Commandant, Historical Section, "LR, 1818–1915," Box 42, RG 127.

41. For a similar occurrence, see U.S. House of Representatives, Hearings before the Subcommittee on Naval Academy and Marine Corps, 191. For a similar modern-day account, see Andrew A. Buffalo, *Swift, Silent and Surrounded: Marine Corps Sea Stories and Politically Incorrect Common Sense*, vol. 1 (Riverview, FL: S&B Distribution, 2010), 214. For a scholarly treatment of the subject see Simon J. Bronner, *Crossing the Line: Violence, Play and Drama in Naval Equator Traditions* (Amsterdam: Amsterdam University Press, 2006).

42. Miles M. Oviatt, *A Civil War Marine at Sea*, ed. Mary P. Livingston (Shippensburg, PA: White Mane, 1998), 66. For the role of African Americans in the Navy during the Civil War, see David L. Valuska, *The African American in the Union Navy, 1861–1865* (New York: Garland, 1993).

43. Captain John Broome, USMC, to Capt. James Palmer, USN, copy sent to Col. Cmdt. John Harris 11 Dec. 1862, "LR, 1818–1915," RG 127. In 1880, for example, Lt. George Elliott married Annie Badger, the daughter of naval officer Oscar Badger and sister of naval officer Charles Badger. Elliott's groomsmen included four men in the Navy as well as two Army artillery officers. Only one of his groomsmen was a Marine. "A Wedding in High Life," *Washington Post*, 7 Jan. 1880. Also see "Married," *New York Times*, 18 Jun. 1859, 5; and "Lieut. Neville's Wife Happy," *New York Times*, 14 Jun. 1898, 1. For suggestions of friendship and other family between the branches, see "The Cowie-Gedney

Wedding," *Washington Post*, 16 Feb. 1881, 4; and "Linked for Life," *Washington Post*, 19 Oct. 1882, 1. For a naval officer whose ushers included one line officer, one engineer, and two Marine officers, see "Shepard-Watt," *The Sun*, 16 Oct. 1893, 6.

44. "On the Expediency of Merging the Marine Corps into the Artillery or Infantry of the Army," *American State Papers: Military Affairs*, vol. 4 (Washington: Gales and Seaton, 1860), 275. For an account accusing Marine officers of being especially guilty of this tendency see "Article V. Report of the Secretary of the Navy to the President of the United States, Dec. 1, 1829," *North American Review* 31 (Apr. 1830): 363. Also see Millett, *Semper Fidelis*, 61.

45. U.S. Congress, *Statutes at Large*, Vol. 4, Ch. 132, Section 2 (approved 30 Jun. 1834), 23rd Cong., 1st. Sess. (Boston: Charles C. Little and James Brown, 1846).

46. Philo Classiarius Miles, "The New Regulations of the Marine Corps," *Army and Navy Chronicle*, Feb. 11, 1836, 93. For similar comments see "Statement of Brevet Lieutenant Colonel Freeman, of the Marine Corps, complaining of the operation of the regulations of the Navy, under the law of 1834," *American State Papers: Military Affairs* 4:835–37. After two months had passed since putting Marine officers more directly under the commanding naval officer of navy yards where Marines acted as sentries and guards, he believed the act had "humiliate[d] and degrade[d]" the Corps.

47. "The Marine Corps," *Army and Navy Chronicle*, 11 Feb. 1836, 89. For the 1818 regulation see *Public Documents*, vol. 3 (Washington, D.C.: Gales and Seaton, 1836), 7. "The Marine Corps," *Army and Navy Chronicle*, 11 Feb. 1836, 89. For the 1818 regulation see *Public Documents*, vol. 3 (Washington, D.C.: Gales and Seaton, 1836), 7. 30 Jun. 1834, 725, which provided for money to be used to build a barracks outside the Navy Yard if needed. U.S. Congress, *Statutes at Large*, Vol. 1, Ch. 12, Section 1 (approved 27 March 1794), 3d Cong., 1st session (Boston: Charles C. Little and James Brown, 1850).

48. Lieutenant John G. McReynolds, *Remarks and Suggestions on the Organization and Re-organization of the Marine Corps* (Brooklyn: Lees and Foules, 1847), 3. For negative images of Royal Marine officers in novels written by a former Royal Navy officer, see William Nugent Glascock, *Land Sharks and Sea Gulls*, vol. 2 (Philadelphia: Lea and Blanchard, 1838), 23–24. Naval officers probably borrowed this depiction from British naval officers, who were sometimes served by Marines while at sea. See Basil Hall, *Fragments of Voyages and Travels*, vol. 3 (Edinburgh: Robert Cadell, 1832), 285–86.

49. Historiography on the Corps' contributions during the Civil War is divided. Marine historians have taken a mixed view of the Corps' participation in the Civil War. Robert Heinl suggests the Corps played a very marginal role (*Soldiers of the Sea*, 71). Alan Millett points to the successes of Marine gun crews and, to a lesser extent, Marine landing parties (*Semper Fidelis*, 100).

David Sullivan's more recent four-volume series seeks to illuminate the Corps' contributions during the war. Much of his proof, however, derives from the formulaic after-action reports of naval officers, which do not explain how Marines contributed anything distinctive. See *The United States Marine Corps in the Civil War*, 4 vols. (Shippensburg, PA: White Mane, 1997).

50. Oviatt, *Civil War Marine*, 89. The lowest-ranking seamen and Marines shared 35 percent of the prize money. See William H. Roberts, *Now for the Contest: Coastal and Oceanic Naval Operations in the Civil War* (Lincoln: University of Nebraska Press, 2004), 103.

51. Officers had a slightly less monotonous experience, in part because of a wider range of social activities. For accounts emphasizing the social aspects of officers' wartime experiences, see Frederick Peet, *Personal Experiences in the Civil War* (New York: F. T. Peet, 1905), 75; and Frank L. Church, *Civil War Marine: A Diary of the Red River Expedition, 1864* (Washington, D.C.: Government Printing Office, 1975). At its peak in 1875 the Navy had about 51,000 sailors compared to the Corps' peak number of fewer than 4,000. During the war 148 Marines were killed in action while 131 were wounded. By comparison, 2,112 sailors were killed in action while 1,170 were wounded. The likelihood of being killed in action was almost 4 percent for both sailors and Marines.

52. Henry O. Gusley, *The Southern Journal of a Civil War Marine: The Illustrated Note-Book of Henry O. Gusley*, annotated and ed. Edward T. Cotham Jr. (Austin: University of Texas Press, 2006), 63. Gusley was not the only Marine to use the word "monotony" in his diary; see Oviatt, *Civil War Marine*, 12. Other published accounts of the war written by enlisted Marines include C. Carter Smith Jr., *Two Naval Journals, 1864, at the Battle of Mobile Bay. The Journal of a Confederate Sailor aboard the CSS* Tennessee *and the Journal of a U.S. Marine aboard the USS* Hartford (Chicago: Wyvern Press of S.F.E., 1964).

53. Pvt. Lawrence Carpenter to Col. Cmdt. John Harris, USMC, 15 Jun. 61, Office of the Commandant, Historical Section "LR, 1818–1915," Box 42, RG 127. Similarly, Henry Meredith asked for a discharge on the grounds of his "ambitions to succeed in life." Pvt. Henry Meredith to Col. Cmdt. John Harris, USMC, 16 Jun. 1861, Office of the Commandant, Historical Section, "LR, 1818–1915," Box 41, RG 127. Also see Lt. Col. Ward Marston to Col. Cmdt. John Harris, 18 Jun. 1862, Office of the Commandant, Historical Section, "LR, 1818–1915," Box 41, RG 127.

54. Private Henry Meredith to Col. Cmdt. John Harris, USMC, 16 Jun. 1861, Office of the Commandant, Historical Section, "LR, 1818–1915," Box 41, RG 127.

55. About 2,200 Marines deserted, and of those about 550 returned on their own to the Corps. David Stephen Heidler, Jeanne T. Heidler, and David J. Coles, *Encyclopedia of the American Civil War: A Political, Social, and*

Military History (New York: W. W. Norton, 2000), 1251. About 200,000 soldiers are thought to have deserted during the war, 40 percent of whom were returned to their units. Also see Thomas R. Kemp, "Community and War: The Civil War Experience of Two New Hampshire Towns," in Maris A. Vinovskis, ed., *Toward a Social History of the American Civil War: Exploratory Essays* (New York: Cambridge University Press, 1990): 41; McPherson, *Ordeal by Fire*, 468. For discussions of desertion, see Major John G. Reynolds to CMC, 28 April 1861, Office of the Commandant, Historical Section, "LR, 1818–1915," Box 41, RG 127; Major John G. Reynolds to Governor Andrew, 27 April 1861, Office of the Commandant, Historical Section, copy in "LR, 1818–1915," Box 42, RG 127. Many enlisted Marines seem to have deserted because of ethnic ties while others sought to join other services to be promoted.

56. Soldiers could find their service just as dull, and more than ten thousand transferred to the Navy by the end of the war. Michael J. Bennett, *Union Jacks: Yankee Sailors in the Civil War* (Chapel Hill: University of North Carolina Press, 2004), 15.

57. L. W. Forney to Secretary of the Navy Gideon Welles, 4 Jan. 1864, copy in Office of the Commandant, Historical Section, "LR, 1818–1915," Box 43, RG 127; Robert Huntington to Father, 30 Mar. 1865, Robert Huntington Papers, Box 1, MCHD.

58. Chester G. Hearn, *Ellet's Brigade: The Strangest of Them All* (Baton Rouge: Louisiana State University Press, 2000); Heinl, *Soldiers of the Sea*, 77. The Mississippi Marine Brigade consisted of infantry, artillery, and cavalry. It served the purpose of conducting short landing operations to subdue transportable Confederate artillery and other Confederate forces seeking to attack naval vessels. For a further description of their tasks, see "Ellet's Marine Brigade," *Philadelphia Inquirer*, 29 Nov. 1862, 2. Ironically, its commander, Albert D. Ellet, received the rank of brigadier general, which ranked above the Corps' commandant, Col. John Harris.

59. James E. Valle, *Rocks and Shoals: Naval Discipline in the Age of Fighting Sail* (Annapolis, MD: Naval Institute Press, 1980), 104; McKee, *Gentlemanly and Honorable Profession*, 258, 259; Christopher M. Bell and Bruce A. Elleman, *Naval Mutinies of the Twentieth Century: An International Perspective* (London: Frank Cass, 2003), 1; Secretary of the Navy J. C. Dobbin, quoted in M. Almy Aldrich, *History of the United States Marine Corps* (Boston: Henry L. Shepard, 1875), 114; Millett, *Semper Fidelis*, 100. For morale during blockade duty, see Valle, *Rocks and Shoals*, 102.

60. For the military's struggles with public relations during the Civil War, for example, see Scott M. Cutlip, *Public Relations History: From the 17th to the 20th Century* (Hillsdale, NJ: Lawrence Erlbaum Associates, 1995), 134–37.

61. *Public Ledger*, 12 Sep. 1861, 4, emphasis in original; *Philadelphia Inquirer*, 2 March 1863; *Public Ledger*, 17 Sep. 1862, 4.

62. *Philadelphia Inquirer*, 11 March 1864, 7, and 22 April 1864, 6. By contrast, an Army ad published on the same page offered the inducement of a commissioning. For a similar Marine ad emphasizing the benefits of service, especially for "soldiers," see *Public Ledger*, 11 Jun. 1866, 3. This ad suggests the Corps sought recruits from those who had served in the Army. The Corps would continue to seek former soldiers as well as Marines to reenlist. *New York Herald*, 24 April 1875, 11.

63. Gary Rutledge, "The Rhetoric of United States Marine Corps Enlisted Recruitment: A Historical Study and Analysis of the Persuasive Approach Utilized" (M.A. thesis, University of Kansas, 1974), 50. Gary Rutledge dates the "Wanted" poster to 1866 and claims that Henry Cochrane had five hundred copies printed while on recruiting duty in Chicago (52).

64. Mark E. Neely and Harold Holzer, *The Union Image: Popular Prints of the Civil War North* (Chapel Hill: University of North Carolina Press, 2000), 50–51; Bennett, *Union Jacks*, 14, 156–57; Harold Langley, *Social Reform in the United States Navy, 1798–1862* (Annapolis, MD: Naval Institute Press, 1967), 185–204.

65. In 1864, for example, the Department of the Navy published ads seeking men for the "Naval Service and Marine Corps." Untitled, *New Hampshire Sentinel*, 14 Apr. 1864, 3; "Local Matters," *Boston Daily Advertiser*, 30 March 1864, 1.

66. For the confusion regarding bounties for Marine recruits during the Civil War, see John W. Butterfield, *A Digest of Decisions in the Office of the Second Comptroller of the Treasury*, 3rd ed. (Washington, D.C.: Government Printing Office, 1869), 37–38. Also see James W. Geary, *We Need Men: The Union Draft in the Civil War* (DeKalb: Northern Illinois University Press, 1991).

67. For general works on Civil War recruiting, see Eugene C. Murdock, *One Million Men: The Civil War Draft in the North* (Madison: State Historical Society of Wisconsin, 1971); and *Patriotism Limited: The Civil War Draft and the Bounty System, 1862–1865* (Kent, OH: Kent State University, 1967).

68. Sgt. B. W. Hopper to Col. Cmdt. John Harris, 24 Feb. 1862, Office of the Commandant, Historical Section, "LR, 1818–1915," Box 42, RG 127.

69. Linderman, *Embattled Courage*, 376; Capt. James Lewis to Col. Cmdt John Harris, 5 Oct. 1863, Office of the Commandant, Historical Section, "LR, 1818–1915," Box 43, RG 127; Maj. John Broome to Col. Cmdt. John Harris, 30 Jul. 1865, Office of the Commandant, Historical Section, "LR, 1818–1915," Box 44, RG 127; Bennett, *Union Jacks*, 14. For naval recruiting that played up this reality, see Bennett, 17–18.

70. Millett, *Semper Fidelis*, 99; Heinl, *Soldiers of the Sea*, *80*–83; Google books: Ensign William L. Rodgers, "Notes on the Naval Brigade," *Proceedings* 14 (1888): 58; Millett, *Semper Fidelis*, 95; Adm. David Porter to Col. Cmdt. John Harris, 17 Nov. 1863, Office of the Commandant, Historical Section, "LR, 1818–1915," Box 43, RG 127.

71. The Army's primary attack on the fort was ultimately successful. "Wilmington," *New York Herald*, 19 Jan. 1865, 1. One of Porter's sons who accompanied him to Fort Fisher would serve in the Corps. "Col. C.P. Porter Dead," *Washington Post*, 21 May 1914, 2.

72. George Dewey, *Autobiography of George Dewey, Admiral of the Navy* (New York: Charles Scribner's Sons, 1913), 135.

73. Capt. L. L. Dawson to Col. Cmdt. John Harris, 27 Jan. 1865, Office of the Commandant, Historical Section, "LR, 1818–1915," Box 44, RG 127; One Thousand and One Marines to Editor of the *Herald*, *New York Herald*, 21 Jun. 1866, 1. In his memoir, Dahlgren recalled how three Marine officers stated how they did not want to put their men in danger by "attacking works." Dahlgren commented that he found this "rather hurtful. What are marines for?" Madeleine Vinton Dahlgren, *Memoir of John A. Dahlgren, Rear Admiral United States Navy* (Boston: James R. Osgood, 1882), 407.

74. "U.S. Army" to the Editor, *Army and Navy Journal*, 30 Jun. 1866, 713.

75. First Lt. P. C. Pope to Col. Cmdt. John Harris, 30 Jul. 1863, Office of the Commandant, Historical Section, "LR, 1818–1915," Box 43, RG 127; Flag Officer Samuel F. Du Pont to Col. Cmdt. John Harris, 25 March 1862, "LR, 1818–1915," RG 127.

76. Quoted in Millett, *Semper Fidelis*, 92; *Senate Journal*, 37th Cong., 34rd Sess., 22 December 1862, 67. Harris had made similar comments in response to Garland's request that Marines receive Army instead of Navy rations. See Col. Cmd. John Harris to Maj. Augustus Garland, 18 Jun. 1863, copy in "LR, 1818–1915," RG 127.

77. "A Word for the Marine Corps," *Philadelphia Inquirer*, 29 Jul. 1863, 4.

78. Like observers of the U.S. Marines, British observers felt that the Marines had not received enough recognition. See Glascock, *Naval Sketch-Book*, 266; and "The Royal Marines," *Colburn's United Service Magazine* 153 (1880): 221. For a similar "contempt" between Royal Marines and British sailors see Glascock, 267. For the argument over whether it was easier to turn sailors into soldiers or vice versa, see Glascock, 270.

79. Rear Adm. Henry Walke, *Naval Scenes and Reminiscences of the Civil War in the United States* (New York: F. R. Reed, 1877), 243.

80. See, for example, "The Marine Corps," *Army and Navy Journal*, 6 March 1875, 472. Army officers, equally worried about budgetary cuts, formed the Military Service Institution of the United States in 1878 to lobby Congress. Stephen

Skowronek, *Building a New American State: The Expansion of National Administrative Capacities, 1877–1920* (New York: Cambridge University Press, 1982), 92.

81. Even the band, though, was not considered sacrosanct by at least one congressman. For a congressman's humorous defense of the band that ensured the amendment to abolish it was shot down, see *Harper's New Monthly Magazine*, Jul. 1876, 318.

82. "Sitting Bull Brevities," *Kalamazoo Gazette*, 26 August 1876, 1. While the article explained how many Marine officers hoped for the opportunity to aid the Army in subduing Native Americans, the headline suggested the Corps was an organization interested largely in appearance.

83. The article was almost as critical of the Navy, describing it as a "fraud" and the Corps as a "shameful fraud upon the Navy." *Cincinnati Daily Enquirer*, 29 Dec. 1875, 4. *North American Review*, 2 Jan. 1867, 2; and "The Marine Corps," *The Sun*, 2 Jan. 1867, 1.

84. The Recruiting Publicity Bureau would address the alternate definition of the USMC acronym in the early twentieth century. See "Why the Marines Prosper," *Bulletin*, Sep. 1917, 18; and another publication likely tied to the bureau: Willis John Abbot, *Soldiers of the Sea: The Story of the United States Marine Corps* (New York: Dodd, Mead, 1918), 4. "Top-Heaviness," *Washington Post*, 22 Dec. 1877, 2. Also see *Idaho Daily Avalanche*, 19 Jan. 1876, 2.

85. Marines, however, argued they had fewer officers per enlisted men than other branches. The Army had one officer for every thirteen and one-third men, the Navy one for every five and one-third men, and the Corps an officer for every twenty-seven men. "The Marine Corps," *ANJ*, 31 Jan. 1874, 391. Also see Shulimson, *Marine Corps' Search*, 21, for politicians' ability to influence where officers were stationed.

86. "Absolute Inutility," *Washington Post*, 2 February 1878, 2. For the increasing commonality of this kind of sexualized language during the course of the nineteenth century that "unsexed a man, made him bisexual, or turned him into a woman," see E. Anthony Rotundo, *American Manhood: Transformations in Masculinity from the Revolution to the Modern Era* (New York: Basic Books, 1993), 271–72.

87. For similar suggestions see a letter to the editor written by Subscriber, "Abuses in the Marine Corps," *Washington Post*, 8 Feb. 1882, 2. For the newspaper's desire for more commissions from the ranks for all branches, see "Give Merit a Chance," *Washington Post*, 21 Jan. 1881, 2.

88. "A Mellifluous Marine," *Washington Post*, 27 Aug. 1878, 1. The journalist might have sought to overturn ideas of class in the Marine Corps, but he maintained common ideas about race. The enlisted Marine stated that if rumors were true he would not be enlisting again. Upon hearing that a "colored man" might be

commissioned, the journalist responded in "utter amazement." For society's generally negative view of the military, especially officers, see Charles A. Byler, *Civil-Military Relations on the Frontier and Beyond, 1865–1917* (Westport, CT: Praeger, 2006), 1–20.

89. The *ANJ*, while supportive of the Corps' continued existence, generally agreed with the journalist and the purported conclusion of the Marine, writing that the "trouble with the marines is simply this, that while they have always and the best noncommissioned officers and privates to be found anywhere in the service," their way of choosing officers was "radically wrong." *ANJ*, 9 Jan. 1875, 344. For a similar perspective, see Clipping, 1 Aug. 1869, Henry Cochrane Papers, MCHD.

90. The Army lagged behind some European nations in promoting from within the ranks during the nineteenth century. Ernest F. Fisher, *Guardians of the Republic: A History of the Non-Commissioned Officer Corps of the U.S. Army* (Mechanicsburg, PA: Stackpole Books, 2001), 83. Noncommissioned officers began seeking legislation promoting their commissioning as early as the 1820s, but this legislation did not make much headway until 1847 during the Mexican-American War when Congress allowed for noncommissioned officers who had served bravely on the battlefield to become officers. Fisher, 86. Thirty-four of the Army's 2,863 officers serving during the war were promoted this way. In 1851 Congress established an examination system for qualified noncommissioned officers seeking promotions. Fisher, 91.

91. First Lieutenant Henry Cochrane, USMC, to Col. W. C. Church, Editor, 10 March 1875, Henry Cochrane Papers, Box 13, MCHD. He stressed that "*in two years the Marine Corps could be made the Horse Guards of America*" (emphasis in original). Through a number of internal and rather simple improvements, such as replacing the current commandant and commissioning officers only from West Point. First Lieutenant Henry Cochrane, USMC, to Col. W. C. Church, Editor, 20 Nov. 1875, Henry Cochrane Papers, Box 13, MCHD. His use of the word "ancient" represented a departure from the more common use of the word by officers to suggest a more sentimental attachment to their institution. The word "old" was often used as well, which I discuss later.

92. *New York Herald*, 11 Oct. 1871, 3; "Marine Recruiting Rendezvous," 8 Jul. 1872, Clipping, Henry Cochrane Papers, Box 1, MCHD. For similar sentiments, see "Recruiting Rendezvous," 17 Sep. 1872, Clipping, Henry Cochrane Papers, Box 1, MCHD.

93. Shulimson, *Marine Corps' Search*, 16; the continuation of this trend of getting "statements" can be seen in Capt. George Collier to First Lieutenant Henry Cochrane, 7 Jan. 73, Henry Cochrane Papers, Box 4, MCHD. The *ANJ* seemed to think the possibility of the Corps being incorporated to be a remote one, suggesting Marine officers might be overreacting and paying attention to "unfounded" reports. *ANJ*, 9 Jan. 1875, 344, and 12 Dec. 1874, 281.

94. First Lieutenant Henry Cochrane, "A Resuscitation or a Funeral," 1 Oct. 1875, 5–6, Henry Cochrane Papers, MCHD. The term "Adonis" might have emphasized Marine officers' reputation as dancers; see "Brilliant Private Ball," *The Times* (Philadelphia), 17 Feb. 1887, 1.

95. Cochrane similarly argued that it was this lack of esprit that explained the Corps' struggles. Cochrane suggested that officers move away from the traditional method of publicizing the Corps: "gathering certificates of character from naval officers." They needed to find their own voices. Quoted in Shulimson, *Marine Corps' Search*, 17.

96. Cochrane wondered if the Corps' image was so wrecked that it might be better to "sink forever the despised name" of the Marine Corps and "rebaptize" it the "United States Naval Artillery." Quoted in J. Robert Moskin, *The U.S. Marine Corps Story* (New York: Little, Brown, 1990). Cochrane's pamphlet set out a number of ways to reorganize the Corps and rescue it from public mockery, from improving the quality of officers to ensuring faster promotions. None of Cochrane's ideas was terribly original; still, he wanted reform ardently enough that he promised to donate up to five hundred dollars if necessary to make these ideas a reality. Cochrane, "A Resuscitation or a Funeral," 5–6.

97. Cochrane, 5–6. The Army also struggled with drawing up a "concise plan for reform" in the 1870s and thinking ahead to new missions. Mark R. Grandstaff, "Preserving the 'Habits and Usages of War': William Tecumseh Sherman, Professional Reform, and the U.S. Army Officer Corps, 1865–1881, Revisited," *Journal of Military History* 62, no. 3 (Jul. 1998): 536.

98. *ANJ*, 26 February 1876, 468.

99. Shulimson, *Marine Corps' Search*, 10, 203. For historiography on the Navy's professionalization, see Mark C. Hunter, "The U.S. Naval Academy and Its Summer Cruises: Professionalization in the Antebellum U.S. Navy, 1845–1861," *Journal of Military History* 70 (Oct. 2006): 963–94.

100. For some of their efforts and discussions, though, see Captain Richard Collum to First Lieutenant Henry Cochrane, 26 May 1875 and 1 Jun. 1875, Henry Cochrane Papers, Box 4, MCHD. In the 26 May letter, Collum noted he had requested a Gatling gun and planned to become an expert with it in case his detachment needed to use it in Asia. He also reminisced about when he and Cochrane had been stationed together in 1864 and the changes they had hoped to implement. In the next letter sent in June, he described Cochrane as "my oldest and nearest friend in the Corps." He also encouraged him to seek out a teaching position in tactics at the Naval Academy, believing "*that* should be assigned to the Corps" (emphasis in original). Also see Henry Clay Cochrane and Richard R. Neill, "Uniform of the Marine Corps," *ANJ*, 21 December 1872, Henry Cochrane Papers,

Box 37, MCHD; Henry Cochrane, "A New Uniform for the Marine Corps," *ANJ*, 22 Feb. 1873, Henry Cochrane Papers, Box 37, MCHD. For Neill's guidebook see "Various Naval Items," *ANJ*, 1 March 1873, 454. Also see Shulimson, *Marine Corps' Search*, 73.

101. Grandstaff, "Preserving," 535. Historians have argued about when the Army professionalized. William Skelton believes this process began before the Civil War. See William B. Skelton, *An American Profession of Arms: The Army Officer Corps, 1784–1861* (Lawrence: University Press of Kansas, 1992). Samuel P. Huntington has argued that apolitical officers largely isolated from society began professionalizing in the 1880s. See *The Soldier and the State: The Theory and Politics of Civil-Military Relations* (Cambridge: Belknap Press, 1981). Edward Coffman suggests that the end of frontier wars brought Army officers together to think about professionalization and that they did so within the framework of larger societal changes beginning in the 1890s. See "The Long Shadow of *The Soldier and the State*," *Journal of Military History* 55 (Jan. 1991): 69–82. Mark Grandstaff suggests that antebellum reform efforts were stopped by the Civil War and not immediately picked up after the war because the demographics of the officer corps had changed significantly. By the 1880s, however, officers who had served before the Civil War would articulate a peacetime purpose of the Army based on education and preparing for future wars. Grandstaff, "Preserving," 521–45.

102. Ronald H. Spector, *Professors of War: The Naval War College and the Development of the Naval Profession* (Newport, RI: Naval War College Press, 1977), 3. Also see Allan R. Millett, *Military Professionalism and Officership in America* (Columbus, OH: Mershon Center, 1977).

103. Organizational structure explains some of these differences. Cavalry officers, for example, preferred to write regimental histories emphasizing their contributions rather than those of the Army as a whole. See, for example, George Price, "Chapter from the History of Our Army," *United Service*, Jul. 1870, 438–45.

104. Captain Richard Collum to First Lieutenant Henry Cochrane, 14 Oct. 1877, Henry Cochrane Papers, Box 5, MCHD: "I am quite sure that you and the other gallant officers and men of '*ours*' will accept my heartfelt praise and admiration for your continuing zeal, gallantry and devotion to duty displayed during the late riots. . . . my heart stirred with emotions of joy and pride when I received the news of the *splendid* conduct." Emphasis in original.

105. Luce supported the idea of sending Marine officers to West Point in the introduction to Collum's work and, according to Collum, in

personal conversations. Captain Richard Collum to First Lieutenant Henry Cochrane, 14 Oct. 1877, Henry Cochrane Papers, Box 5, MCHD; Aldrich, *History*, 30; Collum, *History* (1890), 21. Luce was not the only naval officer to hold this opinion; see Aldrich, *History*, 85.

106. The Corps did not choose this route, however, with future Marines beginning to attend the Naval Academy in 1882.

107. Captain Richard Collum to First Lieutenant Henry Cochrane, 14 Oct. 1877, 27 Jan. 1874, 25 Feb. 1875, Henry Cochrane Papers, Box 5, Box 4, MCHD; Edwin H. Simmons, "A History of Marine Corps Histories," *Naval History* 17 (Feb. 2003): 34. In his February letter, Collum asked Cochrane if he had received the copy of "our" work, suggesting that Cochrane had played an important role.

108. In 1877 Collum asked Cochrane to save any papers relating to the Corps' role in quelling the recent labor riots and complained, again, about how Aldrich had condensed his work excessively, thereby omitting "some important parts." Captain Richard Collum to First Lieutenant Henry Cochrane, 14 Oct. 1877, Henry Cochrane Papers, Box 5, MCHD.

109. Captain Richard Collum to First Lieutenant Henry Cochrane, 27 Jan. 1874, 21 Feb. 1873, Henry Cochrane Papers, Box 4, MCHD. In this case, Collum referred to reports of the Marines' appearance at a presidential inauguration.

110. Karsten, *The Naval Aristocracy*, 205–7. For this shift in the late nineteenth century due, in part, to mass production of items, see Gerald J. Baldasty, *The Commercialization of News in the Nineteenth Century* (Madison: University of Wisconsin Press, 1992), 53.

111. Lieutenant Richard S. Collum to Lt. Harris, 12 Dec. 1861, Office of the Commandant, Historical Section, LR, 1817–1915, Entry 42, Box 42.

112. Captain Richard Collum to First Lieutenant Henry Cochrane, 21 Feb. 1873, Henry Cochrane Papers, Box 4, MCHD.

113. Luke Gibbons, "Race against Time: Racial Discourse and Irish History," in *Cultures of Empire: Colonizers in Britain and the Empire in the Nineteenth and Twentieth Centuries*, ed. Catherine Hall (New York: St. Martin's Press, 2000), 216. For one example of such a historical approach, see Morgan, "From a Death to a View: The Hunt for the Welsh Past in the Romantic Period," in *Invention of Tradition*, ed. Eric Hobsbawm and Terence Ranger (Cambridge: Cambridge University Press, 2002), 43–100. Hobsbawm, "Introduction," 7.

114. For this tendency in society as a whole, see T. J. Jackson Lears, *No Place of Grace: Antimodernism and the Transformation of American Culture, 1880–1920* (Chicago: University of Chicago Press, 1981), 159.

115. Aldrich, *History*, 21, 30. Shulimson considers the Luce essay to be the "most remarkable feature of the Aldrich history." Shulimson, *Marine Corps' Search*, 16–17. See "Notices," *Marine Corps Gazette*, November 1996, 10. For a similar article focused solely on the Navy, see Rear Admiral Stephen B. Luce, "The Dawn of Naval History," *Proceedings* 24 (1898): 441–50.

116. Keith M. Brown, "Imagining Scotland," *Journal of British Studies* 31 (Oct. 1992): 417. This "yearning" for the past was also a theme in naval literature, with naval officers romanticizing the days of sail. See, for example, E. Z. Bowline, "Whiffs from an Old Sailor's Pipe," *United Service*, April 1880, 486–91.

117. Aldrich, *History*, 33.

118. See Captain George Collier to First Lieutenant Henry Cochrane, 7 Jan. 73, Box 4, Henry Cochrane Papers, MCHD. He wrote that he was engaged in "getting statements . . . to save our old corps, as we will be either abolished or so much reduced in rank" at any time. Also see Captain Richard Collum to First Lieutenant Henry Cochrane, 14 Oct. 1877, Henry Cochrane Papers, Box 5, MCHD. Collum wrote of "our dear old Corps." For this trend continuing through the early twentieth century, see Sgt. Frank Stubbe, "Wilkes-Barre Opinions," *Bulletin*, Jan. 1916, 13.

119. Henderson quoted in Heinl, *Soldiers of the Sea*, 43; Commander Joshua R. Sands, USN, to Brig. Gen. Archibald Henderson, USMC, 27 Jul. 1852, in U.S. Senate, Senate Document 1, 32d Congress, 2d Session (1852), 593, emphasis in original; Schein, *Organizational Culture and Leadership*, 16.

120. Hobsbawm, "Introduction," 4.

121. 1st Lt. A. S. Taylor, recognizing Cochrane's leadership in the matter, wrote to ascertain how much progress he was making. See Taylor to First Lieutenant Henry Cochrane, USMC, 10 May 1874, Box 4, Henry Cochrane Papers, MCHD.

122. First Lieutenant Henry Cochrane, USMC, to Major John C. Cash, USMC, 20 March 1874; First Lieutenant Henry Cochrane to General [Zeilin?], 24 May 1873, Henry Cochrane Papers, MCHD.

123. "Reform Versus Change of Uniform," *Army and Navy Journal*, 4 January 1873, 325; Scott Hughes Myerly, *British Military Spectacle: From the Napoleonic Wars through the Crimea* (Cambridge: Harvard University Press, 1996), 44 and 75; First Lieutenant Henry Cochrane, USMC, to Major John C. Cash, USMC, 20 March 1874, Henry Cochrane Papers, MCHD.

124. *ANJ*, 15 March 1873, 490. Although this letter was written anonymously, given Cochrane's statement (discussed later in this chapter) about his anonymous contributions to the *ANJ*, it seems unlikely that anyone else could have written it. "A New Uniform for the Marine Corps," *ANJ*, clipping, Henry

Cochrane Papers, MCHD. Also see First Lieutenant Henry Cochrane to Colonel William Church, 15 Oct. 1873, Henry Cochrane Papers, MCHD.

125. First Lieutenant Charles F. Williams, USMC, to First Lieutenant Henry Cochrane, USMC, 26 Aug. 1872 and 5 Jan. 1872, Henry Cochrane Papers, MCHD. Similarly, Capt. George Collier hoped to see "that damned full dress of ours sent to the devil." Collier to First Lieutenant Henry Cochrane, 7 Jan. 73, Box 4, Henry Cochrane Papers, MCHD. For background on the New York 7th Regiment's uniform see Fred Porter Todd, "The Centennial of a Uniform," *Journal of the American Military History Foundation* 1 (winter 1937–38): 195–98. The 7th Regiment seems to have paid excessive attention to its uniform. A discussion over changing its hat in 1842 caused so much controversy that the regiment decided that all changes to the uniform must be approved by two-thirds of its members. As one historian wrote in his history of the 7th Regiment, no discussion had "ever provoked so fierce and bitter a controversy." Col. Emmons Clark, *History of the Seventh Regiment of New York, 1806–1889*, vol. 1 (New York: Seventh Regiment, 1890), 264.

126. First Lieutenant C. L. Sherman to First Lieutenant Henry Cochrane, 3 Dec. 1872, Box 3, Henry Cochrane Papers, MCHD. In particular, he noted that the enlisted chevrons, the symbol of rank, should be red instead of yellow, as that was the only "proper facing of the Corps."

127. Lt. Col. Charles H. Cureton, "Parade Blue, Battle Green," in Marine Corp Heritage Foundation, *The Marines* (Quantico, VA: Marine Corps Heritage Foundation, 1998), 112 and 139–41; First Lieutenant Henry Cochrane, "Marine Corps," *Naval Encyclopedia*, 474.

128. By contrast, the Marine Corps' current dress uniform remained very similar over the course of the twentieth century. The Corps takes pride in this consistency. For example, its website notes that the uniform's buttons have been used since 1804. The uniform, the Corps claims, is the "most distinctive uniform in the military." It is one of the most powerful symbols to Marines of the Corps' corporate identity. The original wording of "in the military" is no longer available at the following site: http://www.marines .com/main/index/makingmarines/culture/symbols/dress_blues (accessed 25 Apr. 2010). The rhetoric recently has been toned down. See "Dress Blues" on Legendary Uniforms; available online at https://www.marines.com/ who-we-are/our-values/battle-worn.html (accessed 26 Mar. 2019).

129. Harold Leslie Peterson, *The American Sword, 1775–1945* (Mineola, NY: Dover Publications, 2003), 170.

130. First Lieutenant Charles F. Williams to First Lieutenant Henry Cochrane, 5 Jan. 1872 or 26 Aug. 1872, Box 3, Henry Cochrane Papers, MCHD; Captain George Collier to Captain Henry Cochrane, 7 January 1873, Box 4, Henry Cochrane Papers, MCHD. Collier wrote that not in "a *single instance*"

(emphasis in original) should the Corps "follow the Army." Collier also informed Cochrane that the current commandant had told him that when he retired he would be replaced by a "soldier" who had commanded the Army of the Potomac.

131. He stated his preference for the sword under the "old regulation, brass sheath," suggesting he did not agree with the adoption of the Army's sword. Captain Richard Collum to First Lieutenant Henry Cochrane, 12 Aug. 1872, Box 3, Henry Cochrane Papers, MCHD.

132. Millett, *Semper Fidelis*, 112. Comdt. Jacob Zeilin also invented the Corps' symbol, the eagle, globe, and anchor, which became part of the uniform in 1875. Collum stated that the symbol, which he described as a "metal hemisphere on an anchor and surmounted by an eagle," was adopted in 1869. Collum, *History* (1890), 304.

133. Millett, *Semper Fidelis*, 112. The first motto meant "By Land, By Sea," the other "Always Faithful." For this interpretation of the motto, see "Marines' Motto Fruit of Bravery from Tripoli to the Halls of the Montezumas Was Earned," *Duluth News-Tribune*, 9 Jun. 1907, 11.

134. Pvt. Philip O'Neill to Colonel John Reynolds, 7 Jul. 1865, copy in "LR, 1818–1915," Office of the Commandant, Historical Section, Box 44, RG 127.

135. Major James Forney, "The Marines," *United Service*, April 1889, 397.

136. For this transformation to a battleship fleet, see Kenneth Hagan, *This People's Navy: The Making of American Sea Power* (New York: Free Press), 193–227. While the transition away from sail enabled ships to avoid a dependence on wind, for example, they required a ready access to coal, which necessitated the development of refueling bases overseas. The Corps was not the Navy's only target. Since the 1840s the Navy had struggled to amalgamate officer and enlisted engineers into its institutional fabric. For the difficulties of incorporating engineers into the Navy's culture see Hagan, 108 and 118, and Harry P. Huse, "The Question of Naval Engineers," *Proceedings* 28 (1903): 911–16. For the transition from sail to steam, see Donald L. Canney, *Frigates, Sloops, and Gunboats, 1815–1885*, vol. 1; and *Ironclads, 1815–1885*, vol. 2 (Annapolis, MD: Naval Institute Press, 1990–1993); and James C. Bradford, ed., *Captains of the Old Steam Navy: Makers of the American Naval Tradition, 1840–1880* (Annapolis, MD: Naval Institute Press, 1986).

137. Lieutenant Commander Allan D. Brown, "Prize Essay, Naval Education," *Proceedings* 5 (1879): 321. See the similar comments of Lieutenant Commander Goodrich in the ensuing "Discussion," 379.

138. Millett, *Semper Fidelis*, 122. For a detailed study see Frederick S. Harrod, *Manning the New Navy: The Development of a Modern Naval Enlisted Force, 1899–1940* (Westport, CT: Greenwood Press, 1978).

139. See especially William Fullam, "The Organization, Training, and Discipline of the Navy Personnel as Viewed from the Ship," *Proceedings* 22 (1896): 77, 91 and 109–11. "Americans in the Navy: Important Changes Asked for by the Blue Jackets," *Baltimore Sun*, 7 Jan. 1891, 1.

140. Ensign A. A. Ackerman, Discussion of Lt. William F. Fullam, "The Systems of Naval Training and Discipline Required to Promote Efficiency and Attract Americans," *Proceedings* 16 (1890): 505.

141. Lieutenant J. F. Meigs, USN, to Lieutenant William Fullam, USN, 15 Nov. 1890, William Fullam Papers, LOC.

142. See A Lieutenant, USN, "Style in the Navy," *United Service* 4 (April 1881): 490–98. The article mentioned the "Style," 497. Also see W. T. Truxtun, "Reform in the Navy," *United Service*, April 1880, 450–51; "Lieut. Fullam's Paper: It Is Being Discussed throughout the Navy," *New York Times*, 7 Dec. 1890, 2; Capt. Harry Glass, USN, to Lieutenant William Fullam, USN, 7 Dec. 1890, William Fullam Papers, LOC. Glass, however, found Fullam to be excessively critical of Marines. While supporting Fullam, Capt. P. F. Harrington, however, believed he was "on the losing side" because the Corps had too many supporters. Capt. P. F. Harrington, USN, to Lt. William Fullam, USN, 11 April 1896, William Fullam Papers, LOC. For similar sentiment see Capt. Richard Wainwright to Lt. William Fullam, USN, 5 May 1896, William Fullam Papers, LOC.

143. Naval Department, *New York Times* to Lieutenant William Fullam, USN, 22 Nov. 1890, William Fullam Papers, LOC. For the commandant's protest to the Secretary of the Navy for Fullam's attacks, see 14 April 1896, Press Copies of Letters Sent, 1895–1898, RG 127. For an Engineer Yeoman writing to object to Marines in public correspondence, see Commandant Charles Heywood to Secretary of the Navy, 21 May 1896, Press Copies of Letters Sent, 1895–1898, RG 127.

144. Admiral Stephen B. Luce, USN, to Lieutenant William Fullam, USN, 24 Nov. 1896, William Fullam Papers, LOC; Captain W. S. Schley, "Official Report on the Behavior of the U.S.S. Baltimore," *Proceedings* 18 (1893): 246.

145. For discussion of the need for the Royal Marines, see G. A. Schomberg, "Are the Royal Marine Forces a Necessary Auxiliary to the Royal Navy," *Journal of the Royal United Service Institution* 15 (April 1871): 486–507; G. A. Shomberg, "Shall We Retain the Marines," *Nineteenth Century: A Monthly Review* 13 (May 1883): 795–803.

146. In the version edited by Aldrich, Nicolas had been mentioned by name. Nicolas' preface begins: "From an early period a practice has prevailed in many of the continental armies, for each regiment to keep regular records of its services and achievements; but it is only of recent date that this emulative principle has been encouraged in the British service, and hence arises

the difficulty of obtaining any authentic account of their origin, or of their subsequent proceedings." Nicolas, *Historical Record*, vii. Richard Collum writes: "A custom has prevailed throughout the armies of Europe to keep regular record of the services and achievements of their regiments and corps. This principle has not obtained in our own country, hence a great difficulty arises in presenting an authentic account of the services of any branch of our establishment either military or naval." Collum, *History* (1890), 7.

147. One commandant looked to the Royal Marines as a model for the United States to emulate. See Commandant to Secretary of the Navy, 9 Oct. 1896, Press Copies of Letters Sent to the Secretary of the Navy, 1895–1899, Box 2, RG 127.

148. The 1875 work had begun with the Revolutionary War. See Aldrich, *History*, 9. For mention of these Marines, see John Russell Bartlett, *Records of the Colony of Rhode Island and Providence Plantations in New England: 1741 to 1756*, vol. 5 (Providence: Knowles, Anthony and Col., State Printers, 1860), 30 and 119. For two groups that similarly emphasized links to their role in the American Revolution, see Michele Gillespie, "Memory and the Making of a Southern Citizenry: Georgia Artisans in the Early Republic," and Anne Sarah Rubin, "Seventy-six and Sixty-One: Confederates Remember the American Revolution," in W. Fitzhugh Brundage, ed., *Where These Memories Grow: History, Memory and Southern Identity* (Chapel Hill: University of North Carolina Press, 2000), 35–77 and 85–105, respectively.

149. *ANJ*, 13 March 1875, 490; "History of the Marine Corps," *ANJ*, 16 Jan. 1891, 333.

150. James Forney, "The Marines," *United Service: A Quarterly Review of Military and Naval Affairs*, April 1889, 393.

151. The term describes something that is "indeterminate" or "not easily classified or understood." See Paul Beale, ed., *A Dictionary of Slang and Unconventional English*, 8th ed. (New York: Routledge, 1984), 785; and Kwong Ki Chiu, *A Dictionary of English Phrases with Illustrative Sentences* (New York: A. S. Barnes, 1881), 331.

152. Forney, "The Marines," 394.

153. Forney, 397. Despite his apparent proclivity for writing—based on his observations from a yearlong trip abroad, he had submitted a lengthy report in 1873 summarizing his conclusions about the conditions of European Marine forces—this was his first foray into writing articles for publication. Shulimson, *Marine Corps' Search*, 14. Almost 75 percent of the paper focused on the Royal Marines.

154. Forney, 400.

155. Edgar S. Maclay, *A History of the United States Navy, from 1775 to 1894*, vol. 1 (New York: D. Appleton, 1894), 21. The phrase was frequently used

in headlines. One of the earliest that did not draw on the typical tension between sailors and Marines is perhaps an article recounting the commandant's desire to enlist more Marines. See "Tell It to the Marines," *Washington Post*, 30 Oct. 1894, 9.

156. "Marines on Shipboard: An Important Factor in a Navy," *New York Times*, 7 April 1889, 16. "Jack" was a nickname for a sailor. This article made its way into a number of other papers, including the *Great Falls Tribune* in Montana, which ran the article with the headline "Told of the Marines: An Important Though Much Abused Factor in a Navy," 5 Jul. 1889, 3. Also see just a few examples of the same article, including "Marine on Shipboard: They Constitute an Important Factor," *Los Angeles Times*, 9 Jun. 1889, 6; "Told of the Marines: An Important though Much Abused Factor in a Navy," *The Leader Courier* (Kingman, Kansas), 25 May 1889, 1. Far more were published in papers across the United States. The journalist's hazy assignation of the Marines to the Navy demonstrated the problem the Corps had of clearly demarcating its institutional independence to observers.

157. "Our New Navy Crippled," *New York Times*, 10 May 1891, 1; "Everyone Should Work," *New York Times*, 25 Jun. 1891, 9. Also see "Marines and Bluejackets: Difficulties in Finding Accommodations on Board Modern Warships," *The Times* (Philadelphia), 10 Jun. 1894, 7, for descriptions of the Marines as "idlers."

158. Letter to the Editor, "Marines on Board Ship," *New York Times*, 3 Mar. 1892, 9. For other letters in this blitz, see Fair Play to the Editor of the *New York Times*, "The American Seaman," *New York Times*, 14 Jan. 1892, 10; and Fair Play to the Editor of the *New York Times*, "Watch Them Coal Ship and Then Decide Whether You Would Be a Bluejacket," *New York Times*, 15 Feb. 1892, 3. For a precedent for the use of the term "fair play," see "Sailors Ask for Fair Play," *The Times* (Philadelphia), 7 Jan. 1891, 4. An examination of letters to the editor would be interesting to determine the extent to which this was more of a national phenomenon. On the same page as one of the April letters, for example, is a letter written by a self-proclaimed "Alabama Democrat." See An Alabama Democrat to Editor of the *New York Times*, "A Southerner's View," *New York Times*, 4 April 1892, 9.

159. Fair Play to the Editor of the *New York Times*, "Justice for the Bluejackets," *New York Times*, 28 Mar. 1892, 3. A follow-on letter to the editor pointed out less serious military offenses to argue that, again, Marines misbehaved more than sailors. See Gun Captain to Editor of the *New York Times*, "Bluejackets and Marines," *New York Times*, 4 April 1892, 9.

160. "Weak Spots in Our Navy," *The Sun* (New York), 14 Jun. 1896, 3. The Corps' Uniform Board approved "canvas working clothes" so that Marines could help in this task. "The Marine Corps," *ANJ*, 28 May 1892, 699.

161. Fair Play to the Editor of the *New York Times*, "Watch Them Coal Ship," *New York Times*, 15 Feb. 1892, 3.

162. Con Marrast Perkins, "The Last of the Drums," *St. Nicholas: An Illustrated Magazine for Young Folks*, Jul. 1897, 711–12, 715.

163. The Army's *Infantry Drill Regulations*, revised in 1904, for example, included a section on "drum signals." *Infantry Drill Regulations, United States Army* (New York: Army and Navy Journal, 1904), 234–42. The Army continued to have field music until shortly before World War II, when it was no longer needed for communication. Donald E. Mattson and Louis D. Walz, *Old Fort Snelling: Instruction Book for Fife with Music of Early America* (Saint Paul: Minnesota Historical Society Press, 1974), 6.

164. Rudyard Kipling, "Soldier an' Sailor, Too," *McClure's Magazine*, 481–82. For works on Rudyard Kipling, see Charles Allen, *Kipling Sahib: India and the Making of Rudyard Kipling* (New York: Little, Brown, 2008); William B. Dillingham, *Rudyard Kipling: Hell and Heroism* (New York: Palgrave Macmillan, 2005); Zohreh T. Sullivan, *Narratives of Empire: The Fiction of Rudyard Kipling* (New York: Cambridge University Press, 2003).

165. Kipling wrote that "there isn't a job on the top o' the earth the beggar don't know, nor do" and that "'E isn't one o' the reg'lar Line, nor 'e isn't one of the crew." The poem was told from the perspective of soldiers who, despite differences, appreciated that they were "brothers" to them. Rudyard Kipling, "Soldier an' Sailor Too," *The Works of Rudyard Kipling: The Seven Seas* (New York: D. Appleton, 1899), 152–54.

166. "Pfeifer's Triumph," *Maine Farmer*, reprint from *New York Sun*, 27 Aug. 1896, 6. The article made its way all the way to Honolulu. See *Honolulu Star-Bulletin*, 27 Nov. 1896, 7. Other newspapers that ran the article included *Edwardsville Intelligencer* (Illinois), *North Adams (MA) Transcript*, *Sterling Daily Gazette* (Sterling, IL), *Ohio County News* (Hartford, KY); and *Fort Wayne (IN) News*.

167. For an attack on traditions, see "Sailors Ask Fair Play," *The Times* (Philadelphia), 7 Jan. 1891, 4.

Chapter 2. Internalization

1. Telegram, John Philip Sousa to Commandant Charles Heywood, 14 April 1902 in Philippines Subject File, Marine Corps Historical Center, Washington, D.C. For a description of the Corps' band performances highlighting Marine wives as well, see "At the Marine Barracks," *Evening Star* (Washington, D.C.), 22 Jul. 1889, 9.

2. For this process in Great Britain, see Graham Dawson, *Soldier Heroes: British Adventure, Empire, and the Imagining of Masculinity* (New York: Routledge, 1994).

3. Laura Wexler, *Tender Violence: Domestic Visions in the Age of U.S. Imperialism* (Chapel Hill: University of North Carolina Press, 2000), 16–17. For the role of journalism in the Spanish-American War, see Charles H. Brown, *The Correspondents' War: Journalists in the Spanish-American War* (New York: Charles Scribner's Sons, 1967); and David Ralph Spencer, *The Yellow Journalism: The Press and America's Emergence as a World Power* (Evanston, IL: Northwestern University Press, 2007). For cultural approaches to imperialism, see Amy Kaplan and Donald E. Pease, eds., *Cultures of United States Imperialism* (Durham, N.C.: Duke University Press, 1993); Amy Kaplan, "Romancing the Empire: The Embodiment of American Masculinity in the Popular Historical Novel of the 1890s,"*American Literary History* 2 (Winter 1990): 659–90; John Carlos Rowe, *Literary Culture and U.S. Imperialism: From the Revolution to World War II* (New York: Oxford University Press, 2000). Useful works in British imperial history include John MacKenzie, *Popular Imperialism and the Military, 1850–1950* (Manchester, UK: Manchester University Press, 1992).

4. See John D. Seelye's *War Games: Richard Harding Davis and the New Imperialism* (Amherst: University of Massachusetts Press, 2003); and Arthur Lubow, *The Reporter Who Would Be King: A Biography of Richard Harding Davis* (New York: Scribner, 1992).

5. "Uncle Sam's Marines Are True Heroes," *The Times* (Philadelphia), 5 Aug. 1900, 30.

6. Millett, *Semper Fidelis*, 134; "The Marine Corps Bill," *Washington Post*, 9 Jan. 1899, 6.

7. "Uncle Sam's Marines Ashore and Afloat Where They Are," *Boston Journal*, 10 April 1898, 9.

8. "Duties of the Marine Guard; All about the Soldier and Sailor Too of the American Navy," *Sioux City Journal*, 1 May 1898, 10. For similar comments about the Royal Marines at this time, see John R. Black, *Young Japan: Yokohama and Yedo*, vol. 2 (London: Trubner, 1881), 387. Black explained how a Royal Marine officer had helped make Japanese Marines into an elite just as they were in Great Britain. Also see "The National Defences," *Fraser's Magazine*, Dec. 1859, 650, and Mrs. J. D. Leather-Culley, *On the War Path: A Lady's Letters from the Front* (London: John Long, 1901), 99. For other positive comments, see Sir Henry Keppel, *A Sailor's Life under Four Sovereigns*, vol. 2 (London: Macmillan, 1899), 305. As an 1872 dictionary explained, Marines had been the "butts of the sailors, from their ignorance of seamanship" but they had become "deserved appreciated as the finest regiment in the service." John Camden Hotten, *The Slang Dictionary* (London: John Camden Hotten, 1872), 156.

9. "Uncle Sam's Sea Soldiers," *Charlotte Observer*, 29 Jan. 1898, 2. Also see W. J. Henderson, "A War-Ship Community," *Scribner's Magazine* 24 (Sep. 1898): 291.

10. Shulimson, *Marine Corps' Search*, 193. For the Army's mobilization difficulties see Graham Cosmas, *An Army for Empire: The United States Army in the Spanish-American War* (College Station: Texas A&M University Press, 2003). The best overview of the war is David Trask's *The War with Spain in 1898* (New York: Macmillan, 1981). For the implications of the Spanish-American War on U.S society and its imperial importance, see Gerald F. Linderman, *Mirror of War: American Society and the Spanish-American War* (Ann Arbor: University of Michigan Press, 1974); and Paul T. McCartney, *Power and Progress: American National Identity, the War of 1898, and the Rise of American Imperialism* (Baton Rouge: Louisiana State University Press, 2006). Kristin Hoganson analyzes the importance of gender to the war in *Fighting for American Manhood: How Gender Politics Provoked the Spanish-American and Philippine-American Wars* (New Haven C.T.: Yale University Press, 2000).

11. Major Charles L. McCawley, USMC to Commandant Brig. Gen. Charles Heywood, USMC, 8 Jan. 1900, "LR, 1818–1915," RG 127, NARA; E. R. Hagemann, "'My Dear Bobby': Letters from a Marine Corps Colonel to His Son during the Spanish-American War," *Marine Corps Gazette* (Nov. 1979), 78.

12. Stephen Crane, *Prose and Poetry* (New York: Library of America, 1975), 1051–57; Stephen Crane, *Wounds in the Rain: A Collection of Stories Related to the Spanish-American War* (London: Methuen, 1900), 189.

13. Michael Robertson, *Stephen Crane, Journalism, and the Making of Modern American Literature* (New York: Columbia University Press, 1997), 139. Michael C.C. Adams has discussed how certain military events become memorialized more so than others, often through art. See *Echoes of War: A Thousand Years of Military History in Popular Culture* (Lexington: University Press of Kentucky, 2002). For the use of this image in its recruiting material as late as 1915, see U.S. Marine Corps Recruiting Publicity Bureau (hereafter USMCRPB), *U.S. Marines: Duties, Experiences, Opportunities, Pay*, 2nd ed. (New York: Chasmar-Winchell Press, 1912); 5th ed. (New York: USMCRPB, 1915).

14. "They Kept at Bay a Much Superior Force," 14 Jun. 1898, *Anaconda Standard*, 2; "Gallant Band is Reinforced: Men and Rapid Fire Guns Landed at Guantanamo for the Brave Marines," *Omaha World Herald*, 14 Jun. 1898, 2; "Bullets Pattering All around Them: The Marines at Guantanamo in Constant Danger," *Anaconda Standard*, 15 Jun. 1898, 1.

15. "The Kind of Men the Marines Are," *Kansas City Star*, 12 Jun. 1898, 1; "The Marine Corps," *Evening Star* (Washington, D.C.), 2 Jul. 1898, 8. Interestingly, the article stressed that it was the Corps' centennial, thus linking the Corps' origins not to its birth as the Continental Marine Corps but to its reestablishment in the new nation.

16. For an example see "The U. S. Marines: the Distinguished Record Made by the Soldiers of the Navy," *New Haven Evening Register*, 19 Aug. 1898, 11.

17. "The Mariners," HQMC Scrapbooks, 1880–1901, Entry 46, RG 127; "He Won A Lieutenancy: A Son of Congressman Butler Gets into the Navy," *Kansas City Star*, 20 May 1898, 5. Ford's letters reflected the influence of late nineteenth-century Marines, especially referring to the Corps as the "oldest" military branch. "Marine Life on the Marblehead," *Sunday World Herald*, 10 Jul. 1898, 5. Until he survived the *Maine*'s destruction in February of 1898, Fords' parents had no idea where he was after his disappearance years earlier. He was awarded the Medal of Honor for participating in the cutting of the underwater cable lines at Cienfuegos under the false name under which he had enlisted of James Meredith.

"Pat Ford Home on Leave," *Omaha World Herald*, 8 Oct. 1898, 4. Ford had enlisted under the false name James Meredith. See Karl Schuon, *U.S. Marine Corps Bibliographical Dictionary: The Corps' Fighting Men, What They Did, Where They Served* (New York: Franklin Watts, 1963), 76–77.

18. "First in the Fight," Clipping, Henry Cochrane Papers, Box 1, MCHD.

19. John Ramsey Graham, "The Marines," in *Spanish-American War Songs*, ed. Sidney A. Witherbee (Detroit: Sidney A. Witherbee, 1898), 392–93.

20. William M. McBride, *Technological Change and the United States Navy, 1865–1945* (Baltimore: Johns Hopkins University Press, 2000), 74. Mahan argued that "the funnels are open to serious injury by guns of that secondary battery, six to eight inch, which there is now a tendency to discard. It has long been my own opinion that the so-called secondary battery is really entitled to the name primary, because its effect is exerted mainly on the personnel, rather than the material of a vessel; and I am glad to find this view supported by the author of the article in Blackwood, though he does not use the same words." Mahan suggests that his view of the importance of secondary batteries was largely unique. The context for this writing was the Russo-Japanese War. A. T. Mahan, "Reflections, Historic and Other, Suggested by the Battle of the Japan Sea," *Proceedings* 32 (Jun. 1906): 441–71.

21. Cmdt. Charles McCawley had been pushing for the Corps to secure this role for almost ten years. In 1893 the institution's new School of Application, which trained future officers and enlisted men, received two six-pound rapid-fire guns of the type found on secondary batteries. Whether or not the School of Application propounded the notion that Marines were naval artillerists, at least one young officer believed this to be the case. See James Breckenridge to Mother, 19 Feb. 1899, James Breckenridge Papers, MCHD.

22. For hints of this competition, see Willard H. Kelly, "Not Private M'Neall," *Washington Post*, 25 Dec. 1898, 12. The seaman wrote to the newspaper to inform them of mistakenly identifying a Marine private instead of a gunner's mate for undertaking a heroic act.

23. Meade eventually was forced into early retirement for writing a "disrespectful" letter to the Department of the Navy. See "President Punishes Meade," *NYT*, 14 Aug. 1903, 1. He appears to have been as eager to clash with Marine officers as he was with naval officers. See "Major Meade Has Been Removed," *Boston Morning Journal*, 30 Dec. 1897, 1.

24. "Report of the Major General Commandant of the United States Marine Corps," *Annual Report of the Navy Department 1898* (Washington, D.C.: Government Printing Office, 1898), 830. Collum's treatment of the war is unusual in that he did not proceed chronologically. First including numerous after-action reports written by Marines about their contributions to naval gunfire, he subsequently began recounting how the Marines had treated Spanish prisoners in the wake of the war. Only at the end did he return to the Corps' role in securing Guantanamo.

25. This belief had begun circulating after Spanish naval officer Capt. Don Antonio Eulate cited the effect of the Marines' secondary batteries on his ship the *Vizcaya*, one of the few ships close enough to American ships to be within range of the batteries. Captain Eulate was quoted in an Associated Press article as saying that the secondary batteries' fire was critical. The article also cited an anonymous Spanish officer who found the batteries' fire to be effective against his vessel. See "Marines Fought Nobly; Their Work at the Secondary Batteries Helped Largely to Destroy Cervera's Fleet," 25 Jul. 1898, 2; James William Buel, *Hero Tales of the American Soldier and Sailor As Told by the Heroes Themselves and Their Comrades, the Unwritten History of American Chivalry* (New York: A. Holloway, 1899), 174. Early reports claimed the secondary batteries were rendered useless by being out of range. "Bombardment of Santiago Particulars of the Second Attack by the American Fleet," *Sioux City Journal*, 13 Jun. 1898, 2.

26. Collum, *History* (1903), 324. Also see the report of Marine Captain Murphy issued by the Navy Department and quoted in "Praise for the Marines," *New York Tiems*, 11 Aug. 1898, 4.

27. Collum, *History* (1903), 331, 333, 325; "Marines Fought Nobly," 2. For a naval account that supports this view, see George Edward Graham, *Schley and Santiago* (Chicago: W. B. Conkey, 1902), 160.

28. Lt. Col. Robert Meade, USMC, to Maj. Charles L. McCawley, USMC, 18 March 1899, Charles L. McCawley Papers, MCHD.

29. Anne Leland, *American War and Military Operations Casualties: Lists and Statistics* (Washington, D.C.: Congressional Research Service, 2010), 2.

30. F. K. Hill, "The Secondary Battery," *Proceedings* 24 (1898): 737–38; Millett, *Semper Fidelis*, 130.

31. The quoted Marine did note that sometimes sailors did not have time to "get behind the steel" nor did they "always want to" in "Marines of Our Navy:

Numerous and Varied Are the Duties Assigned to Them," *Indiana State Journal*, 29 Jun. 1898, 6.

32. "Soldier and Sailor, Too," 24 Jul. 1898, Clipping, Henry Cochrane Papers, Box 1, MCHD.

33. This particular article seems to have been syndicated, as it appeared in more than one newspaper. See "What Marines Are," *Grand Rapids Herald*, 17 Jul. 1898, 12; *Duluth News-Tribune*, 26 Sep. 1898, 4.

34. "Marine Corps: The Naval Officers Ignore Them in Their Reports," *Minneapolis Journal*, 30 Jul. 1898, 1; and *Tacoma Daily News*, 4 Aug. 1898, 3. In 1898 J. S. Van Antwerp was a reporter for the *San Francisco Examiner*, the *Minneapolis Journal*, and the *Minneapolis Time*s. See *Official Congressional Directory*, 2nd ed. (Washington, D.C.: Government Printing Office, 1898), 320–21. For Van Antwerp's reputation, see Charles Austin Bates, *American Journalism from the Practical Side* (New York: Holmes Publishing Company, 1897), 203.

35. Regarding the reports, see, for example, "Their Bravery Recognized: Official Report of Captain Murphy of the Marine Corps," *New Haven Register*, 10 Aug. 1898, 3. The journalist did not specify who in the Navy Department opposed the Corps in "1000 More Marines," *Boston Daily Advertiser*, 10 Oct. 1898, 7.

36. Gustav Kobbe, "Ever Ready to Fight," *Washington Post*, 8 May 1898, 26. For an even earlier editorial supporting the Corps' usefulness from the same newspaper, see "United States Marines," *Washington Post*, 18 Sep. 1892, 4. The newspaper had also used the expression "Tell It to the Marines" in an 1894 article about the commandant's desire to increase the number of enlisted Marines in the service. See "Tell It to the Marines: Col. Heywood Wants More Men to Relieve Them of the Hard Work," *Washington Post*, 30 Oct. 1894, 9.

37. Millett, *Semper Fidelis*, 135. An advanced base would be defended by Marines and designed to support the Navy in offensive operations by providing a safe place for ships to refuel, repair, and accomplish other necessary tasks.

38. The expression "tell it to the Marines" was prevalent enough that one commentator used it in comparing the Army's higher casualty numbers from disease. The author stated that Army officials might claim that "disease was inevitable . . . but, in view of the record made at Guantanamo Bay, we may say to them, seriously and respectfully, rather than flippantly—'Tell that to the marines!'" George Kennan, "George Kennan's Story of the War: The Santiago Campaign," *Outlook*, 22 Oct. 1898, 475. For some of the reasons for the Corps' lower disease rates, see French E. Chadwick, *The Relations of the United States and Spain: The Spanish-American War*, vol. 1 (New York: Charles Scribner's Sons, 1911), 259.

39. Robert Moskin, *The Marine Corps Story* (Boston: Little, Brown, 1992), 90.

40. Karsten, *Naval Aristocracy*; First Lieutenant William Upshur, USMC, to Dr. John N. Upshur, 19 Jan. 1908, William P. Upshur Papers, Southern Historical

Collection, University of North Carolina–Chapel Hill Library (hereafter William Upshur Papers). Emphasis in original.

41. First Lieutenant William Upshur, USMC, to Mrs. John N. Upshur, 8 Aug. 1905, William P. Upshur Papers. For other less direct comments suggesting his Marine identity, see First Lieutenant William Upshur to Dr. John N. Upshur, 12 April 1908, William Upshur Papers.

42. Earl Ellis to Tad, 20 March 1902, 18 April 1902, Earl Ellis Papers, MCHD. The same letter talks about some of the affectations of Marine officers in the Philippines.

43. Carolyn Tyson, ed., *The Journal of Frank Keeler* (Quantico, VA: Marine Corps Museum, Marine Corps Letter Series, No. 1, 1975), 3, 20, 5. There is no indication of when Frank Keeler wrote his journal, though the use of the word "journal" implies it was produced around the time of the Spanish-American War.

44. "Marine Life on the Marblehead," *Sunday World Herald*, 10 Jul. 1898, 5.

45. E. R. Hagemann, " 'My Dear Bobby': Letters from a Marine Corps Colonel to His Son during the Spanish-American War," *Marine Corps Gazette*, Nov. 1979, 78. Huntington also confided to his son that far from being fearless, his Marines were rather "scared" at Guantánamo.

46. For example, see the headline, "Story of the Tien-Tsin Fight: None of the Americans Expected to Escape," *New York Times*, 25 Jul. 1900, 2. One *Washington Post* article wondered if the fifty Marines within the legation were still alive. See "Recruiting the Marines," 21 Jul. 1900, 2. Another article described how seventy-six Marines guarded the legation protecting Westerners. "China Gets Worse: Civil Foreigners in Pekin Are under Arms to Fight," *Morning Oregonian*, 11 Jun. 1900, 1. For frustration with their allies, see "Report of the Major General Commandant of the United States Marine Corps," *Annual Report of the Navy Department 1900* (Washington, D.C.: Government Printing Office, 1900), 1150; "Chinese Opened Fire," *Washington Post*, 19 Jun. 1900, 4. Works on the Boxer Rebellion include Robert Bickers and R. G. Tiedemann, *The Boxers, China, and the World* (Lanham, MD: Rowman and Littlefield, 2007); Jane E. Elliott, *Some Did It for Civilization; Some Did It for Country: A Revised View of the Boxer War* (Hong Kong: Chinese University Press, 2002). For the Marines' experience in China, see George B. Clarke, *Treading Softly: The U.S. Marines in China from the 1840s to 1890s* (Pike, NH: Brass Hat, 1996), especially 19–46.

47. The word "horde" was commonly used to describe the Boxers. See, for example, "Battle Is Going On," *Washington Post*, 24 Jun. 1900, 1; and W. N. Pethick, "The Struggle on the Peking Wall," *Century Illustrated Magazine*, Dec. 1900, 308.

48. "Recruiting the Marines," *Washington Post*, 21 Jul. 1900, 2.

49. U.S. soldiers responded similarly. See Coffman, *Regulars*, 32–33.

50. Diana Preston, *Besieged in Peking: The Story of the 1900 Boxer Rising* (London: Constable, 1999), 144; and William Harllee, *The Marine from Manatee:*

A Tradition of Rifle Marksmanship (Washington, D.C.: National Rifle Association, 1984), 73. For somewhat similar comments from a later period, see James Breckenridge to Mother, 27 Oct. 1908, James Breckenridge Papers, MCHD. Also see Mary Hooker, *Behind the Scenes in Peking* (London: John Murray, 1910), 96. For earlier praise for Japanese soldiers see Collum, *History* (1903), 319.

51. Frederic M. Wise and Meigs O. Frost, *A Marine Tells It to You* (New York: J. H. Sear, 1929), 31.

52. Oscar Upham, "Account of Private Oscar Upham, American Marine," in *China 1900: The Eyewitnesses Speak*, ed. Frederic A. Sharf and Peter Harrington (Mechanicsburg, PA: Stackpole Books, 2000), 167.

53. See Hooker, *Behind the Scenes*, 23, 65, and 186–87.

54. Sgt. George Herbert, USMC, 2 Jul. 1900, George Herbert Personal Papers, MCHD.

55. H. J. Hirshinger, "An American Marine Officer's Trip to China with the China Relief Expedition, Jul., 1900," H. J. Hirshinger Papers, MCHD. For more negative depictions of Marines see one Marine's characterization of his fellow Marines as "'generally demoralized' and 'behaving badly,' with instances of rape, sodomy, and looting, and the brig full." Quoted in Hans Schmidt, *Maverick Marine: General Smedley D. Butler and the Contradictions of American Military History* (Lexington: University Press of Kentucky, 1987), 25.

56. U.S. Marines and Royal Marines had worked together during joint operations in Egypt (1882) and again in Nicaragua (1899), where British and American Marines alternated command and exchanged uniform buttons. Brooks, *Royal Marines*, 185. For the case of the U.S. Army, see Coffman, *Regulars*, 24.

57. Quoted in Charles Lee Lewis, *Famous American Marines: An Account of the Corps* (Boston: L. C. Page, 1950), 183; Heinl, *Soldiers of the Sea*, 140.

58. *Annual Report of the Navy Department 1900* (Washington, D.C.: Government Printing Office, 1900), 1120; Collum, *History* (1903), 407; Thomas, *Old Gimlet Eye*, 67. For the Royal Welch Fusiliers see Robert Graves, *Good-Bye to All That* (New York: Anchor Books, 1989; reprint, 1929), 85. Also see "Home from the Wars," *Washington Post*, 11 January 1901, 11.

59. The relationships forged during these joint operations were not set aside at the end of the expedition. The U.S. Marines subsequently sent official greetings on the national holiday of Wales. Heinl, *Soldiers of the Sea*, 137; Graves, *Good-Bye*, 86.

60. Of course this fiction was harder to proclaim at sea, where Filipino and African American messmen served white officers.

61. Sharf and Harrington, *China 1900*, 218; Karsten, *Naval Aristocracy*, 58. For other manifestations of this sentiment, see C. J. Hicks, "The Life of a Jack Tar," *Independent*, 20 Aug. 1903, 1979.

62. Thomas, *Old Gimlet Eye*, 52. Marines had only one meal to eat per day as they marched toward Peking. See "Report of the Major General Commandant of the United States Marine Corps," *Annual Report* (1900), 1118.

63. H. J. Hirshinger, "An American Marine Officer's Trip to China with the China Relief Expedition, Jul., 1900." H. J. Hirshinger Papers, MCHD. Hirshinger also celebrated the U.S. Army cavalry, describing the cavalry's "reckless dare devil soldiery."

64. John Harllee, *Marine from Manatee*, 65. For other indications of this "contrast" from Waller, see Colonel Littleton Waller, USMC, to Second Lieutenant Edwin McClellan, USMC, 27 Jun. 1910, Edwin McClellan Papers, MCHD. Waller's actions could be interpreted as being more paternalistic than democratic. For the interest he took in enlisted Marines who had served under him in the past, see Littleton Waller to Magill, 27 Dec. 1909, Personal Book, Littleton Waller Papers, MCHD. For a private who considered Waller his only friend, see Littleton Waller to Richards, 26 March 1910, Personal Book, Littleton Waller Papers, MCHD.

65. It is also possible that Waller's decision was motivated by *noblesse oblige*. For this tendency as a pattern in American labor history see Matthew Frye Jacobson, *Barbarian Virtues: The United States Encounters Foreign Peoples At Home and Abroad, 1876–1917* (New York: Hill and Wang, 2000), 133. For one journalist's account that suggested good relations between enlisted men and officers see "Spirit of Harmony among Marines," [1898], Clipping, Henry Cochrane Papers, MCHD.

66. Photograph, Waller Papers, MCHD. On the difficulty of the Boxer Rebellion, see Major Littleton Waller, USMC, to Frank Bearss, 28 Jun. 1901, Littleton Waller Papers, MCHD. He characterized the duty as "one of the most trying known in modern times." See Myerly, *Spectacle*, 115, for how difficult campaigns decreased the differences between officers and men in the British Army. Smedley Butler, from the possibly biased and patronizing perspective of an officer, described how an "easy and friendly relationship prevailed between officers and enlisted men on the march. We were sharing the same hardships." Thomas, *Old Gimlet Eye*, 50 and 71. This source is more problematic because Butler was recalling his memories of the Corps.

67. On smaller naval vessels, for example, Marine sergeants commanded Marine Guards without immediate oversight from Marine officers. "Soldier and Sailor, Too," 24 Jul. 1898, Clipping, Henry Cochrane Papers, Box 1, MCHD. For the increasing attention the Army gave to enlisted soldiers' conditions, see Coffman, *Regulars*, 96–141.

68. Collum, *History* (1903), 359.

69. In recollecting his service, William L. Adams noted how learning the Marines were among the first Western troops to land during the Boxer Rebellion inspired him to enlist. William Llewellyn Adams, *Exploits and Adventures of a Soldier Ashore and Afloat* (Philadelphia: J. B. Lippincott, 1911), 46.

70. Hooker, *Behind the Scenes*, 15; Peter Harrington and Michael Perry, *Peking 1900: The Boxer Rebellion* (Oxford: Osprey, 2001), 82.

71. Sharf and Harrington, "Journal of Mary E. Andrews, American Missionary," 195; Major Thomas Wood, USMC, to General Charles Heywood, USMC, Nov. 6, 1900, LR, RG 127. It seems Wood might have been a bit hasty in writing the second letter, given the original article was published in October and a correction was issued in November.

72. John A. Sleicher to Major Thomas Wood, USMC, Nov. 5, 1900, Encl., Major Thomas Wood to General Charles Heywood, USMC, 6 Nov. 1900, LR, RG 127.

73. *Annual Reports* (1900), 1151.

74. For an overview of the U.S. involvement in the Philippines, see David J. Silbey, *A War of Frontier and Empire: The Philippine-American War, 1899–1902* (New York: Hill and Wang, 2007). For accounts of the U.S. Army, see John Morgan Gates, *Schoolbooks and Krags: The United States Army in the Philippines, 1898–1902* (Westport, CT: Greenwood Press, 1973); Stuart Creighton Miller, *"Benevolent Assimilation". The American Conquest of the Philippines* (New Haven, CT: Yale University Press, 1982); Brian McAllister Linn, *The Philippine War, 1899–1902* (Lawrence: University Press of Kansas, 2000); Coffman, *Regulars*. For a more cultural approach see Angel Shaw and Luis H. Francia, *Vestiges of War: The Philippine-American War and the Aftermath of an Imperial Dream, 1899–1999* (New York: New York University Press, 2002); Julian Go, *The American Colonial State in the Philippines: Global Perspectives* (Durham, N.C.: Duke University Press, 2003); and Paul A. Kramer, *The Blood of Government: Race, Empire, the United States, and the Philippines* (Chapel Hill: University of North Carolina Press, 2006). Also see Warwick Anderson, *Colonial Pathologies: American Tropical Medicine, Race, and Hygiene in the Philippines* (Durham, N.C.: Duke University Press, 2006).

75. Linn, *Philippine War*, 207; Millett, *Semper Fidelis*, 152.

76. John Clifford Papers, MCHD.

77. For Smith's background, see Davd L. Fritz, "Before the 'Howling Wilderness': The Military Career of Jacob Hurd Smith, 1862–1902," *Military Affairs* 43 (Dec. 1979): 186–90; "Major Waller Testifies," *New York Times*, 1 Apr. 1902, 3; Brian Linn, " 'We Will Go Heavily Armed': The Marines' Small War on Samar, 1901–1902," in *New Interpretations in Naval History: Selected Papers from the Ninth Naval History Symposium*, ed. William R. Roberts and Jack Sweetman (Annapolis, MD: Naval Institute Press, 1991), 273.

78. Harry Glenn, "The Pursuit of Captain Victor," *The Wide World Magazine*, Jul. 1903, 316; and Harry Glenn, "The Pursuit of Captain Victor: II," *The Wide World Magazine*, Aug. 1903, 434. Glenn's comments regarding the Marines' love for Waller were stated in the context of the disastrous Samar expedition. For an observer's suggestion that the incidents on Samar made Waller the "idol of fighting men," see Arthur Wallace Dunn, *From Harrison to Harding: A Personal Narrative*, vol. 1 (New York: G.P. Putnam's, 1922), 371.

79. U.S. War Dept., *Annual Reports of the War Department*, vol. 8 (Washington, D.C.: Government Printing Office, 1902), 442.

80. "Attack by Marines," *Army and Navy Register*, 23 Nov. 1901, 418.

81. The Marines' attack was celebrated in a poem published in several newspapers. Ironically, the Marines again were erroneously described as "mariners," continuing the tradition of journalists' and the public's errors regarding spelling the word Marine. See "At Sojoton," *New York Times*, 6 Dec. 1901, 8.

82. Copy of Littleton Waller to Senior Squadron Commander, Cavite, PI, 25 Jan. 1902 Philippine Subject Files, HD. Waller suggested that he had discussed finding a trail several times with Smith but did not say that Smith had ordered him to find a trail.

83. Stanley Karnow, for example, describes Waller as a "scrupulous professional" in *In Our Image: America's Empire in the Philippines* (New York: Ballantine Books, 1989), 191. Also see "The Waller Acquittal," *New York Times*, 15 April 1902, 3. Military historians have debated the extent to which useful lessons can be gleamed from the study of military history. Similarly, military historians have debated about whether they should provide guidance for the military. For examples of this debate, see Martin van Creveld, "Thoughts on Military History," *Journal of Contemporary History* 18 (October 1983): 556, 560–63; and Michael Geyer, "War and the Context of General History in an Age of Total War," *Journal of Military History* Special Issue 57 (October 1993): 147–48.

84. Linn, "We Will Go Heavily Armed," 278.

85. Earl Ellis to Mother, 21 May 1902, Earl Ellis Papers, MCHD; Lt. Col. George Elliott, USMC, to Commandant Brig. Gen. Charles Heywood, USMC, 13 Oct. 1899, "Reports Related to Engagements in the Philippines and China, April 21, 1898 to Jun. 7, 1907," RG 127; Littleton Waller to Frank L. Denny, 10 Jan. 1910, Copy in Personal Book, Littleton Waller Papers, MCHD.

86. One song about the Army's soldiers mocked the Marines' expedition in Samar rhyming: "About another soldier man I'd like to say a word: / He's neither fish nor flesh nor fowl, but he is a bird, / He finds his way o'er foreign seas by sun and moon and star, / But he could not find his way across the Island of Samar. / Chorus: So make way for the web-foot man / The good U.S. Marines. / They need four guides for every man, / Out in the Philippines." This song pointed

to the difficulty of establishing exactly what a Marine did except to travel long distances. It also mocked the purported reliance of Marines on large numbers of guides. The lyrics suggests that where soldiers and Marines served together members of both services were likely to define themselves against each other. W. E. Christian, *Rhymes of the Rookies: Sunny Side of Soldier Service* (New York: Dodd, Mead, 1917), 36.

87. Cameron, *American Samurai*, 7. Unfortunately, this historiography has not been fully developed yet. For some examples of this type of work, however, see James Belich, *The Victorian Interpretation of Racial Conflict: The Maori, the British, and the New Zealand Wars* (McGill-Queen's University Press, 1990); and Streets, *Martial Races*.

88. For example, see Michael Adas, *Machines as the Measure of Men: Science, Technology, and Ideologies of Western Dominance* (Ithaca, N.Y.: Cornell University Press, 1989), especially 184–87, in regard to the connections between Western attitudes and military technology.

89. Historiography on so-called small wars is somewhat limited. See Keith Bickel, *Mars Learning: The Marine Corps' Development of Small Wars Doctrine, 1915–1940* (Boulder, C.O.: Westview Press, 2001); and Roger Beaumont, "Small Wars: Definitions and Dimensions," *Annals of the American Academy of Political and Social Science* 541 (Sep. 1995): 20–35.

90. Charles Calwell, *Small Wars* (Lincoln: University of Nebraska Press, 1996), 21; U.S. War Dept., *Annual Reports for the War Department* (1902), 445; "Defense of General Waller," 2, Waller subject file, Historical Detachment (HD).

91. See, for example, Hoganson, *Fighting for American Manhood*.

92. Gail Bederman, *Manliness and Civilization: A Cultural History of Gender and Race in the United States, 1880–1917* (Chicago: University of Chicago Press, 1995), 22–23 and 44. For Glenn's heroics, see *Annual Reports for the War Department* (1902), 442. The magazine published stories of exotic adventure around the globe.

93. Glenn, "Pursuit of Captain Victor, II," 436. For intimacy during combat, see Santanu Das, *Touch and Intimacy in First World War Literature* (New York: Cambridge University Press, 2006).

94. Anderson, "Trespass Speaks," 1349; "Waller Goes Free," *Baltimore Sun*, 14 April 1902, 1; "Waller Had Very Hard Experience; Himself and Men Starve While Crossing Samar; Native Carriers Get Sulky and Try to Kill Leader of the Famous Expedition," *Duluth News-Tribune*, 13 March 1902, 8.

95. General Chaffee, who had praised Waller so heartily after Sojoton, expressed this sentiment clearly. "Waller Trial Record," *Washington Post*, 15 Jul. 1902, 3.

96. "War in Samar Is Not a Pleasure Trip," *Great Falls (MT) Tribune*, 21 April 1902, 5; "Waller Goes Free," *Washington Post*, 14 April 1902, 1. For discussions of atrocities in the Philippines, see Richard E. Welch Jr., "American Atrocities in

the Philippines: The Indictment and the Response," *Pacific Historical Review* 43 (May 1974), 223–53. Welch emphasizes that the press was slow to react to events in Samar and, even then, relatively forgiving of his actions. See especially pages 244–47. For an account that largely exonerates Waller given the extreme circumstances he faced in Samar, see "Waller Trial Record," *Washington Post*, 15 Jul. 1902, 3. Also see G.K., "The Charges of Cruelty in the Philippines," *Outlook*, 22 Mar. 1902, 711–12.

97. "Maj. Waller Speaks in His Own Behalf," *Los Angeles Times*, 12 Apr. 1902, 3; Captain David D. Porter to Senior Squadron Commander Cavite P.I., 8 Feb. 1902, Philippines Subject Files, HD. A penciled notation on the report suggests Porter intended it for Major Waller. "Friends of Waller Claim Conspiracy," *Los Angeles Times*, 9 March 1902, 4.

98. Linn, *Philippine War*, 317. For the shaping of memories of war see Gary W. Gallagher, *Causes Won, Lost, and Forgotten: How Hollywood and Popular Art Shape What We Know about the Civil War* (Chapel Hill: University of North Carolina Press, 2008).

99. *Annual Reports of the Navy Department for the Year 1902*, 972.

100. Author unknown, n.d., John H. Clifford Papers, MCHD. For a Samar veteran who took immense pride in hearing these words, see Victor Salvatore Jr., "Survivor Recalls Rugged Samar Duty," *Washington Post*, 24. Dec. 1951. For the suggestion that these words were more a product of the Corps' Recruiting Publicity Bureau, see Maj. John L. Zimmerman, "Stand, Gentlemen!," *Proceedings* 75 (March 1949): 289.

101. In suggesting a more formal organization for the Corps, one officer pointed to the march through the jungle as an event that had drawn them together. The "tradition of the way they faced that grave danger" could be maintained by a particular regiment, thereby increasing an individual's pride in belonging. Captain Henry C. Davis, "A Plea for a Permanent Regimental Formation in the United States Marine Corps," *Proceedings* 29 (1903): 214.

102. Writing in 1933, former Marine sergeant Eugene Dooley concluded his comments about the Samar Campaign by stating that the officers he served with "showed good judgment, and I cannot speak too highly of them. They did all that they could do for the sick and wounded men, and . . . [they] suffered just as much hardship as the enlisted men did." See "Letter of Eugene Dooley," 1933, John H. Clifford Papers, MCHD. Also see Glenn, "Pursuit of Captain Victor, II," 464.

103. Even those works that appear relevant focus more on society's experience at large. See Jay Winter and Emmanuel Sivan, eds., *War and Remembrance in the Twentieth Century* (New York: Cambridge University Press, 1999). Other works include Paul Fussell, *The Great War and Modern Memory* (New York: Oxford University Press, 2000); Patrick Hagopian, *The Vietnam*

War in American Memory: Veterans, Memorials, and the Politics of Healing (Amherst: University of Massachusetts Press, 2009); T. G. Ashplant, Graham Dawson, and Michael Roper, eds., *The Politics of War Memory and Commemoration* (London: Routledge, 2000); J. M. Winter, *Remembering War: The Great War between Memory and History in the Twentieth Century* (New Haven: Yale University Press, 2006).

104. Bernard S. Cohn, "Representing Authority in Victorian India," in *Invention of Tradition*, 179.

105. Adams, *Exploits and Adventures*, 143. For the Marines' frustration with counterinsurgency, see Albert Gardner Robinson, *The Philippines: The War and the People, A Record of Personal Observations* (New York: McClure, Phillips, 1901), 350.

106. This was particularly the case for Spanish officers. For similar problems in the U.S. Army, see Linn, *Philippine War*, 64. "Defense of Major General L. W. T Waller," Subject file, Philippines War, HD. Waller contrasts the more civilized way that the Marines cared for wounded Spanish troops during the Spanish-American War with the treachery of insurgents in Egypt, the Philippines, and elsewhere. Also see John Clifford, *History of the First Battalion of U.S. Marines* (Pike, NH: Brass Hat, 1930), 50 and 56. Clifford served as a Marine during the Spanish-American War. Collum notes how the treatment of Spanish prisoners was "characteristic of American methods" in warfare in *History* (1903), 336. Spanish officers even received claret wine during their imprisonment. Collum, 339.

107. Earl Ellis to Father, 8 Aug. 1902, and Earl Ellis to Mother, 24 Feb. 1903, Earl Ellis Papers, MCHD.

108. Benedict Anderson, *Imagined Communities* (New York: Verso, 1991), 151.

109. Quoted in *Army and Navy Journal*, 30 Jan. 1904, HQMC Scrapbook, RG 127, NARA.

110. "Our Marines in the War," *Evening Times*, 15 Oct. 1898, 5. McLemore became the head of the Recruiting Publicity Bureau during World War I. He will be discussed in a later chapter. Headquartered in San Francisco, he established substations in Sacramento and San Jose. An article describing his efforts headlined Rudyard Kipling's phrase "Soldier and Sailor Too." See "Soldier and Sailor Too," *Record-Union* (Sacramento), 27 Sep. 1899, 4.

Chapter 3. Refinement and Elaboration

1. "Defies Police Order to Lower Old Glory," *Indianapolis Star*, 8 August 1907, 3. For a more dramatic account replete with purported quotes of the exchange, see "Old Glory Still Waves," *Eau Claire Leader* (Wisconsin), 10 Aug. 1907, 1. "Gun Keeps Police from Flag," *Chicago Tribune*, 9 Aug. 1907, 5.

2. "Defies Police Order," 3; "Labor Day Plans," *Huntington Herald*, 22 Aug. 1907, 4; "Soldier Life Evidently Does Not Appeal Now," *Call-Leader* (Elwood, IN), 21 Aug. 1907, 5; "Federal against State Authority," *Brooklyn Eagle*, 22 Aug. 1907, 4. For the Army's frustrations and its drop in enlistments from 1905 to 1907, see "Report of the Adjutant General" in *War Department, U.S.A., Annual Reports, 1907,* Vol. 1 (Washington, D.C.: Government Printing Office, 1907), 228. For an early effort at printing a "promotional booklet" see Coffman, *Regulars*, 96.

3. For a recruiter's difficulties, see William Brackett, "When the Corps Was Short," *Bulletin*, Jun. 1915, 3.

4. L. J. Magill to Capt. James Breckinridge, 11 Jan. 1905, James Breckinridge Papers, MCHD.

5. See *Minneapolis Journal*, 14 Mar. 1906, 18; and *Philadelphia Inquirer*, 14 Mar. 1906, 12, for just two of many examples.

6. See "Wanted for U.S. Army," *Salt Lake Herald Republican*, 12 May 1907, 29; "Wanted," *Wichita Daily Eagle*, 6 Jul. 1911, 9; "Wanted," *Philadelphia Inquirer*, 16 Mar. 1913, 36. For just one of many examples of the ads running in close proximity see the *Philadelphia Inquirer*, 19 Jul. 1903, 17.

7. See "Wanted," *Baltimore Sun*, 6 Aug. 1906, 3. There is a Navy help-wanted ad immediately below it. For the same wording, see also "Wanted for the U.S. Marine Corps," *Fort Wayne Daily News*, 27 Dec. 1906, 9; "Wanted," *The Pioneer* (Bemidji, MN), 23 Apr. 1906, 2.

8. *Dallas Morning News*, 2 Nov. 1910, 12. For the use of similar wording in its recruiting posters as early as 1887, see "The Life of a Marine," *Evening Star* (Washington, D.C.), 16 Jul. 1887, 2. This practice was still in use by 1898, including pay charts. See "Recruits for Marine Service," *Wilkes-Barre Record* (Wilkes-Barre, PA), 25 Mar. 1898, 8. This article did not differ dramatically from one published shortly after the conclusion of the Spanish-Cuban American War: untitled, *New York Herald*, 27 Dec. 1898, 15. For similar, albeit less-detailed, classifieds, see *Dallas Morning News*, 14 March 1907, 12; *Kansas City Star*, 21 Oct. 1903, 12; *Philadelphia Inquirer*, 6 March 1904, 1; *Duluth News-Tribune*, 27 March 1905, 6; *Grand Forks Daily Herald*, 1 Feb. 1906, 7; *Morning Oregonian*, 1 Jan. 1912, 17. One ad simply highlighted an opportunity to "see the world." See *Omaha World Herald*, 23 Dec. 1906, 10. By contrast, a 1911 ad placed by the Navy stated that sailors were the "finest body of picked men in the world." For other uses of the same language, see untitled, *Philadelphia Inquirer*, 9 Jul. 1911, 2. Also see *Duluth News-Tribune*, 28 May 1911, 22; *Kalamazoo Gazette*, 2 Jul. 1911, 14; *Wilkes-Barre Times*, 30 Sep. 1911, 2.

9. Inger L. Stole, *Advertising on Trial: Consumer Activism and Corporate Public Relations* (Urbana: University of Illinois Press, 2006), 2–5, 6.

10. "Wanted," *Indianapolis Journal*, 11 Oct. 1902, 8.

11. The contact in the ad was a Marine officer, Capt. J. E. Mahoney. See *Philadelphia Inquirer*, 30 Aug. 1901, 10. Mahoney appears to have copied the ad from his predecessor, Major W. P. Biddle, USMC; *Philadelphia Inquirer*, 16 Aug. 1899, 10; and *Philadelphia Inquirer*, 18 March 1900, 1. The last of these particular ads appears to have been published in 1903. See *Philadelphia Inquirer*, 27 Jun. 1903, 12. An article published the subsequent week made no mention of "U.S. Navy Recruits." See *Philadelphia Inquirer*, 1 Jul. 1903, 10; 21 Aug. 1903, 12; 31 Oct. 1903, 12; 9 Aug. 1905, 10.

12. "Uncle Sam's Efforts to Enlist Naval Fighters in Chicago," *Inter Ocean* (Chicago), 8 Feb. 1903, 39.

13. For other uses of the "important branch" phrasing, see "Our Marine Corps: The Men Who Occupy a Middle Ground between the Army and the Navy," *Inter Ocean* (Chicago), 25 April 1886, 19. See "Recruits for Marine Service," *Wilkes-Barre Record*, 25 Mar. 1898, 8.

14. *ANJ*, 24 Sep. 1904, 421. A search in the database America's Historical Newspapers shows that the words "Marine Corps U.S. Navy Recruits" only appeared in this newspaper, suggesting the extent to which individual officers had latitude in publishing classified advertisements at the local level. Ironically, naval officer Lt. William S. Sims returned from duty as an attaché in France to the USS *Kentucky*, the *Kearsarge's* sister. He found the ship to be an abomination. William M. McBride, *Technological Change and the United States Navy, 1865–1945* (Baltimore: Johns Hopkins University Press, 2000), 49.

15. James Breckinridge to Mother, Jan. 19, 1905, James Breckinridge Papers, MCHD; Stole, *Advertising on Trial*, viii and x. When launched, the *Kearsarge* was noted for its impressive secondary battery, which made it highly advanced at the time. Perhaps this fact explains the vessel's choice for ads. See "Battleship Kearsarge: To Be Most Powerful of the Defenders of American Rights," *New York Times*, 24 Nov. 1895, A20. Or it could have been that Breckenridge had served on the ship. For naval officers' distrust and dislike of businessmen, see Karsten, *Naval Aristocracy*, 187–93.

16. "Army Gossip in Washington," *Omaha Daily Bee* (Nebraska), 1 Nov. 1904, 4. For the suggestion that recruiters often struggled with an extremely limited stock of recruiting posters, see L. J. Magill to Capt. James Breckinridge, 11 Jan. 1905, James Breckinridge Papers, MCHD.

17. "Army Gossip in Washington," *Omaha Daily Bee*, 1 Nov. 1904, 4; "Report of the Adjutant General" in *War Department, U.S.A., Annual Reports, 1907*, Vol. 1 (Washington, D.C.: Government Printing Office, 1907), 238–39; Colonel, Adjutant and Inspector to the Officer in Charge of Recruiting, Buffalo, NY, 3 November 1906, RG 127, Office of the Commandant, Press Copies of Letters Sent, Box 55, Vol. 173, 5 Nov. 1906–26 Dec. 1906.

18. This article shows a mix of words and images: "'Rookies' Now are Being Legally Sought in Parks," *Detroit Free Press*, 8 Aug. 1908, 4. One poster used by the Corps in 1905, for example, highlighted the striking uniforms worn by Marines. For an emphasis on imagery, see "Attractive Bill Posters Put Up by Uncle Sam," *Brooklyn Daily Eagle*, 2 April 1905, 59.

19. Roland Marchand, *Advertising the American Dream: Making Way for Modernity, 1920–1940* (Berkeley: University of California Press, 1985), 235.

20. In 1896 the Corps had 2,676 Marines. With the passage of the Naval Personnel Act (1899) in the wake of the Spanish-American War, it increased to 6,263 Marines. By 1908 it had 9,854 Marines, a number it would more or less maintain until the passage of the National Defense Act of 1916, which increased the institution to 15,630 Marines. Heinl, *Soldiers of the Sea*, 610–11.

21. The Corps was not alone in facing this struggle among the branches. "Attractive Bill Posters," 59; Commandant to the Officer in Charge of Recruiting, 5 November 1906, RG 127, Office of the Commandant, Press Copies of Letters Sent, Box 55, Vol. 173, 5 Nov. 1906–26 Dec. 1906.

22. BG George Elliott to Charles H. Fuller Company, 19 Nov. 1906, and Commandant to Quartermaster, U.S. Marine Corps, 14 Nov. 1906, both in RG127, Office of the Commandant, Press Copies of Letters Sent, Box 55, Vol. 173, 5 Nov. 1906–26 Dec. 1906. Also see Quartermaster to Secretary of the Navy, 26 Nov. 1906 and Commandant to Secretary of the Navy, 6 Dec. 1906, both in RG127, Office of the Commandant, Press Copies of Letters Sent, Box 55, Vol. 173, 5 Nov. 1906–26 Dec. 1906.

23. As early as 1902, two companies had contacted a Navy recruiting officer in Chicago, offering their services in placing ads to get recruits in western newspapers. Although the Bureau of Navigation supported the idea, the secretary of the Navy ultimately rejected it. See Secretary of the Navy to the Bureau of Navigation, 19 Jun. 1902, RG 80 General Correspondence Secretary of the Navy, Entry 14413. Whether this would constitute display advertising is unknown. What is known is that the Navy rejected their services, stating that the Navy would not be following appropriate procedure. This process would be the subject of great concern again in 1912 and 1913. Commandant to Quartermaster, U.S. Marine Corps, 6 Dec. 1906, RG127, Office of the Commandant, Press Copies of Letters Sent, Box 55, Vol. 173, 5 Nov. 1906–26 Dec. 1906.

24. Commandant to Charles H. Fuller Company, 19 November 1906 and Commandant to Secretary of the Navy, 26 Nov. 1906, both in RG127, Office of the Commandant, Press Copies of Letters Sent, Box 55, Vol. 173, 5 Nov. 1906–26 Dec. 1906. By display advertising, it seems that officials meant larger, more distinctive ads as opposed to the more traditional help-wanted ads. For other examples of advertisements masquerading as newspaper articles run

at the same time as the Corps' experiment, see "Piles Cured," *Rockford Daily Register-Gazette*, 25 Jan. 1907, 3. This article ran above another that does not seem to be display advertising but a regular article about the last day of the experiment in Rockford. See "Last Day of Recruits," *Rockford Daily Register-Gazette*, 25 Jan. 1907, 3. See, for example, Cornell University's display advertising campaign in 1920: "University Uses Display Ads," *Fourth Estate*, 14 Feb. 1920, 4.

25. See, for example, a letter suggesting Gamborg-Andresen and the company decide the best towns together. BG George Elliott to Charles H. Fuller Company, 10 Dec. 1906, RG127, Office of the Commandant, Press Copies of Letters Sent, Box 55, Vol. 173, 5 Nov. 1906–26 Dec. 1906. In addition to letters already cited to the Charles H. Fuller Company, see Commandant to Charles H. Fuller Company, 10 December 1906; Commandant to the Officer in Charge of Recruiting, Chicago, IL, 13 Dec. 1906; Commandant to the Officer in Charge of Recruiting, Des Moines, IA, 13 Dec. 1906; Commandant to Officer in Charge, Recruiting District of Illinois, 22 Dec. 1906, all in RG127, Office of the Commandant, Press Copies of Letters Sent, Box 55, Vol. 173, 5 Nov. 1906–26 Dec. 1906. Also see a letter requesting the Navy's medical officers. The commandant expressed his frustration that the Corps' hired civilian doctors would accept recruits only for the Navy's doctors to reject them later. Commandant to Secretary of the Navy, 22 Dec. 1906, RG127, Office of the Commandant, Press Copies of Letters Sent, Box 55, Vol. 173, 5 Nov. 1906–26 Dec. 1906.

26. "Uncle Sam's Efforts to Enlist Naval Fighters in Chicago," *Inter Ocean* (Chicago), 8 Feb. 1903, 39; Capt C. Gamborg-Andresen to Brigadier General, Commandant, 1 Feb. 1907, RG 80, General Correspondence, 1897–1915, Box 835, Entry 24004.

27. "Young Man! You are Wanted!," *Rockford Morning Star*, 17 Jan. 1907, 2. Also see the same article in the *Rockford Daily Register-Gazette*, 17 Jan. 1907, 8; and *Rockford Morning Star*, 20 Jan. 1907, 18.

28. "A Chance for Young Men to See the World," *Rockford Daily Register-Gazette*, 19 Jan. 1907, 2. Also see the same ad in *Rockford Morning Star*, 19 Jan. 1907, 4.

29. Gamborg-Andresen also said there were 25 to 30 other captains in the service who had been enlisted as well before receiving commissions.

30. "From Private to Captaincy," *Rockford Daily Register-Gazette*, 21 Jan. 1907, 1.

31. "Seek Recruits in Naval Service," *Rockford Morning Star*, 2 Jan. 1907, 8.

32. BG Elliott to Secretary of the Navy, 1 March 1907, RG 80, General Correspondence, 1897–1915, Box 835, Entry 24004. The commandant offered no explanation for why the Chicago recruiting office spent so much more money than other districts, with the average cost around Chicago being $70.79 per

recruit versus $36.44 elsewhere. Of that amount, it cost about $18 alone just to transport and feed a new recruit. In May of 1909 the average cost of a recruit was $44.50. Lt. Col. Assistant Quartermaster to Major General, Commandant, U.S. Marine Corps, Headquarters, 16 Jun. 1909, RG 80, General Correspondence, 1897–1915, Box 837, Entry 24004.

The Corps gained 340 recruits that month. The next May it acquired 235 recruits at an average cost of $51.10. Colonel Denny, Quartermaster to Major General, Commandant, U.S. Marine Corps, Headquarters, 18 May 1910, RG 80, General Correspondence, 1897–1915, Box 837, Entry 24004. The following April it obtained 229 recruits at an average cost of $78.49. Major General Commandant to Assistant Secretary of the Navy, 22 May 1911, RG 80, General Correspondence, 1897–1915, Box 837, Entry 24004. In March of 1912 it obtained 273 recruits at a cost of $62.92 per recruit. Major General Commandant to Secretary of the Navy, 13 April 1912, RG 80, General Correspondence, 1897–1915, Box 837, Entry 24004.

33. Capt. C. Gamborg-Andresen to Brigadier General, Commandant, 1 Feb. 1907, RG 80, General Correspondence, 1897–1915, Box 835, Entry 24004.

34. Capt. C. Gamborg-Andresen to Brigadier General, Commandant, 1 Feb. 1907, RG 80, General Correspondence, 1897–1915, Box 835, Entry 24004. See Commandant BG Elliott to Sec of the Navy, 1 March 1907, RG 80, General Correspondence, 1897–1915, Box 835, Entry 24004. Capt. C. Gamborg-Andresen to Brigadier General, Commandant, 1 Feb. 1907, RG 80, General Correspondence, 1897–1915, Box 835, Entry 24004. Many also balked at the required four-year enlistment term because they could not imagine being away from family and friends for so long.

35. Indorsement, Colonel Quartermaster F. L. Denny to Brigadier General, Commandant, U.S. Marine Corps, 28 Feb. 1907, RG 80, General Correspondence, 1897–1915, Box 835, Entry 24004.

36. For the continued characterization of a Marine as a soldier, see, for example, a recommendation letter by Brigadier General, Commandant George Elliott to Whom it May Concern, 21 March 1908, RG127, Office of the Commandant, Press Copies of Letters Sent, Box 75, Vol. 193, 3 Mar. 1908–25 April 1908. The commandant used "soldier" where one would use "Marine" today: "His record as a soldier was clear throughout the whole enlistment."

37. Quartermaster Col. F. L. Denny to Mr. B. F. Peters, Chief Clerk, Navy Department, 27 Feb. 1907, RG 80, General Correspondence, 1897–1915, Box 817, Entry 23362-3; Memorandum to All Recruiting Officers, Assistant Adjutant and Inspector to Mr. L. H. Lowry, 25 Mar. 1908, RG127, Office of the Commandant, Press Copies of Letters Sent, Box 65, Vol. 193, 3 Mar. 1908–25 April 1908.

38. See, for example, the commandant's approval of two recruiting officers' requests on the same day: Commandant George Elliott to Officer in Charge

of Recruiting, Detroit, 21 April 1908, and to Officer in Charge of Recruiting, Buffalo, 21 April 1908, RG127, Office of the Commandant, Press Copies of Letters Sent, Box 65, Vol. 193, 3 Mar. 1908–25 April 1908.

39. Assistant Adjutant and Inspector to Mr. L. H. Lowry, 7 Mar. 1908, Office of the Commandant, Press Copies of Letters Sent, Box 65, Vol. 193, 3 Mar. 1908–25 April 1908; Assistant Adjutant and Inspector to Mr. L. H. Lowry, 7 Mar. 1908; Assistant Adjutant and Inspector to Mr. M. C. Long, 8 April 1908, RG127, NARA. Less familiar with the booklet, perhaps, the commandant's substitute did not make a similar mention. See Assistant Adjutant and Inspector to Mr. M. C. Long, 8 April 1908, Office of the Commandant, Press Copies of Letters Sent, Box 65, Vol. 193, 3 Mar. 1908–25 April 1908, RG127, NARA.

40. Chief of Bureau to Assistant Secretary of the Navy, 1 April 1907, Box 817, Entry 23362–2, RG80, NARA; Secretary of the Navy to BG Elliott, 24 March 1907, RG 80, General Correspondence, 1897–1915, Box 835, Entry 24004, RG80, NARA.

41. Colonel, Quartermaster Frank L. Denny to BG George Elliott, 11 Jun. 1907, RG 80, General Correspondence, 1897–1915, Box 835, Entry 24004.

42. For the differences in costs, see Acting Secretary of the Navy to BG George Elliott, 31 Jul. 1907, RG 80, General Correspondence, 1897–1915, Box 835, Entry 24004. The Corps had known it cost more as early as March. See BG Elliott to Sec of the Navy, 7 March 1907, RG 80, General Correspondence, 1897–1915, Box 835, Entry 24004.

43. Indorsement, BG George Elliott to Secretary of the Navy, 7 Oct. 1907; BG Elliott to Sec of the Navy, 7 March 1907; 9th Indorsement, Quartermaster to BG George Elliott, 6 Sep. 1907; 10th Indorsement, BG George Elliott to Secretary of the Navy, 7 Oct. 1907, all in RG 80, General Correspondence, 1897–1915, Box 835, Entry 24004.

44. Major Rufus H. Lane, Asst. Adjutant and Inspector by Order of BG Elliott to the Secretary of the Navy, 9 August 1907, RG 80, General Correspondence, 1897–1915, Box 835, Entry 24004. No specific examples of excessive Navy advertising were provided.

45. BG Commandant George Elliott to Secretary of the Navy, 8 May 1907, RG 80, Box 817, Entry 23362–4. The reason for this round of correspondence in May is unknown, given that the secretary of the Navy approved display advertising in March. See Secretary of the Navy to the Brigadier General Commandant, 2 March 1907, RG 80, General Correspondence of the Secretary of the Navy, 1897–1915, Box 835, Entry 24004–11.

46. BG Commandant Elliott to Secretary of the Navy, 8 May 1908, RG127, Office of the Commandant, Press Copies of Letters Sent, Box 58, Vol. 179, 4 Mar. 1907–20 May 1907; Commandant George Elliott to Recruiting Officers, 18

May 1907, RG127, Office of the Commandant, Press Copies of Letters Sent, Box 58, Vol. 179, 4 Mar. 1907–20 May 1907.

47. Acting Secretary of the Navy to BG Commandant George Elliott, 11 May 1907, RG 80, Box 817, Entry 23362–4. A January report made in 1908 provided more conclusive proof for the success of display advertising. Lt. Commander R. Shoemaker, USN, Bureau of Navigation, Navy Department to Assistant Secretary of the Navy, 4 Jan. 1908, RG 80, Box 817, Entry 23362–7. Shoemaker wrote that the Navy used the "services of a well-known Advertising Agency" and experimented mainly in "agricultural papers." It then experimented more without the agency, claiming to have had greater success. A delinquent bill owed to an advertising firm sparked the suggestion of how much money could be saved by instituting a system within the Navy to facilitate display advertising. See Assistant Secretary of the Navy to the Chief of the Bureau of Navigation, 23 Nov. 1909, Box 817, Entry 23362–10. By 1910 at least one advertising company was requesting the opportunity to compete for this advertising. See George W. Edwards, the Saint Clair-Edwards Company, to Assistant Secretary of the Navy Beekman Winthrop, 8 Dec. 1910, Box 817, Entry 23362–11.

48. See "Uncle Sam's Marines," *Daily News* (Galveston, TX), 14 April 1907, 23; "The United States Marine Corps," *Houston Post*, 14 April 1907; "Our Marines," *Lima (OH) News*, 10 Jan. 1908, 3. Pinkston was the officer in charge of recruiting in Texas who wrote an article that stated his name but not his affiliation with the Corps. Such an article could have represented the officer's own attempts at display advertising. At this point in his career, Pinkston served on recruiting duty for eighteen months before receiving orders to the Philippines. A journalist praised him for applying better business practices to recruiting, and before going to the Philippines he traveled to the Corps' Headquarters to share his ideas. See "Officers Shifted," *Houston Post*, 19 Aug. 1907, 6. Marine lore incorrectly attributes this motto to the Recruiting Publicity Bureau and, more particularly, a Marine named Paul Woyshner.

49. "Marine Corps Now Complete," *Morning Oregonian*, 29 Dec. 1907, 2; "Plenty of Marine Recruits," *Washington Post*, 11 Dec. 1907, 9. See "Officers Shifted," *Houston Post*, 19 Aug. 1907, 6.

50. "Lively Scramble for New Recruits," *Duluth News-Tribune*, 8 Jan. 1908, 12; "Plenty of Marines: Supply Exceeds Demand—Army and Navy Need Men," *New York Daily Tribune*, 8 March 1908, 8. It is also possible, however, that this popularity was fallout from the popular world cruise of 1907, which attracted the most recruits since the Spanish-American War. "Men Rush to Enlist," *Washington Herald*, 12 Nov. 1907, 3. The Navy, on the other hand, believed it suffered because it had more stringent citizenship standards for recruits. See

"Nine Recruits Join Uncle Sam's Navy," *Duluth News-Tribune*, 5 Oct. 1907, 6. The commandant's annual reports provide further insight into the Corps' strength. The commandant reported in 1906 that he believed the Corps would soon be recruited to "full strength." *Annual Reports* (1906), 1092. Due to "high wages" and plentiful job opportunities, however, the Corps struggled to find recruits throughout 1907. *Annual Report* (1907), 1279. The Corps was full or almost full in 1913 and 1914. See *Annual Reports* (1913), 530; and *Annual Reports* (1914), 463.

In the wake of the Veracruz Incident, however, the Navy halted recruiting while the Marine Corps continued to recruit, suggesting that many were more eager to enlist as sailors than Marines. See "Men Still Sought for Marine Corps," *Montgomery Advertiser*, 2 May 1914, 6. Other newspapers actually recorded a waiting list, one of seventy-eight recruits. "U. S. Marine Corps Recruiting Halted," *Boston Morning Journal*, 10 Jul. 1915, 13; "Recruiting Marines a Simple Proposition," *Columbus Daily Enquirer*, 16 April 1916, 6. Individual recruiting stations broke records despite general economic prosperity, which marked a departure from nineteenth-century recruiting patterns. "Many Recruits Signed Marine Corps Makes New Record in Enlistments," *Oregonian*, 1 Oct. 1916, 14. For economic prosperity see "To Put U. S. Navy in Second Place," *Dallas Morning News*, 1 Oct. 1916, 2; and "Prosperity Hits Navy Increase Era of Business Gain Tends to Keep Enlistments below Normal" *Duluth News-Tribune*, 2 Jun. 1916, 14.

51. Commandant George Elliott to "Sir" (Circular Letter), 15 Jan. 1908, RG127, General Correspondence, 1904–1912, Entry 19162, Box 158.

52. Capt William Harllee to Commanding Officer, Marine Barracks, Navy Yard, Washington, D.C., 28 Feb. 1908, RG127, Office of the Commandant, Historical Section, LR, 1908–1915, Box 56; [Signature illegible] to Commanding Officer, Marine Barracks, Navy Yard, Washington, D.C., 1 Mar. 1908, RG127, Office of the Commandant, Historical Section, LR, 1817–1915, Box 56, Entry 42. The Pittsburgh officer bragged that the Corps secured far better quality recruits than the Army or the Navy. In February, for example, he claimed to have received five hundred applicants, from whom only nine were enlisted.

53. "Macon is Excellent Recruiting Station," *Macon Daily Telegraph*, 2 Feb. 1908, 5; "Macon is Excellent Recruiting Station," *Macon Daily Telegraph*, 2 Feb. 1908, 5; "Call of the Sea Again," *Duluth News-Tribune*, 17 March 1907, 12.

54. Russell Doubleday, *A Gunner aboard the "Yankee" From the Diary of Number Five of the After Port Gun* (New York: Doubleday and McClure, 1898), 214–15.

55. "Uncle Sam's Soldiers of the Sea," *Idaho Statesman*, 26 Sep. 1909, 8.

56. Robert Lindsay, *This High Name: Public Relations and the U.S. Marine Corps* (Madison: University of Wisconsin Press, 1956), 10. Lindsay states that the

bureau was established in 1911, but he includes no primary documents from the time to support his claims about the Corps' publicity during this time. Muster rolls suggest the bureau was established at the end of 1912. See U.S. Marine Corps Muster Rolls, 1893–1958, October 1912, NARA, T977, Roll 89, for the first time a Marine received orders to the Recruiting Publicity Bureau.

57. Elliott attained the position of commandant in May of 1908, so he was relatively new to the position. Records do not make clear what kind of recruiting material the Corps had at this point in time. In 1907 the Corps wrote to an interested applicant that the office was low on printed recruiting material at that time. He could only send him a "circular letter and a printed hand bill relative to the Marine Corps." See Major, Assistant Adjutant and Inspector by Order of the Commandant to Mr. E. T. Geittmann, 5 Aug. 1907, RG 127, Press Copies of Letters Sent, 1895–1898, Vol. 183. The following article claimed that it was never released, however, because by the time McCawley finished the Corps had met its recruiting goals for the year "Plenty of Marines: Supply Exceeds Demand—Army and Navy Need Men," *New York Daily Tribune*, 8 March 1908, 3. However, two months later, the commandant wrote a letter explaining that he would be releasing the pamphlet—to be distributed to potential recruits sparingly due to expense—as soon as pay tables were updated. See BG, Commandant George Elliott to All Recruiting Officers, 13 May 1908, RG 127, General Correspondence 1904–1912, Entry 19162, Box 158.

58. "Marines Ordered to the Indiana," *New York Herald*, 9 Nov. 1895, 6; Commander C. H. Davis, Jr., USN, to Lieutenant William Fullam, USN, 22 April 1896, William Fullam Papers, LOC; [Signature illegible], Navy Department, Office of the Secretary to Lieutenant William Fullam, USN, 20 April 1896, William Fullam Papers, LOC P1030388; "Status," 495, 482–83, and 544.

59. "Record of the Marines," *New York Times*, 23 Oct. 1898, 13; Lt. Col. Robert L. Meade, USMC, to Maj. Charles L. McCawley, USMC, 18 Mar. 1899, Charles L. McCawley Papers, MCHD; Richard Collum, *History of the United States Marine Corps* (New York: L. R. Hamersly, 1903), 332. See "Marines of Our Navy: Numerous and Varied Are the Duties Assigned to Them," *Indiana State Journal*, 29 Jun. 1898, 6; "Duties of the Marine Guard All About the Soldier and Sailor Too of the American Navy," *Sioux City Journal*, 1 May 1898, 10.

60. Commandant Charles Heywood, USMC, to Hon. Theodore Roosevelt, President of the Board of Reorganization of the Navy Personnel, 22 Nov. 1898, Press Copies of Letters Sent to the Secretary of the Navy, 1895–1899, RG 127; "Marines in Panama," *Evening Star* (Washington, D.C.), 26 Dec. 1903, 24; "Too Efficient United States Marine Corps Is Entrusted Guarding and Policing of Caribbean and Southern Seas," *Philadelphia Inquirer*, 13 Feb. 1905, 2.

61. Allan R. Millett and Jack Shulimson, eds., *Commandants of the Marine Corps* (Annapolis, MD: Naval Institute Press, 2004), 157; "Status," 158.

62. "No Marines on Ships: Sailor-Soldiers by New Order to be Kept Ashore," *New York Times*, 13 Nov. 1908, 1.

63. "Officers are Admonished to Cease Comment on President's Marine Order," *Evening Star*, 21 Nov. 1908; "Commander of the U.S. Marine Corps," Clipping, HQMC Scrapbook, RG 127. Under a picture of the commandant, the caption stated that officers considered this the "severest blow" possible to the Corps. For similar remarks see "No Marines on Ships: Corps Assigned to Shore Duties by President," *Washington Post*, 15 Nov. 1908, HQMC Scrapbook, RG 127. Also see A Friend of the Corps, "Passing of the Marine Corps," *New York Sun*, 30 Nov. 1908, HQMC Scrapbook, RG 127. While it is unclear what they discussed, a group of officers stationed in the northeast met secretly for four hours to discuss the order, suggesting that they did not embrace the decision. "Marine Corps Men Gather in Secret," *Washington Evening Times*, 20 Dec. 1908, HQMC Scrapbook, RG 127. Officers present at the meeting included: Col. T. N. Wood, Maj. Charles S. Hill, Capt. Carol Carpenter, Capt. F. M. Buttrick, Col. Frank Halford, Maj. Harry Davis, Maj. Harris Leonard, Capt. T. F. Lyons, and Capt. W. H. Parker.

64. J. J. Meade, "Voice of the People," *Chicago Daily Tribune*, 26 Dec. 1908, 6.

65. "Status," 608, 609, 220, 612, 452, 480, 498; Navy Dept., *Annual Report* (1909), 1029–30; Conrad Reid, "The Marines Are Always in the Way," George C. Reid Papers, MCHD.

66. "Proud Record of the Marine Corps," *New York Daily Tribune*, 29 Nov. 1908, 4. For a similar comment also see "What Duty for Marines," *Boston Transcript*, 2 Dec. 1909, Clipping, HQMC Scrapbook, RG 127. Various committees in the House began fighting over whether or not the Corps should remain part of the Department of the Navy or become integrated into the Army. "Are Marines Land or Water Warriors," *Duluth News-Tribune*, 22 Dec. 1908, 11.

67. "Get Down to Hard Pan: Michigan Men of Marine Corps Taken From Battleships," *Grand Rapids Press*, 16 Nov. 1908, 10; "What Duty for Marines," *Boston* [?] *Transcript*, 2 Dec. 1908, Clipping, HQMC Scrapbook, RG 127.

68. "Marine Corps Has Fine Record," *Morning Telegraph*, 27 Dec. 1908, Clipping, HQMC Scrapbook, RG 127. Similar wording was used in "Marines Have Fought a Hundred Little Wars," *Baltimore Sun*, 6 Dec. 1908, HQMC Scrapbook, RG 127.

69. For the numerous prospects that sought to join the military to serve in China, see "Anxious for China Service. Many Want to Enter the Army or the Marine Corps," *Kansas City Star*, 11 Jul. 1900, 1; "United States Marine Corps. Some Interesting Facts about a Branch of the Naval Service," *Springfield Republican*, 10 Aug. 1900, 5.

70. "Marine Corps Has Fine Record," *Morning Telegraph*, 27 Dec. 1908, Clipping, HQMC Scrapbook, RG 127; "Sea Delights Cut from Marines' Book," *New York Times*, 7 Dec. 1908, 10; Maj Gen, Commandant Elliott to Sir, 16 Nov. 1908, RG 127, Press Copies of Letters Sent, 1895–1898, Vol. 204, 21 Oct. 1908 to 10 Dec. 1908.

71. Outsiders also voiced their concern in private correspondence to the commandant, who informed them that the newspaper coverage was mostly "incorrect and misleading." Captain, U.S. Marine Corps, Aide-de-Camp for Major General Commandant George Elliott to Mrs. N. M. McDaniel, 1 Dec. 1908, RG 127, Press Copies of Letters Sent, 1895–1898, Box 70, Vol. 204, 21 Oct. 1908 to 10 Dec. 1908. For another letter from a concerned observer, see First Lieutenant, U.S. Marine Corps, Aide-de-Camp for Major General Commandant George Elliott to Rev. C. J. Baldwin, D.D., 5 Dec. 1908, RG 127, Press Copies of Letters Sent, 1895–1898, Box 70, Vol. 204, 21 Oct. 1908 to 10 Dec. 1908.

72. Major General Commandant George Elliott, Special Order No. 1, 16 Nov. 1908, RG 127, Press Copies of Letters Sent, 1895–1898, Box 70, Vol. 204, 21 Oct. 1908 to 10 Dec. 1908.

73. For the increasing importance of exercise, see Donald J. Mrozek, *Sport and American Mentality, 1880–1910* (Knoxville: University of Tennessee Press, 1983). For Roosevelt in particular see Mark Dyreson, "Regulating the Body and the Body Politic: American Sport, Bourgeois Culture, and the Language of Progress, 1880–1920," in *The New American Sport History: Recent Approaches and Perspectives*, ed. S. W. Pope (Champaign: University of Illinois Press, 1997), 7, 123, and 131.

74. "Marine Officers Must Run, Says President; Besides Walking, They Will Have to Show Ability as 700-Yard Sprinters," *Philadelphia Inquirer*, 17 Dec. 1908, 1; "Marine Officers Walk 50 Miles," *Portsmouth Herald*, 11 May 1909, 8. One article described how they had established a record, which their fellow officers subsequently beat a few weeks later. See "Marine Corps Officers Establish New Record," *Wichita Daily Eagle*, 27 May 1909, 6; "General Elliott Stops Extraordinary Physical Tests in the Marine Corps," *New York Daily Tribune*, 29 May 1909, 4. For a description of the tests, see "Physical Tests for Marine Corps Officers," *Duluth News-Tribune*, 17 Dec. 1908, 7. In December of 1908 Roosevelt ordered that Marine officers carry out this test every two years. For Waller's description of this test, see Col. Littleton Waller, USMC, to Major General Commandant, USMC, 20 May 1909, RG 127, General Correspondence 1904–1912, Entry 10365, Box 86. Waller justified the attempt by explaining that officers from other branches had completed the test similarly and thus he believed the order meant that three days was the maximum length for the test. 5th Endorsement, Col. Littleton Waller to Maj. Gen. Commandant, 7 Jun. 1909 RG 127, General Correspondence 1904–1912, Entry 10365, Box 86. The commandant had

little patience with Waller's explanations and ordered him to retake the test. 4th Endorsement, Maj. Gen. Commandant to Col. Littleton Waller, 3 Jun. 1909, RG 127, General Correspondence 1904–1912, Entry 10365, Box 86.

75. Perhaps this tendency was enhanced by the practice on board ship of denoting those who did not participate in watch as "idlers" in both the U.S. and Royal Navies. For this definition, see Stephen B. Luce, *Text-Book of Seamanship*, rev. and enlarged by Aaron Ward (New York: D. Van Ostrand, 1884), 293. A number of officers, including Marines, fell under this category. See Charles Nordhoff, *Nine Years a Sailor* (Cincinnati: Moore, Wilstach and Baldwin, 1866), 55–56; and James Fenimore Cooper, *The Two Admirals, A Tale in Two Volumes,* vol. 1 (New York: Stringer and Townsend, 1849), 168. Nordhoff argued that the Marine officer in particular had an easy life on board ship, especially in peacetime. Nordhoff had a more positive view of enlisted Marines, stating they had a "thankless" task of guarding the vessel. Nordhoff, *Nine Years a Sailor*, 57, 120. For general references to Royal Marines as idlers not based on watch, see Francis Davenant, *What Shall My Son Be? Hints to Parents* (London: S. W. Partridge, 1870), 70–71. Davenant argued that by this period the image of Royal Marines had improved.

76. Former commandant Victor H. Krulak believed the Corps should have "welcomed" this decision to expand the Corps' "horizons." See Victor H. Krulak, *First to Fight: An Inside View of the U.S. Marine Corps* (Annapolis, MD: Naval Institute Press, 1999), 12. Also see John G. Miller, "William Freeland Fullam's War with the Corps," *Proceedings* 105 (Dec. 1975): 38–45. Merrill L. Bartlett, "Ben Hebard Fuller and the Genesis of a Modern Marine Corps, 1891–1834," *Journal of Military History* 69 (Jan. 2005): 76. That Fullam sought to have the Marines commanded by a naval officer suggests that Heinl's view that Fullam hoped for the abolition of the Corps is more likely.

77. See, for example, Clipping, *Washington Post*, 29 Dec. 1898, HQMC Scrapbook, RG 127. One newspaper reported that Elliott was interested in looking into the prospect of using Marines on board transports to be ready for any potential conflicts. "Marines Taken from Warships," *Baltimore American*, 13 Nov. 1908, Clipping, HQMC Scrapbook, RG 127.

78. "Army and Navy Gossip," *Washington Post*, 20 Dec. 1908, E2; "Marines Taken from Warships," *Baltimore American*, 13 Nov. 1908, HQMC Scrapbook, RG 127.

79. "Status," 156, 548. Pillsbury made similar comments. He noted that it was not conducive to the sailor's morale to have someone who was in no way a "better" person over him. "Status," 460. When Fullam claimed that the presence of Marines on board ship privileged Marines over sailors, Commandant George Elliott interrupted him. Elliott countered that the fourteen sailors serving on board vessels in the position of master-at-arms were over the Marines and

yet that did not injure the Marines' morale. "Status," 448–50. For others who argued similarly, see "Status," 460, 469, 516. Fullam's argument that Marines be used as advanced base forces was ancillary to his comments; see "Status," 559–60. One naval officer suggested that "select" bluejackets be given the privilege of doing this duty. "Status," 596. Other naval officers believed that sailors would not relish this duty. "Status," 602.

80. "Status," 541–42. Similarly, Fullam stated at a later point in his testimony that journalists tended to mention Marines rather than Marines and sailors when describing landing parties. "Status," 562. A perusal of one landing in 1907, however, reveals that sometimes Marines were mentioned, sometimes bluejackets were mentioned, and sometimes both were mentioned. See "United States May Intervene in War Blue Jackets and Marines Landed Step is Taken to Protect American," *Aberdeen American*, 22 Mar. 1907, 1; "Blue Jackets Landed in Honduras," *Albuquerque Journal*, 22 Mar. 1907, 4; "U.S. Marines in Honduras. Regarded a Diplomatic Move," *Charlotte Observer*, 22 Mar. 1907, 1; "He Lands Marines," *Dallas Morning News*, 22 Mar. 1907, 1; "Navy Takes Precautions to Protect Americans. Bluejackets and Marines Landed from the United States Gunboat," *Duluth News-Tribune*, 22 Mar. 1907, 1; "U.S. Blue Jackets and Marines Landed at Honduran Ports Will Protect Interests of All," *Grand Forks Herald*, 22 Mar. 1907, 1; "Marines Landed in Honduras Cities Gunboats Patrolling Both Coasts of Warring Republics of Central America," *Lexington Herald-Leader*, 22 Mar. 1907, 1. One headline in particular must have satisfied Fullam. See "Fullam Lands Blue Jackets. To Guard American Interests during War," *Montgomery Advertiser*, 22 Mar. 1907, 1.

81. "Status," 491 and 500. For another naval officer's use of the same word, see "Status," 582. Also see "Lieut. Fullam's Paper: It Is Being Discussed throughout the Navy," *New York Times*, 7 Dec. 1890, 2. Captain Charles Badger, USN, however, disagreed. He believed that the force was "homogenous" except for the minor difference in the Marine's uniform. In 1895 the secretary of the Navy had issued a report suggesting that the presence of Marines improved morale by providing a competitive "spirit" on board ship that could improve efficiency. "Status," 640.

82. "Status," 575. The following naval officers testified in favor of the Corps: Rear Admiral Schley, Rear Admiral Willard H. Brownson (ret.), Rear Adm. Royal R. Bradford (ret.), Rear Adm. Caspar F. Goodwin (ret.), Capt. Charles J. Badger, Cdr. Templin M. Potts, and Cdr. Charles A. Grove.

83. Carl Builder has made this argument for many of the choices and decisions made by the other services in *Masks of War*.

84. When asked to explain why the Royal Marines had been removed from the Royal Navy and subsequently reintroduced, Commander Sims cited the British tendency toward "excessive conservatism," the same conservatism that led them

to what he implied as the illogical tendency to wear red coats. "Status," 526. Ful-lam made a similar comment about the extent to which comparisons between the British and U.S. navies were irrelevant because of the extent to which "caste" was a factor in Great Britain. "Status," 564.

85. "Status," 448–49. When questioned as to whether the sailor could serve just as ably on shore as the Marine, Pillsbury agreed that he could. "Status," 458. Another naval officer admitted to not having considered the possible expense or the effect of Marines on this decision. "Status," 475. This led one committee member to suggest dryly that perhaps sailors should be brought ashore to guard naval stations. Naval officer Captain Marshall stated how easy it would be to recruit more bluejackets to fill the duties of Marines both at sea and on shore if the Corps were abolished, which he did not view as problematic given that soldiers could easily take on the Corps' jobs. "Status," 473 and 481. However, Marshall contradicted himself by immediately stating that "marines ha[d] always come to the front when the Army has tumbled down." "Status," 481. For another naval officer who felt that soldiers could easily fill the role of Marines, see "Status," 498. For one critical editorial of Pillsbury's comments see "The Marine Corps," *New York Sun*, 11 Jan. 1909, Clipping, HQMC Scrap-book, RG 127, NARA.

86. Many naval officers believed that the committee did not really want to hear their opinion. The committee's chairman, Representative Thomas Butler, had a son in the Marine Corps, convincing some naval officers that the Corps was nothing more than a respite for the sons of congressional members who could not find employment elsewhere. Heinl, *Soldiers of the Sea*, 156. The image of the nineteenth-century Marine officer as a well-connected supernumerary continued to linger in the minds of some naval officers.

87. The unknown writer did not explain why sailors would be jealous of Marines, other than to also point out that sailors had come to view Marines as "inter-lopers." See "Get Down To Hard Pan," *Grand Rapids Press*, 16 Nov. 1908, 10. As one recruiter stated, Marines did not have to "wash decks or do any such chores." See "Offer No Sea Duty Now," *Kansas City Star*, 24 Nov. 1908, 8. For an example of tensions between sailors and Marines on naval bases, see "Terpsichore Lets War Dogs Loose: Marines at League Island Order Jackies off Dance Floor in Former's Barracks," *Philadelphia Inquirer*, 15 Nov. 1903, 4.

88. Ryan Wadle, *Selling Sea Power: Public Relations and the U.S. Navy, 1917–1940* (Norman: University of Oklahoma Press, 2019).

89. The Corps solicited responses to McLemore's ideas but, to my knowledge, there are few records of these responses. For one that suggested increasing recruiting pay instead, see Officer in Charge, Pacific Coast Recruiting Dis-trict, to Major General Commandant, Washington, D.C., 8 Jan. 1912, RG 127, General Correspondence, Entry 19162, Box 158.

90. Officer in Charge of Recruiting A. S. McLemore to Major General Commandant, 16 Dec. 1911, RG 127, General Correspondence, 1904–1912, Entry 19162, Box 158. Major Magill, who had encouraged Captain Breckenridge's ideas, subsequently endorsed McLemore's plan.

91. To My Dear Chairman, 7 May 1912, RG 80, General Correspondence, 1897–1915, Box 817, Entry 23362–14. The Corps was perhaps even more successful. Despite the rejection of its plan, the Corps generally benefited from their single control under the Secretary of the Navy, which allowed them greater familiarity with different approaches. By contrast, the Army does not seem to have been aware of the Navy and Marine Corps' shift toward display advertising until 1911, when it requested additional information regarding their practices. Acting Secretary of the Navy to the Secretary of War, 2 Sep. 1911, RG 80, General Correspondence, 1897–1915, Box 817, Entry 23362–12. That the acting secretary of the Navy referred the Army's letter to the Marine Corps suggests that display advertising had found a stronger home in that institution than in the Navy. Major General, Commandant, U.S. Marine Corps to Assistant Secretary of the Navy, 1 Sep. 1911, RG 80, General Correspondence, 1897–1915, Box 817, Entry 23362–12. By then, the Corps was in its second year with a new advertising agency: the Collins-Armstrong Advertising Company. In addition to saving more than five hundred dollars outright in the cost of placing newspaper advertisements, it did not have to expend as much clerical work, paying only one voucher instead of one hundred. Still, the Navy had been using a similar company for the past four years. R. J. Tracewell, Comptroller, Treasury Department to the Honorable Secretary of War, 25 April 1912, RG 80, General Correspondence, 1897–1915, Box 817, Entry 23362–13. The Navy, by contrast, by 1912 was using the advertising firm of Street and Finney, considering publications such as *Home Life* to attract recruits.

92. Major General Commandant Biddle to Secretary of the Navy, 12 Nov. 1912, RG 80, General Correspondence of the Secretary of the Navy, Boxes 1708 and 1709, Entry 28369–50. The commandant argued that the treasury said the decision did not include the Marines. The secretary of the Navy sent forth the request to the chairman, Secretary on Naval Affairs, U.S. Senate on 26 Feb. 1913. See RG 80, General Correspondence of the Secretary of the Navy, Box 1118, Entry 26255: 274–24. In November of that year, the commandant argued that the ruling did not apply to the Corps as he tried to get advertising agencies approved once again for fiscal year 1914, requesting $352,000 for recruiting.

Chapter 4. Intensification and Dissemination

1. Sgt. Frank Stubbe, "Wilkes-Barre Opinions," *Bulletin*, Jan. 1916, 14.

2. "There's Nothing a Marine Can't Do," *Columbus Daily Enquirer*, 13 Nov. 1916, 8.

3. There is some evidence that a Lt. L. P. Pinkston, while on recruiting duty in the South, had written the first edition of the pamphlet in 1907 on his own initiative. He subsequently completed it at the Corps' headquarters in Washington, D.C. An article described the book as "surpass[ing] the books of similar character used by the other services." See "United States Navy," *Washington Post*, 3 Nov. 1907, 118. His name is copyrighted on the 1912 edition of *U.S. Marines: Duties, Experiences, Opportunities, Pay*, which is the second edition. See U.S. Marine Corps Recruiting Publicity Bureau (hereafter USMCRPB), *U.S. Marines: Duties, Experiences, Opportunities, Pay*, 2nd ed. (New York: Chasmar-Winchell Press, 1912). Pinkston would subsequently be on recruiting duty again in 1917, showing that Marine officers could fill such duty multiple times, allowing for better recruiting efforts. See "Of Nation is Dinner Theme," *La Grande (OR) Observer*, 27 Mar. 1917, 1. He was described as the head of the Recruiting Publicity Bureau in 1915. See "Cooks Desert Uncle Sam Same as Commuter's Wife," *Pittsburgh Post-Gazette*, 10 Nov. 1915, 2.

4. USMCRPB, *U.S. Marines: Duties, Experiences, Opportunities, Pay*, 2nd ed. (New York: Chasmar-Winchell Press, 1912), 3.

5. Moreover, Pinkston's copyright was now shared with H. C. Snyder, which corresponds to the Corps' muster rolls. See L. P. Pinkston and H. C. Snyder, *U.S. Marines: Duties, Experiences, Opportunities, Pay*, 3rd ed. (New York: Chasmar-Winchell Press, 1913).

6. The bureau did communicate with the Royal Marines on at least one occasion during this time period, with the editor of the Royal Marines' publication *Globe and Laurel* requesting to exchange publications for inspiration. See "Hands across the Sea," *Bulletin*, May 1916, 30. "Our Press Department Rapidly Gaining Favor throughout the Country," *Bulletin*, Jun. 1916, 11.

7. USMCRPB, *U.S. Marines: Duties, Experiences, Opportunities, Pay*, 6th ed. (New York: USMCRPB, 1918), 4. For the importance of Kipling in the Corps, see Thomas F. Carney, "The Kipling Cult," *Marines Magazine* 2, no. 3 (Feb. 1917): 8–9; and another Marine's response to this article defending Kipling's reputation in A. A. Kuhlen, "Kipling," *Marines Magazine* 2, no. 5 (April 1917): 63–64. Other references to Kipling include T. G. Sterrett, "Them Was the Happy Days," *Bulletin*, Nov. 1914, 10.

8. Cpl. Percy Webb, "Service and Study: Marines Can Learn While They Earn," *Bulletin*, Jan. 1917, 6. Webb characterized it as the "big 'two-in-one,'" suggesting the stress the bureau placed on this theme. Also see "The Recruiting Signs," *Bulletin*, Feb. 1917, 20 and "The Recruiting Situation," *Bulletin*, Jun. 1916, 16,

which also characterized it as the "big appeal." This article explained further that the Corps "offers in four years that which the Army and Navy combined offer in eleven." Still, the article pointed out that the Corps' recruiting numbers were "not so good as it should be." This could be explained, the unknown author suggested, by the fact that the Corps required a longer enlistment than either the Army or the Navy. Also see "United States Marine Corps," *Bulletin*, Aug. 1916, 20.

9. For one example of these pamphlet covers, see *U.S. Marines: Duties, Experiences, Opportunities, Pay*, 7th ed. (USMCPB, 1917). "Spokane Reporter Converted: Prefers Marines Because of Their Picture Books," *Bulletin*, March 1916, 5. Importantly, the article mentioned that the reporter's remarks were an "unsolicited testimonial, not in any way inspired" through contact with Marine recruiters. Moreover, the reporter considered the Corps to have more compelling publicity than the Army and the Navy.

10. For example, the Corps printed a calendar that recruiters could distribute to anyone interested. Recruiters would use this opportunity to converse with those seeking calendars, hoping to obtain names of potential recruits. Sgt. Joseph Ascheim, "A Good Way to Get Names for the Publicity Bureau," *Bulletin*, March 1915, 2.

11. One article stated that the bureau sent press releases to 20,000 newspapers. "More Room for Publicity Bureau," *Bulletin*, Jan. 1915, 16. In another article, however, the *Bulletin*'s editor stated that the bureau issued articles twice a week to 3,000 newspapers. "Our Press Department," *Bulletin*, Nov. 1915, 12. In the same issue, however, the *Bulletin* stated that the articles were issued three times a week. "Attention! Everyone!" *Bulletin*, Nov. 1915, 24. The *Bulletin*'s first issue does mention how a sergeant wrote an article for a local paper at that establishment's office.

12. U.S. Marine Corps Muster Rolls, 1893–1958, October 1912, NARA, T977, Roll 89. At this time, the Corps had about 384 men on recruiting duty, distributed as follows: 22 men on recruiting duty in the Central District, 54 at the Recruiting District of Chicago, 26 at the Recruiting District of Detroit, 14 at the Recruiting District of Minnesota, 19 at the Recruiting District of Saint Louis, 18 in the Mountain Recruiting District, 76 at the Recruiting District of the Pacific Coast, 138 in the Recruiting District of Pennsylvania, and 17 at the Southeastern Recruiting District.

13. U.S. Marine Corps Muster Rolls, 1893–1958, February 1913, NARA, T977, Roll 92. Becker had experience both getting recruits and overseeing some kind of training of them, having been a recruiting officer in Chicago and stationed at the Recruit Depot in Norfolk, Virginia. See "Marine Corps," *Washington Times* (Washington, D.C.), 3 Feb. 1913, 7. He subsequently received orders to recruiting duty, this time to Detroit in July of 1913.

"Marine Corps," *Washington Times*, 30 Jul. 1913, 12. Over the next year he would then take charge of recruiting in Saint Louis before being sent to Veracruz. "Lieut. Becker Goes to Join His Company," *Saint Louis Star and Times*, 25 April 1914, 2. Capt. T. H. Brown subsequently received orders to the bureau in Jun. of 1913. "Marine Corps," *New York Times*, 7 Jun. 1913, 16. Like Becker, Brown would also receive orders to Veracruz.

14. See, for example, Navy Department, *Annual Reports of the Navy Department for the Fiscal Years 2012 and 2013* (Washington, D.C.: Government Printing Office, 1913 and 1914), 577–78 and 530–31, respectively. The only account focused solely on the Corps' recruiting and publicity efforts states that sources for the bureau's early efforts are available but does not cite any of them. Lindsay, *This High Name*, 16.

15. "More Room for Publicity Bureau," *Bulletin*, Jan. 1915, 16; U.S. Marine Corps Muster Rolls, 1893–1958, May 1917, NARA, T977, Roll 122, 453–54.

16. "Distribution of Bulletin," *Bulletin*, Nov. 1918, 24.

17. The *Bulletin* abounds with stories about recruiters and their families, which often joked about aspects of military life. See "Marjorie's Madness," *Bulletin*, Nov. 1915, 19. Some recruiters appreciated the quality of family life the Corps enabled. Sgt. L. C. McLauchlin compared the Marine Corps' provisions for married recruiters favorably to those of the Army where he was stationed. "Spokane Letter," *Bulletin*, Dec. 1914, 2. For a more lighthearted commentary on this fear, see "Adios Trabajo," *Bulletin*, April 1915, 15; and "The Bulletin Appreciated in the Western Division," *Bulletin*, Dec. 1914, 11.

18. For the idea that the Corps could improve a man see Gus R. Fisher, "Too Old to be a Marine," *Bulletin*, Jul. 1916, 14; "A Recruiter's Varied Experiences," *Bulletin*, Dec. 1914, 16. For a recruit that enlisted for this reason and found himself in the "presence of many good men" from the beginning, see "He Came Down from Alaska to Enlist," *Bulletin*, Jan. 1917, 22. The *Bulletin* published the thank-you letter he had sent to his recruiting officer.

19. James D. Norris, *Advertising and the Transformation of American Society, 1865–1920* (New York: Greenwood Press, 1990), 47; "Corporal Miller, of Lehman, May be Made Lieutenant," *Wilkes-Barre Times*, Aug. 3, 1916, 8. One recruiter even suggested it was better to be a private in the Corps than an officer in another branch. Sgt. C.W. Herizog, "The Truth Counts," *Bulletin*, Jan. 1915, 13.

20 "Tis Not for Gold We're Here," 16; Sgt. John F. Cassidy, "School for Recruiters at Recruit Depot Is Suggested," *Bulletin*, May 1916, 6. Cassidy used the words "Marine" and "soldier" virtually interchangeably, whereas later Marines largely preferred to use "Marine" only.

21. Norman M. Shaw, "A Plea for Big, Yellow Chevron," *Bulletin*, Sep. 1915, 4; "The Distinguishing Emblem for Recruiters," *Bulletin*, Feb. 1915, 7.

22. "The Bulletin Appreciated in the Western Division," *Bulletin*, Dec. 1914, 11; Louie W. Putnam, "Various Suggestions and Comments," *Bulletin*, Aug. 1916, 22. See the anonymously contributed article by A Marine Recruiter, "Standardizing Our Advertising," *Bulletin*, Jul. 1916, 20.

23. William Brackett, "Sergeant Katcher Has Right Idea," *Bulletin*, Oct. 1916, 22; Frank E. Evans, "Carrying the Message," *Bulletin*, May 1915, 4.

24. "Attention! Everyone!," *Bulletin*, Nov. 1915, 24. Sgt. James F. Taite, USMC, credited Major A. S. McLemore, USMC, for the success of the bureau in "Publicity, Etc.," *Bulletin*, Jan. 1915, 9. "They Know and Won't Tell," *Bulletin*, Jun. 1916, 16. Recruiters had used this technique before the Recruiting Publicity Bureau's establishment, although the extent to which it was officially encouraged is difficult to ascertain. See, for example, "Capt. Harlee's Great Capture," *Dallas Morning News*, 4 Sep. 1907, 12. The *Dallas Morning News* published extensive reports of recruits obtained in the area, suggesting that the recruiting officer for that area had developed especially strong ties with the paper.

25. William E. Parker, "The Recruiting Officer and the Newspaper," *Bulletin*, Jun. 1915, 16. Despite these efforts, some newspapers refused to make clear to the bureau's satisfaction that the Corps was a distinct institution from the Navy. Frank T. Brown, "Publicity Station at P.P.I.E.," *Bulletin*, Oct. 1915, 3.

26. "Wanted to be Submarine," *Bulletin*, Dec. 1914, 11. Also see "Wanted Boy Spanked by Recruiting Officer," *Decatur (IL) Herald*, 28 Nov. 1915, 14. For even earlier indications of this tendency among recruiters, see "Sergeant Bellman's Little Joke Causes Much Wondering," *Buffalo Morning Express*, 8 March 1905, 7. For more lighthearted articles, see "Take Him," *Idaho Statesman*, 17 Jan. 1916, 5; "Ford Jokes Reach Marine Corps," *Charlotte Observer*, 20 Dec. 1915, 6; "Sword Swallower in Navy," *Miami Herald Record*, 30 Jan. 1916, 24.

27. Norris, *Advertising*, 48. "Expert Shark Hunters Organize for Crusade July 21, 1916," *Montgomery Advertiser*, 21 Jul. 1916, 10. An even more bizarre example is the publication of a Marine's prophecy that World War I would end in 1916. The Marine was the aforementioned Thomas Sterrett, then a gunnery sergeant. For just two examples of this press release, see "Sergeant Predicts End of War and an Attack upon U.S," *Grand Forks Daily Herald*, 31 Dec. 1915, 4; and "A Dire Prophecy," *Idaho Statesman*, 2 Jan. 1916, 2.

28. W. W. Sibert, "Down North Carolina Way," *Bulletin*, Aug. 1916, 28; Sgt. B. J. Doherty, "Newspaper Publicity Up Boston Way May Help You," *Bulletin*, May 1916, 4.

29. For contradictory numbers about how many articles it released, see "More Room for Publicity Bureau," *Bulletin*, Jan. 1915, 16; and "Our Press Department," *Bulletin*, Nov. 1915, 12.

30. "Another Luzerne County Boy Makes Good with Marines," *Wilkes-Barre (PA) Times*, 7 Feb. 1916, 2; "Makes a Record," *Charlotte Observer*, 1 Feb. 1916, 6; "Qualifies as Sharpshooter," *Hobart Daily Republican*, 10 Feb. 1916, 4. At least one recruiter seems to have taken a more subdued approach. One article simply stated that Clark "had qualified" as a sharpshooter, and that local recruiters would be following his "career in gunnery with interest." See "Kansas City Boy a Marksman," *Kansas City Star*, 23 Feb. 1916, 6. Another recruiter took a more enthusiastic approach while focusing more on the American tradition of excellence in naval gunnery. See "Olympia Boy Now Sharpshooter in Marine Corps," 29 Feb. 1916, 1. The Wilkes-Barre recruiter issued a similar notice to the press about a month later ("Local Marine Boy Has Straight Aim," *Wilkes-Barre Times*, 4 March 1916, 3), as did the recruiter in Duluth ("Duluthian Qualifies as Expert Rifleman in Marine Corps," *Duluth News-Tribune*, 10 March 1916, 3).

31. The articles mentioned relatives included uncles, sisters, mothers, and fathers. For Marines' discussions of these negative images, see William Brackett, "The Public's Misconception of the Enlisted Man," *Bulletin*, Jan. 1915, 11; C. Hundertmark, "John Boyle, U.S. Marine," *Bulletin*, Jul. 1915, 15. Also see Alfred Reynolds, "The Life of an Enlisted Soldier in the United States Army," (Washington, D.C.: Government Printing Office, 1904), 7, for a similar perspective from the Army.

32. See, for example, "Louis Harvey with Marines," *Grand Forks Herald*, Sep. 19, 1915, 6.

33. For the many newspapers that used the bureau's articles, see "Press Bureau Checks Up and Receives Some Wonderful Replies," *Bulletin*, Aug. 1916, 10. A search of the America's Historical Newspapers Database reveals some of the specific subjects that were discussed and which newspapers were receptive. Papers in Wilkes-Barre, PA, Duluth, MN, and Olympia, WA, for example, published similar articles. The *Miami Herald* made these connections more explicit. It noted that its source for one article was "The Marine Bulletin." This article explained that recruits who had worked as cooks were the most likely to desert. The article noted that "desertions from the marine corps are very light at all times: the average marine considers that the service offers better advantages than anything he could find in civil life . . . and were it not for the cooks the 'oldest branch of the service' would have an almost clean slate with regard to desertions." For another article citing "a Marine Corps Bulletin" as a source, see "The United States Marine Corps," *Charlotte Observer*, 1 April 1916, 4. In focusing on cooks as being the only unsatisfied ones in the Corps, recruiters managed to incorporate important recruiting themes into a short article. "Cooks Will Desert," *Miami Herald*, 18 Nov. 1915, 2. The same article was also published as "Of All Deserters

Cooks Are Called the Worst," *Morning Olympian*; 16 Nov. 1915, 1. The article mentioned "New York" as a byline, thus providing another way to track the influence of the bureau. The *Charlotte Daily Observer* published variations of the bureau's articles in quick succession. After printing a story about Sergeant Major Deaver's retirement on November 26, it printed the experience of a "local boy" in Haiti the next day followed by the article about the probability of cooks deserting the next day, thus helping to keep the Corps constantly before the eyes of newspaper readers in Charlotte. See "With $100,000 Deaver Retires Form Marines," *Charlotte Daily Observer*, 26 Nov. 1915, 9; "Landed in Haiti," *Charlotte Observer*, 27 Nov. 1915, 7; "Cooks Will Desert," *Charlotte Observer*, 28 Nov. 1915, 16.

The *Miami Herald* included a brief article regarding the Corps' history the same day it printed an article concerning the commandant's desire to increase the institution's size. "The U. S. Marine Corps," *Miami Herald Record*, 27 Dec. 1915, 2; and "Will Modify Demands for More Men," 1. The *Morning Olympian* even published more than one release on the same day right next to each other. "7-Year-Old Enlists; Snorers Are Isolated," *Morning Olympian*, 4 Jan. 1916, 4. The Corps took another approach to desertions in 1916, suggesting that those with "artistic temperaments" were especially likely to desert. The emphasis on the masculinity of Marines was intensifying in the years leading up to World War I. "Tapering Fingers Mean Anything but Stability," *Idaho Statesman*, 28 Aug. 1916, 3.

34. See, for example, "Blushing through Our Tan," *Bulletin*, Oct. 1916, 16.

35. "Press Bureau Checks Up," 10, 11. A few made similar comments. In one case the *Wilkes-Barre Times* published two bureau articles on the same page. See "Marine Recruits Prove Tempting to School of Fish," 4 Mar. 1914, 3; and "Local Marine Boy Has Straight Aim," 4 March 1916, 3. It appears that Stubbe, who contributed to the *Bulletin* on several occasions, must have submitted the letter that was the basis for "Marine Recruits Prove Tempting" to the bureau, as it was published the following day in a Charlotte paper. See "Good Liars among Marines," *Charlotte Daily Observer*, 5 March 1916, 9.

36. Frank E. Evans, "First Aids to Publicity," *Bulletin*, Nov. 1914, 2; Norris, *Advertising*, 26; Clarance B. Proctor, "Advertising and Recruiting: Some Publicity Bureau Help," *Bulletin*, Oct. 1916, 6.

37. Important works on advertising include Jackson Lears, *Fables of Abundance: A Cultural History of Advertising in America* (New York: Basic Books, 1994); Roland Marchand, *Advertising the American Dream: Making Way for Modernity, 1920–1940* (Berkeley: University of California Press, 1985); Stephen Fox, *The Mirror Makers: A History of American Advertising and Its Creators* (New York: Morrow, 1984); Daniel Pope, *The Making of Modern Advertising* (New York: Basic Books, 1983); Pamela Walker Laird, *Advertising Progress and the Rise*

of Consumer Marketing (Baltimore: Johns Hopkins University Press, 1998); Stephen Harp, "*Marketing Michelin: Advertising and Cultural Identity in Twentieth-Century France,*" *Business History Review* 76 (Winter 2002): 919–21.

38. Norris, *Advertising*, 22. Ironically, the Marine Corps helped secure many recruits for the Navy both inadvertently and advertently. See Henry R. Dornbush, "Troubles of a Recruiter," *Bulletin*, Jul. 1915, 4.

39. For a discussion of trademarks or branding, see Nancy F. Koehn, "Henry Heinz and Brand Creation in the Late Nineteenth Century: Making Markets for Processed Food," *Business History Review* 73 (Autumn 1999): 349–93.

40. A Marine Recruiter, "Standardizing our Advertising," *Bulletin*, Jul. 1916, 20. One recruiter liked to describe his "hikes" to applicants. See Benjamin Sayers, "Luck, Confidence and Ability are Working Tools of Successful Recruiters," *Bulletin*, Jun. 1916, 3.

41. For example, officer Hiram Bearss was nicknamed "Hiking" for his service in the Philippines. For his biography see Clark, *Hiram Iddings Bearss*, 38 and 97. For other references to hiking see "Long Hike Made by U. S. Marines," *Wilkes-Barre (PA) Times*, Aug. 11, 1916, 2. The article stressed the ability of Marines during a "hike" in the Dominican Republic to adapt to unfavorable conditions in unfriendly settings. Another headline stressed how the "hike" demonstrated the Corps' "ability." See "Good on Land; Too Long March by Marines Sign of Ability," *The State* (Columbia, SC), 13 Aug. 1916, 13. Also see W. E. Christian, *Rhymes of the Rookies: Sunny Side of Soldier Service* (New York: Dodd, Mead, 1917), 30.

42. Frank E. Evans, "The Lure of the Fighting Man," *Bulletin*, Jul. 1915, 1; Percy Webb, "Service and Study: Marines Can Learn While They Earn," *Bulletin*, Jan. 1917, 6; "The Recruiting Signs," *Bulletin*, Feb. 1917, 20; "The Recruiting Situation," *Bulletin*, Jun. 1916, 16.

43. Clifford Bleyer, "Stimulating Recruiting Suggested by an Advertising Expert," *Bulletin*, Dec. 1916, 13.;

44. The professional advertiser appeared especially worried about how mothers would respond to their sons' decisions to join the Corps, reinforcing Lears' argument regarding the assumption that ads more often reached women. T. J. Jackson Lears, *Fables of Abundance*, 209.

45. George Kneller, "Straight from the Shoulder: Handling of the Recruiting Question," *Bulletin*, Feb. 1917, 4. Also see Barnett Neidle, "Recruiting on the Streets Requires Tact and Persistency," *Bulletin*, May 1917, 9.

46. Louis F. Zanzig, "Good Advice from Indianapolis," *Bulletin*, Dec. 1914, 13; "Quality Before Quantity in Final Standing Consideration," *Bulletin*, Oct. 1916, 8; and "Again—Quality before Quantity," *Bulletin*, Feb. 1919, 8.

47. "The Recruiting Situation," *Bulletin*, Jun. 1916, 16. Capt. Frank Evans made a slightly different argument, stating that the superior advertisement was more

important than the reality as to whether the product was superior, in "Carrying the Message," *Bulletin*, May 1915, 4.

48. "Editorial," *Bulletin*, Dec. 1914, 8; Thomas McCrum, "A Few Suggestions from an Old Recruiter to Beginners," *Bulletin*, March 1915, 6; Frank Stubbe, "Some Wilkes-Barre Viewpoints," *Bulletin*, Sep. 1915, 19.

49. Barnett Neidle, "Recruiting on the Streets Requires Tact and Persistency," *Bulletin*, May 1917, 9. While it would be difficult to prove a definite link, a popular recruiting poster of the 1970s depicted a drill sergeant yelling at a recruit with the headline, "We don't promise you a rose garden." See Jennifer Brofer, "We Don't Promise You a Rose Garden," Marines: Official Website of the United States Marine Corps, 21 Feb. 2006, http://www.tecom.marines.mil/News/News-Article-Display/Article/527984/we-dont-promise-you-a-rose-garden/.

50. Norman F. Hatcher, "Thorns and Roses," *Bulletin*, Aug. 1916, 22; "Wants No Rum Hound; Marine Corps Not Refuge for Dipsomaniacs," *The State* (Wheeling, WV), 11 Aug. 1916, 9; "Explain the Service to Everybody," *Bulletin*, Jan. 1915, 13.

51. Norris, *Advertising*, 44; "Only Real Men Can Hope to Join Uncle Sam's Carefully Trained Marine Corps; Four out of Five Applicants Fail," *Wilkes-Barre Times*, 13 Apr. 1916, 7. This approach also overlapped with Progressive ideas regarding morality within military institutions. See, for example, Nancy K. Bristow, *Making Men Moral: Social Engineering During the Great War* (New York: New York University Press, 1996).

52. Louis F. Zanzig, "How to Obtain Good Men," *Bulletin*, March 1915, 18. Lt. Arthur J. Burks expressed a similar idea in "Selling the Corps," *Gazette* 9, no. 2 (Jun. 1924): 115.

53. "Military May Honor Veterans of Civil War with Officer's Salute," *Morning Olympian*, 9 Jun. 1916, 1; John F. Cassedy, "Lack of Publicity," *Bulletin*, Jun. 1915, 5; "Honorable Discharge Buttons," *Bulletin*, Feb. 1917, 3.

54. J. W. McClaskey, "Military Funeral of an Ex-Marine," *Bulletin*, March 1915, 6. Today Marines emphasize that there is no such thing as an ex-Marine, only former Marines, suggesting that at this point this tenet had not been established yet. Still, the Corps was beginning to move toward this trend. A "former" Marine with thirteen years' service wrote in to confirm that he did believe that the phrase "Once a Marine, Always a Marine" was accurate. "Our Letter Writing Friends Provide Much Material for Recruiting Argument," *Bulletin*, Sep. 1916, 13. Another suggested an "Ex-Marines Social Club," *Bulletin*, Feb. 1917, 21. A Navy chaplain and a civilian established an organization for current and retired noncommissioned officers in 1915. See "The Chevron Club," *Bulletin*, Feb. 1915, 12. Also see William A. Rolff, "Semper Fidelis U.S.W.V." *Bulletin*, Oct. 1915, 5.

55. Frank E. Evans, "'The Halls of Montezuma': Call for All Versions of Song," *Bulletin*, Feb. 1916, 7. Evans' article seems to have inspired the bureau to release an article about the Corps' song. See "Favorite Song of the Marines," *Wilkes-Barre Times*, 25 Feb. 1916, 12. Today the Corps is known as the only institution to have a "hymn" rather than a song. At least by 1914 more Marines were beginning to refer to the song as a hymn. See, for example, "'Marines' Hymn' Recalled," *Charlotte Observer*, 26 Apr. 1914, 4.

56. The civilian advertiser in Dec. issue of 1916 similarly recognized the importance of this emotional pull.

57. Quoted in Rutledge, "Rhetoric," 66. For other references to the importance of the Corps being the oldest branch, see Edward A. Callan, "Following Them Up," *Bulletin*, May 1915, 5.

58. Charles Lee, "Soldiers of the Sea," *Overland Monthly and Out West Magazine*, September 1914, 234. The publication's editor, Capt. Fred Marriott of the California National Guardsmen, was one of the Corps' eager supporters, having helped find quality recruits for the Corps in the past. See "New Pacific Coast Publication," *Bulletin*, May 1916, 12.

59. "Our Press Department Rapidly Gaining Favor throughout Country," *Bulletin*, Jun. 1916, 11. The author explained that articles not beginning with "The employment of infantry aboard ship dates back to the Phoenicians," as had been Marines' earlier tendency, helped to ensure publication of its articles.

60. The high literacy rates of the United States no doubt furthered these tendencies. For literacy rates see Norris, *Advertising*, 9. For what appears to be a bureau release regarding the reading preferences of Marines, see "Sea Soldiers of Uncle Sam Not Strong for Light Fiction Books," *Morning Olympian*, 10 May 1916, 1.

61. K. A. Painter Jr., "Recruiting in the Tropics," *Bulletin*, Aug. 1916, 17.

62. "New Marine Corps Publication," *Bulletin*, Jun. 1916, 16. The *Bulletin's* editor envisioned the publication becoming something akin to the Royal Marines' institutional magazine *Globe and Laurel*. See "Editorial," *Bulletin*, May 1915, 8. By 1916 Marines were producing four different magazines. Corporal C. Hundertmark, USMC—who wrote a great deal for the *Bulletin*—became the editor of *Semper Fidelis*, a magazine designed for those connected to the Recruit Depot at Port Royal. Whether he did so under official orders or voluntarily is unknown. The *Marine Corps Gazette* was also established in 1916. This publication of the Marine Corps Association, it is still in existence today, beginning in 1916 with three hundred subscriptions and closing the year with more than five hundred. Of noncomissioned officers, 25 percent from the rank above sergeant joined the association within two weeks of receiving an invitation to join. "The Marine Corps Gazette: Review of December Issue," *Bulletin*, Dec. 1916, 8. Also see "Noncoms May Join Marine Corps Association," *Bulletin*, Sep. 1916, 31. Officers voted by mail to determine whether to allow

highranking noncommissioned officers to join. See "Marine Corps Gazette: New Publication Nearly Ready," *Bulletin*, Feb. 1916, 7.

63. Frank Stubbe, "Some Wilkes-Barre Viewpoints," *Bulletin*, Sep. 1915, 19; Thomas W. Dench, "A Title Suggestion," *Bulletin*, Sep. 1915, 3; "Semper Fidelis," *Bulletin*, Jul. 1915, 16. These publications are discussed in a later chapter.

64. About one-fourth of the Corps' officers were serving together in Cuba at the time. This constituted the most Marine officers to serve together up to this point in history. It was a significant number, considering the extent to which Marine officers were generally scattered on board naval vessels or at naval bases in small contingents. Heinl, *Soldiers of the Sea*, 158. For naval officers' suggestions that permanent regiments could strengthen the Corps' cohesion, see "Status," 525.

65. One article cited the interest of Capt. Harold C. Snyder, the head of the Marine Corps' Recruiting Publicity Bureau in 1913, in the association. See "United States Navy," *Washington Post*, 29 Jun. 1913, ES2. As a major, Snyder would lead the Corps' officer training school in Norfolk and then in Quantico after it moved. This could have allowed him to foster the Corps' identity based on his understanding of it from his time at the bureau. "Marine Corps Promotions," *Washington Post*, 7 Oct. 1917, 3.

66. The Army's individual associations had existed since the nineteenth century. Officers had established the United States Cavalry Association, for example, as early as 1885.

67. Frank E. Evans, "Then and Now," reprint, *Gazette*, Jan. 2001, 52; "Marine Corps Notes," *Washington Post*, 20 Feb. 1916, 13. The association considered allowing noncommissioned officers to join. The outcome of this vote is unknown.

68. "The Marine Corps Association: Its Formation and Object," *Gazette* 1 (March 1918): 73; "Marine Corps Gazette: New Publication Nearly Ready," *Bulletin*, Feb. 1916, 7. The association determined that one of the most effective means of "present[ing] in permanent and authoritative form historical phases of the corps' history that have hitherto been neglected" would be through a publication. Frank E. Evans, "Then and Now," 52; "Marine Corps Association," 75.

69. Advertisement, *International Military Digest* 3 (March 1917): 176.

70. He also served as the association's secretary-treasurer. "Marine Corps Association," *Washington Post*, 26 Sep. 1915, 15.

71. Frank E. Evans, "The Marines Have Landed," *Gazette* 2 (Sep. 1917): 213; Walter N. Hill, "A Haitian Reconnaissance," *Gazette* 8 (Dec. 1923): 34. See Mrinalini Sinha, *Colonial Masculinity: The 'Manly Englishman' and the 'Effeminate Bengali' in the Late Nineteenth Century (New York Manchester University Press, 1995).*

72. A similar story was later published in Julian Street, "The Story of 'Johnnie Poe,'" in *For France*, ed. Charles Hanson Towne (New York: Doubleday, Page, 1917), 116–21.

73. Frank E. Evans, "How the Marine Corps Recalls Sergeant John P. Poe, Jr.," *Gazette* 1 (March 1916): 68–73.

74. See, for example, Navy Dept., *Annual Reports of the Navy Department for the Fiscal Year 1916* (Washington, D.C.: Government Printing Office 1917), 763.

75. 1st Sgt Francis Fisk, USMC, to B. C. Awkerman, 21 Aug. 1916, John J. Awkerman Papers, MCHD. For another example see Capt. Frederick Henry Delano, USMC, to Mother, 24 Feb. 1914, Franklin H. Delano Papers, USAHMI. After his Marines participated in a Mardi Gras event while stopping in the port city of Mobile, Alabama, Delano wrote that although he might not enjoy such events—in part because they made it more difficult for him to maintain control of his Marines—he "suppose[d] they have to be done to keep the service in the public eye." For a description of the events, see "King's Parade Opens Mardi Gras at Mobile. Number of Visitors Estimated at 20,000—Marines and Jackies in March," *Columbus (GA) Daily Enquirer*, 24 Feb. 1914, 1.

Chapter 5. Differentiation

1. "U.S. Marines Work in Any Position," *Philadelphia Inquirer*, 14 Jun. 1914, 10. The article also noted that no other service member had "worked harder . . . nor endured as many hardships" as Marines. For similar rhetoric in the *Bulletin*, see C. Hundertmark, "The United States Marine," *Bulletin*, April 1915, 7.

2. John A. Lejeune, *The Reminiscences of a Marine* (Philadelphia: Dorrance, 1930; reprint, Quantico: Marine Corps Association, 1990), 202.

3. "Who Am I," Paul Woyshner Papers, MCHD.

4. Dave Grossman, *On Killing: The Psychological Cost of Learning to Kill in War and Society* (Boston: Little, Brown, 1995). Recent technological developments, however, are complicating this relationship between distance and killing. See, for example, Joseph L. Campo, *From a Distance: The Psychology of Killing with Remotely Piloted Aircraft*, PhD diss., School of Advanced Air and Space Studies, 2015.

5. See, in particular, Richard Howson, *Challenging Hegemonic Masculinity* (New York: Routledge, 2006).

6. R. W. Connell, *Masculinities*, 2nd ed. (Berkeley: University of California Press), xviii; L. P. Pinkston, "The United States Marine Corps," *Houston Post*, 14 Apr. 1907, 45; "Uncle Sam's Marine Corps: Our Oldest Military Organization with a Brilliant Record," *Detroit Free Press*, 13 Sep. 1908, 40.

7. The 1918 and 1921 landing parties described this relationship as such: "The ship's landing force varies in size and composition, according to the type

of ship. For a ship of the first rate it consists normally of one company of marines (infantry), two companies of bluejacket infantry, and one company of bluejacket artillery, battalion commander and staff, and special details. This constitutes a ship's battalion." See *Landing-Force Manual. United States Navy, 1918* (Washington, D.C.: Government Printing Office, 1918), 219; and *Landing-Force Manual. United States Navy. 1920* (Washington, D.C.: Government Printing Office, 1921), 17.

8. Renda, *Taking Haiti*, 63.

9. Renda, 63, 71.

10. "Want Ads Do the Work," *Times-Democrat* (New Orleans), 26 Oct. 1909, 9.

11. Edwin N. McClellan, "Marines in Nicaragua," *Marine Corps Gazette* 5, no. 2 (Jun. 1921): 164–87; Capt. Patrick H. Roth, "Sailors as Infantry in the US Navy," Naval History and Heritage Command, accessed 3 Jul. 2018, https://www.history.navy.mil/research/library/online-reading-room/title-listalphabetically/s/sailors-as-infantry-us-navy.html; U.S. Congress, Senate, Select Committee on Haiti and Santo Domino, *Inquiry into Occupation and Administration of Haiti and Santo Domingo* (Washington, D.C.: Government Printing Office, 1922), 1674.

12. "Plenty of Marines: Supply Exceeds Demand—Army and Navy Need Men," *New York Daily Tribune*, 8 March 1908, 8.

13. "Bud" Fisher, "Pretty Soft for Jeff in the Navy, Yes, Indeed Pretty Soft," *Tulsa Daily World*, 6 Jun. 1912, 6.

14. For a similar cartoon focused more on advancing American economic interests see "Uncle Sam, the Admirer of U.S. Marines, Should Own This One," *Baltimore American*, 7 Jan. 1912, 12.

15. "Marines and the Navy," n.d., HQMC Scrapbook, RG 127; Damon Runyon, *Rhymes of the Firing Line* (New York: Desmond Fitzgerald, 1912), 35.

16. U.S. Navy Department, *Annual Reports of the Navy Department for the Fiscal Year 1914* (Washington, D.C.: Government Printing Office, 1915), 49.

17. Ironically, the weapons had been purchased in the United States from Remington. John S. D. Eisenhower, *Intervention! The United States and the Mexican Revolution, 1913–1917* (New York: W. W. Norton, 1993), 117.

18. Robert E. Quirk, *An Affair of Honor: Woodrow Wilson and the Occupation of Veracruz* (New York: W. W. Norton and Company, 1962), 83–84; Jack Sweetman, *The Landing at Veracruz: 1914* (Annapolis, MD: Naval Institute Press, 1968), 52–53, 67.

19. The prisoners ironically had been imprisoned because they had resisted military service. Quirk, *Affair of Honor*, 80. Three other sailors would be wounded or killed in the same location that day as they kept communication open between ship and shore. Eisenhower, *Intervention!*, 116.

20. Millett, *Semper Fidelis*, 173.

21. Sweetman, *Landing at Veracruz*, 103; Eisenhower, *Intervention!*, 120, 116–17. For other examples of sailors' proficiency and bravery, see Sweetman, *Landing at Veracruz*, 110–11.

22. Quirk, *Affair of Honor*, 95.

23. Anne Cipriano Venzon, ed., *General Smedley Darlington Butler: The Letters of a Leatherneck, 1898–1931* (New York: Praeger, 1992), 35. Also see George B. Clark, *Hiram Iddings Bearss, U.S. Marine Corps: Biography of a World War I Hero* (Jefferson, NC: McFarland, 2005), 83. Clark points to multiple instances of tensions between Marine and naval officers. See, in particular, pages 30, 85, 91, 102, and 105–6.

24. Capt. William Harllee, USMC, to Col. John A. Lejeune, USMC, "Report on operations at Vera Cruz, Mexico, April 21st, 1914 et. seq.," 1 May 1914, Robert Heinl Papers, MCHD. Naval officers reported favorably on the troops' behavior. See Sweetman, *Landing at Veracruz*, 144.

25. Harllee served at the Chicago recruiting office, leaving in 1907. "Marine Corps Orders," *Evening Star*, 23 Aug. 1907, 3. He returned in 1908 and received attention for keeping the office open until 9 p.m. in order to attract more recruits. "Seeks Clerks as Marines; New Move by Recruiter," *Chicago Tribune*, 9 May 1908, 7. About a month later, he was temporarily assigned to the Marine Corps' rifle team. See "U.S. Marine Corps Orders," *Baltimore Sun*, 5 Jun. 1908, 2.

26. U.S. Navy Department, *Annual Reports of the Navy Department for the Fiscal Year 1914* (Washington, D.C.: Government Printing Office, 1915), 81, 104. Twenty-six sailors and Marines were court-martialed for this offense in each branch. The judge advocate general divided drunkenness into several categories.

27. Quoted in Col. John Lejeune to General George Barnett, 22 May 1914, George Barnett Papers, MCHD.

28. Albert Catlin, *With the Help of God and a Few Marines* (Garden City, NY: Doubleday, Page, 1919), 255. Quirk describes a similar tactic, albeit with more tempered wording. Quirk, *Affair of Honor*, 100. For their lack of this kind of training, see Wise, *A Marine Tells It to You*, 222.

29. Clark, *Hiram Iddings Bearss*, 118. The accidental shooting of a Marine by a high-strung sailor performing guard duty at night probably enhanced this feeling. See "Bravery of Badger's Men," *New York Times*, 24 Apr. 1914, 2. One Marine wrote home informing his parents that about six Marines had been killed, two due to the mistakes of sailors. "Local Boy Writes from Mexico," *Aberdeen Daily News* (South Dakota), 1 May 1914, 5. Also see "What Ryan Saw at Vera Cruz," *Los Angeles Times*, 7 May 1914, 12. For the eagerness of some Marines to shoot without orders, see Harllee, *Marine from Manatee*,

152. For issues between the Navy and Marines regarding the cessation of friendly fire, see Harllee, 153.

30. Thomas, *Old Gimlet Eye*, 202. For a similar suggestion made by a sailor about Marines, although in regard to hunting, see "Surveying in Moro Land," *Our Navy*, Aug. 1914, 55.

31. Lt. Col. Wendell Neville, USMC, to Capt. William Rush, USN, "Report of operations of a battalion of Marines ashore at Veracruz, Mexico from April 21, 1914 to April 30, 1914," 11 May 1914, George Reid Papers, MCHD. Indeed, some naval officers probably would have agreed with Neville. Commander Yates Stirling wrote that sailors simply could never be trained as extensively to fight on land as Marines due to their naval duties. See Commander Yates Stirling, USN, *Fundamentals of Naval Service* (Philadelphia: J. B. Lippincott, 1917), 479. Stirling titled this particular chapter "The Sailor as a Soldier," suggesting how naval officers were still debating how soldierly sailors should be.

32. This claim was made elsewhere in the *Bulletin*. See Francis E. Turin, "Suggested Handbill," *Bulletin*, Dec. 1916, 26. For a Marine who claimed sailors and Marines landed contemporaneously see Caitlin, *With the Help of God*, 254. Also see *Annual Reports of the Navy Dept.* (1914), 141.

33. A. S. Campbell, "Workin' the Suburbs," *Bulletin*, May 1915, 3; Evans, "The Lure of the Fighting Man," 2; *Annual Reports of the Navy Dept.* (1915), 141; "Funston to Land at Vera Cruz To-Day," *New York Times*, 27 Apr. 1914, 3; Quirk, *Affair of Honor*, 106–7; Sweetman, *Landing at Veracruz*, 125. For the initial division of the town between sailors and Marines to occupy it, see "Satisfied with Conditions of the Occupation," *Reading (PA) Times*, 24 Apr. 1914, 1.

34. Millett, *Semper Fidelis*, 174. As Millett does not point to any specific articles, it is difficult to determine how he arrived at this conclusion.

35. Examples of such headlines are numerous. A few include: "Marines Ready to Seize Road to Mexico City," *New York Times*, 24 April 1914, 1; "Battle Scenes at Ojinaga, That Rebels Are Storming; Double Marines on U.S. Warships off East Mexico," *Philadelphia Inquirer*, 9 Jan. 1914, 1; "Marines Ordered from the Zone to Reinforce U.S. Ships; Department Says Change Is Made," *Miami Herald Record*, 9 Jan. 1914, 1; "Uncle Sam Will Not Land Marines at Vera Cruz If Huerta Collapses," *Bellingham (WA) Herald*, 26 Jan. 1914, 1.

36. One large headline, for example, proclaimed, "Gallant Marines under Cover of Perfectly Aimed Guns in the Harbor Take Veracruz." A somewhat smaller headline continued, "Sailors and Marines with Aid of Machine Guns Rush Snipers Losing Six Dead and 30 Hurt." The journalist characterized the Marines' work as gallant in a way that minimized the naval gunfire and did

not mention sailors at all until the smaller headline. *Decatur Herald*, 23 Apr. 1914, 1. See, for example, a headline that mentioned Marines before sailors: "800 Americans at Mercy of Dictator in Capital: Consulate Is Assailed and U.S. Flag Trampled in Mud by Angry Mexicans on Learning of the Landing at Veracruz of Marines and Sailors," *The Sun* (NY), 25 April 1914.

37. "3 Sailors Killed, 25 Wounded in New Vera Cruz Fight," *Washington Post*, 24 April 1914, 1; Henry M. Hyde, "Record of Uncle Sam's Week of Activities against Mexico," *Chicago Daily Tribune*, 26 April 1914, 4. Similarly, the secretary of the Navy grouped sailors and Marines together in stating the number of troops who had landed. See *Annual Report of the Navy Department* (1915), 141.

38. One article did suggest that sailors "behaved as well under fire as the marines," implying that some did expect Marines to outperform bluejackets in military operations of this nature. For articles that mentioned bluejackets and Marines but did not make any qualitative comments suggesting one service performed better than the other, see "American Flag Again Flies Over Vera Cruz," *Los Angeles Times*, 22 April 1914, 11; "Wilson Faces War with a United Mexico," *Los Angeles Times*, 23 April 1914, 11; "Deadly American Marksmen Kill Mexicans by Scores as Battle Rages in Streets and on Rooftops of City," *Washington Post*, 22 April 22, 4. An Associated Press article printed on April 23 received a wide gamut of headlines ranging from "Vera Cruz Quieted by Sharp Shelling and Gallant Work of the Bluejackets," *The Atlanta*, 23 April 1914, 1; "Twelve Marines Slain in 'Peaceful' Occupation," *Los Angeles Times*, 23 April 1914, 15. The article "Days of Fighting in Vera Cruz," *Los Angeles Times*, 24 April 1914, 13, stated that the "most spirited action" of the day was the conquest of the Naval Academy which, once completed, allowed the sailors to continue on. Another article's sub-headline stated that "U.S. Marines landed without opposition" but continued with the statement that after the Mexicans made up their mind to fight back the "Bluejackets . . . Poured in Such a Fire that Mexicans Were Soon in Disorder." See "United States Has Seized Vera Cruz 4 U.S. Marines Killed, 20 Wounded, Over 200 Mexicans Killed in Fight," *Atlanta Constitution*, 22 April 1914, 1. Other headlines that mentioned both sailors and Marines without making any distinctions between the two included: "Take All of Vera Cruz: Americans Complete the Occupation of the City Today following the Arrival of Re-Enforcement," *Kansas City Star*; 22 April 1914, 1; "Stars And Stripes Now Floats over Vera Cruz; Four Americans Killed 20, Wounded; 200 Mexicans Dead," *Albuquerque Morning Journal*, 22 April 1914, 1; "Vivid Description of Vera Cruz Told by Herald's Correspondent United Press Writer Gives Thrilling Account," *Daily Herald* (Biloxi, MS), 13 May 1914, 8. One article did reverse the more usual listing of bluejackets

and then Marines. See "Conflict between United States and Mexico Began Tuesday," *Perry (OK) Republican*, 23 April 1914, 1.

39. Frank E. Evans, "First Aids to Publicity," *Bulletin*, Nov. 1914, 1.

40. "Our Marines No Strangers in Mexico," editorial in *New York Telegram*, 23 April 1914, reprinted in *The Marines ("Soldiers of the Sea") in Rhyme, Prose, and Cartoon* (New York: U.S. Marine Corps Recruiting Publicity Bureau, 1914), n.p. I have not found any evidence to support that these editorials were written by the bureau and then reprinted by the newspapers, but given the bureau's practice of sending out press releases, it is indeed possible.

41. For the continuing power of this theme in the Corps' history through much of the Cold War, see Aaron B. O'Connell, *Underdogs: A Cultural History of the United States Marine Corps, 1941–1965* (PhD dissertation, Yale University, 2009). A poem reprinted in *Marines in Rhyme, Prose, and Cartoon* suggested the Army and the Navy might have "scornful doubt[s]" about the Corps. See *Marines in Rhyme* (1914), n.p.

42. "Hats Off to the Marines!," *Buffalo Courier*, 16 Apr. 1914, quoted in *Marines in Rhyme* (1914), n.p. For a detailed discussion of the phrase "hewers of wood," see Peter Linebaugh and Marcus Rediker, *The Many-Headed Hydra: The Hidden History of the Revolutionary Atlantic* (New York: Beacon Press, 2000), 36–70.

43. Franklin T. Lee, "Soldiers of the Sea," *Overland Monthly*, Sep. 1914, 241; "The Taking of Vera Cruz by American Marines," *World's Work*, Jun. 1914, 126–27.

44. James F. J. Archibald and Berton Braley, "Soldiers and Sailors, Too," *Collier's*, 23 May 1914, 12–13 and 30. The article also expanded on the various "firsts" that Marines loved to stress. Allan Millett characterizes the event as the "first amphibious landing made by American marines." Millett, *Semper Fidelis*, 10. He also notes that Marines encountered little resistance and mentions the presence of fifty sailors. Even Marine historian Robert Heinl, an ardent supporter of the Corps, did not consider this event to constitute real battle. Heinl, *Soldiers of the Sea*, 6. The Marines encountered little resistance, mainly that of "alarmed" residents, and the occupants of the fort quickly fled after firing three shots. See "Extract of a letter from a captain of marines on board the ship Alfred, dated New-London, April 10," *The Remembrancer, or, Impartial Repository of Public Events*, Pt. 2 (London: J. Almon, 1776), 212–13. Even if it could be considered the Navy's first battle, however, it would have been incorrect to assert that the Corps had won the battle single-handedly. As the naval officer who ordered the landing wrote in his after-action report, two hundred Marines had landed under command of a Marine officer while fifty sailors had landed under command of a naval officer. See "Extract of a letter from Esek Hopkins, Esq; commander in

chief of the American fleet, to the President of the Congress, dated on board the ship Alfred, New-London harbour, April 9, 1776," *The Remembrancer*, 211–12.

45. U.S. Marine Corps Recruiting Publicity Bureau, *The Marines in Rhyme, Prose, and Cartoon*, 3rd ed. (New York: USMCRPB, 1917), 5. The first edition was published in 1914.

46. Millett, *Semper Fidelis*, 856; U.S. Navy, *Landing-Force Manual, United States Navy, 1918* (Washington, D.C.: Government Printing Office, 1918), i; U.S. Navy, *Landing-Force Manual, United States Navy, 1920* (Washington, D.C.: Government Printing Office, 1921), 1.

47. Michael T. Coventry, "'Editorials at a Glance': Cultural Policy, Gender, and Modernity in the World War I Bureau of Cartoons," *Review of Policy Research* 24, no. 2 (2007): 97.

48. "2,700 Marines in France to Fight with Allies," *News Journal* (Wilmington, DE), 28 Jun. 1917, 12.

Chapter 6. Democratization

1. Thomas Boyd, *Through the Wheat: A Novel of the World War I Marines* (Lincoln: University of Nebraska Press, 2000), 168; "A Jackie's Rebuke," *Baltimore American*, 19 May 1906, 3. Also see "Music Almost Led to Mutiny," *Duluth News-Tribune*, 17 May 1906, 1.

2. For an overview of the public's perception of the military and various segments of it, see Robert C. Kemble, "Mutations in America's Perceptions of Its Professional Military Leaders: An Historical Overview and Update," *Armed Forces and Society* 34 (Oct. 2007): 29–45. For the strict division between officers and enlistees in the nineteenth century, see Karsten, *The Naval Aristocracy*, 51–52. For the simplistic and somewhat dismissive view of naval officers for sailors, see Karsten, 83–84.

3. It was subsequently turned into a movie. See "Metro Pictures Corps. Photoplay," *Gettysburg (PA) Times*, 22 Mar. 1917, 6.

4. Boyd, *Through the Wheat*, 168.

5. See Ralph D. Paine, *Roads of Adventure* (Boston: Houghton Mifflin, 1922), 441.

6. See, for example, his positive treatment of Kendall's initial commanding officer, Capt. Roy Gildersleeve. Ralph D. Paine, *The Wall Between* (New York: Charles Scribner's Sons), 5, 13, 3–4.

7. Interestingly, the book was adapted into a movie that featured the Army. This was the reverse of what happened for *The Star-Spangled Banner* and *Unbeliever*, which are discussed later in this chapter. See "Garden—The Wall Between," *Washington Herald* (Washington, D.C.), 4 April 1916, 5. However, that could be reflective of public ignorance of the Marine Corps as a distinct

institution. See, for example, "The Wall Between," *Courier-Journal* (Louisville, KY), 21 Sep. 1914, 8. The first line describes the "rigid case rules of the army" before noting the two main characters are Marines.

8. The reviewer also inadvertently confirmed he did not read the novel very carefully. The woman in question was the commanding officer's niece, not daughter.

9. "News from Various Sources," *Bulletin*, Feb. 1916, 19. Sgt. Thomas G. Sterrett had written a similar review the previous year in which he recommended avoiding any notice of the book so as to not encourage additional sales of the book. Thomas G. Sterrett, " 'The Wall Between,' " *Bulletin*, Mar. 1915, 16. Perhaps Sterrett's rank suggests the extent to which he had been co-opted into the Corps' rhetoric. Sterrett subsequently received a commission.

10. See, for example, this rhetoric as early as 1904 in "Marines' Chance Good for Commissions, Now," *Brooklyn Daily Eagle*, 21 Jul. 1904, 13. For Secretary of the Navy Josephus Daniels' emphasis on a democratic culture for both the Navy and the Marine Corps see "Democracy in the Navy," *Altoona (PA) Tribune*, 1 Aug. 1913, 8.

11. For the persistence of military hierarchies from a postmodern perspective, see Larry Allan Van Meter, "The Officer Fetish," (PhD diss., Texas A&M University, 2005), http://oaktrust.library.tamu.edu//handle/1969.1/1366. The Army, for example, focused more on making its soldiers into good citizens. Conversations with Sebastian Lukasik, May 2017. The Navy also moved in this direction due to the personal beliefs of its egalitarian secretary of the Navy Josephus Daniels.

12. William A. Wolff, "Leading Advertising Experts Commend Success of Marines' Publicity Campaign," *Bulletin*, Dec. 1918, 5; " 'Soldier and Sailor, Too': The Marines Are the Real Soldiers of Fortune," *Kansas City Star*, 5 April 1917, 22. This particular article heavily resembled the bureau's releases, evidenced by quotes from Rudyard Kipling, descriptions of the Corps as the oldest U.S. military branch, and several verses of the Corps' hymn. For other references to Kipling, see "Soldiers of the Sea," *Wilkes-Barre Times*, 9 April 1917, 1.

13. "Could You Join the Navy or the Army," *Idaho Register*, 14 April 1916, 3; "Discussion Supplement," *Bulletin*, Feb. 1918, 4; "Again—Quality before Quantity," *Bulletin*, Feb. 1919, 8. The commandant also expressed this wording in his annual report to the secretary of the Navy. See "Report of the Major General Commandant of the United States Marine Corps, 1911," *Annual Reports of the Navy Department* (Washington, D.C.: Government Printing Office, 1912), 533.

14. "Why the Marines Prosper," *Bulletin*, Sep. 1917, 18; Millett, *Semper Fidelis*, 289 and 654.

15. Gerald Clark, letter to "Ed and Family," 16 Dec. 1917, Clark Papers, MCHD; "Major-General Barnett Thanks Newspapers for Marine Corps Publicity," *Greeley Daily Tribune*, 30 April 1917, 1.

16. Provost Marshal General's Bureau, *Report of the Provost Marshal General to the Secretary of War on the First Draft Under the Selective-Service Act, 1917* (Washington, D.C.: Government Printing Office, 1918), 153; McClellan, *The United States Marine Corps in the World War*, 10; *Annual Report of the Surgeon General, U.S. Navy, Chief of the Bureau of Medicine and Surgery to the Secretary of the Navy for the Fiscal Year 1916* (Washington, D.C.: Government Printing Office, 1916), 40.

17. For suggestions of the better quality of the Corps' recruiting material, see "Spokane Reporter Converted," *Bulletin*, Mar. 1916, 5. This is not to say that the public fully understood the Marine Corps' purpose or its relationship to the Navy. Many articles continued to explain the differences between the Corps and the Navy. See, for example, "The Call For Marines; Who The Marines Are," *Colorado Springs Gazette*, 15 May 1917, 9. This particular article drew on the traditional overview provided by Marines, which looked back to the institution's establishment in 1775. Also see a very similar article: "Marines Fine Fighters; Public Now Curious to Learn About Sea Soldiers," *Philadelphia Inquirer*, 6 May 1917, 4. The article stressed the Corps' more traditional roles, such as serving as orderlies and guards at sea rather than emphasizing its expeditionary duties. See "Life of Marine Very Appealing to Average Man; Smartness of Dress and Drill Adds Greatly to Enchantment of the Life," *Wilkes-Barre Times Leader*, 24 April 1917, 12.

18. "Major-General Barnett Thanks Newspapers," 1. For similar wording, see "Marines Want More Men: Evening Ledger Aid Asked," *Evening Public Ledger* (Philadelphia), 24 May 1817, 6. See "Civic Bodies Striving to Wake up America," *Evening Star* (Washington, D.C.), 6 Jun. 1917, 14.

19. "The Power of Publicity," *Bulletin*, Jun. 1917, 11. This article reprinted a *Saint Louis Post-Dispatch* editorial published in May 1916.

20. It is difficult to determine how potential recruits received the Corps' recruiting appeals. Surveys conducted years after World War I reveal a range of motives for entering the war. These responses are somewhat problematic, though, in the extent to which the respondents' perspective might have changed greatly after seeing combat. Former Marines recalled a number of reasons for selecting the Corps, including the desire to be surrounded by people "who knew how to fight." This was the case for PFC George H. Donaldson, 78th Company, 6th Marine Regiment. Others, like Pvt. Anders Peterson, Sixth Machine Gun Battalion, Sixth Marine Regiment, were drawn by the "first to fight" rhetoric. See Department of the Army Questionnaire, World War I Veterans' Survey Project, U.S. Army Military History Institute (hereafter USAMHI).

21. "Every Man in State Urged to Take Hand in Navy Recruiting," *Atlanta Constitution*, 28 April 1917, 6. For tempered language urging practical benefits in a letter to a postmaster and the logic that recruits should join since the Navy could not sail its ships without men, see "Join the Navy," *Box Elder News* (Brigham City, UT), 6 April 1917, 1.

22. Wadle, *Selling Sea Power*; "Every Man in State Urged to Take Hand in Navy Recruiting," *Atlanta Constitution*, 28 April 1917, 6. The Navy would implement a day in 1922 called "Navy Day" whose purpose was less to recruit than it was to acquaint the public with the need for a peacetime Navy. The Navy League also attempted a predecessor in either 1906 or 1907 that it did not repeat until 1922. Author's correspondence with Ryan Wadle, 6 Jun. 2017. Also see "Soldier and Sailor, Too," *Press and Sun-Bulletin* (Binghamton, NY), 8 Jun. 1917, 6.

23. "Registration Day," *Arizona Daily Star* (Tucson), 5 Jun. 1917, 4; "Marine Week Is Observed," *Durham Morning Herald*, 8 March 1917, 8; "National Marine Corps Recruiting Week, June 10–16," *Wilkes-Barre Times Leader*, 22 May 1917, 4.

24. "Every Man in State Urged to Take Hand in Navy Recruiting," *Atlanta Constitution*, 28 April 1917, 6.; "Recruiting Aided by Registration," *Atlanta Constitution*, 7 Jun. 1917, 14; Leo M. Kelly, "Raleigh, N.C., Briefs," *Bulletin*, Jul. 1917, 22; Otto G. Hinz, "Notes from Oakland, Calif.," *Bulletin*, Jul. 1917, 25. Posters were placed on the front and rear of streetcars in Springfield, Illinois. See Homer J. Gravelle, "Big Drive in the Whole Country," *Bulletin*, Jul. 1917, 26.

25. "Way Up Top at Austin," *Bulletin*, Jul. 1918, 29.

26. The article ran in numerous newspapers, including the *Harrisburg Telegraph*, *La Plata (MO) Home Press*, *Coshocton (OH) Morning Tribune*, *Saint Louis Star and Times*, *Waxahachie (TX) Daily Light*, *Stevens Point (WI) Journal*, *Town Talk* (Alexandria, LA), and others. For example, "Loops Loop in Seaplane" *Leavenworth (WA) Edge*, 30 Mar. 1917, 6; "Marine Officer Loops the Loop in Seaplane," *Bulletin*, March 1917, 32.

27. Submarines had only limited submersive capability, but such matters did not preoccupy Marine recruiters unduly. "Questions Hurled at Man on Furlo," *Quantico Leatherneck*, 1 Dec. 1917, 1. For other references that played up the similarities in the words "submarine" and "Marine," see "Today's Minute Men," *The State* (Columbia, SC), 16 April 1917, 7; James S. Carolan, "'One Punch' Sergeant Fighting for Enlistment," *Bulletin*, Aug. 1917, 15. For an article stressing the variety of the Corps' duties which appears to be a Recruiting Publicity Bureau release, see "U.S. Marine Most Diversified Soldier in the World," *Colorado Springs Gazette*, 23 May 1918, 9. A book about the Navy even included a chapter that mentioned that the Marines' motto was There's Nothing I Can't Do. See Elaine Sterne, *Over the Seas for Uncle Sam* (New York: Britton, 1918), 10.

28. See, for example, an article that mentions both the Army and the Navy. The section on the Army recounts the recruiter's frustration and the part on the Corps details a reward of a "swagger" stick for the high school student that can bring in the most recruits. See "Boys of Tech High to Help Recruiting for Marine Corps," *Atlanta Constitution*, 9 Jun. 1917, 5.

29. "Applicants Throng Army, Navy and Marine Corps," *Pittsburgh Daily Post*, 5 Jun. 1917, 4; "Marine Corps Motor on Recruiting Dash," *Evening Ledger* (Philadelphia), 24 May 1917, 6.

30. The only article I have found proclaimed that the Corps recruited nearly two thousand on its first day. See "Nearly 2,000 First Day Marine Week," *Durham Morning Herald*, 14 Jun. 1917, 1. For the Corps' difficulties in Philadelphia on one particular day, see "Ninth Engineers Needs Craftsmen," *Philadelphia Inquirer*, 8 Jun. 1917, 16. With two days left, Chicago recruiters still needed 208 men to meet their quota of 500. See "Two Days Left of Marine Week to Get 208 Men," *Chicago Tribune*, 15 Jun. 1917, 5.

31. "Got 5 Recruits in Marine Week," *Durham Morning Herald*, 17 Jun. 1917, 8; Edwin N. McClellan, *The United States Marine Corps in the World War* (Washington, D.C.: Government Printing Office, 1920), 10; "The Bureau's Own Page," *Bulletin*, 31. Twenty potential recruits had visited the office during the week.

32. "Where There's Action," *Saturday Evening Post*, 5 May 1917, 39.

33. One *Bulletin* contributor proudly noted that Marines devised all of the bureau's slogans. William A. Honing, "War Posters are Silent and Powerful Recruiters," *Bulletin*, Aug. 1917, 4. Also see Charles Cushing, "Campaigning with a Pen for Marine Recruits," *Kansas City Star*, 13 May 1917, 15. The Corps did receive some assistance from professional advertisers, however. See "The Marine Corps Publicity Conference," *Bulletin*, Feb. 1918, 7; "The Bureau's Own Page," *Bulletin*, April 1917, 5; J. C. Armstrong, "Marine Corps Week in Its Larger Meaning," *Bulletin*, Jun. 1917, 3. For the attraction of this slogan, see William A. Honing, "War Posters," *Bulletin*, Aug. 1917, 4.

34. "Coining a New War Cry," *Colorado Springs Gazette*, 13 Jul. 1917, 10; "Col. McLemore Author of 'First to Fight' Slogan," *The Bourbon News* (Paris, Kentucky), 16 Oct. 1917, 2. Lejeune, *Reminiscences of a Marine*, 235. For a similar view, see "Nation to be Placarded with Slogans of War," *Albuquerque Journal*, 24 March 1918, 2.

35. For the extension of this motto to the Corps being "first in everything," see "'Spirit of 1917' Is Shown by Marines," *Gettysburg Times*, 10 Nov. 1917, 5.

36. "Who Will Be First to Fight," *San Jose Mercury Herald*, 8 May 1917, 6; "First to Fight in France," *Bulletin*, Jun. 1917, 16. In surveying the Corps' publicity efforts at the end of the war, professional advertisers believed the institution

had met its promises in a way that should be an example for all marketing. William Almond Wolff, "Leading Advertising Experts Commend Success of Marines' Publicity Campaign," *Bulletin*, Dec. 1918, 6. Harrod discusses how Navy actually shifted ship schedules to live up to "Join the Navy and See the World" before 1917.

37. "'Spirit of 1917' Is Shown by Marines," *Gettysburg Times*, 10 Nov. 1917, 5. For one recruiter's confidence in this poster's appeal see Capt. E. Sears Yates, "Window Cards," *Bulletin*, Aug. 1917, 19. "Today's Minute Men," *The State*, 16 April 1917, 7. The article's content was typical of Recruiting Publicity Bureau releases. "'Spirit of 1917' Is Shown by Marines," *Gettysburg Times*, 10 Nov. 1917, 5.

38. *U.S. Marines: Duties, Experiences, Opportunities, Pay*, 6th ed. (New York: USMCRPB, 1918), 5.

39. The terminology of "globe, anchor and eagle," though, seems to have been the preferred term of the bureau beginning in 1917. The traditional term continued to be used in World War II. See, for example, "Marine Corps Asks for More Women Reserves," *Daily Times* (Davenport, IA), 16 March 1945, 29; Advertisement, "For 167 Years . . . Marines Have Been," *Eau Claire (WI) Leader*, 10 Nov. 1942, 5. For the first mentions of this term that I can find, see an article that came out in 1917 that must have been a Bureau release given its publication in multiple newspapers to include "How to Tell Marines," *Allentown (PA) Leader*, 23 Aug. 1917, 4.

40. "How to Tell Marines," 4. The article capitalized "navy" but not "army." While it used this term in its official material, newspapers often used "eagle, globe, and anchor."

41. "A State of War," *Bulletin*, April 1917, 4. Other recruiters continued to stress service on board naval vessels. See "It's a Life of Adventure is the Lot of the Marine," *Anaconda Standard*, 17 May 1917, 8. Another article anticipated the war would provide plenty of opportunities for Marines to participate in landing parties as well as "clashes at sea." See " 'What Can I Do for My Country?' Enlist To-Day; Join the United States Marine Corps and See Actual Service," *Wilkes-Barre Times*, 9 May 1917, 1. Another article emphasized the Marines' continued service with naval guns while confidently stating the Marines would be the first to land in France. James S. Carolan, "One Punch Sergeant Fighting for Enlistment," *Bulletin*, Aug. 1917, 15. For increased Marine detachments on naval vessels, see Ollie A. Wilson, "Notes from Nashville, Tenn.," *Bulletin*, Jul. 1917, 19. Not all agreed with this view. For his belief that "expeditionary work" was the Corps' central mission, see W. H. Parker, "Adroit Newspaper Publicity," *Bulletin*, May 1917, 6.

42. "'Spirit of 1917' is Shown by Marines," *Gettysburg Times*, 10 Nov. 1917, 5. Outsiders often referred to the institution in the same manner. See "What Others

Say about the Marine Corps," *Bulletin*, Jun. 1917, 3. For just a few examples see "Enlist as Marines; Are Both Sailors and Soldiers, Then," *Grand Forks Herald*, 13 April 1917, 8; editorial, *Quantico Leatherneck*, 14 Nov. 1917, 2.

43. "What Others Say about the Marine Corps," 3.

44. Allan Millett, for example, periodizes the Corps' history as "soldiers at sea," "colonial infantry," "amphibious assault force," and "force in readiness." Millett, *Semper Fidelis*, v–vi.

45. "Marine Corps Wants Men," *Dallas Morning News*, 6 May 1917, 3; "Americans Enlist in Marine Corps in Large Numbers," *Wilkes-Barre Times*, 2 May 1917, 3. Another version of this article began by stressing the adventure an enlistment in the Corps provided. "Marine Recruiter Tells Adventures in Marine Service," *Evening News*, 7 May 1917, 6.

46. Charles Phelps Cushing, "A Cosmopolitan Fighting Man: Assorted Services Indicated in Blue Uniform of Marines," *Kansas City Star*, 29 May 1917, 14; "Who Will be First to Fight?," *San Jose Mercury Herald*, 8 May 1917, 6. To say the Corps had cavalry in a formal sense was a bit of a stretch, though. See "The Secret Is Out There Are Horse Marines," *Duluth News-Tribune*, 13 Jan. 1918, 2. For another article mentioning cavalry, see "Picked Men Are Only Ones Who Can Get in Marines," *Tulsa World*, 28 Jul. 1918, 4. Charles Phelps Cushing described the Corps similarly in "First to Fight on Land or Sea," *The Independent*, 26 May 1917, 371.

47. "Entering Naval Academy by Enlistment in Marine Corps," *Bulletin*, Jan. 1917, 13; letter quoted in "The Marine Officer's School," *Bulletin*, Jul. 1917, 3; C. S. McReynolds, "Odds and Ends from Lusty Files," *Bulletin*, Jan. 1917, 5.

48. "Report of the Major General Commandant of the United States Marine Corps, 1914," *Annual Reports of the Navy Department* (Washington, D.C.: Government Printing Office, 1915), 459–60. As Ryan Wadle argues in *Selling Sea Power*, many, though not all, films set at Annapolis in the interwar period featured the protagonist making friends with the former enlisted man who tested into the academy.

49. "Report of the Major General Commandant of the United States Marine Corps, 1916," *Annual Reports of the Navy Department* (Washington, D.C.: Government Printing Office, 1917), 767; *Annual Report*, 1916, 772–73; "Future Commissions All to Be from the Ranks," *Bulletin*, Aug. 1917, 29.

50. "The U. S. Marine Corps—An Object Lesson of Democracy in the Military," *Wilkes-Barre Times*, Nov. 27, 1916, 8. Also see "Distinguishing Emblem for Recruiters," Dec. 1914, 14. For the suggestion that the Corps was "a little better" than the other branches because its "officers [were] closer to their men, looking out for their welfare," see James F. J. Archibald and Berton Braley, "Soldiers and Sailors, Too," *Collier's*, May 16, 191–94, 12.

51. "'Caste' in Army Bitterly Assailed," *Philadelphia Inquirer*, 9 Jan. 1917, 18. This was not the first time Harllee had used this type of rhetoric. See "Opportunity for Men in Ranks to Win Commissions," *Charlotte Observer*, 18 Dec. 1916, 9.

52. "Coming Up from the Ranks," *Miami Herald*, 5 Jul. 1918, 5. Some enlisted Marines stressed similar themes. Upon leaving his recruiting position for service in France, Sgt. Frank Stubbe wrote that he had been "been treated with more consideration while serving under Captain Patterson than I ever would have received in a like capacity on the outside." See "Farewell from Wilkes-Barre, Pa.," *Bulletin*, Jul. 1917, 19.

53. "Nation to Be Placarded with Slogans of War Today," *Albuquerque Journal*, 24 March 1918, 2. One article explaining Army rank to its readers advised that shoulder straps were "generally the best identification of an officer." See "Rank in the American Army and How It is Ranked," *Anaconda Standard*, 18 Nov. 1917, 8.

54. Beaumont, *Military Elites*, 18 and 21. For this democratizing trend in other armies, see Martin Kitchen, "Elites in Military History," *Elite Military Formations in War and Peace*, ed. Ion A. Hamish and Keith Neilson (Westport, CT: Praeger, 1986), 25.

55. "Advance Base Work at League Island," *Bulletin*, Nov. 1917, 3; "Worth-While Esprit de Corps," *Bulletin*, Jul. 1917, 15. The term "boot camp" was not yet in use, and even Parris Island was then spelled Paris Island. See U.S. House of Representatives, *Hearings before Committee on Naval Affairs of the House of Representatives on Estimates Submitted by the Secretary of the Navy*, 1919 (Washington, D.C.: Government Printing Office, 1919), 865.

56. "Congressman's Son Likes the Service," *Bulletin*, Nov. 1917, 13. The article noted that the son was training with the son of a "millionaire" as well as others with prominent professions. For the Army's critique of the National Guard for its unseemly democratic tendencies, see Jennifer Keene, *World War I* (Westport, Conn.: Greenwood Press, 2006), 50. Denby ultimately did receive a commission. "Former Congressman A Marine," *Bulletin*, May 1917, 32.

57. "Lieut. Col. Gamborg-Andresen: Highest Ranking Officer Promoted from the Ranks," *Bulletin*, April 1917, 1. Also see "Marine Recruiter Wins a Second Lieutenancy," *Bulletin*, March 1918, 23. Gamborg-Andresen had been the recruiter who had worked with the professional advertising company in Chicago in 1906 to 1907 with display advertising.

58. Another film was also released in 1917 that included Marines, but it appears to have had less, if any, direct relationship with the Corps. According to Ryan Wadle's *Selling Sea Power*, Secretary of the Navy Josephus Daniels banned filming on Navy ships and at naval installations during the war. Perhaps the

Recruiting Publicity Bureau's more decentralized New York City location helped it escape this prohibition.

59. Lawrence H. Suid, *Guts and Glory: The Making of the American Military Image in Film* (Reading, MA: Addison-Wesley, 1978), 23.

60. Leslie Midkiff DeBauche, *Reel Patriotism: The Movies and World War I* (Madison: University of Wisconsin Press, 1997), 125; " 'Star-Spangled Banner' Interesting Motion Picture at Grand Theater," *Pueblo (CO) Chieftain*, 13 Jul. 1918, 8.

61. "Two New Marine Corps Films," *Bulletin*, Aug. 1917, 30; Mary Raymond Shipman Andrews, *Three Things: The Forge in which the Soul of a Man Was Tested* (Boston: Little, Brown, 1916), 13.

62. "Great War Film Comes to Rialto for Five Days," *Pueblo (CO) Chieftain*, 6 Jun. 1918, 4.

63. Jan-Christopher Horak, "American Showman: Roxy Rothafel," UCLA Film and Television Archive, https://www.cinema.ucla.edu/blogs/archival-spaces/2013/06/28/american-showman-roxy-rothafe. Rothapfel anglicized his name during World War I.

64. Ross Melnick, *American Showman: Samuel "Roxy" Rothafel and the Birth of the Entertainment Industry, 1908–1935* (New York: Columbia University Press, 2012), 34, 35; "Rothafel Lecture Tour Embraces Wide Territory," *New York Clipper*, 30 Oct. 1915, 42.

65. Melnick, *American Showman*, 152, 35. He also removed the letter "p" from his name either during or after the war to anglicize it more.

66. " 'Sam' Rothapfel, U.S. Marine," *Bulletin*, Feb. 1918, 16.

67. Editorial, *Quantico Leatherneck*, 24 Nov. 1917, 2.

68. One poem made fun of a man with "tango toes," proclaiming, "He thinks he's a man, but he's nothing but clothes. . . . His assets are ten—just his tango toes; The real men laugh while he prances." Stokely S. Fisher, "The Universal Beau," *The Judge* 68 (20 Mar. 1915): n.p.

69. Andrews, *Three Things*, 8.

70. See, for example, Fred W. Staehle, "On Booming Business," *Bulletin*, Feb. 1916, 21. Also see Evans, "The Lure of the Fighting Man," 2.

71. Andrews, *Three Things*, 12, 13, 16.

72. "How You Can Best Serve Your Country in Wartime," *Evening Star* (Washington, D.C.), 11 April 1917, 10.

73. B. J. Rutzen, "Love of the Corps," *Bulletin*, Feb. 1918, 6.

74. For examples of this term's use by Marines, see Henry F. Hayes, A. K. Carrick, and Monkton Dene, "How Necessary is Love of the Corps to Successful Recruiting," Supplement, *Bulletin*, Feb. 1918, 4–6. The Corps also frequently just used the word "spirit" to reference the phenomenon. For one example, see "Chafing at the Bit," *Bulletin*, Feb. 1918, 16.

75. Mark H. Dunkelman, *Brothers One and All: Esprit De Corps in a Civil War Regiment* (Baton Rouge: Louisiana State University Press, 2006), 6.

76. "Join the Marines if you would be a Military Nobleman," *Wilkes-Barre Times*, 10 April 1917, 5. For another mention of "brotherhood," see Harry Baldwin in "Discussion Supplement," *Bulletin*, Feb. 1918, 2. For the influence of medieval notions of brotherhood on the Victorians, see Mark Girouard, *The Return to Camelot: Chivalry and the English Gentleman* (New Haven: Yale University Press, 1981), 41. For this theme within the United States, see Michael C. C. Adams' suggestion that the Spanish-American War "generated a chivalric revival." Also see Marcus Cunliffe's emphasis on a "chevalier" tradition in the United States in *Soldiers and Civilians: The Martial Spirit in America, 1775–1865* (Boston: Little, Brown, 1968), 422.

77. "Man Wanted to Fit This Hat." Recruiting Poster, L.S. Rose Papers, MCHD. The Marine Corps continued to draw on the image of a knight in its advertising well into the 1980s. Michael C. C. Adams, *Echoes of War: A Thousand Years of Military History in Popular Culture* (Lexington: University Press of Kentucky, 2002), 2. Adams also points to the idea of comradeship and its benefit in combat (31).

78. For works on the military and morality during the war, see Nancy K. Bristow, *Making Men Moral: Social Engineering during the Great War* (New York: New York University, 1996). For Colonel Catlin's suggestion that the Americans provided a more moral environment in France than some of the other allies, see Catlin, *With the Help of God*, 27.

79. "Virtue in Uniform," *Quantico Leatherneck*, 2 Feb. 1918, 2; editorial, *Quantico Leatherneck*, 1 Dec. 1917, 2. For others who used the word gentlemen in regard to Marines of all ranks, see "Military Briskness and Courtesy," *Bulletin*, April 1918, 16; and William H. Richardson, "Marines Work Together like Clockwork," *Bulletin*, March 1918, 13. While it had been assumed that officers were gentlemen in the nineteenth century, the idea that enlisted men should be considered gentlemen as well was new. For an enlisted Marine who used the phrase "a soldier and a gentleman," see "Letters from a Marine to His Mother and Father," Malcolm Aitken Papers, U.S. Army Military History Institute. For another who deeply internalized this rhetoric, see Levi Hemrick, *Once a Marine* (Staunton, VA: Clarion, 2013), 31.

80. For the difference between manliness and masculinity, see Bederman, *Manliness and Civilization*, 19; Girouard, *Return to Camelot*, 188. This turn was made easier by the element of brotherhood so essential to knights. Girouard, 217.

81. "How Necessary is Love of the Corps to Successful Recruiting?," discussion supplement, *Bulletin*, Feb. 1918, 2. He perhaps made this link in the context of French soldiers fighting in France. See "Marines Of France—Some War

Memories," *Times Picayune* (New Orleans), 27 Jan. 1918, 43. For the British Army's difficulty in incorporating working-class men during World War I, see Fussell, *Great War and Modern Memory*, 13.

82. "First to Fight," *Arizona Republic* (Phoenix), 30 Apr. 1917, 5; "How Necessary Is a Love of the Corps to Successful Recruiting," discussion supplement, *Bulletin*, Feb. 1918, 1. For the importance of knowing the Corps' traditions, also see Francis E. Turin, "Suggested Handbill," Dec. 1916, 26.

83. Frank Stubbe, "Farewell from Wilkes-Barre, PA," *Bulletin*, Jul. 1917, 19.

84. It also urged recruits to write of their training experiences, and the bureau seized upon those letters in which recruits seemed to have internalized the institution's identity. "Marines on Furlough," *Bulletin*, Jan. 1918, 16; "Make Patriotism Worth While," *Bulletin*, May 1917, 6.

85. "The Marine Corps Publicity Conference," *Bulletin*, Feb. 1918, 7. For other mentions of this spirit see Editorial, *Bulletin*, Dec. 1917, 36; "Thousands Enjoy Big Thanksgiving; Big Feed Here," *Quantico Leatherneck*, 1 Dec. 1919, 1; "Marines' Spirit an Asset, Cooper Says," *Quantico Leatherneck*, 24 Nov. 1917, 1. The word "spirit" also had a slightly different connotation when used in regard to the Corps' "fighting spirit" that purportedly distinguished Marines from other military branches. See "Chafing at the Bit," *Bulletin*, Feb. 1918, 16 and "Soldiers of the Sea," *Wilkes-Barre Times*, 9 April 1917, 1. According to one article a Marine was a "wonder of aggressive action and resourcefulness." See "What Can I Do for My Country?," 1.

86. "Former Congressman," *Cincinnati Enquirer*, 22 Apr. 1917, 1; "Their Deeds Confirm Their Words," *Detroit Free Press*, 23 Apr. 1917, 4; Catlin, *With the Help of God*, 284, 285; "Yanks' Spirit in the War Best Shown by Capt. Denby Letter," *Duluth News-Tribune*, 17 Nov. 1918, 4.

87. Catlin, *With the Help of God*, 15; Clifton Cates to Mom, 1917, Clifton Cates Papers, MCHD.

88. "Well Pleased Marine Writes Sergeant," *Bulletin*, Feb. 1918, 30. Mentions of the Corps' unmatched esprit de corps were not limited to issues of the *Bulletin*. For an enlisted Marine's letters home mentioning spirit, see Arthur Davis to Mother, 7 Jul. 1918, Arthur Davis Papers, MCHD. For an officer's perspective on this "all-pervasive spirit" see Catlin, *With the Help of God*, 32. Also see Josephus Daniels, *Our Navy at War* (New York: George H. Doran, 1922), 216.

89. "The Marine Corps Publicity Conference," *Bulletin*, Feb. 1918, 7. Whereas recruiters previously seem to have debated these issues through the forum of the *Bulletin*, public discussion occurred at this recruiters' conference. Recruiters first visited the recruit training depot at Paris Island, South Carolina then journeyed to Quantico where they witnessed the Corps' more advanced training. William H. Cayan, "Publicity Sergeants' Educational Tour," *Bulletin*,

March 1918, 15. By forming 3,800 "sturdy" Marines into the shape of the globe, eagle, and anchor and photographing them from the air, for example, the Corps tried to keep this symbol in the "limelight." "Keeping Our Corps in the Limelight," *Bulletin*, March 1918, 8.

90. "O Winterfield My Winterfield," *Bulletin*, Dec. 1917, 40; "The Globe, Eagle and Anchor," *Bulletin*, Feb. 1918, 16.

91. William A. Wolff, "Leading Advertising Experts Commend Success of Marines' Publicity Campaign," *Bulletin*, Dec. 1918, 5–6. One article mentioned the symbol along with the Corps' blue uniform as being "unmistakable" symbols of the Corps. See "Keeping Our Corps in the Limelight," *Bulletin*, March 1918, 6–7. Also see Charles Phelps Cushing, "A Cosmopolitan Fighting Man," *Kansas City Star*, 29 May 1917, 14.

92. "Kismet," *Bulletin*, Oct. 1918, 20. The bureau mentioned this "order" in what appeared at the time to be the *Bulletin's* last issue. With the onset of the draft, the bureau ceased its efforts to find recruits. Now, the magazine would become the *Marines' Bulletin*. Its purpose would be to increase the individual Marine's sense of attachment to the Corps, and it would be disseminated by providing each officer and one of every twenty Marines with each issue. "Distribution of Bulletin," *Bulletin*, Nov. 1918, 24. By February of 1919, however, the publication was once again the *Recruiters' Bulletin*.

93. For a similar emphasis on inculcating spirit, see Ben Johnson Cope, "The Marine and His Rifle," *Bulletin*, supplement, Sep. 1917, 16; and Edwin Denby, "Indoctrination with True Corps Spirit," Dec. 1917, 37.

94. Elton E. Mackin, *Suddenly We Didn't Want to Die: Memoirs of a World War I Marine* (Novato, CA: Presidio Press, 1993), 1; emphasis in original. See also Frank E. Goodnough Papers, MCHD.

95. "Join the Marines 'IF' You Can," *Wilkes-Barre Record*, 20 April 1918, 15; Arthur Davis to Aunt Ginnie, 7 Jun. 1918, Arthur Davis Papers, MCHD. Emphasis in original.

96. For recruits who felt this way, see Warren Jackson, *His Time in Hell—A Texas Marine in France: The World War I Memoir of Warren R. Jackson* (Novato, CA: Presidio Press, 2001), 6; Asa J. Smith Diary, 14 Dec. 1917, Asa J. Smith Papers, MCHD. Craig Cameron offers a different interpretation of this tendency, suggesting that instructors made recruits feel insecure because of the Corps' purported inferiority complex. He argues that recruits were taught to "perform to some abstract standard of behavior, a standard so high that it was intended to compensate for the marines' sense of inferiority." See *American Samurai*, 36. More seriously, he charges that the Marines' need to live up to this high standard led them to pay a "price in blood incommensurate with their accomplishments." Others suggest that training of this nature serves a practical purpose, including boosting morale. As Heather Streets has argued, the morale one

gains from an elite identity can pay dividends on the battlefield. See "Identity in the Highland Regiments in the Nineteenth Century: Soldier, Region, Nation," in *Fighting for Identity: Scottish Military Experience, c. 1550–1900*, ed. Steve Murdoch and A. Mackillop (Boston: Brill, 2002), 213–14.

97. Asa J. Smith Diary, 3, 16, and 24 Dec. 1917, Smith Papers; Vincent B. Grube Papers, MCHD; Gerald Clark, 31 Jul. 1917, Gerald Clark Papers, MCHD; Ben Finney, *Once a Marine—Always a Marine* (New York: Crown Publishers, 1977), 17. Also see Victor D. Spark Papers and Gerald Bertrand Clark to Ed and Family, 16 Dec. 1917, Gerald Bertrand Clark Papers, MCHD.

98. Melvin L. Krulewitch, *Now That You Mention It* (New York: Quadrangle, 1973), 28, 23. Also see Jackson, *His Time in Hell*, 4; Carl Andrew Brannen, *Over There: A Marine in the Great War* (College Station: Texas A&M University Press, 1996), 5. Others, however, recalled more practical reasons for choosing the Marine Corps. For some, the institution offered a way to avoid the draft and service in the Army. PFC Brownell, Lessiter and Cpl. Peter P. Bymers, 6th Marine Regiment, Army Service Experiences Questionnaire, World War I Veterans' Survey Project, USAMHI.

99. Chas. W. Alban, letter to Major General George Barnett, 13 Aug. 1918, typescript in George Barnett Papers, MCHD; "The Rivalry," in Henry Berry, *Make the Kaiser Dance* (New York: Doubleday, 1978), 117.

100. John Thomason, *Fix Bayonets!* (New York: Charles Scribner's Sons, 1926), xiii; John Thomason, *Fix Bayonets!* (New York: Charles Scribner's Sons, 1926), xiii; Clark to "Ed and Family," 16 Dec. 1917, Clark Papers, MCHD.

101. Arthur Davis, letter to mother, 24 and 21 Jul. 1918, Arthur Davis Papers, MCHD. Davis served in France but he did not see combat. Quoted in Arthur Davis, letter to Aunt Ginnie, 7 Jun. 1918, Arthur Davis Papers, MCHD.

102. Peter F. Owen, *To the Limit of Endurance: A Battalion of Marines in the Great War* (College Station: Texas A&M University Press, 2007), 2, x, xi, 3. He also implicitly accepts the cultural assumptions of the time regarding the importance of the offensive "spirit" rather than using psychology to understand why men not only fight but keep on fighting. Owen, 91. Such works as Dave Grossman, *On Killing: The Psychological Cost of Learning to Kill in War* (Boston: Little, Brown, 1995) help to illuminate this approach.

103. Albert Catlin, *With the Help of God and a Few Marines* (Garden City, NY: Doubleday, Page, 1919), 14. This story seems to have been popular as similar versions can also be found in Courtney Ryley Cooper, ed., *"Dear Folks at Home": The Glorious Story of the United States Marines in France as Told by their Letters from the Battlefield* (New York: Houghton Mifflin, 1919), xii; "French Playwright Lauds Marine Corps," *Quantico Leatherneck*, 2 Oct. 1918, 1; "Crack American Troops," *Le Figaro*, 27 Aug. 1918,

in *History of the 96th Company, 6th Marines in World War I* (privately published, 1967), Clifton Cates Papers, MCHD. For a similar yet seemingly less embroidered account, see "Wounded Ask for Tooth Brushes and Gum," *Bulletin*, Sep. 1918, 23.

104. See, for example, the responses of Sgt. Taylor Hodnett, Cpl. James O. Clay, Sgt. Edward Howe, "How Necessary is Love of the Corps to Successful Recruiting?," discussion supplement, *Bulletin*, Feb. 1918, 1–12. Sgt. George Mursick did not state that the Corps was the "best" but he did state that the recruiter must convince the potential candidate of this fact. For those recruiters who believed it had the "best" spirit of almost any, see the responses of Sgt. Clarence C. Barry and Sgt. A. K. Carrick, 2 and 4, respectively.

105. Owen, *Limits of Endurance*, 28–29. Owen only cites a lieutenant's interview.

106. Mark Grotelueschen, *The AEF and the Way of War: The American Army and Combat in World War I* (New York: Cambridge University Press, 2006), 207.

107. Owen, *Limits of Endurance*, 206.

108. Jackson, *His Time in Hell*, 27, 238, 119.

109. Janet S. K. Watson, *Fighting Different Wars: Experience, Memory, and the First World War in Britain* (Cambridge: Cambridge University Press, 2007). Boyd served in in the 75th Company, 6th Marines. Boyd, *Through the Wheat*, xiii.

110. Boyd, vi, viii. For Boyd's life, see Brian Bruce, *Thomas Boyd: Lost Author of the "Lost Generation"* (Akron, OH: University of Akron Press, 2006). See, for example, Wen Zhou and Ping Liu, "The First World War and the Rise of Modern American Novel: A Survey of the Critical Heritage of American WWI Writing in the 20th Century" *Journal of Cambridge Studies* 6, no. 2–3 (2011): 121. For some of the literature of this era, see Philip D. Beidler, "The Great Party-Crasher: *Mrs. Dalloway, The Great Gatsby*, and the Cultures of World War I Remembrance" *WLA: War, Literature and the Arts* 24–1 (2013): 25.

111. Boyd, *Through the Wheat*, v and 1–2. Not only is Boyd highly sensitive to the existence of rank, he criticizes the institution's culture as a whole. He describes Marine officers as the "white-collared fighters for democracy" (84). He finds even enlisted leadership hypocritical and hesitant to share the lot of the "common" soldiers (40, 65, and 75). He does consider some officers to be heroes, however, including Major Berton W. Sibley. See "Memorable Portraiture," *The Bookman* (May 1925): 344. Regarding the importance appearance sometimes played in the decision to enlist, also see Joseph Edward Rendinell, *One Man's War: The Diary of a Leatherneck* (New York: J. H. Sears, 1928), 4; and Malcolm D. Aitken, Department of the Army Questionnaire, World War I Questionnaires File, USAMHI.

112. Boyd, *Through the Wheat*, 4–5, 10–11, 45. For critiques of officers, see Boyd, 24, 40, 203–7. Recruiters certainly did not always keep their promises. One Marine who ended up fighting in some of the major battles in France noted he had been promised service in China if he enlisted. Pfc. William A. Dodge, 75th Company, 6th Marine Regiment, World War I Veterans' Survey Project, USAMHI. These surveys were conducted in the 1970s. For more information on this project see Hermine Scholz, *World War I Manuscripts: The World War I Surveys* (Carlisle Barracks: USAMHI, 1986).

113. Boyd, *Through the Wheat*, 10, 48, 45, 40. For the view of Bedford as a coward in combat see Boyd, 115. For his transformation over time, see Boyd, 177.

114. Boyd, 143–50. Bedford loses any semblances of being a leader at this point, but he will rebound.

115. Boyd, 84, 168.

116. Boyd, 142.

117. Boyd, 1, 44–45, 67, 70, vi and viii, 26. Boyd provides this description in the context of his falling asleep on duty. For Adams' treatment of him, see Boyd, 26–28. Adams deals lightly with him in hopes that "some day [he] might make a good soldier" (27–28).

118. In contrast to Harriman and Bedford, Adams walks his horse to encourage his men. Boyd, 213.

119. Boyd, 110–11.

120. See, for example, Thomas Bryan McQuain, *To the Front and Back: A West Virginia Marine Fights World War I* (Westminster, MD: Eagle Editions, 2005), 88, 116, 128–29, 134, 47, 164, 263, 24, 160. Jackson, *His Time in Hell*, 16, 43, 69, 91, 222.

121. Mackin, *Suddenly We Didn't Want to Die*, 156, 74–78, 98. There is only one exception—a sergeant who fearfully leads some replacements on a mission into no man's land.

122. Mackin, 203–4. Also see 226 and 255.

123. Martha L. Wilchinski, "Colonel McLemore to Leave Headquarters Recruiting Head to Go to West Coast," *Bulletin*, April 1919, 3–4 and 22.

124. See, for example, Melvin L. Krulewitch, *Now That You Mention It* (New York: Quadrangle, 1973). By contrast, an account written fifty years after shares many themes with the memoirs here, including its lack of identification with the Corps: Don V. Paradis, *The World War I Memoirs of Don V. Paradis*, Gunnery Sergeant, USMC, ed. Peter F. Owen (Morrisville, NC: Lulu, 2010).

Chapter 7. Hypermasculinization

1. R. M. Duncan, "Dear John," *American Speech* 22, no. 3 (Oct. 1947): 187. The letter, published under the headline, "Breaking the News to Bill," played on the general fear of soldiers and Marines for the infamous Dear John letter announcing a breakup during a boyfriend's overseas combat tour. In this case, however, the twist was, of course, that her decision to join the Marines was almost as shocking as a breakup.

2. Martha Wilchinski, "Breaking the News to Bill," *Bulletin*, Sep. 1918, 26; Stephen J. Ducat, *The Wimp Factor: Gender Gaps, Holy Wars and the Politics of Anxious Masculinity* (Boston: Beacon, 2004), 9.

3. Pamela Wood and Mary Bacon Hale, *Women Marines Association* (Nashville: Turner, 1997), 9.

4. Cynthia Enloe, *Maneuvers: The International Politics of Militarizing Women's Lives* (Berkeley: University of California Press, 2000), 9; Charles Eugene Claghorn, *Women Composers and Songwriters: A Concise Biographical Dictionary* (Lanham, MD: Scarecrow Press, 1996), 235.

5. Anne McClintock, *Imperial Leather: Race, Gender and Sexuality in the Colonial Contest* (New York: Routledge, 1995), 353, emphasis in original; Joan W. Scott, "Rewriting History" in *Behind the Lines: Gender and the Two World Wars*, ed. Margaret Higonnet (New Haven, CT: Yale University Press, 1987), 21.

6. David D. Gilmore, *Manhood in the Making: Cultural Concepts of Masculinity* (New Haven, CT: Yale University Press, 1990), 1.

7. Evans, "The Lure of the Fighting Man," 2; "His Trigger Finger Made No Difference," *Wilkes-Barre Times*, 30 Aug. 1916, 6; John J. Sheradan in "Publicity Sergeant's Educational Tour," *Bulletin*, March 1918, 18.

8. Joshua S. Goldstein, *War and Gender: How Gender Shapes the War System and Vice Versa* (Cambridge University Press, 2001), 264; "Well Done, Recruiters!," *Bulletin*, Aug. 1917, 19. For similar remarks, see a poem suggesting that individual Marines emphasized masculinized rhetoric similarly to recruiters and the Recruiting Publicity Bureau.

   "The Marine," *Quantico Leatherneck*, 27 March 1918, 2; "Fumes from the Incinerator," *Quantico Leatherneck*, 2 Feb. 1918, 2. Also see Cpl. Ollie A. Wilson, USMC, in "My Argument as to Why a Man Should Enlist in the Marine Corps Rather than the Army or the Navy," discussion supplement, *Bulletin*, Oct. 1917, 10.

9. Barnett Neidle, "Recruiting on the Streets Requires Tact and Persistency," *Bulletin*, May 1917, 9; emphasis in original. At the time his article was published, he had been on recruiting duty for more than five years. He wrote in the context of providing the recruit with the unvarnished truth about service life, believing that "if the man is a *man*" he could appreciate what the Corps offered.

10. "Afraid of a Cat Rejected as Marine," *Columbus Daily Enquirer*, 5 Feb. 1917, 1; "Wanted to Fight but Could Not Stand Cats," *Morning Olympian*, 10 Feb. 1917, 4. Another story recounted how a recruiter had made no mention to stop a potential recruit from leaving after the potential recruit began crying after hearing a sentimental song about mothers. "Recruit, Hearing 'Mother' Played, Weeps, Goes Home Refuses to Enlist after Listening Street to Street Piano," *Philadelphia Inquirer*, 1 Jan. 1916, 1. The recruiter noted that someone who burst into tears upon hearing a song might not be the best candidate to endure the sound of "bursting shell[s] in battle." In doing so, the bureau reinforced the theme that it was the organization to join for real fighting. Other examples include "Recruit Couldn't Pass Test but He Had One Good Puzzle," *Morning Olympian*, 13 April 1916, 4. Despite refusing overly sentimental recruits, the Corps apparently felt it needed to show it could be more sympathetic to civilian family members of Marines and even pets. See "Little Girl Pleaded for 'Life' of Dog," *Columbus Daily Enquirer*, 20 Oct. 1916, 6. The article was published in multiple newspapers suggesting it was a Bureau production. Such an article would have furthered the desire of some Marines to ensure that even children understood the role of the Corps. For example, see "Teach Children Duties Marine Corps," *Columbus Daily Enquirer*, 15 March 1916, 1. The impetus for the article appears to have been Sgt. Frank Stubbe's comments to a local newspaper about the need for citizens to understand that the Corps was "distinct" from the Army and the Navy.

11. "Only Real Men Can Hope to Join Uncle Sam's Carefully Trained Marine Corps," *Wilkes-Barre Times*, 13 April 1916, 7. The connection between virile masculinity and service in the Corps intensified greatly several years before the United States entered World War I. For other institutions undergoing related processes, see Gerda W. Ray, "From Cossack to Trooper: Manliness, Police Reform, and the State," *Journal of Social History* 28 (Spring 1995): 565–86; and Arnaldo Testi, "The Gender of Reform Politics: Theodore Roosevelt and the Culture of Masculinity," *Journal of American History* 81 (Mar. 1995): 1509–33.

12. "Young Men Study for Entry into Marine Corps," *Montgomery Advertiser*, 10 Dec. 1916, 2. The article indicated that the night school would be expanded to the Corps' recruiting stations throughout the country.

13. "Marine Corps Bars Flat Feet: 18 out of 100 Applicants Fail," *Duluth News-Tribune*, 4 Nov. 1915, 9. This article appears to be one issued to recruiters who were allowed to elaborate. One sergeant cited these figures to the Duluth paper the same day that a paper in Washington quoted Capt. Frank Evans with almost identical statements. See "'Flat Foot' Keeps 18 per Cent of New Yorkers out of Navy," *Morning Olympian*, 4 Nov. 1915, 1. That the headline mentioned the Navy whereas the article cited the Marine

Corps demonstrated the uphill battle the Corps faced in portraying itself as a distinct institution.

14. For historiography on this subject, see Michael C. C. Adams, *The Great Adventure: Male Desire and the Coming of World War I* (Bloomington: Indiana University Press, 1990); John Pettegrew, *Brutes in Suits: Male Sensibility in America, 1890–1920* (Baltimore: Johns Hopkins University Press, 2007); Gail Bederman, *Manliness and Civilization: A Cultural History of Gender and Race in the United States, 1880–1917* (Chicago: University of Chicago Press, 1996); Anthony Rotundo, *American Manhood: Transformations in Masculinity from the Revolution to the Modern Era* (New York: Free Press, 1994).

15. Gilmore, *Manhood in the Making*, 4–5; August Fredericks, "Notes from Wheeling," *Bulletin*, Jul. 1917, 20; Sgt. John J. Murphy in "My Argument as to Why a Man Should Enlist in the Marine Corps Rather than the Army or the Navy," Supplement, *Bulletin*, Oct. 1917, 6.

16. Patricia Vettel-Becker, "Destruction and Delight: World War II Combat Photography and the Aesthetic Inscription of Masculine Identity," *Men and Masculinities* 5, no. 87 (2002): 1.

17. "The First Girl to Call Men to the Colors," *Pittsburgh Press*, 25 Jun. 1916, 1.

18. The Navy recruited in a similar manner. See Levin Gavin, *American Women in World War I: They Also Served* (Niwot: University Press of Colorado, 1997), 25, for the suggestion that the Recruiting Publicity Bureau consciously sought to use women for these purposes.

19. "Women Can't Serve on Battleships. Many Women Want to Enlist in Marine Corps," *Aberdeen Daily News*, 28 March 1917, 1; Jean Ebbert and Marie-Beth Hall, *The First, The Few, The Forgotten: Navy and Marine Corps Women in World War I* (Annapolis, MD: Naval Institute Press, 2002), 4.

20. "Woman Recruiter Wins Recruits," *Bulletin*, Feb. 1918, 26; W. H. Smith, "Woman Leads Recruiting at K.C.," Aug. 1918, Supplement, *Bulletin*, 1.

21. Linda L. Hewitt, *Women Marines in World War One* (Quantico: History and Museums Division, 1974), 3.

22. Ebbert and Hall, *The First, The Few*, 31; "Yeowomen Must Cut out the Frills," *Pawtucket Times*, 19 Jul. 1918, 16; "Yeowomen Must Not Sit on Desks; Navy Also Bars 'Idle Conversation,'" *Pawtucket Times*, 23 May 1918, 11.

23. "Navy Officers to Salute Yeowomen," *Pawtucket Times*, 17 May 1918, 23; Reference Branch. MCHD, 2007. "Brief History of U.S. Marine Corps Action in Europe during World War I," World War I Centennial, https://www.worldwar1centennial.org/index.php/usmc-in-ww1/850-a-brief-history-of-u-s-marine-corps-action-in-europe-during-world-war-i.html.

24. "8,584 Enter Marine Corps; Jul. Enlistments Bring Recruiting to New High Point," *New York Tribune*, 5 Aug. 1918, 6; "8500 Join the Marines," *New York*

Times, 11 Aug. 1918, 6. The Navy had 431 killed in action and 819 wounded in action. At its peak strength in 1918, the Corps had about 75,000 Marines. See Allan R. Millett, *Semper Fidelis: The History of the United States Marine Corps* (New York: Macmillan, 1980), 628.

25. "All Recruiting Is Stopped in Nation," *Tulsa World*, 10 Aug. 1918, 12. Congress made the request the first month the American Expeditionary Forces participated in significant combat. Hewitt, *Women Marines in World War One*, 4.

26. Congress, House of Representatives, *Enlisted Men between the Ages of 21 and 31 Assigned to Clerical Work in United States Marine Corps*, 65th Cong., 2nd sess., 1917, Doc. No. 1272, 2. The author does not point out this contradiction in publishing the image.

27. "Marine Corps Enlists First Woman," *Anaconda Standard*, 23 Aug. 1918, 4; "Women Clerks to Free Marines who Seek Fight," *New York Tribune*, 14 Aug. 1918, 7; "Girl Joins Devil Dogs," *Evening Star* (Washington, D.C.), 14 Aug. 1918, 1.

28. "1,000 Women Applications Seek to Enlist in the Marine Corps," *New York Tribune*, 5 Sep. 1918, 7. One article suggested some allowances for physical requirements would be lowered. "Women Can Enlist in Marine Corps," *Tulsa World*, Sep. 4, 1918, 10.

29. Millett, *Semper Fidelis*, 291.

30. Charles W. Wootton and Barbara E. Kemmerer, "The Changing Genderization of Bookkeeping in the United States, 1870–1930," *Business History Review* 70, no. 555 :(1996) 4. John Pettegrew, *Brutes in Suits: Male Sensibility in America, 1890–1920* (Baltimore: Johns Hopkins University Press, 2007), 130.

31. "Marines Ask Women to Supplant Males," *Philadelphia Inquirer*, 14 Sep. 1918, 8; "Our New Marines," *Bulletin*, Sep. 1918, 16; "Military Funeral for Girl Marine," *Reading (PA) Times*, 17 Oct. 1918, 6.

32. "Our New Marines," *Bulletin*, Sep. 1918, 16; "Uniform Women Marines Will Wear," *Bulletin*, Sep. 1918, 23.

33. Diary, Raymond Stenbeck Papers, USAMHI; Diary, George Kase Papers, MCHD; "Charming Blonde Seeks to Enlist in Marine Corps," *Washington Times*, 6 Aug. 1918, 15.

34. "Two More Girls Join Marine Corps," *Washington Times*, 15 Aug. 1918, 4.

35. Enloe discusses the lengths that government officials have taken to ensure the uniform conveys suitable messages. *Maneuvers*, 261–72. Carol Burke, *Camp All-American, Hanoi Jane, and the High-And-Tight: Gender, Folklore, and Changing Military Culture* (Boston: Beacon Press, 2004), 94.

36. Millett, *Semper Fidelis*, 308. At one point the Navy appears to have considered requiring females to wear trousers, deciding against it in 1917. See "Yeowomen

of the Navy Need Not Wear Trousers; Government Settles Momentous Question by Designating Uniform," *Philadelphia Inquirer*, 22 April 1917, 1.

37. "Yeowomen Must Put on Uniforms," *Washington Post*, 21 Sep. 1918, 5; "D.C. Must Take $2,000,000 Daily," *Washington Times*, May 3, 1919, 2.

38. "Marinette's First Request is Mirror," newspaper clipping, Frank L. Martin Papers, MCHD; "Those Girl Marines," *Bulletin*, Dec. 1918, 61.

39. "Daniels in Favor of Navy Yeowomen," *Los Angeles Times*, 30 May 1919, 15. The yeowomen had organized a "drilling team."

40. See William H. McNeill, *Keeping Together in Time* (Cambridge, M.A.: Harvard University Press, 1997), 1–2.

41. "Uniform Women Marines Will Wear," *Bulletin*, Sep. 1918, 23; "Girl Marines 100% Girls, These Marine Girls at Washington—Same Duties as Men Who Have," *Grand Forks Herald*, 11 Feb. 1919, 7; Ebbert and Hall, *The First, The Few*, 71.

42. Margaret Higonnet, Jane Jenson, Sonya Michel, and Margaret C. Weitz, eds., *Behind the Lines: Gender and the Two World Wars* (New Haven: Yale University Press, 1987), 41; "Girl Marines 100% Girls," 7.

43. Sonya Michel uses the term "overfeminize" regarding how the U.S. stressed the importance of a maternal role during World War II, but this was not part of the Corps' World War I rhetoric. Sonya Michel, "American Women and the Discourse of the Democratic Family in World War II" in *Behind the Lines*, 160.

44. "Martha the Marine!," *Bulletin*, Nov. 1918, 31.

45. Sonya O. Rose, *Which People's War?: National Identity and Citizenship in Wartime Britain, 1939–1945* (New York: Oxford University Press, 2003), 134.

46. Also see her description as a "fair Marine." Martha Wilchinski, "Fair Marine Learns, 'When Is a Recruit,'" *Bulletin*, Feb. 1919, 9. For official photographs, see Hewitt, *Women Marines in World War One*, 32.

47. "Girl Marines," *Marion (OH) Star*, 1 Feb. 1919, 13.

48. Ebbert and Hall, *The First, The Few*, 55; Edward J. Evans, "Reminiscing on 30," *Leatherneck*, Nov. 1947, 39. Also see *Leatherneck*, 2 Jan. 1919.

49. "Publicity Bureau Notes," *Bulletin*, Oct. 1917, 22; Hewitt, *Women Marines in World War One*, 35–36; Hap Hadley, "Devil Dog Dave," *Anaconda Standard* (MT), 2 Feb. 1919, 46.

50. Martha L. Wilchinski, "Breaking the News to Bill," *Bulletin*, Sep. 1918, 26; Martha L. Wilchinski, "Colonel McLemore to Leave Headquarters Recruiting Head to Go to West Coast," *Bulletin*, April 1919, 4. At the same time, he cautioned against using them in "publicity stunts" in a way that might "embarrass" or "show a lack of good taste."

51. Martha Wilchinski, "The Cruel, Cruel War Hasn't Ended Yet for Corporal Martha," *Bulletin*, Jan. 1919, 14.

52. Rose, *Which People's War*, 123; "Girl Marines," *Marion Star* (Ohio), 1 Feb. 1919, 13; "Smiling Applicants Who Would Join Marines," *Bulletin*, Sep. 1918, 23.

53. Corinne Rockwell Swain, "Mustered Out," *Life*, 20 Feb. 1919, 286.

Epilogue

1. "Inside the Navy: Marines Make Case for Return to 'From the Sea' Ops, Hybrid Warfare," Marine Corps Base, Quantico, 12 Jan. 2009, accessed 2 Mar. 2010, http://www.quantico.usmc.mil/activities/display.aspx?PID=3045and Section=SVG; Millett, *Semper Fidelis*, 547.

2. Annette D. Amerman, "Celebrating 90 Years of Collecting, Preserving, and Promoting of Marine Corps History," *Fortitudine* 34, no. 4 (2009): 19.

3. Giles Bishop, *The Marines Have Landed* (Philadelphia: Penn, 1920), 148.

Bibliography

Manuscript Collections

Geographic and Subject Files, Marine Corps Historical Detachment, Quantico, Virginia

Civil War Reenactment
Littleton Waller Sr.
Mexican-American War
Nicaragua
Philippines War
Recruiting
Spanish-American War
Veracruz Incident

Library of Congress, Washington, D.C.

William Fullam Papers
Thomas Wood Papers

National Archives and Records Administration, Washington, D.C.

Record Group 80
Record Group 127

Oral Histories, Personal Papers Collection, Marine Corps University Research Archives, Quantico, VA

Clifton Cates
George H. Cloud
A. D. Cooley
Edward A. Craig
Marion Dawson
Pedro del Valle
Graves Erskine
George F. Good Jr.
Samuel B. Griffith
John M. Hart
Leo D. Hermle
Thomas Holcomb

Samuel S. Jack
Joseph E. Johnson
Louis R. Jones
James J. Keating
Robert C. Kilmartin
Robert B. Luckey
John H. Masters
John C. McQueen
Vernon E. Megee
Ivan Miller
Richard B. Millin
Ralph Mitchell
John Munn
Alfred H. Noble
Dewitt Peck
Edwin A. Pollock
Bennet Puryear Jr.
William W. Rogers
Joseph A. Rossell
Lawson Sanderson
Alan Shapley
Lemuel Shepherd
Merwin H. Silverthorn
Julian C. Smith
Gerald C. Thomas
Francis Neville West
Thomas A. Worsham
William A. Worton

Personal Papers Collection, Archives Branch, Marine Corps History Division, Quantico, VA

John J. Awkerman Papers
George Barnett Papers
Clarence G. Baumgartner Papers
Hiram Bearss Papers
David Bellamy Papers
John D. Bennett Papers
James P. Berkeley Papers
Louis L. Bloom Papers
James Breckenridge Papers

Smedley Butler Papers
Clifton Cates Papers
Gerald Bertrand Clark Papers
Arthur Clifford Papers
John H. Clifford Papers
Henry Cochrane Papers
Henry Conkey Papers
Edward A. Craig Papers
Richard B. Creecy Papers
Arthur Davis Papers
Henry C. Davis Papers
Perry Kid Dean Papers
Robert Denig Papers
Edward J. Doyle Papers
Joseph E. Duermit Papers
Earl Ellis Papers
David Erickson Papers
C. L. Fairbairn Papers
Logan Feland Papers
Frank Flanders Papers
John E. Fondahl Papers
Donald G. Forbes Papers
Ben Fuller Papers
Joseph Gold Papers
Frank E. Goodnough Papers
Thomas Granley Papers
William B. Greeley Papers
Ralph Greenlee Papers
William H. Greer Jr. Papers
Vincent B. Grube Papers
John C. Harris Papers
Wilbur K. Hassell Papers
C. G. Henry Papers
George Herbert Papers
Frank Hill Papers
H. J. Hirshinger Papers
John A. Hughes Papers
Robert Hunter Papers
Robert Huntington Papers
Arthur B. Jacques Papers

George F. Johnson Papers
George Kase Papers
Allen C. Kelton Papers
Thomas J. Kilcourse Papers
Joseph B. Knotts Papers
Walter F. Kromp Papers
Milton C. Lindsay Papers
Charles G. Lon Papers
Charles H. Lyman Papers
Frank Martin Papers
Charles L. McCawley Papers
George C. McClellan Papers
Frank McCulley Papers
John McHenry Jr. Papers
Carl Berry Mills Papers
Patrick Moran Papers
Joseph Pendleton Papers
Constantine M. Perkins Papers
George Petry Sr. Papers
George Reid Papers
Nicholas Retza Papers
L. S. Rose Papers
William Rossiter Papers
William J. Scheyer Papers
Charles W. Sension Papers
William Shaw Papers
John E. Smiley Papers
Asa J. Smith Papers
J. Earl Snively Papers
Victor D. Spark Papers
Helen Stote Papers
Wilbur S. Talbott Papers
Merrill Thompson Papers
George C. Thorpe Papers
John L. Tunnell Papers
Alexander Vandegrift Papers
Littleton Waller Jr. Papers
Littleton W. T. Waller Sr. Papers
Richard P. Welte Papers
Richard P. Williams Papers

Robert Wilson Papers
Emil Wishnack Papers
Paul Woyshner Papers
John T. Zumwalt Papers

Southern Historical Collection, Louis Round Wilson Special Collections Library, University of North Carolina, Chapel Hill

William Peterkin Upshur Letters, 1898–1928, Collection No. 02645
William Curry Harllee Letters, 1865–1944, Collection No. 01550

U.S. Army Military History Institute, Army Heritage and Education Center, U.S. Army War College, Carlisle, PA

Franklin H. Delano Papers, 1913–1920
Personal Papers Collection
Second Division, 5th Marine Regiment: Malcolm D. Aitken
Second Division, 6th Marine Regiment: William A. Dodge, Lloyd G. Short, Raymond H. Stenback, Lessiter Brownell, Peter P. Bymers
World War I Questionnaires File

Journals and Periodicals

Army and Navy Journal
Bookman
Colburn's United Service Magazine
Collier's Weekly
Globe and Laurel
Indian (newspaper of the 2nd Division, American Expeditionary Forces)
Infantry Journal
Journal of the Royal United Service Institution
Leatherneck
Literary Digest
Marine Corps Gazette
North American Review
Our Navy
Outlook
Printers' Ink
Quantico Leatherneck
Recruiters' Bulletin
Rotarian
Scribner's Magazine

Southern Literary Messenger
Stars and Stripes
United Serve: A Monthly Review of Military and Naval Affairs
United States Naval Institute *Proceedings*
Wide World Magazine

Published Primary Sources

Abbot, Willis J. *Soldiers of the Sea: The Story of the United States Marine Corps.* New York: Dodd, Mead, 1918.

Aldrich, M. Almy. *History of the United States Marine Corps.* Boston: Henry L. Shepard, 1875.

Andrews, Mary Raymond Shipman. *Three Things: The Forge in which the Soul of a Man Was Tested.* Boston: Little, Brown, 1916.

Barnes, John S., ed. *Fanning's Narrative: The Memories of Nathaniel Fanning, an Officer of the Revolutionary Navy.* New York: Naval History Society, 1912.

Barney, Mary, ed. *A Biographical Memoir of the Late Commodore Joshua Barney.* Boston: Gray and Bowen, 1832.

Bates, Charles A. *American Journalism from the Practical Side.* New York: Holmes Publishing Company, 1897.

Berry, Henry, ed. *Make the Kaiser Dance: Living Memories of a Forgotten War; The American Experience in World War I.* New York: Doubleday, 1978.

Blake, Robert Wallace. *Bayonets and Bougainvilleas: A Memoir of Major General Robert Blake, USMC, 1894–1983.* Bloomington, IN: 1st Books, 2001.

Boyd, Thomas. *Through the Wheat: A Novel of the World War I Marines.* Lincoln: University of Nebraska Press, 2000.

Brannan, John. *Official Letters of Military and Naval Officers of the United States during the War with Great Britain.* Washington City: Way and Gideon, 1823.

Brannen, Carl Andrew. *Over There: A Marine in the Great War.* College Station: Texas A&M University Press, 1996.

Brown, Frederick. *From Tientsin to Peking with the Allied Forces.* London: Charles H. Kelly, 1902.

Buel, James W. *Hero Tales of the American Soldier and Sailor as Told by the Heroes Themselves.* New York: W. W. Wilson, 1899.

Burks, Arthur J. *Land of Checkerboard Families.* New York: Coward-McCann, 1932.

Burrows, Julius. "History of the Marine Corps." Senate Document 719, 60th Congress, 2nd Session. Washington, D.C.: Government Printing Office, 1909.

Butler, Smedley, and Arthur J. Burks. *Walter Garvin in Mexico.* Philadelphia: Dorrance, 1927.

Caitlin, Albert. *With the Help of God and a Few Marines.* Garden City, NY: Doubleday, Page, 1919.

Calwell, Charles. *Small Wars: Their Principles and Practice.* Lincoln: University of Nebraska Press, 1996.

Carter, William A., and Pascal J. Plant. *Tale of a Devil Dog.* Washington, D.C.: Canteen Press, 1920.

Clifford, John. *History of the First Battalion of U.S. Marines.* Portsmouth, NH: Brass Hat, 1930.

Collings, Kenneth. *Just for the Hell of It.* New York: Dodd, Mead, 1938.

Collum, Richard S. *History of the United States Marine Corps.* Philadelphia: L. R. Hamersly, 1890.

———. *History of the United States Marine Corps.* Philadelphia: L. R. Hamersly, 1903.

Cooper, James Fenimore. *The Two Admirals: A Tale in Two Volumes.* Vol. 1. New York: Stringer and Townsend, 1849.

Cowing, Kemper F., comp., and Courtney Ryley Cooper, ed. *Dear Folks at Home: The Glorious Story of the United States Marines in France as Told by Their Letters from the Battlefield.* New York: Houghton Mifflin, 1919.

Craige, John Houston. *Black Bagdad.* New York: Minton, Balch, 1933.

———. *Cannibal Cousins.* New York: Minton, Balch, 1934.

———. *What the Citizen Should Know about the Marines.* New York: W. W. Norton, 1941.

Crane, Stephen. *Wounds in the Rain: A Collection of Stories related to the Spanish-American War.* London: Methuen, 1900.

Cronon, David. *The Cabinet Diaries of Josephus Daniels, 1913–1921.* Lincoln: University of Nebraska Press, 1963.

Daggett, Aaron. *America in the China Relief Expedition.* Kansas City, Mo.: Hudson-Kimberly, 1903.

Dahlgren, Madeleine Vinton. *Memoir of John A. Dahlgren, Rear-Admiral United States Navy.* Boston: James R. Osgood, 1882.

Dana, Richard Henry, Jr. *Two Years before the Mast: A Personal Narrative.* Boston: Houghton Mifflin, 1911.

Davenant, Francis. *What Shall My Son Be? Hints to Parents.* London: S. W. Partridge, 1870.

Davis, John, and John Moore. *The Post-Captain: Or, the Wooden Walls Well Manned.* New York: Joseph M'Cleland, 1828.

De Vere, Bud. *Lions, Leathernecks, and Legacies.* Newington, VA: DeVere Press, 1992.

del Valle, Pedro. *Semper Fidelis: An Autobiography.* Hawthorne, CA: Christian Book Club of America, 1976.

Drury, W. P. *In Many Parts: Memoirs of a Marine.* London: T. F. Unwin, 1926.

———. *The Peradventures of Private Pagett.* London: Chapman and Hall, 1915.

Evans, Frank E. *Daddy Pat of the Marines: Being His Letters from France to His Son Townie.* New York: Frederick A. Stokes, 1919.

Evans, Robley D. *A Sailor's Log: Recollections of Forty Years of Naval Life.* New York: D. Appleton, 1908.

Fallows, Samuel T. *The Progressive Dictionary of the English Language.* Chicago: Progressive Publishing, 1885.

Finney, Ben. *Once a Marine—Always a Marine.* New York: Crown, 1977.

Ford, Worthington C., ed. *Journals of the Continental Congress, 1774–1789.* Washington, D.C.: Government Printing Office, 1905.

Fox, Wesley L. *Marine Rifleman: Forty-Three Years in the Corps.* Dulles, VA: Brassey's, 2003.

Franklin, Irwin R. *Knights of the Cockpit: A Romantic Epic of the Flying Machines in Haiti.* New York: Dial Press, 1931.

Glascock, William Nugent. *Naval Sketch-Book: The Service Afloat and Ashore.* Vol. 1. Philadelphia: E. L. Carey and A. Hart, 1835.

Graves, Robert. *Good-Bye to All That.* Revised 2nd ed. 1929; New York: Anchor Books, 1985.

Gulberg, Martin G. *A War Diary.* Chicago: Drake Press, 1927.

Hamersly, Lewis R. *The Records of Living Officers of the U.S. Navy and Marine Corps.* Philadelphia: J. B. Lippincott, 1870.

Hancock, H. Irving. *Dave Darrin at Vera Cruz; or, Fighting with the U.S. Navy in Mexico.* Philadelphia: Henry Altemus, 1914.

Harbord, James G. *Leaves from a War Diary.* New York: Dodd, Mead, 1925.

Hitt, Neil. *Devil Dog Ballads.* Baltimore City, MD: Baltimore City Printing and Binding, 1919.

Holloway, Abraham. *Hero Tales of the American Soldier and Sailor as told by the Heroes Themselves and Their Comrades.* New York: W. W. Wilson, 1899.

Hooker, Mary. *Behind the Scenes in Peking.* London: John Murray, 1910.

Jackson, Warren R. *His Time in Hell: A Texas Marine in France.* Novato, CA: Presidio Press, 2001.

Jodon, James K. *My Four Years in the U.S. Marines.* New York: Vantage Press, 1970.

Krulewitch, Melvin L. *Now That You Mention It.* New York: Quadrangle, 1973.

Leech, Samuel. *Thirty Years from Home; or, A Voice from the Main Deck.* Boston: Charles Tappan, 1844.

Leland, Anne. *American War and Military Operations Casualties: Lists and Statistics.* Washington, D.C.: Congressional Research Service, 2010.

Leland, Charles G., ed., *A Dictionary of Slang, Jargon, and Cant.* New York: George Bell and Sons, 1897.

Lejeune, John A. *The Reminiscences of a Marine.* Philadelphia: Dorrance, 1930. Reprint, Quantico, VA: Marine Corps Association, 1990.

Letcher, John Seymour. *One Marine's Story.* Verona, VA: McClure Press, 1970.

———. *Good-bye to Old Peking: The Wartime Letters of U.S. Marine Captain John Seymour Letcher, 1937–1939.* Edited by Roger B. Jeans and Katie Letcher Lyle. Athens: Ohio University Press, 1998.

Luce, Stephen B. *Text-Book of Seamanship.* Rev. and enlarged by Aaron Ward. New York: D. Van Ostrand, 1884.

Mackin, Elton E. *Suddenly We Didn't Want to Die: Memoirs of a World War I Marine.* Novato, CA: Presidio Press, 1993.

March, William K. *Company K.* New York: Smith and Haas, 1933.

McClellan, Edwin N. *The United States Marine Corps in the World War.* Washington, D.C.: Government Printing Office, 1920.

McQuain, Thomas Bryan. *To the Front and Back: A West Virginia Marine Fights World War I.* Westminster, MD: Eagle Editions, 2005.

Melville, Herman. *White-Jacket or the World in a Man-of-War.* New York: United States Book Company, 1892.

Miller, J. Michael. *My Dear Smedley: Personal Correspondence of John A. Lejeune and Smedley D. Butler, 1927–1928.* Quantico, VA: Marine Corps Research Center, 2002.

Nordhoff, Charles. *Nine Years a Sailor.* Cincinnati: Moore, Wilstach and Baldwin, 1866.

Oviatt, Miles M. *A Civil War Marine at Sea: The Diary of Medal of Honor Recipient Miles M. Oviatt.* Edited by Mary P. Livingston. Shippensburg, PA: White Mane Publications, 1998.

Paine, Ralph D. *The Wall Between.* New York: Charles Scribner's Sons, 1914.

Parry, Francis Fox Parry, Col. *Three-War Marine: The Pacific, Korea, Vietnam.* Pacifica, CA: Pacifica Press, 1987.

Porter, David D. *Memoir of Commodore David Porter of the United States Navy.* Albany, NY: J. Munsell, 1875.

Post, Charles Johnson. *The Little War of Private Post: The Spanish-American War Seen Up Close.* Lincoln: University of Nebraska Press, 1999.

Pottle, Frederick Albert. *Stretchers: The Story of a Hospital Unit on the Western Front.* New Haven, CT: Yale University Press, 1929.

Registers of the Commissioned and Warrant Officers of the United States Navy and Marine Corps. Washington, D.C.: Government Printing Office. 1856, 1861, 1866, 1871, 1876, 1881, 1886, 1891, 1896, 1901, 1906, 1911, 1916, 1921.

Rendinell, Joseph E., and George Patullo. *One Man's War: The Diary of a Leatherneck.* New York: J. H. Sears, 1928.

Reynolds, Alfred. *The Life of an Enlisted Soldier in the United States Army.* Washington, D.C.: Government Printing Office, 1904.

Riseley, James. *Uncle Jim, USMC: Recollections of Lt. Gen. James P. Riseley, United States Marine Corps (Ret.).* Roswell, NM: Privately published, 1991.

Russell, Thomas Herbert. *Mexico in Peace and War.* Chicago: Reilly and Britton Syndicate, 1914.

Scanlon, William T. *God Have Mercy on Us! A Story of 1918.* Boston: Houghton Mifflin, 1929.

Scarbrough, Byron. *They Called Us Devil Dogs.* Privately published, 2005.

Shoup, David M. *The Marines in China, 1927–1928: The China Expedition which Turned out to Be the China Exhibition, A Contemporaneous Journal.* Hamden, CT: Archon Books, 1987.

Shunk, Caroline S. *An Army Woman in the Philippines and the Far East.* Kansas City, Mo.: Franklin Hudson, 1914.

Sledge, Eugene B. *China Marine: An Infantryman's Life after World War II.* New York: Oxford University Press, 2003.

———. *With the Old Breed: At Peleliu and Okinawa.* New York: Oxford University Press, 1990.

Smith, Charles R., ed. *The Journals of Marine Second Lieutenant Henry Bulls Watson, 1845–1848.* Washington, D.C.: History and Museums Division, Headquarters, U.S. Marine Corps, 1990.

Society of the First Division. *History of the First Division during the World War, 1917–1919.* Philadelphia: John C. Winston, 1922.

Sterne, Elaine. *Over the Seas for Uncle Sam.* New York: Britton, 1918.

Stirling, Yates. *Fundamentals of Naval Service.* Philadelphia: J. B. Lippincott, 1917.

Thomas, Lowell. *Old Gimlet Eye: The Adventures of Smedley D. Butler as Told to Lowell Thomas.* New York: Farrar and Rinehart, 1933.

Thomason, John W., Jr. *Fix Bayonets!* New York: Charles Scribner's Sons, 1926.

———. *Jeb Stuart.* Lincoln: University of Nebraska Press, 1994.

———. *Red Pants and Other Stories.* New York: Charles Scribner's Sons, 1927.

———. *Salt Winds and Gobi Dust.* New York: Charles Scribner's Sons, 1934.

Tomlinson, Everett T. *Sergeant Ted Cole, United States Marines.* Boston: Houghton Mifflin, 1919.

Tyson, Carolyn, ed. *The Journal of Frank Keeler.* Quantico: Marine Corps Museum, 1975.

U.S. House of Representatives Committee on Naval Affairs, Hearings. "Status of the Marine Corps." January 7–15, 1909, 60th Congress, 2nd Session. Washington, D.C.: Government Printing Office, 1909.

U.S. Marine Corps Recruiting Publicity Bureau. *U.S. Marines: Duties, Experiences, Opportunities, Pay.* 2nd ed. New York: Chasmar-Winchell Press, 1912.

———. *U.S. Marines: Duties, Experiences, Opportunities, Pay.* Various editions. New York: U.S. Marine Corps Recruiting Publicity Bureau, 1913–1918.

———. *The U.S. Marines in Rhyme, Prose, and Cartoon.* Various editions.

U.S. Navy Department. *Annual Report of the Secretary of the Navy.* Washington, D.C.: Government Printing Office, 1860–1922.

———. *Landing-Force Manual. United States Navy. 1918.* Annapolis, MD: Naval Institute Press, 1918.

———. *Landing-Force Manual. United States Navy. 1920.* Washington, D.C.: Government Printing Office, 1921.

U.S. War Department. *Annual Report of the Secretary of War.* Washington, D.C.: Government Printing Office, various years.

Vandegrift, Alexander Archer. *Once a Marine: The Memoirs of General A. A. Vandegrift, United States Marine Corps, as Told to Robert B. Asprey.* New York: Norton, 1964.

Williams, Robert H. *The Old Corps: A Portrait of the U.S. Marine Corps between the Wars.* Annapolis, MD: Naval Institute Press, 1982.

Wise, Frederic M. *A Marine Tells It to You.* New York: J. H. Sears, 1929; reprint, Quantico, VA: Marine Corps Association, 1981.

Young, James Rankin. *Reminiscences and Thrilling Stories of the War by Returned Heroes.* Chicago: Wabash Publishing House, 1898.

Published Secondary Sources

Adams, Michael C. C. *Echoes of War: A Thousand Years of Military History in Popular Culture.* Lexington: University Press of Kentucky, 2002.

———. *The Great Adventure: Male Desire and the Coming of World War I.* Bloomington: Indiana University Press, 1990.

Allen, Charles. *Kipling Sahib: India and the Making of Rudyard Kipling.* New York: Little, Brown, 2008.

Alvarez, Eugene. *Parris Island.* Charleston: Arcadia Publishing, 2002.

Anderson, Benedict. *Imagined Communities: Reflections on the Origin and Spread of Nationalism.* New York: Verso, 1991.

Anderson, Warwick. *Colonial Pathologies: American Tropical Medicine, Race, and Hygiene in the Philippines.* Durham, NC: Duke University Press, 2006.

———. "The Trespass Speaks: White Masculinity and Colonial Breakdown." *American Historical Review* 102 (Dec. 1997): 1343–70.

Arms, Linda C. "Through the Looking Glass: A Historic Era of Transformation." *Marine Corps Gazette*, Nov. 2006: 61.

Arnold, David. "Inventing Tropicality." In *The Problem of Nature: Environment, Culture and European Expansion,* edited by David Arnold, 141–68. Oxford: Blackwell, 1996.

Asprey, Robert B. *At Belleau Wood.* New York: G. P. Putnam's Sons, 1965.

Attridge, Steve. *Nationalism, Imperialism and Identity in Late Victorian Culture: Civil and Military Worlds.* New York: Palgrave Macmillan, 2003.

Axelrod, Alan. *Miracle at Belleau Wood: The Birth of the Modern U.S. Marine Corps.* Guilford, CT: Lyons Press, 2007.

Balendorf, Dirk Anthony, and Merrill Lewis Bartlett. *Pete Ellis: An Amphibious Warfare Prophet, 1880–1923.* Annapolis, MD: Naval Institute Press, 1997.

Barde, Robert E. *The History of Marine Corps Competitive Marksmanship.* Washington, D.C.: Marksmanship, G-3 Division Headquarters, U.S. Marine Corps, 1961.

Barnett, Correlli. *Britain and Her Army: A Military, Political and Social History of the British Army, 1509–1970.* London: Cassell, 1970.

Bartlett, Merrill L. "Ben Hebard Fuller and the Genesis of a Modern Marine Corps, 1891–1834." *Journal of Military History* 69 (Jan. 2005): 73–91.

———. *Lejeune: A Marine's Life, 1867–1942.* Annapolis, MD: Naval Institute Press, 1991.

Bartov, Omer. *Hitler's Army: Soldiers, Nazis, and War in the Third Reich.* New York: Oxford University Press, 1992.

Beaumont, Roger. "Small Wars: Definitions and Dimensions." *Annals of the American Academy of Political and Social Science* 541 (Sep. 1995): 20–35.

Beaumont, Roger A. *Military Elites: Special Fighting Units in the Modern World.* Indianapolis: Bobbs-Merrill, 1974.

Beede, Benjamin R., ed. *The War of 1898 and U.S. Interventions, 1898–1934: An Encyclopedia.* New York: Garland, 1994.

Beisner, Robert. *From the Old Diplomacy to the New, 1865–1900.* 2nd ed. Wheeling, IL: Harlan Davidson, 1986.

Belich, James. *The Victorian Interpretation of Racial Conflict: The Maori, the British, and the New Zealand Wars.* New York: Oxford University Press, 1986.

Bermann, Karl. *Under the Big Stick: Nicaragua and the United States since 1848.* Boston: South End Press, 1986.

Bickel, Keith B. *Mars Learning: the Marine Corps' Development of Small Wars Doctrine, 1915–1940.* Boulder: Westview Press, 2001.

Bickers, Robert, and R. G. Tiedemann. *The Boxers, China, and the World.* Lanham: Rowman and Littlefield, 2007.

Blumberg, H. E., comp. *Britain's Sea Soldiers: A Record of the Royal Marines during the War, 1914–1917.* Devonport, UK: Swiss, Naval and Military Printers and Publishers, 1927.

Bogle, Lori Lyn. "TR's Use of PR to Strengthen the Navy." *Naval History* 21 (Dec. 2007): 26–31.

Bourke, Joanna. *Dismembering the Male: Men's Bodies, Britain, and the Great War.* London: Reaktion Books, 1998.

———.   *An Intimate History of Killing: Face-to-Face Killing in Twentieth Century Warfare* London: Granta, 1999.

Bradford, James, ed. *Crucible of Empire: The Spanish-American War and Its Aftermath.* Annapolis, MD: Naval Institute Press, 1993.

Braudy, Leo. *From Chivalry to Terrorism: War and the Changing Nature of Masculinity.* New York: Alfred A. Knopf, 2003.

Braybon, Gail, and Penny Summerfield. *Out of the Cage: Women's Experiences in Two World Wars.* London: Pandora, 1987.

Bristow, Nancy K. *Making Men Moral: Social Engineering during the Great War.* New York: New York University Press, 1996.

Brodsky, G. W. Stephen. *Gentlemen of the Blade: A Social and Literary History of the British Army since 1660.* New York: Greenwood Press, 1988.

Brooks, Richard. *The Royal Marines, 1664 to the Present.* Annapolis, MD: Naval Institute Press, 2002.

Brown, Charles H. *The Correspondents' War: Journalists in the Spanish-American War.* New York: Charles Scribner's Sons, 1967.

Brown, Ronald. *A Few Good Men: A History of the Fighting Fifth Marines.* New York: Ballantine Books, 2003.

Bruce, Brian. *Thomas Boyd: Lost Author of the "Lost Generation."* Akron: University of Akron Press, 2006.

Bruce, Robert B. *A Fraternity of Arms: America and France in the Great War.* Lawrence: University Press of Kansas, 2003.

Brundage, W. Fitzhugh, ed. *Where These Memories Grow: History, Memory, and Southern Identity.* Chapel Hill: University of North Carolina Press, 2000.

Burke, Carol. *Camp All-American, Hanoi Jane, and the High-And-Tight: Gender, Folklore, and Changing Military Culture.* Boston: Beacon Press, 2004.

Burke, Peter J., Timothy J. Owens, and Richard T. Serpe, eds. *Advances in Identity Theory and Research*. New York: Kluwer, 2003.

Calder, Bruce. *The Impact of Intervention: The Dominican Republic during the U.S. Occupation of 1916–1924*. Austin: University of Texas Press, 1984.

Cameron, Craig M. *American Samurai: Myth, Imagination, and the Conduct of Battle in the First Marine Division, 1941–1951*. New York: Cambridge University Press, 1994.

Campbell, James S. "'For You May Touch Them Not': Misogyny, Homosexuality, and the Ethics of Passivity in First World War Poetry." *ELH* 64 (Fall 1997): 823–42.

Caplan, Jane C. *Written on the Body: The Tattoo in European and American History*. Princeton, NJ: Princeton University Press, 2000.

Capozzola, Christopher. "The Only Badge Needed Is Your Patriotic Fervor: Vigilance, Coercion, and the Law in World War I America." *Journal of American History* (Mar. 2002): 1354–82.

Carby, Hazel. *Reconstructing Womanhood: The Emergence of the Afro-American Woman Novelist*. New York: Oxford University Press, 1987.

Carnes, Mark C., and Clyde Griffen, eds. *Meanings for Manhood: Constructions of Masculinity in Victorian America*. Chicago: University of Chicago Press, 1990.

Carpenter, Dennis, and Frank Bisogno. *Anyone Here a Marine? Popular Entertainment and the Marines*. Great Neck, NY: Brightlights Publications, 1992.

Cash, W. J. *The Mind of the South*. New York: Vintage Books, 1991.

Cerasini, Marc. *Heroes: U.S. Marine Corps Medal of Honor Winners*. New York: Berkley Books, 2002.

Chambers, John Whiteclay, II. *To Raise an Army: The Draft Comes to Modern America*. New York: Free Press, 1987.

———. *The Tyranny of Change: America in the Progressive Era, 1890–1920*. New Brunswick, NJ: Rutgers University Press, 2000.

Chandler, Alfred D. *The Visible Hand: The Managerial Revolution in American Business*. Cambridge, MA: Belknap Press of Harvard University Press, 1977.

Chisholm, Donald. *Waiting for Dead Men's Shoes: Origins and Developments of the U.S. Navy's Officer Personnel System, 1793–1941*. Stanford: Stanford University Press, 2001.

Claghorn, Charles Eugene. *Women Composers and Songwriters: A Concise Biographical Dictionary*. Lanham, MD: Scarecrow Press, 1996.

Clancy-Smith, Julia, and Frances Gouda, eds. *Domesticating the Empire: Race, Gender and Family Life in French and Dutch Colonialism*. Charlottesville: University Press of Virginia, 1998.

Clark, George B. *Devil Dogs: Fighting Marines of World War One.* Novato, CA: Presidio Press, 2000.

———. *Devil Dogs Chronicle: Voices of the 4th Marine Brigade in World War I.* Lawrence: University Press of Kansas, 2013.

———. *Hiram Iddings Bearss, U.S. Marine Corps: Biography of a World War I Hero.* Jefferson, NC: McFarland, 2005.

———. *Treading Softly: U.S. Marines in China, 1819–1949.* Westport, CT: Praeger, 2001.

———. *With the Old Corps in Nicaragua.* Novato, CA: Presidio Press, 2001.

Clifford, James. *Routes: Travel and Translation in the Late Twentieth Century.* Cambridge, MA: Harvard University Press, 1997.

Clifford, Kenneth J. *Progress and Purpose: A Developmental History of the U.S. Marine Corps, 1900–1970.* Washington, D.C.: History and Museums Division, Headquarters, U.S. Marine Corps, 1973.

Coffman, Edward M. "The Long Shadow of *The Soldier and the State.*" *Journal of Military History* 55 (Jan. 1991): 69–82.

———. *The Old Army: A Portrait of the American Army in Peacetime, 1784–1898.* New York: Oxford University Press, 1986.

———. *The Regulars: The American Army, 1898–1941.* Cambridge, MA: Belknap Press, 2004.

———. *The War to End All Wars: The American Military Experience in World War One.* Lexington: University Press of Kentucky, 1998.

Cohen, Anthony, ed. *Signifying Identities: Anthropological Perspectives on Boundaries and Contested Values.* New York: Routledge, 2000.

Cohen, Eliot. *Citizens and Soldiers: The Dilemmas of Military Service.* Ithaca: Cornell University Press, 1985.

Cohen, Paul A. *History in Three Keys: The Boxers as Event, Experience, and Myth.* New York: Columbia University Press, 1997.

Cohen, Robin. *Global Diasporas: An Introduction.* Seattle: University of Washington Press, 1997.

Condit, Kenneth W., and Edwin T. Turnbladh. *Hold High the Torch: A History of the 4th Marines.* Washington, D.C.: History and Museums Division, Headquarters, U.S. Marine Corps, 1960.

Connelly, Thomas L. *The Marble Man: Robert E. Lee and His Image in American Society.* Baton Rouge: Louisiana State University, 1977.

Conner, Valerie J. *The National War Labor Board: Stability, Social Justice, and the Voluntary State in World War I.* Chapel Hill: University of North Carolina Press, 1983.

Cooper, Frederick. *Colonialism in Question: Theory, Knowledge, and History.* Berkeley: University of California Press, 2005.

Cooper, Frederick, and Ann Laura Stoler. *Tensions of Empire: Colonial Cultures in a Bourgeois World.* Berkeley: University of California Press, 1997.

Cooper, Norman V. *A Fighting General: The Biography of Gen Holland M. "Howlin' Mad" Smith.* Quantico, VA: Marine Corps Association, 1987.

Corbett, Philip. "When Every Letter Counts." *After Deadline.* 19 Feb. 2009. http://topics.blogs.nytimes.com/2009/02/18/when-every-letter-counts/.

Cornebise, Alfred E. *Soldiers-Scholars: Higher Education in the AEF, 1917–1919.* Philadelphia: American Philosophical Society, 1997.

Cosmas, Graham A. *An Army for Empire: The United States Army in the Spanish-American War.* 2nd ed. College Station: Texas A&M University Press, 1998.

Crossley, Pamela Kyle. *A Translucent Mirror: History and Identity in Qing Imperial Ideology.* Berkeley: University of California Press, 1999.

Cunliffe, Marcus. *Soldiers and Civilians: The Martial Spirit in America 1775–1865.* Boston: Little, Brown, 1968.

Curtin, Philip D. *Death By Migration: Europe's Encounter with the Tropical World in the Nineteenth Century.* New York: Cambridge University Press, 1989.

Dawes, James. *The Language of War: Literature and Culture in the U.S. from the Civil War through World War II.* Cambridge, MA: Harvard University Press, 2002.

Dawson, Graham. *Soldier Heroes: British Adventure, Empire and the Imagining of Masculinities.* New York: Routledge, 1994.

Dickson, Paul. *War Slang: American Fighting Words and Phrases since the Civil War.* 2nd ed. Washington, D.C.: Brassey's, 2004.

Dillingham, William B. *Rudyard Kipling: Hell and Heroism.* New York: Palgrave Macmillan, 2005.

Donovan, James A., Jr. *The United States Marine Corps.* New York: Frederick A. Praeger, 1967.

Dorsey, Leroy G. *We Are All Americans, Pure and Simple: Theodore Roosevelt and the Myth of Americanism.* Tuscaloosa: University of Alabama Press, 2007.

Dower, John W. *Embracing Defeat: Japan in the Wake of World War II.* New York: W. W. Norton and Free Press, 1999.

———. *War without Mercy: Race and Power in the Pacific War.* New York: Pantheon Books, 1986.

Ducat, Stephen. *The Wimp Factor: Gender Gaps, Holy Wars and the Politics of Anxious Masculinity.* Boston: Beacon, 2004.

Duncan, R. M. "Dear John." *American Speech* 22 (Oct. 1947): 187.

Ebbert, Jean, and Marie-Beth Hall. *The First, The Few, The Forgotten: Navy and Marine Corps Women in World War I.* Annapolis, MD: Naval Institute Press, 2002.

Eisenhower, John S. D. *Intervention! The United States and the Mexican Revolution, 1913–1917.* New York: W. W. Norton, 1993.

———. *So Far from God: The U.S. War with Mexico, 1846–48.* Norman: University of Oklahoma Press, 1989.

Elliott, Jane E. *Some Did It for Civilization; Some Did It for Country: A Revised View of the Boxer War.* Hong Kong: Chinese University Press, 2002.

Elshtain, Jean Bethke. *Women and War.* New York: Basic Books, 1987.

Enloe, Cynthia. *Bananas, Beaches and Bases: Making Feminist Sense of International Politics.* Berkeley: University of California Press, 2000.

———. *Maneuvers: The International Politics of Militarizing Women's Lives.* Berkeley: University of California Press, 2000.

Feld, Maury D. *The Structure of Violence: Armed Forces as Social Systems.* Beverly Hills, CA: Sage Publications, 1977.

Finney, Charles G. *The Old China Hands.* Garden City, NY: Doubleday, 1961.

Fleming, Keith. *The U.S. Marine Corps in Crisis.* Columbia: University of South Carolina Press, 1990.

Fletcher, Marvin. *The Peacetime Army, 1900–1941: A Research Guide.* Westport, CT: Greenwood Press, 1988.

Foos, Paul. *A Short, Offhand, Killing Affair: Soldiers and Social Conflict during the Mexican American War.* Chapel Hill: University of North Carolina Press, 2002.

Ford, Nancy Gentile. *Americans All! Foreign-Born Soldiers in World War I.* College Station: Texas A&M University Press, 2001.

Fowler, William M., Jr. *Jack Tars and Commodores: The American Navy, 1783–1815.* Boston: Houghton Mifflin, 1984.

Fox, Stephen. *The Mirror Makers: A History of American Advertising and its Creators.* New York: Morrow, 1984.

Freidel, Frank. *The Splendid Little War.* Boston: Little, Brown, 1958.

French, David. *Military Identities: The Regimental System, the British Army and the British People, c. 1870–2000.* New York: Oxford University Press, 2005.

French, Shannon E. *The Code of the Warrior: Exploring Warrior Values Past and Present.* Lanham, MD: Rowman and Littlefield, 2003.

Frenkel, Stephen. "Jungle Stories: North American Representations of Tropical Panama." *Geographical Review* 86 (July 1996): 317–33.

Frevert, Ute. *Nation in Barracks: Modern Germany, Civil Conscription and Civil Society.* Translated by Andrew Boreham and Daniel Bruckenhaus. New York: Berg, 2004.

Fuller, J. G. *Troop Morale and Popular Culture in the British and Dominion Armies, 1914–1918.* Oxford: Clarendon Press, 1990.

Fussell, Paul. *The Great War and Modern Memory*. New York: Oxford University Press, 1975.

Gallagher, Gary W. *Causes Won, Lost, and Forgotten: How Hollywood and Popular Art Shape What We Know about the Civil War*. Chapel Hill: University of North Carolina Press, 2008.

Gallagher, Gary W., and Alan T. Nolan, eds. *The Myth of the Lost Cause and Civil War History*. Bloomington: Indiana University Press, 2000.

Ganoe, William A. *The History of the United States Army*. New York: Appleton, 1924.

Gates, John M. *Schoolbooks and Krags: The United States Army in the Philippines, 1898–1902*. Westport, CT: Greenwood Press, 1973.

Gavin, Levin. *American Women in World War I: They Also Served*. Niwot: University Press of Colorado, 1997.

Geary, James W. *We Need Men: The Union Draft in the Civil War*. DeKalb: Northern Illinois University Press, 1991.

Gibbs, Christopher. *The Great Silent Majority: Missouri's Resistance to World War I*. Columbia: University of Missouri Press, 1998.

Gilmore, David D. *Manhood in the Making: Cultural Concepts of Masculinity*. New Haven: Yale University Press, 1991.

Gilmore, Glenda. *Gender and Jim Crow: Women and the Politics of White Supremacy in North Carolina, 1896–1920*. Chapel Hill: University of North Carolina Press, 1996.

Gilmour, David. *The Long Recessional: The Imperial Life of Rudyard Kipling*. New York: Farrar, Straus and Giroux, 2002.

Girouard, Mark. *The Return to Camelot: Chivalry and the English Gentleman*. New Haven: Yale University Press, 1981.

Go, Julian. *The American Colonial State in the Philippines: Global Perspectives*. Durham, NC: Duke University Press, 2003.

Goldstein, Joshua. *War and Gender: How Gender Shapes the War System and Vice Versa*. New York: Cambridge University Press, 2001.

Grandstaff, Mark R. "Preserving the 'Habits and Usages of War': William Tecumseh Sherman, Professional Reform, and the U.S. Army Officer Corps, 1865–1881, Revisited." *Journal of Military History* 62, no. 3 (July 1998): 521–45.

Gray, J. Glenn. *The Warriors: Reflections on Men in Battle*. Lincoln: University of Nebraska Press, 1998.

Griffith, Tom, and Libby Robin, eds. *Ecology and Empire: Environmental History of Settler Societies*. Seattle: University of Washington Press, 1998.

Grossman, Dave. *On Killing: The Psychological Cost of Learning to Kill in War*. Boston: Little, Brown, 1995.

Grotelueschen, Mark E. *The AEF Way of War: The American Army and Combat in World War I.* New York: Cambridge University Press, 2007.

Hagan, Kenneth. *This People's Navy: The Making of American Sea Power.* New York: Free Press, 1991.

Hall, Catherine. *Civilising Subjects: Colony and Metropole in the English Imagination, 1830–1867.* Chicago: University of Chicago Press, 2002.

Hall, Marie-Beth. *The First, The Few, The Forgotten: Navy and Marine Corps Women in World War I.* Annapolis, MD: Naval Institute Press, 2002.

Hard, Curtis V. *Banners in the Air: The Eight Ohio Volunteers and the Spanish-American War.* Kent, OH: Kent State University Press, 1988.

Harllee, William. *The Marine from Manatee: A Tradition of Rifle Marksmanship.* Washington, D.C.: National Rifle Association, 1984.

Harp, Stephen. "Marketing Michelin: Advertising and Cultural Identity in Twentieth-Century France." *Business History Review* 76 (Winter 2002): 919–21.

Harries-Jenkins, Gwyn. *The Army in Victorian Society.* London: Routledge and Kegan Paul, 1977.

Harrod, Frederick S. *Manning the New Navy: The Development of a Modern Naval Enlisted Force, 1899–1940.* Westport, CT: Greenwood Press, 1978.

Harwell, Richard, ed. *A Confederate Marine: A Sketch of Henry Lea Graves with Excerpts from the Graves Family Correspondence, 1861–1865.* Tuscaloosa, AL: Confederate Publishing, 1963.

Heinl, Robert D. *Soldiers of the Sea: The U.S. Marine Corps, 1775–1962.* Annapolis, MD: Naval Institute Press, 1962.

Hewitt, Linda L. *Women Marines in World War One.* Washington, D.C.: History and Museums Division, Headquarters, U.S. Marine Corps, 1974.

Higonnet, Margaret, Jane Jenson, Sonya Michel, and Margaret C. Weitz, eds. *Behind the Lines: Gender and the Two World Wars.* New Haven: Yale University Press, 1987.

Hilsabeck, Walter G. Letter to *Military History* (June–July 2009): 7.

Hobsbawm, Eric. *Nations and Nationalism since 1780: Programme, Myth, Reality.* New York: Cambridge University Press, 1990.

Hobsbawm, Eric, and Terence Ranger, eds. *The Invention of Tradition.* Cambridge: Cambridge University Press, 2002.

Hoffman, Jon T. *Chesty: The Story of Lieutenant General Lewis B. Puller, USMC.* New York: Random House, 2002.

Hoganson, Kristin. *Fighting for American Manhood: How Gender Politics Provoked the Spanish-American and Philippine-American Wars.* New Haven, CT: Yale University Press, 1998.

Houlding, J. A. *Fit for Service: The Training of the British Army, 1715–1795.* Oxford: Clarendon Press, 1981.

Huelfer, Evan A. *The "Casualty Issue" in American Military Practice: The Impact of World War I.* Westport, CT: Praeger, 2003.

Hunt, Michael H. *Ideology and U.S. Foreign Policy.* New Haven: Yale University Press, 1987.

Ignatiev, Noel. *How the Irish Became White.* New York: Routledge, 1995.

Ion, A. Hamish, and Keith Neilson. *Elite Military Formations in War and Peace.* Westport, CT: Praeger, 1986.

Jacobson, Matthews F. *Barbarian Virtues: The United States Encounters Foreign Peoples at Home and Abroad, 1876–1917.* New York: Hill and Wang, 2000.

———. *Whiteness of a Different Color: European Immigrants and the Alchemy of Race.* Cambridge: Harvard University Press, 2000.

James, Pearl, ed. *Picture This: World War I Posters and Visual Culture.* Lincoln: University of Nebraska Press, 2009.

Janowitz. Morris. *The Professional Soldier: A Social and Political Portrait.* New York: Free Press, 1960.

Johannsen, Robert W. *To the Halls of the Montezumas: The Mexican War in the American Imagination.* New York: Oxford University Press, 1985.

Kammen, Michael. *Mystic Chords of Memory: The Transformation of Tradition in American Culture.* New York: Alfred A. Knopf, 1991.

———. "The Problem of American Exceptionalism: A Reconsideration." *American Quarterly* 45 (Mar. 1993): 1–43.

Kaplan, Amy. "Romancing the Empire: The Embodiment of American Masculinity in the Popular Historical Novel of the 1890s." *American Literary History* 2, no. 4 (Winter 1990): 659–90.

Kaplan, Amy, and Donald E. Pease, eds. *Cultures of United States Imperialism.* Durham: Duke University Press, 1993.

Karnow, Stanley. *In Our Image: America's Empire in the Philippines.* New York: Ballantine Books, 1999.

Karsten, Peter. "Armed Progressives: The Military Reorganizes for the American Century." In *Building the Organizational Society: Essays on Associational Activities in Modern America,* edited by Jerry Israel, 197–232. New York: Free Press, 1972.

———. *The Naval Aristocracy: The Golden Age of Annapolis and the Emergence of Modern American Navalism.* New York: The Free Press, 1972.

———, ed. *Recruiting, Drafting, and Enlisting: Two Sides of the Raising of Military Forces.* New York: Routledge, 1998.

Kasson, John F. *Houdini, Tarzan, and the Perfect Man: The White Male Body and the Challenge of Modernity in America.* New York: Hill and Wang, 2001.

Keene, Jennifer. *Doughboys, the Great War, and the Remaking of America.* Baltimore: Johns Hopkins University Press, 2002.

———. *World War I.* Westport, CT: Greenwood Press, 2006.

Kemble, Robert C. *The Image of the Army Officer in America: Background for Current Views.* Westport, CT: Greenwood Press, 1973.

———. "Mutations in America's Perceptions of Its Professional Military Leaders: An Historical Overview and Update." *Armed Forces and Society,* Oct. 2007, 29–45.

Kennedy, David M. *Over Here: The First World War and American Society.* New York: Oxford University Press, 1980.

Kimmel, Michael. *Manhood in America: A Cultural History.* New York: Free Press, 1996.

Kindsvatter, Peter S. *American Soldiers: Ground Combat in the World Wars, Korea, and Vietnam.* Lawrence: University Press of Kansas, 2003.

King, Desmond S. *Making Americans: Immigration, Race, and the Origins of the Diverse Democracy.* Cambridge, MA: Harvard University Press, 2003.

Koehn, Nancy F. "Henry Heinz and Brand Creation in the Late Nineteenth Century: Making Markets for Processed Food." *Business History Review* 73 (Autumn 1999): 349–93.

Kramer, Paul A. *The Blood of Government: Race, Empire, the United States, and the Philippines.* Chapel Hill: University of North Carolina Press, 2006.

———. "Empires, Exceptions, and Anglo-Saxons: Race and Rule between the British and United States Empires, 1880–1910." *Journal of American History* 88 (Mar. 2002): 1315–53.

Krulak, Victor H. *First to Fight: An Inside View of the U.S. Marine Corps.* Annapolis, MD: Naval Institute Press, 1999.

La Bree, Clifton. *The Gentle Warrior: General Oliver Prince Smith, USMC.* Kent, OH: Kent State University Press, 2001.

Lacy, Linda Cates. *We Are Marines! World War I to the Present.* Jacksonville, NC: Tar Heel Chapter, NC-1, Women Marines Association, 2004.

LaFeber, Walter. *The New Empire: An Interpretation of American Expansion, 1860–1898.* Ithaca: Cornell University Press, 1998.

Laird, Pamela Walker. *Advertising Progress and the Rise of Consumer Marketing.* Baltimore: Johns Hopkins University Press, 1998.

Lane, Jack C. *Armed Progressive: General Leonard Wood.* San Rafael, CA: Presidio Press, 1978.

Langley, Lester D. *The Banana Wars: United States Intervention in the Caribbean, 1898–1934.* Wilmington: Scholarly Resources, 2001.

Lawson, Jacqueline E. "'She's a Pretty Woman . . . for a Gook': The Misogyny of the Vietnam War." *Journal of American Culture* 12 (Fall 1989): 55–65.

Lears, Jackson. *Fables of Abundance: A Cultural History of Advertising in America.* New York: Basic Books, 1994.

Leed, Eric J. *No Man's Land: Combat and Identity in the World War I.* London: Cambridge University Press, 1979.

Lewis, Charles Lee. *Famous American Marines: An Account of the Corps.* Boston: L. C. Page, 1950.

Lighter, Jonathan. "The Slang of the American Expeditionary Forces in Europe, 1917–1919: An Historical Glossary." *American Speech* 47 (1971): 5–142.

Linderman, Gerald F. *Embattled Courage: The Experience of Combat in the American Civil War.* New York: Free Press, 1987.

———. *The Mirror of War: American Society and the Spanish-American War.* Ann Arbor: University of Michigan Press, 1974.

Lindsay, Robert. *This High Name: Public Relations and the U.S. Marine Corps.* Madison: University of Wisconsin Press, 1956.

Link, Arthur S., and Richard L. McCormick. *Progressivism.* Arlington Heights, IL: Harlan Davidson, 1983.

Linn, Brian. *Guardians of Empire: The U.S. Army and the Pacific, 1902–1940.* Chapel Hill: University of North Carolina Press, 1997.

———. *The Philippine War, 1899–1902.* Lawrence: University Press of Kansas, 2000.

———. "'We Will Go Heavily Armed': The Marines' Small War on Samar, 1901–1902." In *New Interpretations in Naval History: Selected Papers from the Ninth Naval History Symposium,* edited by William R. Roberts and Jack Sweetman, 273–92. Annapolis, MD: U.S. Naval Institute Press, 1991.

Lipset, Seymour Martin. *American Exceptionalism: A Double-Edged Sword.* New York: W. W. Norton, 1997.

Loren, Patricia. *Imperial Identities: Stereotyping, Prejudice and Race in Colonial Algeria.* New York: I. B. Tauris, 1999.

Love, Robert W. *History of the U.S. Navy, Volume 1, 1775–1941.* Harrisburg, PA: Stackpole Books, 1991.

Lubow, Arthur. *The Reporter Who Would Be King: A Biography of Richard Harding Davis.* New York: Scribner, 1992.

Lucas, J. Christopher, ed. *James Ricalton's Photographs of China during the Boxer Rebellion.* Lewiston, NY: Edwin Mellen Press, 1990.

Lunn, Joe. "'Les Races Guerrieres': Racial Preconceptions in the French Military about West African Soldiers during the First World War." *Journal of Contemporary History* 34 (Oct. 1999): 517–36.

Lynn, John A. *Battle: A History of Combat and Culture.* Boulder: Westview Press, 2003.

MacKenzie, John. *Popular Imperialism and the Military, 1850–1950.* Manchester: Manchester University Press, 1992.

MacLean, Nancy. *Behind the Mask of Chivalry: The Making of the Second Ku Klux Klan.* New York: Oxford University Press, 1994.

Madsen, Deborah L. *American Exceptionalism.* Jackson: University Press of Mississippi, 1998.

Maguire, Peter. *Law and War: An American Story.* New York: Columbia University Press, 2001.

Marchand, Roland. *Advertising the American Dream: Making Way for Modernity, 1920–1940.* Berkeley: University of California Press, 1985.

Marolda, Edward J. *Theodore Roosevelt, the U.S. Navy, and the Spanish-American War.* New York: Palgrave, 2001.

Marshall, S. L. A. *Men against Fire: The Problem of Battle Command.* Norman: University of Oklahoma Press, 2000.

McCartney, Paul T. *Power and Progress: American National Identity, the War of 1898, and the Rise of American Imperialism.* Baton Rouge: Louisiana State University Press, 2006.

McClellan, Edwin. *Uniforms of the American Marines, 1775 to 1829.* Washington, D.C.: Marine Corps History and Museums Division, Headquarters Marine Corps, 1982.

McClintock, Anne. *Imperial Leather: Race, Gender and Sexuality in the Colonial Contest.* New York: Routledge, 1995.

McPherson, James. *For Cause and Comrades: Why Men Fought in the Civil War.* New York: Oxford University Press, 1998.

McNeill, William H. *Keeping Together in Time.* Cambridge: Harvard University Press, 1997.

Meigs, Mark. *Optimism at Armageddon: Voices of American Participants in the First World War.* New York: New York University Press, 1997.

Melnick, Ross. *American Showman: Samuel "Roxy" Rothafel and the Birth of the Entertainment Industry, 1908–1935.* New York: Columbia University Press, 2012.

Metcalf, Clyde H. *A History of the United States Marine Corps.* New York: G. P. Putnam's Sons, 1939.

Miller, John G. "William Freeland Fullam's War with the Corps." *U.S. Naval Institute Proceedings* 105 (Dec. 1975): 38–45.

Miller, Stuart Creighton. *"Benevolent Assimilation": The American Conquest of the Philippines.* New Haven, CT: Yale University Press, 1982.

Millett, Allan R. *In Many a Strife: General Gerald C. Thomas and the U.S. Marine Corps, 1917–1956.* Annapolis, MD: Naval Institute Press, 1993.

———. *The Politics of Intervention: The Military Occupation of Cuba, 1906–1909.* Columbus: Ohio State University Press, 1968.

———. *Semper Fidelis: The History of the United States Marine Corps.* New York: Free Press, 1991.

Millett, Allan R., and Peter Maslowski. *For the Common Defense: A Military History of the United States of America.* New York: Free Press, 1994.

Millett, Allan R., and Jack Shulimson, eds. *Commandants of the Marine Corps.* Annapolis, MD: Naval Institute Press, 2004.

Minott, Rodney G. *Peerless Patriots: Organized Veterans and the Spirit of Americanism.* Washington, D.C.: Public Affairs Press, 1962.

Montross, Lynn. *The United States Marines: A Pictorial History.* New York: Bramhall House, 1959.

Moran, John B. *Creating a Legend: The Complete Record of Writing about the United States Marine Corps.* Chicago: Moran/Andrews, 1973.

Moskin, J. Robert. *The U.S. Marine Corps Story.* Boston: Little, Brown, 1990.

Mrozek, Donald J. *Sport and American Mentality, 1880–1910.* Knoxville: University of Tennessee Press, 1983.

Murdoch, David H. *The American West: The Invention of a Myth.* Reno: University of Nevada Press, 2001.

Murdoch, Steve, and A. Mackillop, eds. *Fighting for Identity: Scottish Military Experience c. 1550–1900.* Boston: Brill, 2002.

Murphy, Paul L. *World War I and the Origins of Civil Liberties in the United States.* New York: Norton, 1979.

Myerly, Scott Hughes. *British Military Spectacle: From the Napoleonic Wars through the Crimea.* Cambridge: Harvard University Press, 1996.

Nisbett, Richard E., and Dov Cohen. *Culture of Honor: The Psychology of Violence in the South.* Boulder: Westview Press, 1996.

Noble, Dennis L. *The Eagle and the Dragon: The United States Military in China, 1901–1937.* New York: Greenwood Press, 1990.

Nobles, Gregory H. *American Frontiers: Cultural Encounters and Continental Conquest.* New York: Hill and Wang, 1997.

Norris, James D. *Advertising and the Transformation of American Society, 1865–1920.* New York: Greenwood Press, 1990.

O'Connell, Aaron B. *Underdogs: The Making of the Modern Marine Corps.* Cambridge: Harvard University Press, 2012.

O'Gara, Gordon Carpenter. *Theodore Roosevelt and the Rise of the Modern Navy.* Princeton, NJ: Princeton University Press, 1943.

Owen, Peter. *To the Limits of Endurance: A Battalion of Marines in the Great War.* College Station: Texas A&M University, 2007.

Ownby, Ted. *Subduing Satan: Religion, Recreation & Manhood in the Rural South, 1865–1920.* Chapel Hill: University of North Carolina Press, 1990.

Partridge, Eric. *A Dictionary of Catch Phrases British and American, from the Sixteenth Century to the Present Day.* New York: Routledge, 1986.

Pencak, William. *For God and Country: The American Legion, 1919–1941.* Boston: Northeastern University Press, 1989.

Pettegrew, John. *Brutes in Suits: Male Sensibility in America, 1890–1920.* Baltimore: Johns Hopkins University Press, 2007.

Pickus, Noah M. J. *True Faith and Allegiance: Immigration and American Nationalism.* Princeton, NJ: Princeton University Press, 2005.

Pope, Daniel. *The Making of Modern Advertising.* New York: Basic Books, 1983.

Porch, Douglas. *The French Foreign Legion: A Complete History of the Legendary Fighting Force.* New York: Harper Perennial, 1992.

Possner, Roger. *The Rise of Militarism in the Progressive Era, 1900–1914.* Jefferson, NC: McFarland, 2009.

Pratt, Mary Louise. *Imperial Eyes: Travel Writing and Transculturation.* New York: Routledge, 1992.

Preston, Diana. *Besieged in Peking: The Story of the 1900 Boxer Rising.* London: Constable, 1999.

Quirk, Robert E. *An Affair of Honor: Woodrow Wilson and the Occupation of Veracruz.* New York: W. W. Norton, 1962.

Rainey, Buck. *The Reel Cowboys: Essays on the Myth in Movies and Literature.* Jefferson, NC: McFarland, 1996.

Reardon, Carol. *Pickett's Charge in History and Memory.* Chapel Hill: University of North Carolina Press, 1997.

Reckner, James R. *Teddy Roosevelt's Great White Fleet.* Annapolis, MD: Naval Institute Press, 1988.

Renda, Mary. *Taking Haiti: Military Occupation and the Culture of U.S. Imperialism.* Chapel Hill: University of North Carolina Press, 2001.

Rickards, Maurice. *Posters of the First World War.* New York: Walker, 1968.

Rodgers, Daniel T. *Atlantic Crossings: Social Politics in a Progressive Age.* Cambridge, MA: Belknap Press of Harvard University Press, 1998.

Roediger, David R. *The Wages of Whiteness: Race and the Making of the American Working Class.* New York: Verso, 1991.

Rose, Sonya O. *Which People's War?: National Identity and Citizenship in Wartime Britain, 1939–1945.* New York: Oxford University Press, 2003.

Rosenfeld, Harvey. *Diary of a Dirty Little War: The Spanish-American War of 1898.* Westport, CT: Praeger, 2000.

Rotundo, E. Anthony. *American Manhood: Transformations in Masculinity from the Revolution to the Modern Era.* New York: Basic Books, 1993.

Rowe, John Carlos. *Literary Culture and U.S. Imperialism: From the Revolution to World War II.* New York: Oxford University Press, 2000.

Rowlinson, Michael, and J. Hassard. "The Invention of Corporate Culture: A History of the Histories of Cadbury." *Human Relations* 46 (1993): 299–326.

Rudnick, Lois P., Judith E. Smith, and Rachel Lee Rubin, eds., *American Identities: An Introductory Textbook.* New York: Blackwell, 2006.

Ruppert, Jack. *One of Us: Officers of Marines—Their Training, Traditions, and Values.* Westport, CT: Praeger, 2003.

Sackmann, Sonja A. "Uncovering Culture in Organizations." *Journal of Applied Behavioral Science* 27 (September 1991): 295–317.

Said, Edward. *Culture and Imperialism.* New York: Vintage Books, 1994.

———. *Orientalism.* New York: Vintage Books, 1979.

Santelli, Gabrielle M. Neufeld. *Marines in the Mexican War.* Washington, D.C.: History and Museums Division, Headquarters, U.S. Marine Corps, 1991.

Schein, Edgar H. *Organizational Culture and Leadership.* 4th ed. San Francisco: Jossey-Bass, 2010.

Schivelbusch, Wolfgang. *The Culture of Defeat: On National Trauma, Mourning, and Recovery.* New York: Henry Holt, 2001.

Schmidt, Hans. *Maverick Marine: General Smedley D. Butler and the Contradictions of American Military History.* Lexington: University Press of Kentucky, 1987.

———. *The United States Occupation of Haiti, 1915–1934.* New Brunswick, NJ: Rutgers University Press, 1971.

Scholz, Hermine. *World War I Manuscripts: The World War I Surveys.* Carlisle Barracks: USAMHI, 1986.

Schuon, Karl. *U.S. Marine Corps Bibliographical Dictionary: The Corps' Fighting Men, What They Did, Where They Served.* New York: Franklin Watts, 1963.

Secunda, Eugene, and Terence P. Moran. *Selling War to America: From the Spanish-American War to the Global War on Terror.* Westport, CT: Praeger, 2007.

Seelye, John D. *War Games: Richard Harding Davis and the New Imperialism.* Amherst: University of Massachusetts Press, 2003.

Sexton, William T. *Soldiers in the Sun: An Adventure in Imperialism.* Harrisburg, PA: Military Service Publishing, 1939.

Sharf, Frederic A., and Peter Harrington, eds. *China 1900: The Eyewitnesses Speak.* Mechanicsburg, PA: Stackpole Books, 2000.

Shaw, Angel, and Luis H. Francia. *Vestiges of War: The Philippine-American War and the Aftermath of an Imperial Dream, 1899–1999.* New York: New York University Press, 2002.

Sheffield, Gary D. *Leadership in the Trenches: Officer-Man Relations, Morale, and Discipline in the British Army in the Era of the First World War.* New York: St. Martin's Press, 2000.

Shenk, Gerald E. *"Work or Fight": Race, Gender, and the Draft in World War One.* New York: Palgrave Macmillan, 2005.

Showalter, Dennis F. "Evolution of the U.S. Marine Corps as a Military Elite." *Marine Corps Gazette* (Nov. 1979): 44–58.

Shulimson, Jack. "The Influence of the Spanish-American War on the U.S. Marine Corps." In *Theodore Roosevelt, the U.S. Navy, and the Spanish-American War*, edited by Edward J. Marolda, 81–93. New York: Palgrave, 2001.

———. *The Marine Corps' Search for a Mission, 1880–1898.* Lawrence: University Press of Kansas, 1993.

———, ed. *Marines in the Spanish-American War, 1895–1899: Anthology and Annotated Bibliography.* Washington, D.C.: History and Museums Division, Headquarters, U.S. Marine Corps, 1974.

Shulman, Mark R. *Navalism and the Emergence of American Sea Power, 1882–1893.* Annapolis, MD: Naval Institute Press, 1995.

Simmons, Edwin H. "'I Will Hold': An Appreciation of Gen Clifton B. Cates." *Marine Corps Gazette* (November 2002): 88–96.

———. "Leathernecks at Soissons." *Naval History*, Dec. 2005: 24–33.

———. *The United States Marines: The First Two Hundred Years, 1775–1975.* New York: Viking Press, 1975.

Sinha, Mrinalini. *Colonial Masculinity: The "Manly Englishman" and the "Effeminate Bengali" in the Late Nineteenth Century.* New York: Manchester University Press, 1995.

Skelton, William B. *An American Profession of Arms: The Army Officer Corps, 1784–1861.* Lawrence: University Press of Kansas, 1992.

Skowronek, Stephen. *Building a New American State: The Expansion of National Administrative Capacities, 1877–1920.* New York: Cambridge University Press, 1982.

Slotkin, Richard. *Lost Battalions: The Great War and the Crisis of American Nationality.* New York: Henry Holt, 2005.

———. *The Myth of the Frontier in Twentieth-Century America.* Norman: University of Oklahoma Press, 1998.

Smith, Charles R. *Marines in the Revolution: A History of the Continental Marines in the American Revolution, 1775–1783.* Washington, D.C.: Government Printing Office, 1975.

Smith, Justin Harvey. *The War with Mexico.* 2 vols. New York: Macmillan, 1919.

Snyder, R. Claire. *Citizen-Soldiers and Manly Warriors: Military Service and Gender in the Civic Republic Tradition.* New York: Rowman and Littlefield, 1999.

Spencer, David Ralph. *The Yellow Journalism: The Press and America's Emergence as a World Power.* Evanston, IL: Northwestern University Press, 2007.

Spiers, Edward M. *The Late Victorian Army, 1868–1902.* Manchester: Manchester University Press, 1992.

Stallings, Lawrence. *The Doughboys: The Story of the AEF, 1917–1918.* New York: Harper and Row, 1963.

Stallman, R. W., and E. R. Hagemann, eds. *The War Dispatches of Stephen Crane.* New York: New York University Press, 1964.

Stanley, Peter. *White Mutiny: British Military Culture in India.* New York: New York University Press, 1998.

Stoler, Ann Laura. *Carnal Knowledge and Imperial Power: Race and the Intimate in Colonial Rule.* Berkeley: University of California Press, 2002.

Strasser, Susan. *Satisfaction Guaranteed: The Making of the American Mass Market.* New York: Pantheon Books, 1989.

Sturkey, Marion F. *Warrior Culture of the U.S. Marines.* Plum Branch, SC: Heritage Press International, 2002.

Suid, Lawrence H. *Guts and Glory: Great American War Movies.* Reading, MA: Addison-Wesley, 1978.

Sullivan, Zohreh T. *Narratives of Empire: The Fiction of Rudyard Kipling.* New York: Cambridge University Press, 2003.

Sweetman, Jack. *The Landing at Veracruz, 1914.* Annapolis, MD: Naval Institute Press, 1968.

Swindler, Ann. "Culture in Action: Symbols and Strategies." *American Sociological Review* 51 (April 1986): 273–86.

Taillon, Paul Michel. "'What We Want Is Good, Sober Men': Masculinity, Respectability, and Temperance in the Railroad Brotherhoods, c. 1870–1910." *Journal of Social History* 36 (Winter 2002): 319–38.

Tedlow, Richard. *New and Improved: The Story of Mass Marketing in America.* New York: Basic Books, 1990.

Testi, Arnaldo. "The Gender of Reform Politics: Theodore Roosevelt and the Culture of Masculinity." *Journal of American History* 81 (Mar. 1995): 1509–33.

Trask, David F. *The AEF and Coalition Warmaking, 1917–1918.* Lawrence: University Press of Kansas, 1993.

———. *The War with Spain in 1898.* New York: Macmillan, 1981.

Trice, Harrison M., and Janice M. Beyer. "Studying Organizational Cultures through Rites and Ceremonials." *Academy of Management Review* 9 (Oct. 1984): 653–69.

Vagts, Alfred. *A History of Militarism, Civilian and Military.* Revised ed. New York: Free Press, 1959.

Valle, James E. *Rocks and Shoals: Naval Discipline in the Age of Fighting Sail.* Annapolis, MD: Naval Institute Press, 1980.

van Creveld, Martin. "Thoughts on Military History." *Journal of Contemporary History* 18 (October 1983): 549–66.

Venzon, Anne Cipriano, ed. *General Smedley Darlington Butler: The Letters of a Leatherneck, 1898–1931.* New York: Praeger, 1992.

Verhey, Jeffrey. *The Spirit of 1914: Militarism, Myth, and Mobilization in Germany.* New York: Cambridge University Press, 2000.

Vettel-Becker, Patricia. "Destruction and Delight: World War II Combat Photography and the Aesthetic Inscription of Masculine Identity." *Men and Masculinities* 5, no. 1 (2002): 80–102.

Wakefield, Wanda E. *Playing to Win: Sports and the American Military, 1898–1945.* Albany: State University of the New York Press, 1997.

Ward, Larry W. *The Motion Picture Goes to War: The U.S. Government Film Effort during World War I.* Ann Arbor: University of Michigan Press, 1985.

Watson, Janet S. K. *Fighting Different Wars: Experience, Memory, and the First World War in Britain.* New York: Cambridge University Press, 2004.

Weigley, Russell F. *The American Way of War: A History of United States Military Strategy and Policy.* New York: Macmillan, 1973.

———. *History of the United States Army.* Bloomington: Indiana University Press, 1984.

Welch, Richard E., Jr. "American Atrocities in the Philippines: The Indictment and the Response." *Pacific Historical Review* 43 (May 1974): 223–53.

Wexler, Laura. *Tender Violence: Domestic Visions in an Age of U.S. Imperialism.* Chapel Hill: University of North Carolina Press, 2000.

Wiebe, Robert H. *The Search for Order, 1877–1920.* New York: Hill and Wang, 1967.

Williams, William Appleman. *The Tragedy of American Diplomacy.* New York: W. W. Norton, 1972.

Willock, Roger. *Lone Star Marine: A Biography of the late Colonel John W. Thomason, Jr., U.S.M.C.* Princeton, NJ: Privately published, 1961.

Winter, Denis. *Death's Men: Soldiers of the Great War.* London: Allen Lane, 1978.

Winter, Jay. *Remembering War: The Great War between Memory and History in the Twentieth Century.* New Haven: Yale University Press, 2006.

———. *Sites of Memory, Sites of Mourning: The Great War in European cultural history.* Cambridge: Cambridge University Press, 1995.

Winter, Jay, and Antoine Prost. *The Great War in History: Debates and Controversies, 1914 to the Present.* New York: Cambridge University Press, 2004.

Winter, Jay, and Emmanuel Sivan, eds. *War and Remembrance in the Twentieth Century.* New York: Cambridge University Press, 1999.

Wise, James E., Jr., and Anne Collier Rehill. *Stars in the Corps: Movie Actors in the United States Marines.* Annapolis, MD: Naval Institute Press, 1999.

Wise, Jennings C. *The Turn of the Tide: American Operations at Cantigny, Chateau Thierry, and the Second Battle of the Marne.* New York: Henry Holt, 1920.

Wood, Pamela, and Mary Bacon Hale. *Women Marines Association.* Nashville: Turner, 1997.

Wootton, Charles W., and Barbara E. Kemmerer. "The Changing Genderization of Bookkeeping in the United States, 1870–1930." *Business History Review* 70 (Winter 1996): 541–86.

Woulfe, James B. *Into the Crucible: The Making of a 21st Century Marine.* New York: ibooks, 1998.

Wynn, Neil A. *From Progressivism to Prosperity: World War I and American Society.* New York: Holmes and Meier, 1986.

Zeiger, Susan. *In Uncle Sam's Service: Women Workers with the American Expeditionary Force, 1917–1919.* Ithaca, NY: Cornell University Press, 1999.

Zieger, Robert H. *World War I and the American Experience.* New York: Rowman and Littlefield, 2000.

Index

Adams, John R. (literary character), 169–70

advanced bases: Marines' securing of, 5, 56, 63, 70–72, 94, 232n37, 253n79; during Spanish-American War, 12

advancement, 14, 29, 94. *See also* commissions

advertising: advertising agencies, 13; billboards, 84; blueprints for, 110; Charles H. Fuller Company, 86; after Civil War, 31, 31fig.3, 32fig.4, 37–38; during Civil War, 30–31; classified ads, 82–84; disguised as newspaper articles, 13, 243–44n24, 247n48; Gunning System of, 84; help-wanted ads, 13, 197; recruiting posters, 84; traditional, 143, 144n12; use of superlatives in, 109

AEF (American Expeditionary Force). *See* American Expeditionary Forces (AEF)

affiliation, 5–6, 9–10, 93, 160, 164

aggressive rhetoric: challenges to, 138; of commercial marketing, 41; female service and, 179, 183, 186; Marine image and, 15, 80, 98, 282n85; public ignorance and, 5; in recruiting methods, 13

Aldrich, M. Almy, 40

American Expeditionary Forces (AEF): attempts to subsume Corps, 164; at Belleau Woods, 8, 166; Corps' incorporation into, 6, 147, 165; democratic rhetoric and, 197–98; Lejeune and, 119; Marines' uniform requirement under, 161; recruitment and, 290n25

American Revolution, 20, 47, 62, 130, 145

amphibious mission, 4–5, 20, 37, 48, 59, 147, 271n44

anchor. *See* emblem (globe, eagle, and anchor)

ancient Greek marines, 12, 37, 41–42, 47, 103, 113

Anderson, Benedict, 78

Anderson, E. A., 125

Anderson, Warwick, 75

Andrews, Mary Raymond Shipman, 150

antiflogging campaigns, 33

Archibald, James F. J., 130

Army and Navy Journal (periodical), 2, 34–35, 39, 47

Balangiga, Massacre of, 71

Barbary States pirates, 21

Barnett, George: on clerical duty, 182–83; on commissions, 148; on historical records, 199; Lejeune to, 127; on manpower, 139; Marine Week, 140–41; on morale, 145

Barry, Clarence, 159

Bartle, Marcia, 184

bayonets, 1, 35, 179, 201n2

Becker, Otto, Jr., 104

Bederman, Gail, 75

Belleau Wood, Battle of, 8, 165–67, 203n21

Bennett, Michael, 34

Bigler, E. L., 98

Bishop, Giles, 200

Blake, D. W., 160

Boxer Rebellion, 65–70, 79, 87, 137, 233n46

Boyd, Thomas, 166–70

Braley, Berton, 130

Branch, John, 24

Breckenridge, James, 81

British Expeditionary Force, 152

Brooklyn, 27

Broome, John, 26–27

brotherhood rhetoric, 14, 149, 150–56, 159, 165, 205n36, 281n80

Buchanan, Allen, 124

Builder, Carl, 3

Bulletin (periodical). *See Recruiters' Bulletin* (periodical)

Burke, Carol, 185

Burkett, Thomas (literary character), 137–38

Butler, Smedley, 68, 125–26, 127

Butler, Thomas, 186

Callan, Edward, 112

Cameron, Craig, 7–8, 74, 203n21, 283n96

Campbell, A. S., 128

Carlisle, Julian, 161

Carpenter, Lawrence, 29

censorship, 165

Chaffee, Adna R., 68, 71, 72

Chamberlain, Sergeant, 159–60

Charles H. Fuller Company, 86

China Relief Expedition, 54, 66–70

Christy, Howard Chandler, 178–79, 178fig.16, 180fig.16

"Christy girl" poster, 178–79, 178fig.16, 180fig.16, 187, 189

Cienfuegos, Battle of, 230n17

Civil War: advertising after, 9; Army professionalization during, 210n101; Army-Corp merger considerations during, 147; Corps' role in, 211n49, 212n51, 212n55, 213n58; Corps' survival after, 2; developments before, 23; esprit de corps during, 158; Fort Fisher assault, 34; identity during, 45, 147; identity issues, 45, 147, 196; landing operations after, 4; limited land service during, 12; Marine image after, 24, 35–36, 196; Marine sea service during, 27–29; mutiny concerns during, 30; professionalization and, 219n101; recruiting ads after, 31, 32fig.4, 33; recruiting ads during, 30–31, 31fig.3; recruiting posters, 84; recruiting practices, 82; Red Badge of Courage (Crane), 57, 58; veterans of, 80, 108, 112

Clark, Gerald, 139

clerical positions, 15, 182–83, 187, 188fig.18, 189, 193

Climb to the Shoulder Straps slogan, 136, 149, 150fig.13, 279n53

coaling: expense of, 46; Marine image and, 64, 129; as Marines' duty, 95; Marine-sailor tensions and, 50; refueling bases for, 5, 12, 223n136

Cochrane, Henry Clay: anonymous contributions of, 221n124; Collier correspondence with, 221n118, 222n125, 222n130; Collum correspondence with, 41, 96, 218n100, 219n104, 220nn108–9, 223n131; on Hundred Hours' War, 56; influence of, 79; on

Marine image reform, 2, 37–39, 82, 196, 199, 218nn95–96; Rutledge on, 214n63; on secondary battery role, 60; Taylor correspondence with, 221n121; on uniform revisions, 43–44

Coffman, Edward, 219n101

Collier, George, 222n125, 222n130

Collum, Richard: Cochrane correspondence with, 41, 96, 218n100, 219n104, 220nn108–9, 223n131; on Corps' origins, 94; History of the United States Marine Corps, 40–43, 47–48, 51, 53, 60–61, 102–3, 200; image reform and, 2, 196, 199; influence of, 79; legacy of, 112; on Mameluke sword, 44, 223n131; Meade's echoing of, 96

combat: combat imagery in recruiting posters, 134fig.10; combat trauma, 8; comradeship in, 281n77; conduct in, 22, 67; democratic rhetoric and, 164–65, 169–70, 171, 172; drilling and, 186; effect of losses in, 1; female support of men in, 183; imagery of, 122–23, 131, 178, 178fig.16, 179; land combat, 55, 74, 127; male Marine unfit for, 182; participation in, 3, 131, 166, 199; promise of, 145, 156, 167; proving worth in, 174; realities of, 10, 33–34, 127, 274n20; rhetoric of, 21, 127; risk in, 9, 122, 123, 170; sea combat, 59, 61, 120; ship-to-ship combat, 20

commissions: debates over, 37, 43; democratization and, 147–50, 154, 171, 172; Naval Academy and, 39, 43, 63, 148; of noncommissioned officers, 217n90; patronage/influence in appointing, 37, 137; recruitment and, 69, 106, 147, 154, 214n62; reforms over, 39; during WWI, 205n37

conscription, 141. See draft

Continental Army, 20

Continental Congress, 206n6, 208n25

Continental Marines, 20, 229n15

Conway, James, 198

courts-martial, 53, 72–73, 126, 156, 208n25, 268n26

Crane, Stephen, 54, 57–58, 67

Crane, William M., 23

Cushing, Charles, 147, 278n46
Cuzco Well, Battle of, 56–58, 57fig.5

Daniels, Josephus, 150, 181
Davis, Arthur, 162, 163
Davis, C. H., Jr., 95
Davis, Richard Harding, 54
Dawson, L. L., 34
dead marine (term), 26
Dear Folks at Home (Cowing and Cooper),
    1–2, 201n2
Dear John letters, 174–75, 194–95, 287n1
Deaver, James, 106
democratic rhetoric: female service and,
    181; flexible approach and, 199; dur-
    ing imperial service, 67–68; internal
    limits of, 197–98; need for, 136; in
    recruitment posters, 134fig.10, 168;
    use of, 14, 197; during War of 1812,
    21–22
democratization, 136–73; commissions
    and, 147–50, 154, 171, 172; external
    image and, 136; female service com-
    parison to, 176; internal identity and,
    136; internal limits of, 197–98; non-
    commissioned officers and, 167–68,
    170, 172, 197; recruiting pamphlets
    and, 149; slogans and, 149; U.S. Con-
    gress and, 147, 148
Denby, Edwin, 150, 160
Dench, Thomas W., 113
Dewey, George, 34, 53–54
Dickins, R., 61
division of labor, regendering of, 15, 175.
    See also clerical positions
Dolphin, 56–57
draft: avoiding associations with, 145;
    conscription, 141; Corps enlistment
    and, ix, 139, 162, 163, 284n98; debates
    on, 141; exemptions, 154; Harllee's
    advocation of volunteers over, 148;
    institution of, 33; recruitment and,
    182, 283n92; resistance to, 139; U.S.
    reliance on, 182
Ducat, Stephen J., 174
Dunkelman, Mark, 158

eagle. *See* emblem (globe, eagle, and
    anchor)

eliteness: emphasis on, 139, 146, 147;
    enlistment as path to, 154; enlistment
    selectivity and, 139; female service
    and, 176; image of, 4, 6, 7, 8, 9, 198;
    institutional tradition and, 8; physical
    requirements and, 139, 176, 183,
    283n96; Recruiting Publicity Bureau
    and, 9, 111, 149; reinforcement of
    image of, 13, 41, 54, 106, 111, 186–87,
    200; shared vision of, ix, 3, 60, 134, 196
Elliott, George F., 56, 73, 85, 95, 97, 103
Ellis, Earl, 64, 73, 77
emasculation imagery, 178–79
emblem (globe, eagle, and anchor), 146,
    161–62, 191, 223n132, 277nn39–40,
    283n89
enlisted men: advancement for, 14, 106,
    115; during Civil War, 29; commis-
    sions for, 148, 149, 205n37; Corps'
    trust in, 69; desertion by, 213n55; in
    East India Company Army, 204n30;
    enlisted recruiters, 106–7; field-grade
    officers and, 198; Frigate Act of 1794
    and, 21; as gentlemen, 281n79; institu-
    tional culture and, 10–11, 136–67;
    military hierarchy and, 106, 136,
    138, 147, 149; negative images of, 37,
    109; officers per, 216n85; Recruiting
    Publicity Bureau and, 11, 104, 156;
    relations with officers, 14, 68, 76–77,
    136–37, 156, 157fig.14, 198, 235n66,
    239n102; Renda on, 204n29; School
    of Application training for, 230n21; in
    Tripoli War, 44
enlistment: chose of over commission,
    149–50; in Corps over Army, ix;
    female enlistment, 181–87, 194, 198;
    of first female Marines, 15, 175; in
    Latin America, 113; legislative shifts
    and, 148; reasons for, 34, 64, 81, 89,
    92, 137, 167; recruiters' incentives
    per, 100; recruitment limitations and,
    90; reenlistment, 93, 126, 214n62;
    selectivity of, 139; social status and,
    29, 154, 168, 170; term of, 33
Enloe, Cynthia, 175, 193
Erie, 19, 23, 24
esprit de corps: Collum on, 41; Dunkelman
    on, 158; *Gazette* (periodical) and, 114;

esprit de corps *(cont.)*
indoctrination into, 162–63; Meade on, 96; in New Navy, 47; recruit training and, 14, 149; Sands on, 42; Waller on, 68. *See also* brotherhood rhetoric

Evans, Frank, 112, 114, 128

Evans, Robley D., 95

Evening Post (periodical), 25

Executive Order 969, 96–101, 146

existence justification, 8–9, 12, 47–48, 73, 147, 196, 198

existential crisis: approach to, 2, 4, 5, 13; during 1870s, 12; institutional tradition and, 8; Recruiting Publicity Bureau and, 5–6; after Spanish-American War, 13

expeditionary mission, 3, 4, 5, 55, 122, 198–99

external image: *Bulletin* (periodical) and, 105–6; democratization and, 136; emphasis on, 5; female service and, 176; imperial service influences on, 54; warfare influences on, 5, 15, 198

female service: challenges of, 185; in clerical positions, 198; Corps' rhetoric on, 175–76, 187, 188fig.18, 189, 190fig.19; democratization comparison, 176; drilling, 186–87; emasculation imagery and, 178–79; equality issues and, 198; female volunteer recruiters, 179; hypermasculinization and, 15; on inactive duty, 194–95; in Navy, 181–82; newspaper articles on, 184–85, 186, 189–90; physical requirements, 183; recruiting discourse for, 183–84; recruits, 183; resistance to, 184; as temporary, 194–95; training, 183; uniforms, 185–86; volunteer recruiters, 181; during WWI, 174–95, 198; WWI enlistments, 175; yeowomen, 181–82, 185–86, 290n36

feminized imagery, in recruiting posters, 178–79, 178fig.16, 180fig.16

fighting style: comparisons of, 7, 9, 54, 58, 121, 123; Cushing on, 147; depictions of, 131, 134fig.10; as first to fight, 145; image and, 8; Meade on, 61–63; popular culture on, 59; recruitment

and, 197; spirit of, 282n85, 284n102; during Veracruz Incident, 123–30, 140, 270n38

film: brotherhood in WWI era films, 150–56; clichés and, 151; importance of, 172; interwar films, 278n48; Naval ban on wartime filming, 279n58; recruiting and, 80–81; *Star-Spangled Banner, The* (1917 short film) (Griffith), 141, 150–51; *Unbeliever, The* (1918 film) (Crosland), 150–56, 171; *Wall Between, The* (Paine), 272n7

First to Fight slogan, 134fig.10, 139, 145, 149, 162, 274n20, 278n46

Fisk, Francis, 116

Fitzgerald, F. S., 166–67

Fletcher, Frank F., 124

flexibility of image, 5, 6, 8, 9, 14

Forbidden City, 69

Ford, Patrick (AKA James Meredith), 58, 230n17

Foreign Legion, 146

Forney, James, 29, 45, 48–49, 51

Fort Fisher assault, 34

France: Belleau Wood, Battle of, 8, 165–67, 203n21; female service and fighting in, 174, 182, 183–84, 187, 191; institutional identification and, 138, 142; Marine combat losses in, 1–2, 182; Marine image and fighting in, 14, 15, 135, 165, 168–69, 172–73; Marines' experiences in, 14–15; recruitment and service in, 145–46, 160, 164, 166, 277n41, 286n112; uniforms in, 161, 191. *See also* World War I

Frigate Act of 1794, 21

Fullam, William, 96, 99

Fulton, Robert, 45

Gallagher, Joseph, 93

Gamborg-Andresen, Carl, 86–89, 92, 103

Ganoe, William, 40

Garland, Augustus, 35

Gatling guns, 218n100

Gazette (periodical), 114–16, 264n62, 265n68

gender issues: Corps' manipulation on, 195; feminized imagery in recruitment posters, 178–79, 178fig.16, 180fig.16, 181; hegemonic masculinity, 121–22, 176; regendering of division of labor, 15, 175; sanctioning of gender difference, 175. *See also* masculine military narrative

Gentlemanly and Honorable Profession, A (McKee), 19

Ghent, Treaty of, 22

Gibson, Charles Dana, 189

Gibson Girl imagery, 189, 190fig.19

Glenn, Harry, 71, 75

globe. *See* emblem (globe, eagle, and anchor)

Globe and Laurel (periodical), 113

Guantánamo: battle at, 54–58; effects on Corps, 78; landing operations at, 122; Marines at, 62–63, 65, 232n38, 233n45; Marines' securing of, 94, 231n24; recruitment and, 79

Haiti, 115, 123, 127, 204n29, 261n33

"Halls of Montezuma, The" (Marine Corps hymn), 112, 129, 145, 264n55

Harllee, William, 92–93, 126, 148

Harriman, Kerfoot (literary character), 167–68

Harrington, F. H., 54–56

hegemonic masculinity, 121–22, 176

help-wanted ads, 13, 197

Henderson, Archibald, 42

Herbert, George, 67

Herbert, Hilary A., 60, 95

Heywood, Charles, 60

Hicks, William (literary character), 167–70

hiker image, 109–10

Hill, F. K., 62

Hill, Walter N., 115

Hirshinger, H. J., 67, 68

historical origins: ancient Greek marines and, 12, 37, 41–42, 47, 103, 113; institutional identification and, 196; in recruitment posters, 145; Royal Marines and, 103; value of early histories, 2

Historical Record of the Royal Marine Forces (Nicolas), 47

History of the United States Army, The (Ganoe), 40

History of the United States Marine Corps (Collum), 40–43, 47–48, 53, 60–61, 102, 200

Hobsbawm, Eric, 43

Hopper, B. W., 33

horse marine (term), 26

House Naval Affairs Committee, 98, 101

Huerta, Victoriano, 123–24

Hull, Isaac, 22

Hundred Hours' War, 56, 58

Huntington, Robert, 29, 56, 65, 219n101

hymn of Marine Corp, 112, 129, 145, 264n55

hyperbole, use of, 13, 119–20, 164

hyperbolic rhetoric, 127

hypermasculinization of institutional culture, 15, 174–95

identity issues, 170; affiliation, 5–6, 9–10, 93, 160, 164; female service and, 15, 183, 195; identity rejection during WWI, 137; individual identity components, 10; Marine-sailor identity conflict, 6, 14; Marine-soldier identity conflict, 6–8, 196, 198; Recruiting Publicity Bureau and, 102–16; during WWI, 164. *See also* Recruiting Publicity Bureau

image reform: Collum and, 2, 196, 199; feminized imagery in recruitment posters, 178–79, 178fig.16, 180fig.16, 181; flexibility of image, 5, 6, 8, 9, 14; Recruiting Publicity Bureau influence on, 102–16; WWI Victorian imagery, 131, 134. *See also* masculine military narrative; publicity efforts; Recruiting Publicity Bureau; romanticized imagery

imperial service: Boxer Rebellion, 65–70, 79, 87, 137; China Relief Expedition, 54, 66–70, 79; enlisted men during, 115; hegemonic masculinity and, 122; image strengthening from, 5; landing parties during, 122; mission(s) and, 8, 12, 54, 63; Philippine-American War, 54, 64–65, 70–77, 78, 79, 109. *See also* Spanish-American War

impressment, 22, 25, 207n17

Indian Mutiny of 1857 (Sepoy Mutiny), 77

Indiana, 61

institutional identification: enlisted men and, 10–11, 136–67; existential crisis and, 8; France and, 138, 142; historical origins and, 196; hypermasculinization and, 15, 174–95; uniforms and, 222n128; World War I and, 10, 13, 164

institutional identity, uniforms as symbol of, 222n128

interdiction mission, 20

internal identity: democratization and, 136; emphasis on, 5; intensifying, 12; strengthening of, 2, 198

internal integration, 2, 54

jack of all trades, 95, 147, 161

Jackson, Andrew, 28

Jackson, Warren, 166

James, William, 177

Johnson, Opha M., 184, 185

Jones, Thomas, 24

journalists: debates and, 25; on female service, 184, 187; negative representations by, 36–37; during Spanish-American War, 57–59, 61–63; Veracruz Incident, 128–29; yellow journalism, 54

"Justice," 25

Karamanli, Hamet, 44

Karsten, Peter, 63

Kase, George, 184–85

Kearsarge, 84

Keeler, Frank, 64–65

Keever, J. K., 24

Kendall, John (literary character), 137–38, 150

Kipling, Rudyard, 51–52, 65, 97, 103–4

Knapp, H. S., 46

Kneller, George, 110–11

Krulewitch, Mel, 162

Landicutt, Philip (literary character), 152, 153–55

Landing Force Manual, 131

landing operations: after Civil War, 4; during Civil War, 211n49, 213n58; Fort Fisher assault, 34; globally after Civil War, 4–5; at Guantánamo, 122; during imperial service, 122–23; joint, 14; landing force manuals, 131

Leatherneck (periodical), 189, 191

Lefty the chauffeur (literary character), 154, 155–56

Legation Quarter siege, 66–69, 233n46

Legion of Honor, 159

Leibrand, Lela, 189, 191

Lejeune, John A., 113, 119–20, 127, 130, 145

Leonard, Harry, 98

Leslie's Weekly (periodical), 69

letters: censorship of, 165; Collum's correspondence, 39; condolence letters, 116; in congressional testimony, 1; on Corps' future, 34–35; *Dear Folks at Home* (Cowing and Cooper), 1–2, 201n2; Dear John letters, 165, 174–75, 194–95, 287n1; to editors, 50, 69, 226n158, 226nn158–59; hyperbolic rhetoric in, 127; by "Justice," 25; Marine image, 63–65, 201n2, 233n45; Marine-sailor identity conflict, 58; Marine-soldier identity conflict, 163; officers letter of support, 38; recruitment and, 81, 140, 282n84; on regulations, 28; as sources, 10, 166; by Stewart, 25–26

Lewis, James, 30–31

Lewis, Sinclair, 167

Linderman, Gerald, 33–34

Lindsay, Robert, 10

Linn, Brian, 73, 76

Lohmiller, C. J., 104–5, 105fig.7

Luce, Stephen B., 42, 206n6

Lukbán, Vicente, 70

Mackin, Elton, 170–71

Madero, Francisco I., 124

Magill, L. J., 81

Mahan, Alfred Thayer, 46, 230n20

Maine, 55, 230n17

Mameluke sword, 44, 223n131

Manila Bay, Battle of, 53–54

manpower requirements: costs of, 88; female service and, 175, 179; impressment and, 207n17; increase in, 139; of Navy, 179; recruitment and, 139–40; after Spanish-American War, 85; WWI increase in, 139

Marblehead, 56

"Marine, The" (Runyon), 78

Marine Band, 36, 53, 216n81

Marine Corps Association, 264n62, 265nn67–68; creation of, 113–14

Marine Corps Gazette (periodical), 114–16, 264n62, 265n68

Marine Guard, 24, 28, 64

Marine Week, 140–42, 172

Marines in Rhyme, Prose, and Cartoon (pamphlet), 129, 130

marksmanship, 20, 22, 23, 67, 108, 127, 129, 142, 160, 164, 165, 176. *See also* sharpshooters

Marvel, Oral R., 108

masculine military narrative, 119–35; changes in, 15; clerical positions and, 183; emasculation imagery and, 178–79; female service and, 15, 187, 195; hypermasculinization, 15; Marine image and, 62, 67; physical standards and, 139; real men rhetoric, 176–77, 198; in recruiting pamphlets, 104; in recruiting posters, 134fig.10; refining of, 173; rowboats, 131, 132fig.8; rowboats and, 14

Mass, Gustov, 125

Mayflower, 113

Mayo, Henry T., 124

McCalla, Bowman, 56, 69

McCawley, Charles, 95, 230n21

McClintock, Anne, 175

McKee, Christopher, 19, 23, 26

McLaughlin, C., 112

McLemore, A. S., 79, 87, 100, 106–7, 145, 171–72

Meade, J. J., 96, 97

Meade, Robert, 60, 61

Meigs, John F., 46

Meredith, Henry, 29

Meredith, James (AKA Patrick Ford), 58, 230n17

messaging: negative messaging, 2, 36–37, 38, 45, 107–11, 123; in newspapers, 5; positive messaging, 5, 175

Mexican government, 123–25

Mexican Naval Academy, 125, 270n38

Mexican Revolution, 123–25

Mexican-American War, 217n90

military hierarchy, 14, 27–28, 149, 174; enlisted men and, 106, 136, 138, 147, 149; flaunting of, 138; recruitment needs and, 136

Military Service Institution of the United States, 215n80

Millett, Allan, 11, 125, 128, 206n6, 206n8, 211n49, 271n44, 278n44

mission(s): amphibious mission, 4–5, 20, 37, 48, 59, 147, 271n44; decreasing in explaining, 54, 196; difficulty claiming, 8, 47–48, 59, 73–74, 196; difficulty defining, 19–20, 35, 37, 38, 42; existence justification and, 8–9, 12, 47–48, 73, 147, 196, 198; expeditionary mission, 3, 4, 5, 55, 122, 198–99; imperial service, 8, 54, 63; interdiction mission, 20; motto and, 45; naval artillery, 196; Navy's issues with, 22–23, 99, 196, 198–99; opposition to increase in, 63; overemphasize of, 6; overlap of, 4, 6, 37, 97; pacification duties, 70–71; primary, 3; recruiters' focus on variety of, 107, 110, 114, 146, 277n41; sharpshooters, 3, 23, 49, 60, 260n30; shipboard security, 3, 96, 99, 101, 196; traditional, 5, 8, 12, 13, 82; uniform and, 43; WWI wartime mission, 14–15, 198

Mississippi River Marine Brigade, 30

morale: improving of, 68, 283n96; presence of Marines and, 6, 24, 30, 252n79, 253n81; sustaining of, 145, 163, 168

mottos: By Land, By Sea motto, 223n133; debates about, 43; Once a Marine, Always a Marine (unofficial motto), 92, 161; *Semper fidelis* motto, 45, 50, 92, 94, 113, 223n133

movies. *See* film

Murtaugh, Colonel, 80, 101

mutiny, 30, 77, 196

Myerly, Scott Hughes, 43

Myers, John T., 67

Naval Academy, 278n48; Collum's preference for West Point over, 40; commissioning from, 39, 43, 148; films set at, 278n49; imperial service and,

Naval Academy (*cont.*)
63; Marine attendance at, 220n106; teaching assignments at, 218n100
Naval Academy, Mexican, 125, 270n38
Naval Appropriations Act of 1916, 148
Naval Personnel Act of 1900, 69
Naval Personnel Bill of 1900, 63
Naval War College, 39
Navy, Department of: advertising practices, 100–101, 214n65, 247n47; authorization for fleet under, 21; coexistence with Navy under, 81, 91, 199; debates over Corps under, 250n66; Marine superiority rhetoric and, 100; Marine-naval officer tensions, 21; on Marines under naval officers, 28; Meade and, 231n23; opposition to Marine presence, 63, 232n35; secondary batteries and, 60
Navy Day, 275n22
negative representations: after Civil War, 2, 36–37, 38; in cartoons, 123; in 1880s and 1890s, 45; recruiters' frustration with, 107–11
Neptune Celebration, 27
Neville, Wendell C., 124, 127–28
New York Sun (periodical), 52
New York Times (periodical), 49–50
Newark, 66
Newberry, Truman, 90–91
newspaper articles: ads disguised as, 13, 243–44n24, 247n48; democratic rhetoric, 149–50, 156, 158; on female service, 184–85, 186, 189–91; hyperbolic rhetoric, 102, 119; on Legation Quarter siege, 66–69, 233n46; Marine image and, 54, 55, 58, 62, 128–30, 142, 144, 216n82; Marine image in, 36; Marine-sailor identity conflict, 100, 226nn155–56; on military efficiency, 37; negative messaging in, 49–50, 63, 216n83; "Pfeifer's Triumph" (*New York Sun*), 52, 227n166; positive messaging in, 229n15, 232n36; recruitment and, 80–81, 86–87, 92–95, 107–10, 120, 140, 141, 142, 144, 156, 158; "Red Badge of Courage Was His Wig-Wag Flag, The" (Crane), 57–58; on secondary battery role, 231n25

newspapers: help-wanted ads in, 13, 197; letters by officers in, 50, 236n71; negative messaging in, 2, 36–37, 38, 45, 107–11, 123; oldest military service claim in, 94; positive messaging in, 5, 128–30, 140, 141, 175
Nicholas, Samuel, 20
Nicolas, Paul, 47
noncommissioned officers: advancement and, 94, 115, 148, 217nn89–90; democratization and, 167–68, 170, 172, 197; organizations for, 263n54, 264n62, 265n67
Norris, James D., 109
Nova Scotia, 20

O'Bannon, Presley, 44
officers: as gentlemen, 136, 281n79; per enlisted men, 216n85; relations with enlisted men, 14, 136, 156, 157fig.14, 198; relations with officers, 239n102
Old Gimlet Eye (Butler and Thomas), 125–26
Once a Marine, Always a Marine (unofficial motto), 92, 161, 263n54
O'Neill, Phillip, 45
Oviatt, Miles, 27
Owen, Peter, 163, 167, 284n102

pacification duties, 70, 71
Paine, Richard, 136, 137–38, 150, 172
Painter, K. A., 113
Panama Canal, 96
Panther, 56
Payne, Edna, 179, 181
Pettegrew, John, 183
"Pfeifer's Triumph" (*New York Sun*), 52, 227n166
Philippine-American War, 54, 64–65, 70–77, 78, 79, 109
physical requirements, 148, 176–77, 183, 251n74, 290n28; female service and, 183; physical tests, 98, 139, 251n74
Pillsbury, John E., 99
Pinkston, L. P., 92
Poe, John P., 115
Pope, P. C., 35
Porter, David, 34, 71
Proctor, Clarance, 109

professionalization: Anderson on, 78; associations and, 40; debates on, 39; defined, 39; democratic rhetoric and, 165, 167–68, 171; historical origins and, 2–3, 114, 202n8; Naval War College and, 39; publications and, 40, 114; spirit of, 208n28; of U.S. Army, 2, 219n101

public recognition: of Army, 33, 87, 108; of Navy, 108; *Recruiters' Bulletin* (periodical) and, 141; Recruiting Publicity Bureau and, 5–6, 13; Spanish-American War and, 12; trademarks and slogans, 13; WWI, 1

publicity efforts: affection for Corps, ix; after Spanish-American War, 13; aggressive methods of, 15; focus on, 5; societal depictions of Corps and, 136; spearheading of, 5; U.S. Navy's impact on, 80–101; before WWI, 102. *See also* Recruiting Publicity Bureau

Putnam, Louie W., 107

Quantico, Virginia, 152, 160
Quantico Leatherneck, 153, 158
Quick, John, 57–58
Quirk, Robert, 125

Rahrig, Mildred, 181
real men rhetoric, 189, 190fig.19; masculine military narrative, 176–77, 198
real women rhetoric, 184
recruiters: challenges of, 102; on female service, 184; female volunteer recruiters, 179, 181; frustration of, 107; imperial service influences on, 54–55, 79
Recruiters' Bulletin (periodical): advertising in, 110–11; cartoons in, 157, 161; contributions to, 106–7; covers, 15–16, 191–93; as creative outlet, 113; democratic rhetoric, 148, 150, 153; on female enlistment, 175, 184, 186, 187, 189–95, 198; *Marine Corps Gazette* (periodical) and, 114, 264n62; newspapers' use of articles from, 260–61n33; public recognition and, 141; recruiters' use of, 104–8, 164; as

research source, 10–11; on Veracruz Incident, 128, 130; *Wall Between, The* (Paine) review, 138; during WWI, 145
recruiting pamphlets: democratization and, 149; pre-WWI rhetoric of, 6, 102–3; for recruitment, 95; as response to critiques, 38–39; Veracruz Incident and, 129
recruiting posters: after Civil War, 31, 31fig.3, 32fig.4, 33; combat imagery in, 134fig.10; Cuzco Well, Battle of, 57fig.5; feminized imagery in, 178–79, 178fig.16, 180fig.16; First to Fight slogan on, 162; historical origins in, 145; rowboats in, 131, 132fig.8; U.S. Navy, 133fig.9
Recruiting Publicity Bureau, 94, 101, 126, 171; aggressive methods of, 13; democratic rhetoric challenges, 138; elite image stressing by, 13, 147; establishment of, 5–6, 13, 95, 102, 113, 116, 120, 197; female Marines at, 175; female service and, 184–85; films and, 151; image of eliteness and, 6, 9; influence of, 102–16; Marine Week, 141; officer-enlisted relations at, 156; *Recruiters' Bulletin*, 10–11; rhetoric of, 1, 162, 166; role of, 13; sexualized imagery, 189, 190fig.19; slogans, 13, 145; trademarks, 13; *Unbeliever, The* (1918 film) (Crosland) and, 152. *See also* publicity efforts
recruitment: Civil War era practices, 82, 84; of college-educated, 163–64; costs of, 88; foundation myths narrative and, 5; after Spanish-American War, 13; U.S. Navy recruitment, 275n22. *See also* advertising; recruiters; recruiting pamphlets; recruiting posters; Recruiting Publicity Bureau
Red Badge of Courage, The (Crane), Civil War, 57, 58
"Red Badge of Courage Was His Wig-Wag Flag, The" (Crane), 57–58
Reiter, George C., 56
Renda, Mary, 122, 204n29
retirees, 112, 263n54
Reynolds, Edward, 26
Reynolds, John G., 35

rhetoric, of leadership, 1
Richardson, J. S. Stewart, 119
romanticized imagery, 54, 58, 93, 104, 114,
    115, 141, 158–59, 161–62, 170, 189,
    221n116
Roosevelt, Theodore, 6, 75, 82, 96–98,
    251n74
Rose, Sonya O., 194
Rosie the Riveter, 175
Rothafel, Samuel, 152–53, 155
rowboats, 14, 131, 132fig.8
Royal Marines, 4, 21, 36, 42, 45, 47, 48, 51,
    67, 97, 103, 113, 161, 208n25
Royal Navy, 22, 47, 208n25
Royal Welch Fusiliers, 67
Runyon, Damon, 78
Rush, W. R., 124, 125
Russians, 66, 67
Rutzen, B. J., 156

Samar, 70–77, 78, 237n86
Sampson, William T., 59
Sands, Joshua, 42
Santiago, Battle of, 59, 60, 87
Schein, Edgar, 2–3
Schley, W. S., 47
School of Application, 230n21
sea service: during Civil War, 27–29;
    Executive Order 969, 96–101, 146;
    in recruitment posters, 146; removal
    from, 6, 11, 95, 96–99, 146; tradition
    of, 110, 146, 196
secondary batteries: Mahan on importance
    of, 230n20; during Spanish-American
    War, 12, 59–60; training, 230n21
self-identification, ix, 6, 14, 33, 164
self-promotion: Collum on, 40; Marine
    Week as, 140–42, 172
Selling Sea Power (Wadle), 278n49, 279n58
Semmes, Raphael, 29
Semper fidelis motto, 45, 50, 92, 94, 113,
    223n133
Sepoy Mutiny (Indian Mutiny of 1857), 77
sexualized imagery, 189, 190fig.19
sharpshooters, 3, 20, 23, 49, 60, 260n30
Shaw, Norman, 106
Sherman, C. L., 44, 222n126
shipboard security, 3, 96, 99, 101, 196
Shulimson, Jack, 4, 40

Shulman, Mark, 4
slogans: Climb to the Shoulder Straps
    slogan, 149, 150fig.13; creation of,
    13; democratization and, 149; First to
    Fight slogan, 134fig.10, 145, 149, 162
Smith, Jacob H., 70, 71
Snyder, Harold, 104
Snyder, Harold C., 113
social Darwinism, 176
social status, during WWI, 138
"Soldier an' Sailor Too" (Archibald and
    Braley), 130
"Soldier an' Sailor Too" (Kipling), 51–52
Sousa, John Philip, 53
Spain, 55
Spanish-American War, ix, 8–9, 12–13,
    53–79; challenges of, 79; Cienfuegos,
    Battle of, 230n17; Cuzco Well, Battle
    of, 56–58, 57fig.5; democratic spirit of
    Corps and, 137, 147; disease casual-
    ties, 232n38; effect of Marines' batter-
    ies fire, 231n25; Guantánamo, 231n24,
    233n45; help-wanted ads after, 82;
    influence of, 4–5, 70, 93, 114–15, 120,
    122, 164; Keeler's journal, 233n43;
    Maine, 55, 230n17; Manila Bay, Battle
    of, 53–54; manpower requirements
    after, 85; "Marine, The" (Runyon), 78;
    Santiago, Battle of, 59, 60, 87; treat-
    ment of prisoners, 231n24, 240n106.
    See also Guantánamo
Sparks, Victor, 163
Spector, Ronald, 39
spirit of Corps. See also esprit de corps
standards, level of, 38, 91, 126, 139, 155,
    158, 176, 183–84, 247n50, 283n96
Star-Spangled Banner, The (1917 short film)
    (Griffith), 141, 150–51
steamships, 12, 19, 23, 45–46, 83, 223n136
Stenback, Raymond, 184
Sterrett, Thomas, 156
Stewart, Charles, 25–26
Streets, Heather, 283n96
Stubbe, Frank, 102, 160
Suid, Lawrence H., 151
Sullivan, David, 212n49
superiority rhetoric, 13, 35, 64–65, 99, 109,
    120, 126–27, 147, 163–64, 262n47
Swain, Corinne Rockwell, 194–95

symbols, 223n132; focus on, 43, 161–62; globe, eagle, and anchor emblem, 146, 161–62, 191, 223n132, 277nn39–40, 283n89; Mameluke sword, 44, 223n31; Recruiting Publicity Bureau and, 13; rowboat as, 14, 131, 132fig.8; use of in recruiting pamphlets, 146

Taite, James, 113
Taylor, A. S., 221n121
"tell it to the Marines" expression, 48–49, 63, 209n35, 232n36, 232n38
Texas Rangers, 146
This High Name (Lindsay), 10
Thomas, Lowell, 125–26
Thomason, John, 162–63
Three Things, The (Andrews), 150–52, 154, 155
Through the Wheat (Boyd), 166–70
trademarks, 13, 109–10, 161. *See also* slogans
traditions: Mameluke sword, 44, 223n31; preservation of, 44; *Semper fidelis* motto and, 45; traditional mission(s), 5, 8, 12, 13, 82
training: esprit de corps and, 14, 149; female service and, 183, 186–87; indoctrination into Corps' culture, 136–37, 149; at Quantico, 160–61; School of Application, 230n21
Tripoli War, 44

Unbeliever, The (1918 film) (Crosland), 150–55, 171
uniforms: ceremonial uniforms, 179; coaling uniform, 50; combat uniforms, 178; debates over, 43–44, 106, 222n125; enlistment decisions and, 187; for female service, 185–86, 187, 191–93, 192fig.20, 195; institutional identity and, 222n128; for yeowomen, 185
United Service (periodical), 48
Upham, Oscar, 66–67
Upshur, William, 63–64
U.S. Army: AEF attempts to subsume Corps into, 164, 165; *Army and Navy Journal* (periodical), 2, 34–35, 39, 47; Army-Marine Corps relations, 15, 27–28, 36, 59, 73; articles by officers of, 48; in China, 69; comparisons to, 4, 5, 6, 54, 64–65, 94, 109, 113; Continental Army, 20; critiques of, 63; Fort Fisher assault, 34; *History of the United States Army, The* (Ganoe), 40; identity issues, 14, 29, 37, 198; land service, 20, 21; Marine officers transfers to, 29; Marines serving with, 48, 97; Marine-sailor identity conflict, 104; Marine-soldier identity conflict, 6–8, 51, 68, 104, 110; Mississippi River Marine Brigade, 30; mobilization and deployment timeframes, 54, 55; need to outdo, 1; officers, 68, 72; overlap with, 4, 6, 37, 78, 97; pacification duties, 71; in Philippines, 70, 72, 73; potential merger with, 2, 11–12, 13, 25, 34–35, 36, 97; professionalization approach of, 2, 219n101; public recognition, 33, 87, 108; recruiting men from, 126; recruitment for, 30, 33, 80, 82–83, 84, 88, 92, 97; sword of, 44; uniform revisions, 43, 106. *See also* American Expeditionary Forces (AEF)
U.S. Congress: Army-Corp merger considerations by, 27, 35, 36, 147, 208n25; authorizations for naval vessels, 20, 21, 23; bounty authorization, 33; conscription debates, 141, 148; debates over Corps, 250n66; democratization and, 147, 148; ending of active recruitment, 182, 290n25; establishment of Continental Marines, 20; legislation on commissions, 217n90; lobbying, 215n80; Marine expansion approval, 63, 139; Navy-Marine Corps relations and, 27–28, 35, 100, 120; New Navy funding, 46; recruiting poster approval by, 84; request on clerical positions, 182; on steamship use, 46
U.S. Marine Corps: Army-Marine Corps relations, 15, 27–28, 36; centennial of, 229n15; establishment of, 21; Marine-sailor identity conflict, 110; Marine-soldier identity conflict, 110; Navy-Marine Corps relations, 27–28, 35, 100, 120; potential merger with Army, 2, 11–12, 13, 25, 34–35, 36

U.S. Navy: articles by officers of, 48; Bureau of Navigation, 91–92; Christy recruiting posters, 179, 180fig.16; comparisons to, 4, 6, 109, 113; Marines serving with, 48; Marine-sailor identity conflict, 6, 12, 51, 110; Navy Day, 275n22; Navy-Marine Corps relations, 27–28, 35, 59, 100, 120; New Navy, 46–47; opposition to Marine presence, 6, 11, 12, 13; overlap with, 4, 6, 37, 78, 97, 198; professionalization approach of, 2; public recognition, 108; recruiting men from, 126; recruiting posters, 131, 133fig.9; tensions between Corps and, 6, 11, 12, 197; use of Marines, 4–5; yeowomen, 181–82, 185–86, 290n36
U.S. Treasure Department, 100–101
USN Bureau of Navigation, 91–92

value of traditions, belief in, 1
Van Antwerp, J. S., 62–63
Vanderbilt, 29
Veracruz Incident, 119–30, 140, 270n38
volunteerism, 141, 179, 181

Wadle, Ryan, 275n22, 278n49, 279n58
Walker, Henry, 35–36
Wall Between, The (Paine), 136, 137–38, 147–48, 150, 172
Waller, Littleton, 53, 61, 63, 66, 68, 70, 71–77, 98, 113
war movies. *See* film
War of 1812, 11, 19–20, 21, 22; developments after, 23; images from, 33; impact of legacy of, 25; letters by officers, 50

Warrington, Lewis, 22–23
Washington Evening Star, 156
Washington Post (periodical), 233n46
West Point Military Academy, 40, 43
"Who Am I" (1916 pamphlet cover), 6, 7fig.1
Wilchinski, Martha, 174–75, 187, 189, 190fig.19, 193–94, 195
Williams, Alexander S., 72
Williams, Charles, 43–44
Wilson, Woodrow, 123–24
Wood, Thomas, 69
World War I: American Expeditionary Forces, 6; Belleau Wood, Battle of, 8, 165–67, 203n21; democratic rhetoric during, 137, 138; democratization during, 136–73; external image and, 135, 198; historical records of, 199; institutional identification and, 10, 13, 164; Marines' experiences of, 14–15, 137, 166–73; publicity and recruitment for, 9, 79, 84, 131, 136; recruitment posters, 178–81, 178fig.16, 179fig.17, 181; rhetoric of, 291n43; US entry into, 135, 139–40, 144–46, 156, 160. *See also* female service; France
World War II, 7, 194, 277n39, 291n43

yeowomen, 181–82, 185–86, 290n36

Zanzig, Louis F., 111
Zeilin, Jacob, 223n132

About the Author

Dr. Heather Venable is an assistant professor of military and security studies in the Department of Airpower at the United States Air Force's Air Command and Staff College. As a visiting professor at the U.S. Naval Academy, she taught naval and Marine Corps history. She graduated with a BA in history from Texas A&M University and received an MA in American history from the University of Hawai'i. She received her PhD in military history from Duke University.